Group Model Building

Group Model Building

Facilitating Team Learning Using System Dynamics

Jac A. M. Vennix

University of Nijmegen, The Netherlands

JOHN WILEY & SONS

Chichester · New York · Brisbane · Toronto · Singapore

Other Wiley Editorial Offices

John Wiley & Sons, Inc., 605 Third Avenue,
New York, NY 10158-0012, USA

Jacaranda Wiley Ltd, 33 Park Road, Milton,
Queensland 4064, Australia

John Wiley & Sons (Canada) Ltd, 22 Worcester Road,
Rexdale, Ontario M9W 1L1, Canada

John Wiley & Sons (Asia) Pte Ltd, Clementi Loop #02-01
Jin Xing Distripark, Singapore 129809

Large portions of the case description of the health care project in Chapter Six have previously been
published in: Morecroft, John D. W., and J. D. Sterman (eds.), *Modeling for learning organizations.*
Copyright © 1994 by Productivity Press Inc., PO Box 13390, Portland, OR 97213-0390, (800) 394-6868.
Reprinted by permission.

The case description on the Dutch fleet problem in Chapter Six has previously been published in:
Group decision and negotiation as building consensus in strategic decision making: system dynamics as
a group support system, *Group Decision and Negotiation, vol. 4 (4)*, 1995, 335–355. Copyright © by
Kluwer Academic Publishers. Reprinted by permission of Kluwer Academic Publishers.

Library of Congress Cataloging-in-Publication Data

Vennix, Jac A. M.
    Group model building : facilitating team learning using system
dynamics / Jac A. M. Vennix.
        p. cm.
    Includes bibliographical references and index.
    ISBN 0-471-95355-5 (cloth)
    1. Decision-making, Group—Mathematical models.   2. Management—
Employee participation—Mathematical models.   I. Title.
HD30.23.V47   1996
658.4´036—dc20   96–11166
                                                          CIP

British Library Cataloguing in Publication Data

A catalogue record for this book is available from the British Library

ISBN 0-471-95355-5

Typeset in 10/12pt Times by Dorwyn Ltd, Rowlands Castle, Hants
Printed and bound in Great Britain by Biddles Ltd, Guildford and King's Lynn
This book is printed on acid-free paper responsibly manufactured from sustainable forestation, for
which at least two trees are planted for each one used for paper production.

to Loes

Contents

Contents ———————————————————————————————— ix

Acknowledgements

Team learning is increasingly recognized as a critical factor in tackling strategic problems. Facilitated (computer supported) meetings to support learning in strategic teams are booming. The literature uses a variety of terms to refer to this phenomenon: group (decision) support systems (GDSS), group communication systems (GCS), facilitated meetings, and computer supported cooperative work (CSCW) to name only a few. This book deals with one specific kind of group decision support, i.e. building system dynamics models with management teams to tackle strategic problems. Group model-building, as it is called, covers a variety of topics, including human information processing, the construction of system dynamics models, individual and team learning, and, last but not least, group process and group facilitation.

As is the case with many books, this book is also at least in part the result of discussions with like-minded people both inside and outside the university. One group outside the university, which I would like to thank, is the 'Q group' of 'Rijkswaterstaat'. This group initiates an organizational change process to enhance the strategic abilities of their management teams. Gerhard Schwarz initially involved me in the work done by this group and I have found discussions with him both profound and stimulating. Bert Keijts and, in particular, Ad de Rooij, introduced systems thinking and system dynamics in the so-called Nostradamus project, the first cycle in the process of organizational change. Later on their work was taken over by Peter Struik and his colleagues, in the CREOPS project, and here too I found that discussions with this group frequently matched in quality with discussions at the university.

When I was still at Utrecht University, Kees Takkenberg first made me fully aware of the importance of the concept of organizational platform and commitment with decisions in the context of group decision support. In Utrecht I have also worked together for a number of years with Wim Scheper. Although I have been in Nijmegen now for over three years, we still collaborate regularly and Wim has made the effort to read previous versions of the manuscript when they were still in their early stages. Apart from his thorough theoretical knowledge on several of the issues discussed in this book, he is a person who is not easily satisfied and, in the spirit of the genuine scientific researcher, continues to ask questions until something is fully understood. Wim's comments and suggestions have had a profound influence on the contents of the book. This also holds for Tom Ikink's comments. Fortunately, Tom also starts asking questions where many others have stopped their thinking process. Discussions with Tom, in particular on the nature of (social) reality and group processes, have not only clarified my own thinking but have also significantly affected the book's content as well as its framework. Several other colleagues have read (parts of) the manuscript and provided comments and suggestions for improvement. Etiënne Rouwette created a link between the world of Group Decision Support and attitude research. As the reader will notice, I consider the latter topic extremely important in relation to group model-building. Hans van Kuppevelt was closely involved in the housing association project described in this book. Not only did he assist in conducting the group model-building sessions, he has also monitored and recorded what actually happened during the model construction process and in that way helped to shape up the chapters in which the housing association project is discussed. Later on in this project Erwin van Schaik joined us and took the effort to read the final manuscript and in particular the chapters on the housing association. In this respect I am also greatful to Johan van Dorssen of Marco Polis who took the time and effort to read the first complete draft of the chapter on the housing association project.

A special word of thanks goes to my friend David Lane, who took the effort to read the entire manuscript and to provide me with both general comments and detailed criticism. David can draw from a rich background in a number of scientific disciplines as well as practical consultancy experience. As a result, my discussions with him on the content and the framework of the book have not only guarded me from potential inconsistencies, but have also significantly increased the book's quality. One reason for this is that, while reviewing the manuscript, David applied the same high standards as he does to his own scientific work. But, not only have I valued David's comments and suggestions, I also appreciate his many stimulating remarks to get the book published. These encouragements proved to be extremely welcome as it is the last straw that breaks the camel's back.

As I, quite by accident, found out later, Colin Eden had served as one of the two anonymous reviewers for Wiley. I am grateful to Colin for reading a couple of early sample chapters and, later on in the process, the first draft of the entire manuscript. Both times, Colin was generous enough to write down his comments. Drawing from both his theoretical knowledge and his extensive practical experience in the realm of group decision support, Colin's remarks and suggestions have been extremely valuable and helpful.

Several persons have helped with a number of more tangible tasks. Eveliene Kuipers conducted the main part of the literature searches and her work was taken over by her friend Judith Ladenstein, when Eveliene had to start her internship. Both have done a tremendous job in creating order in the chaos of key words and literature references that I provided them with. Judith also helped in designing the first drafts of the figures in the book. The final touch to the manuscript was given by Cécile Thijssen. With her organized way of working and well developed feeling for lay-out she both designed the final figures and prepared the manuscript for the publisher. Her work has improved the book's appearance in an important way.

Finally, I have to thank my wife Loes, not only for her continuous support and understanding, but also because she was willing to put her amazing talent to assess a manuscript, simultaneously at a global and at a minutely detailed level, at my disposal, in spite of her own demanding job. This book is dedicated to you.

Introduction

Every organization regularly faces strategic problems. Choices have to be made which can have far reaching (often unanticipated) consequences, choices which may affect the whole organization. In earlier days strategic decisions were frequently made by one person at the top of the organization. However, the 'command and control' organization has largely had its day. Increasingly, teams become the critical building blocks upon which the performance of modern organizations depend. As a result strategic problems are nowadays addressed by teams rather than individuals, not only because the 'command and control' organization has become obsolete but also because the complexity and uncertainty of the problem will overwhelm the cognitive capacities of any one individual. Moreover, several strategic problems may be interrelated thus increasing the complexity of the problems. This has led a number of authors to coin the term 'messy' problems. A typical characteristic of this type of problem is that different people hold widely dissimilar views of the situation and as a result they define problems differently.

Research has convincingly shown that differences of viewpoint can be very productive. They may help to challenge implicit assumptions about situations and thus help to prevent a premature problem definition. The more different perspectives are taken into account, the smaller the chances of premature problem definition and 'solving the wrong problem'. The point is well made by Hogarth. As he put it: '. . . actively seek to frame problems from multiple perspectives in order to avoid being overly influenced by any particular one. Seeing problems from many perspectives can, of course, add to the conflict of choice. However, such conflict is usually preferable to being manipulated. Put succinctly, the advice is "Frame or be framed!"' (Hogarth, 1987, 109). In other words, differences of opinion should be seen as beneficial.

At the same time however, most of us have also experienced ways in which differences of opinion can give rise to lengthy and frustrating discussions. This is particularly the case when individual team members seem convinced that their perspective is correct and others must be wrong. These situations may not only give rise to prolonged, inefficient discussion, they may even lead to deadlocks in a decision making situation. As a result an organization's readiness to act may be severely threatened, which provides competitors with an opportunity to create a competitive advantage.

When individual team members are convinced that they are right, this gives rise to a climate in which team members primarily argue for their own opinions rather than listen to each other. The resulting sphere is one of trying to win the discussion rather than trying to learn from the perspectives of other team members. Several authors of strategic decision making have pointed out that effective strategic decision making largely depends on the ability of team members to learn from each other in order to build a shared perspective (Checkland; 1981, 1985). Former head of the Shell Group Planning, De Geus, is quite compelling about the role of learning. In his view learning might prove to be the only sustainable competitive advantage for organizations in the future (de Geus, 1988).

Team learning presupposes that people are willing to question their opinions. As a result team leaders who want to create learning teams are confronted with issues such as: how to create a situation in which team participants start to doubt their ideas rather than stubbornly clinging to their own opinions. How to create an atmosphere in which team members attempt to learn from each other rather than trying to 'win' the discussion by conspicuously demonstrating their (by definition limited) knowledge. How to create a shared understanding of a problem in a team. And last but not least: how to foster consensus on an issue and how to create commitment with a strategic decision.

Stated differently, from a systems point of view the question is how to make team members collaborate in such a way that the whole is more (rather than less) than the sum of its parts, since, all else being equal, underachievement of teams will automatically lead to underperformance for the organization as a whole. A conclusion which indicates that these issues are by no means trivial. Finding the right way to address them can dramatically improve team performance as well as the organization's effectiveness.

However, as might be anticipated, the questions discussed above defy a quick and simple answer. Improving the performance of strategic decision making teams is not a simple matter, exactly because of the complexity of problems and limitations in human information processing capabilities. Methods and techniques which may support a team in grappling with a messy problem are required to accomplish this. Over the course of the decades a number of methodologies have been developed. These are generally considered to belong to the realm of soft operations research (soft OR). A number of well-known methods include soft systems methodology (SSM), strategic options development and analysis (SODA), strategic choice, robustness analysis, hypergame analysis, and strategic assumption surfacing and testing (SAST). Each of the above methods starts from different underlying theoretical assumptions and employs different methods and tools. A full discussion of differences and similarities of system's methodologies and their applicability to messy problems is beyond the scope of this book. The interested reader is referred to Rosenhead (1989), Eden and Radford (1990), Flood and Jackson (1991), and in particular to the special issue of *System Dynamics Review* on system's thinkers and system thinking (Richardson, Wolstenholme and Morecroft, 1994).

This book discusses group model-building as one approach to increase team performance when tackling strategic, messy problems. Group model-building is based on the system dynamics methodology. It focuses on building system dynamics models with teams in order to enhance team learning, to foster consensus and to create commitment with a resulting decision. A central idea of the book is that when problems become more complex all team members will, by necessity, have a limited view of the problem. What is needed is to enhance learning within the team in order to expand the view of the problem and to identify courses of action in which all team members will feel confident and to which they all feel committed.

ASSUMPTIONS UNDERLYING GROUP MODEL-BUILDING

This book takes as its starting point the assumption that system dynamics can be used as a method to systematically elicit and share mental models in teams. The process of building a model starts from the different perceptions of the participants. One underlying idea is that people's mental models are limited by human information processing capabilities. System dynamics can be helpful to elicit and integrate mental models into a more holistic view of the problem and to explore the dynamics of this holistic view.

A second underlying idea is that people have a strong tendency to think in terms of causal processes (Weiner, 1985; Shoham, 1990). Every proposed policy to alleviate a problem contains one or more hidden causal assumptions about the effects of policy interventions. In general, however, people tend to think in simple causal chains rather than networks of related variables. It is rare for people to see more than one cause of a problem. As Dörner (1980) points out, people have difficulty in identifying interconnections and thinking in causal nets. In general people tend to concentrate on parts rather than wholes. They seem to disregard interconnections between different elements in a system. And if they want to see problems more holistically they generally lack the expertise or rigour to identify and structure the relations between elements in the system. In that sense system dynamics can be helpful to create a more adequate problem description by eliciting the hidden causal assumptions that all of us automatically hold and by integrating these into a more complete problem representation. The primary goal is not to build *the* model of *the* system, but rather to get a group engaged in building a system dynamics model of a problem in order to see to what extent this process might be helpful to increase problem understanding and to devise courses of action to which team members will feel committed.

Stated differently, group model-building is a process in which team members exchange their perceptions of a problem and explore such questions as: what exactly is the problem we face? How did the problematic situation originate? What might be its underlying causes? How can the problem be effectively tackled? An important characteristic of group model-building (and system dynamics in general) is that 'fact' is separated from 'value'. The primary focus is descriptive and diagnostic: the way team members think a system works is separated from the question how they would like a system to work. And this separation in itself often proves helpful to clarify the strategic debate as will be shown in the examples presented in this book.

Although this book takes system dynamics as the underlying methodology it differs substantially from most system dynamics textbooks. This book largely focuses on the process of *group model-building* rather than just system dynamics. In group model-building the model is created in close interaction with a group of policy makers or managers. The purpose is to support a decision making group in structuring a messy problem and designing effective policies to deal with it. As a result this book will not only focus on the system dynamics methodology. Although knowledge of system dynamics and experience in building models is a prerequisite for group model-building, and will thus be discussed at length, such knowledge is in itself not sufficient to assist the team learning process. To be effective in group model-building an awareness of the reasoning behind this approach is required. In other words one needs to be aware of the theoretical assumptions underlying group model-building. The first chapter will discuss this theoretical framework, which is (amongst others) derived from research in the realm of human information processing and behavioural decision making. Furthermore, group model-building, by definition, implies working with small groups. This requires certain skills which sometimes are at right angles with the skills needed for constructing system dynamics models. As a result, considerable attention will be devoted to such topics as factors promoting and impeding group performance. These are derived from the field of small group research, which deals with such subjects as group dynamics, group conflict, and group process techniques. I do have to point out that more than any other book on soft OR or system dynamics this book emphasizes the importance of the group interaction process in arriving at shared learning, consensus and commitment. It is a central premise of this book that group interaction processes determine, to a large extent, the performance of the group in tackling messy problems. As a result, I will extensively discuss the role of group facilitation, since the facilitator has been shown to be of primary importance in increasing the effectiveness of a group (e.g. Vennix, Scheper and Willems, 1993).

GOALS OF GROUP MODEL-BUILDING

Group model-building can be considered as an organizational intervention process, i.e. a process of coming 'between or among persons, groups or objects for the purpose of helping them.' (Argyris, 1970). The question can be raised: to help with what or for what purpose?

In the standard view of policy making it is frequently assumed that problem solving is the business of defining problems, generating alternatives and making a choice. Several authors have pointed out that messy problems cannot be solved but rather are resolved (Checkland, 1981) or finished (Eden, 1987) when a satisficing solution is developed. Problem management (Bryant, 1989) or finishing problems is thus: '. . . also contrary to the common view that problem solving is solely about the generation and evaluation of alternatives and final choice from among them. . . . Instead it suggests that decision making is influenced by the way in which issues are presented, the identification of their significance, their exploration as the group constructs a shared understanding of them, and the point at which a negotiated settlement is likely.' (Eden, 1992a, 204). What is required is a process of decision making in which mental models are communicated, tested and changed in such a way that a shared definition of the problem results. In that respect Eden (1992a) has pointed out that group decision support systems need to support both the substantive and the procedural rationality. In other words, it needs to address both analysis of the problem and attitudes of participants.

The question what group model-building with system dynamics is supposed to accomplish, will be addressed in more detail now. It must be understood that the ultimate goal of the intervention is *not* to build a system dynamics model. The system dynamics model is a *means* to achieve other ends. In the previous section I have argued that model-building serves the purpose of putting people in a position to learn about a messy problem. It is not enough if individuals learn, rather it is team learning which should be enhanced. The learning process should create a shared social reality (Phillips; 1984; 1989) and result in a shared understanding of the problem and potential solutions (Eden, 1992a; Senge, 1990).

However, learning is not enough. Another important goal of the intervention should be to foster consensus within the team which, by the way, should not be confused with compromise. Consensus refers to unanimous agreement about a decision while compromise alludes to a settlement reached by mutual concessions. Group model-building strives for agreement among team members rather than compromise. In order to prevent another misunderstanding at this point, group model-building does not foster *premature* consensus. As we will see elsewhere in this book premature consensus and concurrence seeking negatively affect decision quality. The goal of group model-building is to create consensus *after* sufficient deliberation and contrasting of viewpoints has taken place. As will be seen, consensus will almost automatically emerge when the group model-building has been conducted properly.

Reaching consensus is important because as Schein (1969) points out (unanimous) agreement on a decision will also create a sufficient basis for a decision and commitment with its implementation. Acceptance of a decision and commitment are important with regard to implementation of the decision. Implementation does not automatically follow from issuing an order to carry out a decision. As far back as 1938 Chester Barnard pointed out: 'It is surprising how much that in theory is authoritative, in the best of organizations in practice lacks authority—or, in plain language, how generally orders are disobeyed.' (Barnard, 1938, 162). His analysis of the basis of authority is quite opposite to what it means to most people in everyday life. As he points out: 'Therefore, under this definition the decision as to whether an order has authority or not lies with the persons to whom it is addressed, and does not reside in "persons of authority" or those who issue these orders.' (Barnard, 1938, 163). A couple of pages later he goes even further and concludes: 'There is no principle of executive conduct better established in good organizations than that orders will not be issued that cannot or will not be obeyed. Executives and most persons of experience who have thought about it know that to do so destroys authority, discipline, and morale.' (Barnard, 1938, 167).

Even deciding by majority vote (in particular if the majority only slightly exceeds half of the group) there is the danger that a number of team members will be unsatisfied and hence commitment with the decision is low. In this sense a distinction is frequently made between a decision's quality and its effectiveness. It is stated that the effectiveness (E) of a decision is not only determined by its quality (Q) but also by its acceptance (A) by the people who will have to implement it (Majone, 1984; Zakay, 1984). Hence, the shorthand notation: $E = Q \times A$. From this formula it follows that if either the quality of a decision or its acceptance comes close to zero the effectiveness will also approach zero.

In summary, one may conclude that three purposes can be identified with regard to group model-building. The first is to create a climate in which team learning can take place in order to enhance understanding of the problem. The second is to foster consensus. Finally, the intervention should help to create acceptance of the ensuing decision and commitment with the decision (see also Hart et al., 1985; Eden, 1992b). The remainder of this book is devoted to demonstrating how group model-building can accomplish these goals.

READERSHIP

This book is meant for professionals who want to become acquainted with group model-building as a means to support strategic decision making groups. Three types of readerships can be distinguished. First, there are those who are already familiar with system dynamics, but who want to increase the effectiveness of their model-building efforts by working more closely with client groups in the model-building process. I also consider students who have taken one or more courses in system dynamics to belong to this group. This group might benefit in particular from the chapter on human information processing and problem definition, ways to design group model-building projects, the chapters on group process and group facilitation as well as the cases presented in the final chapters. These readers might consider skipping the two chapters on system dynamics model-building.

The second type of readership are those individuals who are familiar with working with groups, but who are unfamiliar with system dynamics and group model-building. This group will find useful information on system dynamics model-building, group facilitation in the context of group model-building as well as a number of group model-building cases that may serve as examples. For those who are unexperienced with system dynamics I have included suggested titles for further study in a separate appendix, as well as a number of exercises to develop basic system dynamics model-building skills.

The third type of readership are those who have recently become familiar with ideas on team and organizational learning and systems thinking, but who have not yet had a chance to attempt to put these ideas in practice. For this group the book will provide a number of useful ideas and methods as well as tangible examples of group model-building projects showing its power when team learning becomes important for the organization's survival. I hope it will raise their interest and their inclination towards the application of system dynamics in their own work.

FRAMEWORK OF THE BOOK

In the first chapter, a number of potential recurrent flaws are discussed in the process of constructing complex, messy problems by people in organizations. These derive partly from the system dynamics viewpoint, partly from empirical research on human information processing and behavioural decision making and partly from the personal experience of the author. The second and third chapters focus on the system dynamics methodology. Chapter 2 briefly discusses the history of system dynamics, its core assumptions, and the first stages in system dynamics model-building: problem identification and constructing a conceptual model. The chapter closes with a brief discussion of system's archetypes as well as the merits and dangers of qualitative system dynamics in a group model-building context. Chapter 3 discusses the basics of quantitative system dynamics. This chapter includes the subsequent stages of model-building, i.e. model formulation, parameter estimation, model analysis and policy experiments with the system dynamics model. Both Chapters 2 and 3 contain a number of exercises with which the non-system dynamicist can develop basic system dynamics model-building skills.

Chapter 4 takes a look at a number of important decisions which have to be made in the context of helping teams to tackle messy problems by means of group model-building. Although there are many real world problems which can be fruitfully studied through system dynamics, this does not hold for all problems. A critical (and difficult) question which needs to be addressed is whether system dynamics is suited to tackle a particular problem. And if so, is a quantitative model (and simulations) required or will a qualitative model suffice? Other questions relate to the design of the project. For instance, does one start from scratch with the group or does the model-builder first construct a preliminary model which the group can employ as a starting point? Other relevant questions include: how many persons must be involved in the process and who? Will preparatory interviews be needed? Each of these questions will be discussed in Chapter 4. In order to assist the reader I will provide a number of guidelines on how to conduct effective interviews and I will introduce the reader to the use of so-called workbooks which prove to be effective to keep the model-building project on track, in particular when the group becomes larger.

In Chapter 5 we will turn our attention to the more intangible aspects of group model-building: group process and group facilitation. As mentioned before, in many group model-building projects, facilitator behaviour proves to be the crucial element in turning the project into a succes. The more the situation becomes pluralistic the more important becomes the facilitator role. Chapter 5 will discuss appropriate facilitation behaviour in the context of group model-building.

Chapters 6 and 7 will discuss a number of real life examples of group model-building projects. Chapter 6 will focus on qualitative, while Chapter 7 will discuss quantitative system dynamics. Chapter 8 will show the process of model analysis and policy experiments with a system dynamics model. I have chosen to present three projects which differ considerably in their approach to group model-building. This choice was made deliberately in order to demonstrate that, although system dynamics model-building proceeds in a more or less standard fashion, group model-building can take on a variety of forms depending on such things as the type of problem, organizational characteristics, and time and budget constraints. The chapters demonstrate how a particular form of group model-building can be carefully designed to meet a number of project constraints. In other words group model-building projects are tailor-made rather than ready-made. Since no two problem situations are alike the cases will also demonstrate that the results from a group model-building process can be quite unpredictable and hard to anticipate. The outcome is frequently not a clear cut decision, but a change of perspectives on the problem, which in turn may affect the organization's choice.

In Chapter 9 I will summarize the main points and provide some guidelines on how to put things into practice for the practitioner who has become interested in the subject.

A final remark relates to the names of software packages mentioned throughout the book. Stella and Ithink are copyrighted to, and registered trademarks of, High Performance Systems Inc., 45 Lyme Road, suite 300, Hanover, New Hampshire 03755, USA. Powersim is a trademark of ModellData AS, PO Box 642, N-5001 Bergen, Norway. Professional DYNAMO is a trademark of Pugh-Roberts Associates Inc., 41 William Linskey Way, Cambridge, MA 02142, USA. And, finally, Vensim is a trademark of Ventana Systems, 149 Waverley Street, Belmont MA 02178, USA.

Chapter 1

Individual and Organizational Problem Construction

INTRODUCTION

There is convincing evidence that humans consciously or unconsciously select information to construct problem definitions. The information selection process is frequently guided by already existing ideas and opinions. Humans typically select information which confirms their beliefs rather than look for information which might refute their opinions. Existing beliefs can thus be maintained, in spite of contradictory information. For reasons of reduction of mental efforts, contradictory information is generally ignored. In addition, research in the realm of behavioural decision making has revealed that people are constrained by limitations in information processing capabilities. Human beings have been shown to be biased in information selection and to employ a large number of simplifying heuristics to process information. This has been demonstrated to hold for rather simple, static and well-structured problems. It is reasonable to assume that things become worse when one has to deal with dynamic problems in complex systems. Humans typically tend to simplify problems to a large extent, for instance by ignoring potential dynamic effects of selected strategies.

This chapter takes a closer look at recurrent flaws when humans and organizations try to deal with messy problems. As an introduction let us first take a look at an example of a strategic, messy problem from one of the group model-building projects we conducted for a client organization and see what we can learn about the nature of messy problems.

MESSY PROBLEMS: AN EXAMPLE

Between January 1991 and December 1993 I was involved in the so-called 'Nostradamus' management development program at the Dutch Directorate

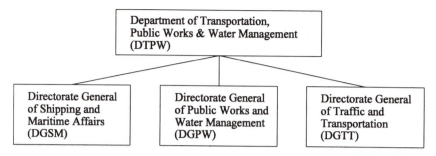

Figure 1.1   Organizational Structure of DTPW

General of Public Works and Water Management (DGPW). DGPW is a government agency which belongs to the Department of Transportation, Public Works and Water Management (DTPW). Besides DGPW, there is a Directorate General of Traffic and Transportation (DGTT) and one for Shipping and Maritime Affairs (DGSM). The interconnection between these departments is depicted in Figure 1.1

The objective of the management development program in DGPW was to improve strategic thinking skills of their 25 management teams. For this purpose scenarios, the hexagon method and (qualitative) system dynamics were used in the training program, which consisted amongst others of a two-day workshop. (For literature on the use of scenarios in strategic decision making see: Schoemaker (1993), de Geus (1988), Wack (1985a and b), Schwartz (1991) and Vennix et al. (1994). For more information on the hexagon method the reader is referred to Hodgson (1992). Lane (1993) provides an example of the use of hexagons to focus a system dynamics study.) I was specifically hired by the DGPW to facilitate system dynamics group model-building sessions to support strategic discussions within management teams. During one of the group model-building demonstration session at DGPW two persons of the Directorate General of Shipping and Maritime Affairs (DGSM), who were also present, approached me enquiring if I was interested in conducting a couple of model-building sessions for the Long Term Strategy Group of DGSM. I was told that the issue to be modeled was related to the Dutch-registered merchant fleet. We agreed that we would have a meeting in the next week and as a preparation to our meeting they sent me a couple of documents relating to the Dutch-registered merchant fleet.

The Problem of the Dutch-registered Merchant Fleet

From way back the Netherlands have been a major maritime nation and have always played an important role in the maritime transportation of goods all over the world. Since the Second World War, however, things have changed dramatically for traditional maritime nations. The capacity of the world merchant fleet has increased fourfold, while at the same time the US and the European share in this fleet have gradually but persistently decreased. The Dutch share in the world fleet decreased from more than 4% to less than 1% in 1990 (Voorlopige Raad voor Verkeer en

Waterstaat, 1992, 4). These dramatic changes have, among others, been caused by differences between countries with regard to wage costs, fiscal policies and safety requirements. For economic reasons many ship-owners were compelled to resort to so-called 'flags of convenience' (e.g. Liberia and Panama). In particular, during the 1960s competition for the Dutch commercial fleet increased significantly. It was, however, not until the beginning of the 1970s that the Dutch government adopted a policy to protect the Dutch-registered fleet by means of investment premiums and tax incentives. The policy seemed a success, because until the mid 1980s the size of the Dutch commercial fleet stabilized at about 800 vessels, while at the same time the Northwest European fleet decreased by about 50% (in tonnage). However, due to the rapidly decreasing economic situation after the mid 1980s, the Dutch govern-ment was forced to introduce new financial aid programs in order to encourage vessels to continue to fly the Dutch flag and to maintain employment in the mar-itime sector. In 1987 it was decided to continue and further increase the investment premiums on the construction of new vessels and the tax exemption programme. The latter aimed at reducing gross wage costs of crews. In addition, a number of regulations regarding crew composition were relaxed. Again these measures seemed succesful; the decreasing trend in the number of ships flying the Dutch flag stabilized and even showed a slight increase in 1990. This recovery did not last though. After 1990 the decline in the size of the Dutch fleet resumed. Once again a new financial aid program seemed to be required to reverse this trend. Several studies were conducted to identify policies which could increase the viability of the Dutch fleet. These studies indicated that the existing investment and tax programs had to be both diversified and expanded to be effective (DGSM, 1992).

However, as my spokespersons told me in our meeting, the political scene had changed radically in a couple of years. In comparison with 1987 the government was now much less inclined to continue financial support to the Dutch-registered mer-chant fleet. One reason was the large budget deficit which had to be reduced. Another was the fact that in the recent past several cases had been made public in which the government had provided large sums of subsidies to insolvent companies. In retrospect these proved to be a waste of the tax payer's money. Since financial aid programs for the Dutch fleet had not been very succesful in the past, the secretary of the Department of Transportation and Public Works (DTPW) was probably afraid of being accused of 'pouring the tax payer's money down the drain'. By the end of 1991 the financial support program was drawing near the end of its term. Both the Secretary of Finance and the Secretary of DTPW seriously con-sidered ceasing financial aid to the Dutch-registered merchant fleet.

A number of people in DGSM regarded this as a hasty decision. In fact it was one group, the Sea Fleet Policy Unit (SFPU) within DGSM, who was most worried about the 'decreasing fleet size problem'. This unit is largely responsible for the Dutch-registered merchant fleet. Termination of the financial aid program would jeopardize their position within DGSM. In addition many within this Unit felt that support for the Dutch fleet could not just simply be abandoned, since in the long run this would mean giving up the position of the Netherlands as a historical maritime nation. People within the SFPU felt strongly that something needed to be done to stop the reduction of vessels flying the Dutch flag. As early as the beginning of 1991 they started to prepare a policy document to obtain renewed governmental support for financial aid programs to protect the Dutch fleet.

The group in which these strategic discussions were conducted (i.e the Long Term Strategy Group) consisted of the heads of the various units within the department of DGSM. Within this Long Term Strategy Group (LTSG) there were sharp differences of opinion. Apart from the Dutch commercial fleet, DGSM is also responsible for two other strategic areas. The first is related to the Dutch ports (i.e. Rotterdam and Amsterdam) and involves such tasks as further innovation in the ports, maintaining safety, and gearing activities and transportation modalities to one another. The second area concerns the advancement of safe and swift shipping traffic in the North Sea. Those involved in these latter two strategic areas had strong doubts about the viability of the Dutch commercial fleet. They basically agreed with the secretary of DTPW to abandon government support and were not inclined to back up the policy document of the Sea Fleet Policy Unit (SFPU). In their view the Dutch fleet was 'history' and the other two strategic issues would prove to be much more critical in a rapidly changing world, where rather than a large commercial fleet, issues like telematics, logistics and 'floor to floor management' would become increasingly important. These individuals proposed to cease interference with the Dutch fleet altogether in order to be able to more fully concentrate future activities of the agency on the other two strategic areas.

By the beginning of 1992 this discussion had lasted for more than a year and the Long Term Strategy Group obviously was not able to reach a consensual decision. On the contrary, it seemed that over time arguments and positions had become more rigid. It was at this point in time that I was approached with the request to conduct a couple of group model-building sessions within DGSM. Since the secretary of DTPW had suggested stopping the financial aid program and a decision by the Lower and Upper Chamber was approaching, time was very limited. As a result there was no time to conduct preparatory interviews. Instead three sessions of three hours each were planned over the course of six weeks, in which a qualitative system dynamics model in the form of a causal loop diagram would be constructed. It was agreed that after three sessions the group model-building process would be evaluated and a decision would be taken whether to continue model-building or not.

The fact that no preparatory interviews were held, meant that I was not aware of the sharp differences of opinion within DGSM. This clearly surfaced during the first model-building session when I introduced the problem to be modeled. When I tried to start the model-building process in the first session, the introduction of the 'fleet problem' immediately gave rise to a heated debate in which several persons indicated that this was only a minor problem and that instead the focus should be on more important problems, i.e. those related to the Dutch coast and the Dutch ports. Some participants held very strong opinions about this matter, which gave rise to an intense discussion and lack of consensus on what problem to model. It looked as if the discussion would get stuck at the beginning of the first session.

To overcome this apparent deadlock I asked several group members why they considered the 'fleet problem' unimportant. Their answers suggested to me that they saw the 'fleet problem' as an isolated phenomenon, largely unrelated to other strategic problems. This is a situation which frequently occurs in decision making groups. I suggested to the group that it might probably make little difference which subject would be taken as a starting point for model-building. From a systems point of view they would most probably prove interrelated and the other strategic areas would automatically come into focus during the construction of a model of the Dutch fleet. This (at least temporarily) convinced most of the sceptic group members and a deal was made that if 'their problems' would not surface within a couple of sessions we would rediscuss this issue. As a result of this decision the problem of the Dutch-registered merchant fleet was taken as our preliminary starting point. Much to the surprise of the participants, in three sessions of three hours each the group, guided by a facilitator, constructed a model which demonstrated that all three strategic areas were intricately interrelated. In other words, a decision taken in any of these three areas would severely affect the other two. More specifically the model revealed that abandoning the Dutch fleet might in the long run also damage the other two strategic areas (particularly the position of the Dutch harbours), an insight which the group had not realized before. The group model-building process thus catalized strategic discussions and consensus was reached during these three sessions to try to maintain support for the Dutch fleet. As a result, a policy document was drafted for the Secretary of DTPW, requesting to maintain the financial support program for the Dutch fleet. This document was discussed by the Lower and Higher Chambers. Obviously the arguments in the document were convincing, because it was decided that subsidies for the Dutch merchant fleet would be continued, albeit for a limited period of five years.

The construction of the system dynamics model created an effective learning atmosphere in which new insights on the strategic problems were gained. It helped reconcile conflicts of interest by looking at the problem from a systems point of view. In Chapter 6 the methodological aspects of this case will be discussed in more detail. There I will demonstrate how the results were accomplished and to what extent group model-building in fact produced these results. For now let us use this case description to demonstrate a number of typical characteristics of strategic, messy problems.

MESSY PROBLEMS: 'THE REALITY OF MULTIPLE REALITIES'

One of the most pervasive characteristics of messy problems is that people hold entirely different views on (a) whether there is a problem, and if they agree there is, (b) what the problem is. In that sense messy problems are quite intangible and as a result various authors have suggested that there are no 'objective' problems, only situations defined as problems by people. (See for instance: Ackoff (1981), Checkland (1981), Checkland and Scholes (1990), Eden, Jones and Sims (1983), and Bryant (1989).) This is also revealed by the DGSM case, discussed in the previous section. People held widely different views, which makes problem definition a grey area. Indeed, in the first session I had arrived in what Schön (1987) has called the 'swampy lowland' of organizational problems, where problems defy a purely technical solution, and where various people define situations differently. In other words 'reality' as people experience it, is not a passive image of some objective world 'out there'. Rather from the wealth of information that is available, human beings actively select and interpret information and thus construct their 'model of reality'. As a result the interventionist is typically confronted with a situation of multiple realities (Schutz, 1962; Checkland, 1981).

Interpreting Situations

Numerous experiments in psychology have confirmed the existence of selective perception (Johnson Abercrombie, 1960; Hogarth, 1987). For instance, people see things according to what they expect to see. Davis and Sinha (1950) have shown that differential previous information leads to dramatically different interpretations of the 'same' empirical phenomenon. In this case people were asked to describe what they saw in Brueghel's painting 'The Village Wedding'. Before subjects were shown the painting, however, one group had to read a story about a feud between two families, which resulted in the killing of the head of one of the two families, and a subsequent wedding party between the son of the deceased father and the daughter of the father's murderer. A control group did not read the story. The description and interpretation of Brueghel's painting differed significantly between the two groups.

Other experiments have shown that people can easily be led to believe something. Naftulin, Ware and Donnely (1973) describe an experiment to show the ambiguous value of subjective evaluations in educational settings. Their hypothesis was that an experienced group of educators would indicate to be satisfied with and to have learned from a lecture despite the fact that the lecturer would convey primarily meaningless and irrelevant content. In order to test this hypothesis the researchers '. . . selected a professional actor who looked distinguished and sounded authoritative; provided him with a sufficiently ambiguous title, Dr Myron L. Fox, an authority on the application of mathematics to human behaviour; dressed him up with an impressive curriculum vitae, and presented him to a group of highly trained educators.' (Naftulin, Ware and Donnely, 1973, 631). This Dr Fox presented a lecture to two different groups. His talk consisted of '. . . an excessive use of double talk, neologisms, non sequiturs, and contradictory statements. All this was to be interspersed with parenthetical humor and meaningless references to unrelated topics.' (Naftulin, Ware and Donnely, 1973, 631–632). The results showed that most people in his audience were quite impressed and highly satisfied with what they had learned during the lecture. Even when informed about the purpose of the study subjects indicated that Dr Fox had stimulated interest in the subject.

In other words when people are induced to believe certain things this will affect the interpretation of subsequent information. This type of process has, for example, also been identified in personnel selection interviews. Tucker and Rowe (1979) provided three groups of students with exactly the same information about a potential applicant by means of transcripts of interviews. The transcripts described a number of past successes and failures of the applicant. However, before giving the students the transcripts of the interviews one group received a favourable letter of reference about the applicant, a second group received a neutral letter and a third group received an unfavourable letter of reference. Students in the group that received the unfavourable letter showed the tendency to blame the applicant for past failures (the applicant was considered to show low effort, low ability, and a weak personality) and to give the person less credit for past successes. On the other hand students who received the favourable letter of reference showed the reverse tendency (although to a lesser extent): the applicant was given more credit for past successes. For instance, he was supposed to have succeeded because of his efforts, abilities or personality. Simultaneoulsy, failures were attributed to external influences like bad luck, and task difficulty. When subjects had to make a decision whether to accept the applicant or not, the results showed that the fewer the subjects attributed past successes to the applicant the higher the chances of being rejected and vice versa. Likewise, the more the subjects attributed past failures to the applicant the higher the chances of being rejected, while attributions of past failures to external circumstances led to a higher chance of being accepted. In short, differences in previous information (i.e. letter of reference) leads people to interpret the same information (i.e. transcripts of an interview) in markedly different ways, which subsequently leads to significant differences in the final decision whether to hire a person or not.

Examples like these stem from laboratory research and are purposefully induced by an experimenter. Some people might question the validity of the results, because they were obtained in an artificial environment. However, there is ample evidence that indicates that processes like selective perception and interpretation permeate our daily life. People incessantly select and interpret information on the basis of their experience and background. As we have seen in the DGSM case, a manager's view of the organization and its problems is powerfully determined by that person's place in the organization. More generally, a production manager 'sees' different problems than a financial manager, and a R&D manager 'sees' different problems than a personnel manager (March and Simon, 1958; Russo and Schoemaker, 1989). This even holds in simulated circumstances when there is no real conflict of interest involved. Dearborn and Simon (1958) for instance asked research subjects to write a brief statement on what they considered to be the most important problem in the Castengo Steel Company case. The most important problem was defined as the problem a new president would have to deal with first, when entering the company. Since this study involves a written case, all subjects were provided with exactly the same information. Yet, the authors found significant differences in problem definitions. Managers tended to select problems which corresponded with their background. For instance, sales managers tended to mention sales as the most important problem, whereas production managers tended to mention production problems. Even in this case where subjects were asked to look at the problem from a company wide perspective they obviously had internalized the criteria of selection so deeply that they 'automatically' selected problem definitions which matched their professional background.

Not only are people biased in information selection, research has also revealed that people tend to be biased in recollecting past events. An example is the so-called 'hindsight bias' phenomenon (Fischhoff, 1975). Recollection of predictions people make before an event takes place, are influenced by their beliefs whether events have taken place after the fact. For instance, Fischhoff and Beyth (1975) conducted an experiment in which they asked a number of students to predict the probability of a number of events which might take place during President Nixon's first visit to the People's Republic of China. Some time after this visit had taken place they asked the same group of students what they thought they had predicted a couple of months before. It proved that the recollection of subjects' past predictions was heavily influenced by their belief whether certain events had actually occurred.

In a related vein, studies of eyewitness testimonies in legal proceedings have demonstrated that people frequently report what they think they should have seen rather than the 'facts' (Hogarth, 1987). For instance, in recollecting information the so-called availability heuristic has been demonstrated: information with salient characteristics can be more easily remembered than less salient information. In short, contrary to what many people believe, memory is not just simply a mechanism which stores and retrieves information. Rather memory is a device which actively reconstructs the past in order to fit in with current beliefs and opinions.

These examples reveal that there is convincing scientific evidence that the human mind actively constructs reality rather than passively stores and recalls information, which is received through the senses. Since different individuals interpret situations differently, this in turn leads to differences in people's 'mental models' and differences in opinion about the nature of reality. (Note: the question might be raised whether a contradiction exists between the point of view of the subjective nature of reality and 'scientific evidence' about this subjective nature. The scientific evidence creates the impression of objective truth. A sceptic might argue that after all, scientific evidence is gathered by human beings which will also be subject to processes of selective perception and recollection. However, an important difference between everyday and scientific knowledge, which is gained through empirical research, is that in the latter case the way knowledge is created has to adhere to specific rules and procedures. One of these rules is that the way knowledge was gained should be open to inspection by others and be replicable. If previous results are replicated by others, and we agree with the rules and methods by which the results were generated then we would have to accept the results. This implies that we have arrived at intersubjective knowledge, i.e. knowledge on which we agree rather than objective knowledge.)

Differences of opinion might be resolved relatively easily in cases where we have consensus on the way to interpret situations. For instance, if a couple of managers argue about the exact level of inventory they can simply find out by counting the number of items in stock. In this case differences of opinion might be settled easily. Note that in this respect some authors use the term physical reality, i.e. '. . . those things regarded as empirically determinable by objective or, in our Western tradition, "scientific" tests.' (Schein, 1988, 89). The problem with this is that, as Schein himself argues, what is considered to be physical reality, in other words what can be established empirically, differs between cultures. As an example he refers to the studies of Castaneda (e.g. Castaneda, 1968) who was taught for several years by the Yaqui indian brujo don Juan. I would like to refer the interested reader to the excellent discussion of Castaneda's works by Silverman (1975). Actually there are two problems. The first is whether something can be established empirically, and second, if we agree on the first issue, how something might be established empirically. If you and I disagree on something we would have to get consensus on both the previous questions in order to be able to empirically establish what the 'truth' is. And that is where the problem lies, although this issue was not too obvious in the inventory problem. But even in simple circumstances differences of opinion might arise. Take for instance the unemployment problem. If we define unemployed persons as those persons who are officially registered, we obtain a different number of unemployed than in the case where we would also like to include those persons who do not even bother to register, because they consider the chances of obtaining work as too slim. And what does it mean to be officially registered? Frequently only those people, looking for part-time jobs exceeding 20 hours per week are considered to be unemployed. In other words even when deciding on such a seemingly clear-cut issue as the number of unemployed it is not simply a matter of counting heads. The number of unemployed persons is determined by the definition we use and no empirical test can be employed to decide what definition to use!

Thus far I have discussed situations in which 'facts' had to be established. Matters become more complicated when we do not deal with simple 'facts', but when we are concerned with values. Suppose in the inventory example that one manager argues that inventory is too high and another that it is too low. The first person might be a financial manager who is primarily occupied with the cost of inventory. The second person might be a sales manager whose primary interest is to avoid delivery delays. In this case it is not a simple question of counting the number of items in stock. Obviously, the two managers attach different meaning to the level of inventory. For one person it means costs, which have to be kept as low as possible. For the other it means a safe reservoir which guarantees low backlog, immediate deliveries and satisfied customers. In this case, for instance, the sales manager has an implicit assumption that low inventory will lead to delivery delays and thus to unsatisfied customers. Stated differently, in this example the question is not 'simply' to establish some 'fact', rather people hold implicit models, including 'facts', (causal) arguments, values etc. And although in principle, these implicit models might be empirically tested, there is also the pragmatic argument whether such a test can be accomplished within a reasonable time and without undesirable risks.

Implicit assumptions were also observed in the DGSM case with which this chapter opened. Some people held the assumption that concentrating on the Dutch fleet led to a dispersion of efforts within the organization. These persons wanted to abandon the Dutch fleet and concentrate the organization's resources more fully on the other two strategic areas, which would then expand more rapidly. This in turn was deemed necessary because of anticipated changes in the transportation process of goods in the future. However, the group model-building sessions came to challenge this implicit assumption. Not only did it prove untenable, rather the opposite proved to be true: the less efforts devoted to the Dutch fleet, the higher the likelihood that the other two strategic sectors would decline.

In general, organizational decision making processes are permeated with implicit assumptions and arguments. In another project that I recently conducted with a number of colleagues for the Royal Dutch Medical Association (RDMA) there were differences of opinion on the membership level. Although the number of doctors becoming members of the RDMA was still rising slightly, it was declining when compared to the absolute growth in the number of doctors in the Netherlands. The proportion of doctors becoming a member of the RDMA had been decreasing from 90% in the 1970s to about 50% in the 1990s. Although in this case there was little disagreement about the actual membership level, there were differences about its meaning. Some considered it important for the organization to have a high number of members. In their view the RDMA was to be the organization for *all* doctors in the Netherlands rather than just a subset. One of the reasons backing up this viewpoint was that a low membership level would encroach upon the organization's legitimacy. Others, however, were less convinced of this need. In their view a high membership level would attenuate the organization's goals. They held the opinion that the organization ought to have an unambiguous mission and clear policies. This would then automatically attract members agreeing with this mission statement, while rebuffing others. And that was exactly what they wanted. Not only were there different beliefs with regard to the need for a high membership level, there were also sharp discrepancies in opinion on the causes of the low membership level. A variety of causes were mentioned, including high membership dues, processes of individualization in society in general, and also, interestingly enough, the high numbers in the membership which attenuated RDMA's goals, which in turn made the organization unattractive to a number of doctors!

In short, when dealing with messy problems, consensual guidelines on how to interpret situations are lacking and there is more room for idiosyncratic, personal interpretations of situations. If, for instance, you are a workaholic you might easily be led to believe that many people in your organization are unmotivated to work. At the same time some of your (non workaholic) colleagues might be convinced that most people's motivation in the organization is quite high. In contrast to the inventory example (where I can count the actual number of items in stock) in this situation, it is more difficult to get agreement on the 'empirical facts'. Typically, as a result of processes of selective perception you as a workaholic might see instances in which people are *not* at work, rather than those situations in which they are.

Now, if there were only differences in perceptions this need not be particularly disturbing for an organization. However, organizations are supposed to coordinate individual efforts into organized action. And the latter becomes problematic because differences in individual realities lead to differences in individual behaviour, which may jeopardize organized action.

Creating (Social) Reality

Thus far we have been concerned with the reality in people's minds. However, if this reality in people's minds is intangible what does it mean that something is real for a person? The answer to this question was most succinctly stated by the sociologist Thomas in what later came to be known as the Thomas theorem: 'If men define situations as real, they are real in their consequences.' (Thomas and Thomas, 1928, 572.) A vivid example of this is the fear many people had when Columbus sailed out to the west. Many people were convinced that the earth was flat and if Columbus would go off too far in a western direction he would literally fall off the earth. To us this seems unimaginable or even ridiculous. However, to the people in those days this was what reality looked like and hence their reluctance to sail too far to the west. In other words, believing that the earth is flat becomes a reality, which in turn affects people's behaviour. And this is exactly the meaning of the Thomas theorem. If, for instance, I am convinced that people in organizations are primarily concerned with playing power games, this conviction is part of my reality and will determine my actions. I might for instance (implicitly) decide that I will have to participate in this game in order not to become a victim of it. Or to provide another example, if I am convinced that people in general cannot be trusted, this will make me suspicious about other people's behaviour and I will act accordingly. Under these circumstances matters become more complicated, because my own behaviour in turn might create the very reality as I perceive it, a phenomenon known as the self-fulfilling prophecy (Johnson Abercrombie, 1960; Jones, 1977; Watzlawick, 1984).

In general, a self-fulfilling prophecy refers to a situation in which an expectation (i.e. my definition of a situation) leads to behaviour, which in turn produces the situation the way I defined it. Einhorn (1980) provides a hypothetical example of a waiter in a busy restaurant who lacks the time to provide good service to all the customers in his station. Suppose this waiter tacitly assumes (maybe partly based on previous experience) that well-dressed people leave larger tips than ill-dressed people. If we suppose that the quality of the service has an effect on the size of the tip (which in some countries is not at all an unreasonable assumption) one can imagine what the outcome will be and how the waiter is reinforced in his judgement about the likelihood of certain people leaving poor tips. For the waiter in this example, it might be difficult to uncover that he continually acts to reinforce his own beliefs. Only if he was aware of his behaviour and its potential effects would he be in a position to radically change his behaviour and to test the hypothesis about the relationship between the way people are dressed and the amount of tips they leave. In other words the waiter in this example would have to perform an experiment to try to refute his hypothesis in order to be sure that he is correct. However, this seems difficult for human beings because people tend to look for information which confirms their viewpoint rather than to look for evidence which might refute it (Hogarth, 1987). It follows that a self-fulfilling prophecy can be quite difficult to uncover and can persist for a long time without a person being aware of it.

Examples of self-fulfilling prophecies are not only found in the individual, but also at more aggregated levels. Merton for instance argued that the dynamics of ethnic and racial conflict in America of his days could largely be explained by the self-fulfilling prophecy (see Merton, 1957). Another example at an aggregated level stems from economics. Investment decisions made by managers will be based, at least partly on expectations about future economic developments, which cannot be known with certainty before the fact. Hence a manager has to make a judgement about future economic developments and next decide whether or not to invest in a new technology. If a sufficiently large proportion of managers have optimistic expectations about the future and decides to invest, these investments themselves might lead to a favorable economic development, something which was supposed to happen in the first place. Unfortunately many econometric models do not incorporate these expectations about the future, and thus miss this self-fulfilling prophecy phenomenon in economics, simply because no data about them are available or the phenomena are considered not to belong to the realm of economics (Pen and Gemerden, 1977, 116).

A sceptic might argue that proof of the self-fulfilling prophecy is predominantly anecdotal and that these processes lack any empirical evidence. However, many empirical studies have demonstrated the working of self-fulfilling prophecies in the classroom. Rosenthal and Jacobson (1968) for instance conducted an experiment in which teachers were told that a certain test could identify those 20% of students who would make above average intellectual progress in a coming school year. Before the teachers met the new students, they were handed the names of these 'above average' students, which were picked randomly from the student list! At the end of the school year however, these students showed a real above-average increase in intelligence. In addition, the faculty stated that these students distinguished themselves from their fellow students by their intellectual curiosity. Although this particular experiment received much criticism, it has been replicated many times (avoiding the pitfalls of the original study), with similar findings. Baker and Crist (1971), summarizing this line of research, commented that the question was not so much *whether* expectancy effects operate, but rather *how* they function. Over the decades further research revealed that teachers treat pupils in different ways, based on their original expectations, and thereby create differences in performance which in turn confirm their original expectations (Jussim, 1986). Similar mechanisms of the self-fulfilling prophecy have been identified in selection recruitment interviews (Dipboye, 1982). And surprisingly, self-fulfilling prophecies have also been demonstrated in the training of rats (Rosenthal, 1966) and even earthworms (Cordaro and Ison, 1963).

The conclusion that the self-fulfilling prophecy is a ubiquitous phenomenon of social life seems to be reinforced. Rather than a rare phenomenon, research indicates that quite frequently our expectations create the very reality the way we perceive it (Jones, 1977; Watzlawick, 1984). But the relationships between expectations, behaviour and social reality can be so subtle and elusive that we fail to recognize the self-fulfilling prophecy even when it happens in front of our own eyes. This subtlety is, for instance, demonstrated in an ingenious experiment by Farina, Allen and Sal (1968). Previous research had revealed that stigmatized people (in this case people who have been mentally-ill) are treated differently by fellow human beings than 'normal' people. One could be led to believe that this might be natural and that it is caused by the actual stigma. However, Farina, Allen and Sal (1968) elegantly demonstrated that differential treatment between stigmatized and non-stigmatized people can be based solely on beliefs. They had subjects (in the control condition) copy a feigned 'normal' life history note. Persons in the experimental condition were asked to copy a concocted life history indicating that the subject was, for instance, mentally ill. The experimenter then pretended to bring this note to a second person with which the first person would have to interact later. For persons in the control condition this was actually done. In other words the second person actually received a normal life history. However, for subjects in the experimental condition the experimenter switched the notes, i.e. the note indicating the stigma was replaced by a 'normal' life history. As a result, in the experimental condition, the second person (receiving the note) was actually provided with a 'normal' life history, similar to those in the control condition. In other words, in the experimental condition the first person (who had written the note) was led to believe that the second person (receiving the note) thought him to be mentally ill, while in fact this was *not* the case, because the notes had been switched by the experimenter. Recordings of the subsequent interactions revealed significant differences in dyadic interaction between experimental and control conditions. In the experimental condition for instance, people initiated fewer contacts with the stigmatized as compared to the control condition. The authors conclude that obviously if one believes that someone else thinks one is stigmatized, one *expects* the other to behave in a specific way and in behavioural terms one obviously gives off cues that lead others to confirm one's expectations.

To summarize the above discussion, people build 'mental models' of their environment and in turn base their behaviour on these mental models, thereby creating situations which are subsequently interpreted as reality. This line of reasoning is summarized in Figure 1.2.

For reasons of simplicity I have (a) distinguished two persons A and B, and (b) made a distinction between three different elements: individual reality, behaviour and environment. Let us start with A's individual reality or mental model. The mental model contains A's view of reality. The term mental model should be interpreted broadly to include attitudes as well. It produces and contains descriptions, interpretations and explanations of situations which A perceives in the environment. This mental model is constructed and maintained by selecting and interpreting information from the environment. As stated, this selection process is itself guided by the existing mental model and subject to the 'law' of looking for confirming evidence, hence the dashed arrow. In addition, internally the mental model is subject to selective memory and distortion. In other words, there is ample opportunity for different human beings to construct and maintain different mental models of the 'same' external situation.

We have also seen that beliefs in a mental model will in turn affect a person's behaviour, which create situations in the environment. From these situations a person selects information and builds a model of reality, subject to the processes and restrictions mentioned before. A similar process could be described for person B. In that sense, although not depicted that way in the figure, I do have to point out that B's behaviour is part of the environment for A and vice versa. As a consequence, every statement or act by B is interpreted by A, which will lead to a specific behaviour by A, which is in turn interpreted by B etc.

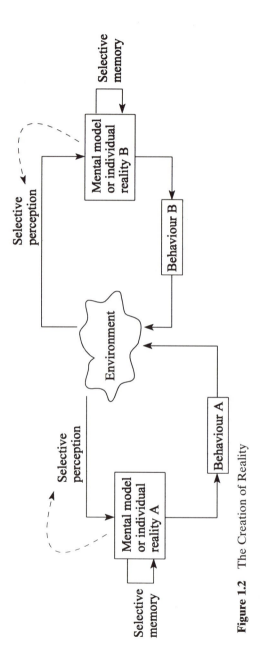

Figure 1.2 The Creation of Reality

I do have to point out that this is a simple model of the construction of reality, which might be questioned at first sight. The reader might for instance argue that frequently what people say they do, does not match their actual actions and vice versa. We are often surprised by the fact that people say they will do A but instead they act in manner B. A teacher might for instance say that he is not there to teach but rather to help his students learn while in fact through his actions it becomes clear that he is 'just' teaching. In other words a distinction needs to be made between so-called espoused theories and theories in use (Argyris and Schön, 1978; Argyris, 1992). The first refers to my verbalization of my beliefs about reality, while the second is obviously the theory which actually guides my behaviour. Both theories frequently do not match, while research shows that people are largely unaware of the discrepancy between what they say they do and their actual behaviour. Typically, what people are aware of is discrepancies between statements and behaviour in others! (see Argyris, 1992).

The second complication is that the way I interpret situations is not only determined by intrapsychic processes like selective perception, but is also largely determined by how others interpret situations in the environment. Stated differently, for the interpretation of situations and the definition of reality, most of us are dependent on the way that others in our environment interpret situations. This was for instance quite convincingly demonstrated in a series of experiments conducted by Asch (1963). Subjects in these experiments were placed in small groups. These groups were then put in a room and two sets of cards were presented to them. One card displayed a single line (the standard) and the other card three lines of different length, one of which was equal in length to the standard. Subjects were asked to indicate which of the three lines on the second card was equal in length to the standard. However, except for one person all group member were confederates who were instructed to give the wrong answer. It proved that if these confederates gave their (wrong) answers first, this produced almost 40% wrong answers for non-confederates, although control subjects, performing the task alone achieved a score of about 100% correct answers. The results of these experiments showed that a large proportion of people tended to concur with the opinion of the majority. In other words, the way others perceive reality in turn (at least in part) affects our view of it, through their (verbal or non-verbal) behaviour. What is seen as real by individuals is thus also partially influenced by what others in our environment think is real. In other words everyday reality presents itself as an intersubjective world which is shared with others (Berger and Luckmann, 1966). Frequently this social reality definition is not put to the test. As Hogarth points out: 'It has been suggested, for instance, that illusory correlation persists in situations where people do not receive good feedback concerning their judgements and where others share the same illusions. Thus instead of feedback concerning actual outcomes, each person both reinforces and is reinforced by the illusions of the others. In many organizations, common beliefs are precisely of this nature.' (Hogarth, 1987, 114.)

Thus far I have discussed the phenomenon of the self-fulfilling prophecy. To make matters more complicated, on the opposite side we have the so-called self-denying prophecy. Here people act in such ways as to refute the original definition of the situation. If for instance the Planning Bureau predicts a large budget deficit for the government, the government starts a 'reduction of expenses' programme. If succesful this programme will falsify the initial prediction. In another situation the Secretary of Education announces that a large surplus of dentists is expected in the near future. The actual result might be a shortage of dentists after a number of years. A phenomenon known more generally as the hog cycle.

The previous paragraphs demonstrate that we have to be careful not to take things for granted and seeing things as simple 'facts'. In particular expectancies in social interaction can easily and unconsciously create a self-fulfilling prophecy. In many cases our actions quite literally create the reality as we perceive it. In the chapter on group facilitation (Chapter 5) I will indicate how this point of view complicates appropriate facilitation behaviour. But as Merton (1957, 477) already cogently pointed out: 'Such are the perversities of social logic.'

Sharing and Aligning Mental Models: Creating a View of the Whole

The previous sections show that problems are subjective constructions where definitions can vary widely between different people of the same organization. Differences of viewpoint are the result of various factors, e.g. differences in personality, in the way one was raised, in professional training, and because people belong to different departments in an organization. The case discussed at the beginning of this chapter confirms the notion that selective perception and conflict of interest is frequently induced by a person's position in an organization. In addition, many people are less interested in the organization's goals than concerned about their careers, 'covering their ass' policies, covering up mistakes, a win-lose fight orientation, and one-upmanship power games (Janis, 1989). It is no wonder that a number of scholars have developed the notion of non-rational behaviour in organizational decision making. Lindblom (1959) has become famous for his 'science of muddling through' emphasizing incremental decision making. Cohen, March and Olsen (1972) launched their 'garbage can model' of organizational decision making (see also March and Olsen, 1976). These models of decision making in organizations are clearly in line with what was said before. People have different mental models of problems and these models in turn affect the way they will behave. All else being equal, the larger the discrepancies between managers' mental models in an organization the more lack of shared vision, the more divergence in behaviour and the higher the dispersion of organizational energy. This in turn impedes the effective operation of the organization, because it will induce a lack of cooperation.

As a result various authors have pointed out that one of the most important goals in structuring messy problems is the creation of a shared reality and problem definition among the group of problem owners (Checkland, 1981; Phillips, 1984; Eden, Jones and Sims, 1983). As Checkland and Scholes point out: 'What is in short supply in organizations is an organized sharing of perceptions sufficiently intense that concerted action gets taken corporately.' (Checkland and Scholes, 1990, 79.) Alternatively, it is sometimes argued that the goal of the intervention is to create shared meaning. (For the difficulties involved in the concept of shared meaning and its measurement see Scheper (1991), Scheper and Faber (1994) and Chapter 6.)

The purpose of an intervention is thus to share and align mental models in order to foster concerted action. Rather than devoting one's time to the construction of strategic plans the focus must instead be on the process of changing mental models itself, i.e. on the creation of a learning process within a team. Or as de Geus (1988) cogently puts it: 'At Shell, planning means changing minds, not making plans.'

Rather than declining in importance it seems that the problem of creating a shared reality will only increase with the coming of the new organization, which largely consists of 'knowledge workers'. Drucker points out that in this type of organization the old command and control coordination mechanism will become obsolete. One important management problem will become to create: '. . . a common vision, a view of the whole. . . . It [the organization] needs a view of the whole and a focus on the whole to be shared among a great many of its professional specialists, certainly among the senior ones.' (Drucker, 1988, 51; see also Espejo, 1994.)

It is exactly the integration of different, and by necessity partial, visions which group model-building attempts to accomplish. This was cleary demonstrated in the DGSM case (and will be discussed in more methodological detail in Chapter 6). This case illustrated that what at first sight is perceived as a conflict of interest at the level of an organizational unit might be considered common ground at the level of the whole organization. Group model-building in this case was successful in providing people with a view of the whole (rather than to concentrate on the separate parts), and thereby foster concerted action.

SEEING PARTS INSTEAD OF THE WHOLE: PIECEMEAL SOLUTIONS

Given the way human beings process information, an holistic view is the exception rather than the rule. A number of cognitive limitations induce people to focus on parts rather than the whole, particularly when they are not trained in systems thinking. This frequently gives rise to piecemeal solutions to complex problems. To illustrate the process of piecemeal engineering and its dangers let me provide an example from a project we conducted for a regional health care insurance organization in the Netherlands.

In the 1980s cost reduction was an important issue in Dutch health care. Various organizations made attempts to develop policies to reduce health care costs. In that context a colleague of mine and I were approached by a person from a regional health care insurance organization (HCIO) in the Netherlands. He asked us whether we would be able to statistically correct 'raw referral rates' of individual general practitioners (family doctors). A referral rate indicates the percentage of patients referred to a medical specialist by a general practitioner in a certain period. The so-called 'corrected referral rate' would have to take into account differences in the composition of a general practitioner's population. If the relevant data are available (which was the case) this is not a very complicated statistical procedure. However, before agreeing to correct the data we asked him for what purpose he needed these corrected referral rates. He explained that these were required for their new policy programme aimed at cost reduction. The Dutch health care system is structured in such a way that people suffering complaints first have to see their general practitioner (or family doctor). The general practitioner decides whether or not a person will be referred to a medical specialist. In other words the general practitioner (working in the so-called first echelon) functions as a kind of gatekeeper for the so-called second echelon (containing medical specialists and hospitals).

Once people are referred to a medical specialist cost per patient increases rapidly. The organization had embarked on a policy to try to reduce referral rates in order to reduce health care costs. To accomplish this, several so-called medical advisors from this organization had been talking to individual general practitioners in the region, in particular those with referral rates above average. The discussion had in general focused on the question what caused their high referral rates and whether the general practitioner was of the opinion that something could be done to reduce these. In a number of cases general practitioners had replied that their higher referral rates were caused by the fact that their practice population contained more older patients and more women compared to the populations of other general practitioners. The 'raw' referral rates were thus useless in the discussion with general practitioners, because these could easily be refuted. Hence the idea to correct raw referral rates for compositional factors of the general practitioner's practice population. It was expected that, after correction, discussions with general practitioners having above-average referral rates, would be more effective in convincing these general practitioners to reduce referral rates.

Typically in this case people had conceived of a potential solution for the health care cost problem and had started to implement it, without giving the problem ample thought. Several studies in organizational decision making have revealed that problems are frequently prematurely defined. Russo and Schoemaker (1989) discuss the tendency of decision makers to 'plunge in' (i.e. reaching conclusions before the problem has been given ample thought) as the first of their 10 'decision traps'. A well-known statement by Alfred Sloan runs as follows: 'Gentlemen, I take it we are all in complete agreement on the decision here . . . Then I propose we postpone further discussion of this matter until our next meeting to give ourselves time to develop disagreement and perhaps gain some understanding of what the decision is all about.' In other words decision making is deliberately postponed in order to prevent premature problem definition, since the way a decision is framed significantly affects subsequent choices (Tversky and Kahneman, 1981).

From our point of view, as researchers, this was exactly what might be happening in the health care insurance organization. Their plan would mean that the organization was going to intervene in the health care system without taking into account potential undesirable side-effects of this intervention. Rather than solving the problem, these side-effects sometimes make matters worse. A nice example is provided by the introduction of the so-called 'medicijnenknaak' ('prescription dollar') in the Netherlands. Its purpose was to reduce health care cost by having patients pay part (i.e. dfl. 2.50) of the prescription fees. What actually happened however, was that general practitioners increased the volume per prescription which eventually led to an increase in prescription costs rather than a reduction (Post and Been, 1988).

What these examples convincingly demonstrate is that even when there is no immediate conflict of interest, people still tend to take a narrow view on a problem. They do not tend to perceive problems as being part of a larger system. As a consequence one designs piecemeal solutions which aim to solve the problem, but in fact produce results which sometimes makes matters even worse.

Situations like these can effectively be prevented by inviting people to think of the consequences of changes in the system. Hence, during the discussion with the HCIO person we asked the following question: 'Let us suppose that you will be successful in convincing general practitioners to try to reduce referral rates, and referral rates will actually start falling, what do you think will happen then?' To be honest, we did not have to wait long for an answer. The person we spoke to was convinced that medical specialists, confronted with a decrease in the number of incoming patients, would, for instance, intensify treatment on their patients in order to keep up their income level. The latter reaction might actually reverse the cost reduction effects the organization hoped for. Once this insight took form people started to doubt the usefulness of their efforts to reduce health care costs in this manner. The result of the discussion was that they abandoned their policy of approaching family doctors and instead started focusing on the larger picture, the structure and dynamics of the health care system. The construction of a system dynamics model proved very helpful in this respect. Initially, a large number of people were invited to participate in this model construction process. Hence, we had to specifically develop a delphi-based procedure in order to structure the group model-building process. Chapter 6 will discuss this process in more detail. For now, let us return to the topic of piecemeal solutions.

There are several reasons why people do ignore 'the larger system'. One is that, as mentioned above, many people are not trained in systems thinking. Another is the limited information processing capacity of the human mind. People tend to (un)consciously reduce complexity in order to prevent information overload and to reduce mental effort (Hogarth, 1987).

One of the first authors to call attention to limited information processing in human decision making was Herbert Simon. He coined the term 'bounded rationality' to contrast it with objective rationality. Bounded (or procedural) rationality is adaptive within the constraints of the situation and limited by the information processing capacities of the decision maker. It is characterized by an incomplete search for information, and is terminated when a satisfactory (not an optimal) solution to the problem is found (Simon, 1948; 1985).

Empirical research in cognitive psychology and in the tradition of behavioural decision making has largely confirmed and elaborated these notions. Miller was one of the first to empirically demonstrate limitations in information processing in individuals (Miller, 1956; Gardner, 1987). He pointed out that in general people can only hold seven (plus or minus two) chunks of information in their short-term memory. Another bottleneck is the limited attention span of individuals. As Simon points out: 'Before [this] information can be used by the deliberative mind, however, it must proceed through the bottleneck of attention—a serial, not parallel, process whose information capacity is exceedingly small.' (Simon, 1985, 302.) In other words in any decision making process only a limited amount of information is selected and subsequently used to define a problem and to make a choice. Heuristics are applied to reduce the mental efforts involved in processing information. A well-known heuristic, which has been found time and again in a number of decision making experiments, is 'anchoring and adjustment' (Kahneman, Slovic and Tversky, 1982). For instance a prediction about next year's sales is made by taking a certain value as an anchor (e.g. last year's sales) and by adjusting this value (taking the new circumstances into account) to predict next year's sales. Typically, people tend to be biased towards the anchor and thus provide conservative estimates. Experiments have shown that even randomly selected anchors significantly affect a subsequent choice. Estimations of the percentage of African countries in the United Nations are significantly correlated with a previous figure derived from spinning a wheel of fortune (Tversky and Kahneman, 1974). Russo and Schoemaker (1989) provide an example in which the last three digits of a person's telephone number affects this person's estimate of such a seemingly unrelated issue as the year in which Attila the Hun was defeated.

The 'anchoring and adjustment' heuristic is only one of a large number of 'biases and heuristics' which have been identified by psychologists in the field of behavioural decision making. Other such biases and heuristics include for example: the representativeness heuristic (probabilities are evaluated by the degree to which A resembles B), the availability heuristic (i.e. salient information is more easily remembered), illusory correlation, the illusion of control, and hindsight bias which was discussed previously (see Kahnemann, Slovic and Tversky, 1982; Hogarth, 1987). Some people argue that it is best to prevent the above biases and heuristics by employing groups for decision making rather than individuals. The argument goes that different individuals will cancel out each others' biases. However, research has revealed that groups tend to show the same type of biases as individuals and hence they will not arrive at higher quality decisions (Stasson et al., 1988). In short, the results from this type of research are quite disturbing and depressing (Hogarth, 1987, 197).

Some have argued that this is a premature conclusion. A number of the above experiments have been criticized because of the fact that in reality people do not make discrete decisions. Rather decision making processes are continuous. It follows that people receive feedback on the effects of decisions and they can subsequently adapt their behaviour and correct failures. This brings us to the important topic of learning on the basis of experience.

LEARNING FROM THE PAST AND FROM ONE'S OWN EXPERIENCE

A lot has been written on the topic of learning. Here I am primarily concerned with learning from experience in the sense of understanding problems and designing courses of action with regard to messy problems.

Folk wisdom states that people learn from experience. In particular we are supposed to learn from our mistakes. As the well-known saying goes: once bitten twice shy. Everyday experience largely confirms this notion. We can all provide numerous illustrations of learning by experience from our own past. Learning in these circumstances, however, presupposes a certain degree of control over events. Lack of control can give rise to the phenomenon of learned helplessness. In a couple of interesting experiments Overmier and Seligman (1967) and Seligman and Maier (1967) demonstrated this phenomenon. One group of dogs was placed in a shuttle box with two compartments separated by a barrier. The floor on either side could be electrified by the experimenter. If this was done the dogs quickly learned to jump to the other, unelectrified, side. This does not seem very special. The experiment was however repeated with a group of dogs which had been subjected to a classical conditioning procedure. These dogs were taught to associate a certain tone with an inescapable electric shock while restrained in a harness. When later placed in the two compartment shuttle box these dogs failed to escape the electric shock. In other words from these experiments it appears that if one has learned that to respond to a certain situation is pointless, this will initiate a mechanism called 'learned helplessness'. In other words, lack of a feeling of control might prevent learning in the future in similar situations.

But even in circumstances when control of the situation is not restrained, learning from mistakes can be seriously impeded. One mechanism which obstructs learning is looking for confirming evidence. Remember the waiter who, looking for confirming evidence, never came to know that it was his own behaviour which induced people to leave tips, rather than the way they were dressed.

Another example derives from personnel selection (Hogarth, 1987). In selecting personnel for a job, only candidates who adhere to the job demands will be selected and one can never be sure whether the persons who were not selected would have done better or worse than the selected candidate. In other words we do not have any evidence which might refute the accuracy of our choice. Moreover, once a person is appointed the manager who selected the candidate will affect subsequent performance by giving special attention and training and thus runs the risk of creating a self-fulfilling prophecy. Stated differently, in the case of personnel selection we do not receive appropriate feedback as to whether our decision was correct or not. The feedback we do receive is biased by our own actions. We might be inclined to believe we have selected the best candidate for the job while in fact the person's performance is largely the result of our own actions, e.g. the special training we provided. In addition, the situation is quite ambiguous because a variety of factors will affect the candidate's performance. It follows that success/failure attribution would make correct interpretation of effects difficult, since people show the tendency to attribute failure to bad luck and success to their own skills (Hogarth, 1987). This might also explain the persistent phenomenon of people's overconfidence in their own judgements (see Lichtenstein, Fischhoff and Phillips, 1982).

In everyday language: if the candidate's performance leaves something to be desired then people show the tendency to attribute this to factors outside of their control. If, on the other hand, the candidate performs well then humans are inclined to attribute this to their own personnel selection skills. This attribution error deprives humans of powerful learning experiences. As Brehmer points out:

> When we have to learn from outcomes, it may, in fact, be almost impossible to discover that one really does not know anything. This is especially true when the concepts are very complex in the sense that each instance contains many dimensions. In this case there are too many ways of explaining why a certain outcome occurred, and to explain away failures of predicting the correct outcome. Because of this, the need to change may not be apparent to us, and we may fail to learn that our rule is invalid, not only for particular cases but for the general case also. (Brehmer, 1980, 228–229).

In other words, when decision making situations are complex and ambiguous, learning from experience might be more exceptional than most of us would be inclined to assume.

With regard to messy problems matters are even more complicated. In the candidate selection process there might be experience from previous similar selection processes which might be helpful. Messy problems on the other hand typically are unique and there is simply no previous experience. As Rittel and Webber point out: 'Every solution to a wicked problem is a "one-shot operation"; because there is no opportunity to learn by trial-and-error, every attempt counts significantly.' (Rittel and Webber, 1973, 163.) The one-shot character of wicked problems was clearly demonstrated in the examples I presented before. The decision to cease the financial aid to the Dutch fleet has no precedent. Assessing its consequences cannot be based on previous experience. A similar case can be made for the decision to attempt to reduce the family doctors' referral rates. Often one has to take a decision, without really knowing what will happen. When confronted with messy problems, we often lack any experience to guide us in the decision making process.

'But isn't it true that the process can be monitored and decisions can be adapted based on the feedback one receives from the systems behaviour?' the reader might ask. A manager can observe the effects and adapt one's decisions. This, however, presupposes that one has a clear understanding of the causal relationships in the system: one needs to know which interventions lead to what effects. The difficulty lies in the fact that inferring causality is impeded when contiguity between cause and effect is low (Einhorn and Hogarth, 1986), a ubiquitous phenomenon in social systems. In other words, the effects of our actions might take a long time to materialize (particularly in systems with long delays in feedback effects) and thus prevent the possibility for learning (Senge, 1990). Moreover, experiments have revealed that even when the feedback system is known, people tend to largely ignore this information in dynamic decision making (Sterman, 1989a and b; Diehl and Sterman, 1995). Ignoring feedback processes can produce detrimental effects. This is not only demonstrated in laboratory research but also in field studies, as we will see in the next section.

Given the fact that wicked problems are one-shot operations it becomes extremely important to study the problem as completely as possible. Simulation is a powerful technique to gain a deeper understanding of a problem. As the coming chapters will show, however, there are cases in which it becomes virtually imposs- ible to build a quantified model of the problem under consideration, e.g. because of lack of time or because of the complete intangibility of the problem. In these cases the best one can do is to build a qualitative model in order to gather insights from many different angles, i.e. to have different people in a management team voice their opinions and insights, and surface and test underlying assumptions as carefully as possible. If conducted properly this means the team will go through a learning process about the problem. Insight in the problem is enhanced through this learning process. But in teams there are also strong barriers to learning. In the coming chapters we will see that one of the greatest enemies of team learning is a defensive attitude. Many team discussions can be characterized as a battle of wits, in which the ultimate goal seems to be to win the discussion, rather than to better understand the problem. Frequently the idea is that some opinions are right and others are wrong. For most of us, having to admit in a discussion that we are wrong is an embarrasing situation. As a result many of the everday processes in organizations are concerned with what Argyris (1990) calls defensive routines. Faced with an embarrasing situation people normally start a so-called face-saving operation. Again, through this routine we are depriving ourselves and others of a powerful learning experience. Rather, through face-saving, we continue our incompetence. The only competence which is trained and improved is the face-saving skill. It follows that there are powerful barriers to effective learning, which are not easily overcome. In the chapter on group facilitation I will emphasize the need to create an open communication atmosphere in order to overcome some of these barriers.

IGNORING FEEDBACK PROCESSES AND DYNAMICS IN SYSTEMS

As pointed out, people tend to ignore feedback processes while at the same time feedback is a ubiquitous characteristic of life. As stated by Powers: 'All behaviour involves strong feedback effects whether one is considering spinal reflexes or self- actualization. Feedback is such an all-pervasive and fundamental aspect of be- haviour that it is as invisible as the air we breathe. Quite literally it is behaviour— we know nothing of our own behaviour but the feedback effects of our own out- puts.' (Powers, 1973, 351.) Powers suggests that its invisibility is one of the reasons why most people tend to ignore feedback processes. It is only those great minds who have given extensive thought to complex social phenomena who are capable of identifying feedback processes. This is most succinctly put by Richardson in his book on the history of feedback thought in the social science and systems theory: '. . . great social scientists are feedback thinkers, and great social theories are feedback thoughts.' (Richardson, 1991, 2).

Feedback is a process in which action and information in turn affect each other. Again we quote Richardson: 'The essence of the concept . . . is a circle of interac- tions, a closed loop of action and information. The patterns of behaviour of any two variables in such a closed loop are linked, each influencing, and in turn responding to the behaviour of the other. Thus the concept of the feedback loop is intimately linked with the concepts of interdependence and circular causality, ideas with a rich history in the social sciences'. (Richardson, 1991, 1.) Thinking in terms of circular causality or feedback processes is not a common habit of policy makers. Axelrod (1976), who extensively studied the cognitive maps of political elites, found that feedback loops were largely absent in these maps. Vennix (1990) and Verburgh (1994) found that even after extensive training in feedback model-building, feedback loops were still very infrequent in the cognitive maps of participants (see also Kenis, 1995). It seems difficult for the human mind to entertain feedback loops just as it is to simultaneously hold unbalanced paths. The latter means that in a cognitive map there are at least two distinct paths, with opposite signs, from a policy to a goal variable. Let me explain this by means of an example, which is visualized in Figure 1.3.

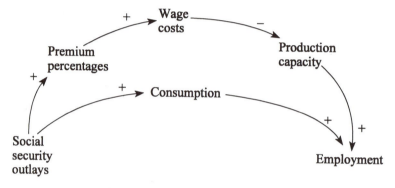

Figure 1.3 Causal Diagram with Unbalanced Paths

Figure 1.3 is an example of a causal diagram. A causal diagram takes the form of variables which are linked by arrows. The variable at the tail of the arrow is considered to have a causal effect on the variable at the point. Arrows are further denoted by a '+' or a '–' sign. A '+' sign represents a so-called positive causal relationship, which indicates that both variables change in the same direction (i.e. both increase or decrease). The diagram for instance shows that an increase in consumption will raise employment. And conversely a fall in consumption will decrease employment.

On the other hand a '–' sign denotes a negative relationship, which indicates that both variables change in opposite directions. As the diagram for instance indicates: the higher (lower) the wage costs the lower (larger) the production capacity. (Sometimes model-builders replace the '+' sign by an 's' for 'same', i.e. both variables change in the same direction. The '–' sign is sometimes replaced by an 'o' for 'opposite' direction.)

Suppose that the policy variable (i.e. the variable under the control of the policy maker) is the amount of social security outlays and the goal variable is employment. Then one path (i.e. chain of causal arguments) might read as follows: the higher the social security outlays, the higher the premium percentages, the higher the wage costs, the lower production capacity and the less employment. The other path reads as: the higher the social security outlays, the higher consumption and the more employment. If our goal would be to increase employment, the first path dictates to decrease social security outlays (leading to lower premium percentages, lower wage costs, more production capacity and more employment), while the second prescribes to increase outlays (leading to more consumption and more employment). Clearly, without quantification it is difficult to calculate outcomes and to make a choice whether to increase or decrease premium percentages. Since the human mind suffers from the inability to make this type of calculation quickly, there is the tendency to rule out imbalancedness by ignoring one of the two paths (Axelrod, 1976; Vennix, 1990). In comparison with feedback loops, imbalancedness is still relatively easy to handle. If people are not capable of holding imbalanced paths, we might well anticipate that they will certainly not be able to hold more than one or two feedback loops in their maps. This is because in the case of feedback loops, in particular with different signs, it would become extremely tedious for the human mind to derive dynamic conclusions from the cognitive map. Hence, the almost complete absence of feedback loops in cognitive maps.

Hall (1984) has clearly demonstrated the potential detrimental effects of ignoring feedback effects in a case study of the demise of the *Saturday Evening Post*. Policies to halt the decrease of the number of subscribers to the paper were based on the partial and biased cognitive map of the promotion circulation department. The policies developed by this department were built on an inaccurate and incomplete perception of the processes underlying the collapse in subscriptions. In order to increase the number of subscribers this department executed a policy of expanding the circulation promotion budget while at the same time increasing advertising rates to pay for this. However the latter gave rise to a loss of advertising, a slimmer magazine and hence loss of new trial readers who did not continue their subscription. And in turn a smaller circulation made the *Saturday Evening Post* less attractive to potential advertisers. As Hall (1984) concludes: '. . . the policy elite of the old *Saturday Evening Post* seemed to be oblivious to the recursive relationships that tightly coupled readers, advertising sales and magazine pages. It resulted in an unstable system.' And: '*It is a perpetual enigma that a complex organization . . . can coordinate such a rich array of highly specialized activities* (from editing to printing) *and yet formulate its major policy decisions on out-of-date maps of causality containing untested beliefs and the simplest of arguments.* Furthermore it seems that once these maps become established, they are difficult to change and require a crisis or substantial turnover of senior managers to effect any radical revision.' (Hall, 1984, 923.) This example clearly demonstrates that ignoring feedback processes can produce disastrous results.

In the health care case that I discussed before we have another illustration of ignoring feedback. The reader will recall that the health care insurance organization attempted to reduce referral rates to decrease health care costs. During the model-building process it was shown that, apart from prescribing drugs, general practitioners have three distinct possibilities when a patient comes to visit them:

send a patient back home; order a patient back (e.g. come back to see me again in two weeks) or refer the patient to a medical specialist. As stated before one had initially focused on this third possibility as a means of cost reduction. However, in the course of building the model it became clear that one factor affecting the general practitioner's referral rate is his workload. The higher the workload the higher the referral rate. The latter implies that if the organization's policy would be successful (i.e. referral rates would actually drop) this would leave more patients with the general practitioner, augment the general practitioner's workload which might in turn lead to higher referral rates and thus in the long run undermine the effectiveness of the policy. In short, we are confronted with a feedback loop in which an original reduction of referral rates would in the longer run lead to increase in referral rates.

During the model-building process it was also discovered that the phenomenon of ordering patients back was much more important than initially thought. In the past health care insurance organizations had never been very interested in this phenomenon. For mandatorily insured patients a standard fee per patient is paid to a general practitioner once a year, regardless of the number of times a patient visits his family doctor. From a financial point of view the frequency with which a patient is ordered back was not very interesting. That was also one of the reasons why the organization's database did not contain any data on this phenomenon. However, through the model-building process it became clear that the phenomenon of ordering patients back is directly related to a general practitioner's workload (i.e. the more patients ordered back, the higher the workload) and thus indirectly also to the referral rate via this workload. It was assumed that general practitioners used ordering patients back as a strategy to control their workload: the higher the workload, the less patients are ordered back in order to reduce the workload. So, in fact a family doctor has at least two distinct possibilities to adjust an experienced high workload to a desired workload: increasing the referral rate or decreasing the fraction of patients ordered back. Reducing the workload through an increase of the referral rates is however to no avail in the longer run. Referred patients, at some point in time, will be referred back to their family doctor by the medical specialist.

In other words, the organization's original policy (reducing referral rates) could put in motion a number of feedback processes which would undermine its effectiveness, dynamic processes which the organization had largely neglected. It seemed that important feedback processes in the health care system were ignored.

As stated above, thinking in terms of feedback processes is difficult, particularly for the non-trained. Most readers have probably had difficulty in keeping track of the arguments in the previous paragraphs. One reason for this is the fact that I have discussed the structure of a complex system by means of written language which is sequential in nature. You as a reader are forced to translate this sequential message into a mental picture of the structure of the system, which can almost only be accomplished by rereading it several times or by slowing down the pace of reading. As some authors have pointed out, visualising information helps to keep track of complex structures (Larkin and Simon, 1987; Lippitt, 1983;

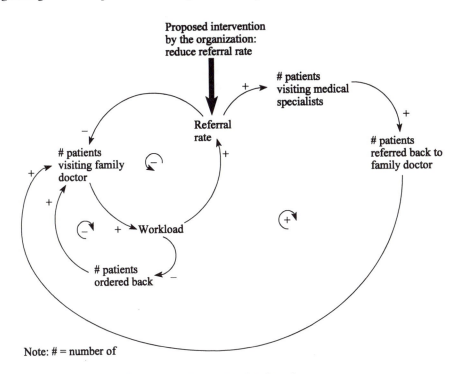

Note: # = number of

Figure 1.4   Causal Loop Diagram of Part of Health Care System

Anderson, 1980). In system dynamics this fact is also emphasized by Wolstenholme: 'A good system diagram can formalise and communicate a modeller's mental image and hence understanding of a given situation in a way that the written language cannot.' (Wolstenholme, 1982, 547). The reader may judge the accuracy of this statement by studying the flow diagram in Figure 1.4. This figure contains a graphical representation in the form of a causal loop diagram of the previous health care discussion.

The diagram makes it easier to trace the feedback loops. In the upper left hand corner the reader may find the loop which was discussed first in the above paragraphs: reducing referral rates (the proposed policy by the HCIO) leads to a higher number of patients at the family doctor, a higher workload and hence more referrals. This is a so-called negative or balancing loop. An increase (decrease) in the original variable is counteracted throughout the loop. Another balancing loop that was discussed is the one from the number of patients visiting the family doctor, through workload to number of patients ordered back and again to number of patients visiting the family doctor. In other words an increase in workload at the consultation hour is counteracted by ordering less patients back. The third loop indicates the (partial) uselessness of referrals as a policy to alleviate workload: more referrals leads to more patients visiting medical specialists, who after some time will be referred back to the family doctor and will thus again increase his workload. In the next chapter, where the system dynamics methodology will be discussed, we will explain the use and the construction of causal loop diagrams and the types of feedback loops in more detail.

The examples that I have presented in this section reveal at least two things. First, people do not tend to think in terms of feedback processes, which can have deleterious consequences, as in the case of the *Saturday Evening Post*. Simultaneously the health care example shows that thinking in terms of feedback processes *before* policies are implemented, can alter one's perception of a problem dramatically and prevent implementation of a policy which might produce undesirable consequences. Second, when it comes to the structure of complex systems, visualization can help in enhancing people's information processing capabilities. Building diagrams also has the advantage that it forces people to express their worldviews more accurately. This brings me to two other important issues in structuring messy problems. The first is that people in general employ ill-defined concepts, which frequently leads to miscommunication. The second is that people also frequently employ tacit (causal) assumptions about a problem, which do not hold even when constructing a causal loop diagram. Let me further illustrate the usefulness of causal loop diagramming in uncovering tacit assumptions and improving communication by a couple of examples.

TACIT CAUSAL ASSUMPTIONS AND AMBIGUITY OF EVERYDAY LANGUAGE

Frequently a problem formulation contains one or more hidden assumptions, which will not hold under scrutiny. Since this happens quite often, it is no wonder that Mason and Mitroff designed a specific procedure, which aims exactly at surfacing and testing hidden assumptions in strategic decision making (Mason and Mitroff, 1981). Constructing causal loop diagrams is particularly helpful to surface and test *causal* assumptions. Remember, for instance, that in the DGSM case, with which this chapter opened, a number of people held the tacit causal assumption that abandoning the support for the Dutch fleet would enable them to focus more on the other two strategic areas, which could then be expanded more fully. As mentioned previously the model-building process revealed that they might be wrong. Model-building assisted to surface and refute the above tacit causal assumption. Below I will present a more elaborate example which shows both the sloppiness with which people employ concepts and the way in which hidden assumptions can play a role in problem definition. The example is taken from the Nostradamus project which was carried out for the Directorate General of Public Works and Water Management (DGPW). As shown in Figure 1.1, DGPW is part of the Department of Transportation, Public Works and Water Management (DTPW). The reader will recall that the Nostradamus management training programme aimed at improving the strategic decision making skills of management teams within DGPW. As a start of the Nostradamus management training project a small project staff conducted about 25 interviews in the first months of 1991 with a number of key persons from within and outside the organization. From these interviews a number of future dilemmas for DGPW was formulated. One of these dilemmas read as follows:

> In what ways can DGPW go along with the development to bring the policy making process closer to the Dutch citizen and at the same time guarantee that the Netherlands will preserve a high quality (wet and dry) infrastructure?

This sentence is clearly framed as a dilemma, i.e. as a choice between two equally desirable objectives (Hampden-Turner, 1990): going along with the trend to bring policy making closer to Dutch citizens while simultaneously maintaining the quality of the infrastructure. There are at least two tacit (non-causal) assumptions and one implicit causal assumption in the way the dilemma is formulated. The first (non-causal assumption) is that the policy making process obviously is too far from the citizen and this gap has to be closed. The question is whether this is true and why this would be the case. The second is that a high quality infrastructure is needed (which may sound reasonable, but it is an assumption anyway). The third, hidden (causal), assumption in this dilemma is that accomplishing one thing (i.e. bringing policy making closer to the citizen) will 'automatically' lead to detrimental effects for the other, i.e. deteriorate the quality of the infrastructure. If this assumption is true (as the dilemma assumes it is) then in a causal loop diagram it should show up as a negative path connecting the first to the second. In other words in the causal loop diagram one would have to find one or more causal relationships in the form of a path leading from 'closeness of policy making process to citizen' through one or more other variables to 'quality of infrastructure', indicating that bringing the policy making process closer to the Dutch citizens would negatively affect the quality of the infrastructure.

An ad hoc group composed of eight persons from various departments of DGPW used this dilemma to test the effectiveness of system dynamics model-building for the Nostradamus programme. The discussions within this group revealed several interesting things. The first is that in one of the sessions a debate arose about the meaning of the concept 'taking policy making closer to the citizen'. This was caused by the fact that at the start of the discussion a number of persons were talking about decentralization rather than the concept 'policy making closer to the citizen'. This led the facilitator to ask the question whether these two could be supposed to mean the same thing or whether a distinction would have to be made between the two. As could be expected the latter proved to be true and the modelling exercise was initially continued with the concept 'policy making closer to the citizen' since this appeared in the formulation of the dilemma. The second interesting phenomenon was that the hidden causal assumption in the dilemma could not be confirmed through the causal loop diagram. In other words no chain of causal arguments could be built by the group to support the assumption that bringing the policy making process closer to the citizen would actually jeopardize the quality of the infrastructure. This hidden assumption however was related to the decentralization phenomenon. It was expected that decentralization (rather than taking the policy making process closer to the citizen) would cut up the construction and maintenance of the main infrastructure and thus affect its quality. The discussion thus gave rise to the introduction of two concepts rather than one: decentralization and bridging the gap between the policy making process and the citizen. The first was roughly defined as bringing responsibilities and policy making to lower levels of government (e.g. from national to provincial or local level). The second as the degree of perceived influence of the Dutch citizen on the policy making process.

Building a causal loop diagram automatically leads to questions about potential causes of phenomena, i.e. to answer why questions, because one will look for incoming arrows for a variable. Hence, the question: why would the government be interested in bringing the policy making process closer to the Dutch citizen? Or stated differently: what are the causes of the government's desire to bring the policy making process closer to the Dutch citizens? The group felt that the primary reason for this was that the government held the assumption that it would help in closing the so-called gap between politics and citizens. It was tacitly assumed that by decentralization (obviously confused with bringing policy making closer to the citizen) the gap between politics and citizens could be reduced.

The model-building group came up with quite a different conclusion. As a consequence of the model the discussion circled around the question of what caused the political apathy of Dutch citizens and what affected the perceived influence on politics? After some deliberation the group came up with the following argument: the Dutch citizen is not satisfied with the performance of the Dutch government and the political process. Most citizens feel that their influence on the policy making process is rather low if not zero. This gives rise to frustration which in turn leads to a decrease in political interest. A decrease in the latter will in turn lower the level of participation in politics which will again decrease the perceived degree of influence. This feedback process (which was part of the causal loop diagram) is depicted in the right hand side of Figure 1.5.

From its character, this feedback process implies that a process of increasing frustration will reinforce itself, leading to less and less citizen participation. It would thus be important to attempt to stop this self reinforcing process. In the subsequent step of the process a number of factors were identified which affect variables in the feedback loop. These have also been depicted in Figure 1.5. For instance the better the feedback to the Dutch citizen about why specific decisions are made, the higher the perceived influence on the policy making process.

From this causal loop diagram a number of policy variables could be identified, i.e. variables which could potentially be under the control of DGPW. These are indicated by the ellipses. According to the group these variables were within the discretion of DGPW and might be used to attempt to stop the process of increasing frustration and decreasing political participation.

Let me point out by the way that the question is not whether this causal loop diagram is valid or not. The figure represents only a small part of the whole diagram, which was produced by the group. The example is presented to show how prematurely and sloppy strategic problems (or dilemmas) can be defined, even when they have previously been committed to paper. Rather than taking the framing of the dilemma for granted the model-building exercise revealed various flaws in its formulation and gave rise to some interesting conclusions:

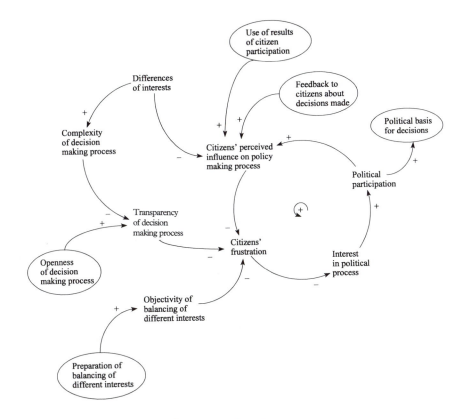

Figure 1.5 Part of Causal Loop Diagram of DGPW Dilemma

● there is no dilemma between taking the policy making process closer to the citizen and the quality of the infrastructure;
● there might be a dilemma between decentralization and quality of infrastructure, but this should be the subject of further study rather than to be taken for granted;
● decentralization will not automatically take the policy making process closer to the citizen in the sense that perceived influence of the citizen will increase (as was tacitly assumed). Or stated differently:
● increasing the Dutch citizen's concern for political matters should not be accomplished by decentralization but rather by measures such as providing feedback about decisions made by government, or by explicitly using results of citizen participation in the decision making process.

The preceding sections demonstrate that one has to watch out for hidden assumptions as well as sloppy use of language in problem definition. In particular one has to be aware of the fact that the same concept, even if it is committed to paper, can mean quite different things to different people. In that sense language is quite ambiguous. Below is another example from a workshop we did for another management team in the context of the DGPW Nostradamus project. It reveals that even a written problem definition can give rise to very different interpretations once going down on the ladder of abstraction.

Before being allowed to participate in the Nostradamus training programme each management team was requested to produce a consensual written problem statement for the workshop. One of these statements from one of the participating teams read as follows: 'What is the added value for a regional unit of DGPW in an ever enlarging Europe?'

It had taken this team at least a couple of hours (but probably more) to get a compromise on this problem statement. Now the problem is both strategic as well as extremely interesting and the group wanted to start by generating answers to this question. However, as was revealed in a couple of hours it proved to be very ill-defined. As we will see in the coming chapters, when starting to build a causal loop diagram the first problem is to define concepts and find concrete variables. So my first assignment to the group was to think of indicators from which one might assess what the added value of their work was anyway. After the group had had a couple of minutes to write down their ideas in silence, I asked each person of the group in turn to name one indicator from their list, which I subsequently put on a flip-chart. The result was that after 10 minutes and one round we had as many different indicators as there were persons in the team. Most people were amazed to find out that ideas ranged so widely. They thought they had already done a good job in defining their problem. They were very much unaware of the fact that the more abstract the concepts one employs the larger the chances of miscommunication in the group. Even when committed to paper problem formulations may contain many ambiguous concepts, which may have quite a different meaning to different people.

SUMMARY

In this chapter I have discussed the nature of messy problems and identified a number of flaws in structuring and defining messy problems in organizations. Typically, people may hold widely divergent views on a problem. Differences in viewpoints are the result of selective perception and selective memory. I have also indicated that frequently we tend to create the very (social) reality the way we expect it to be. Hence, from an interventionist point of view it becomes important to induce people to articulate their mental models, share these with other team members and critically examine them in an effort to create a shared and better understanding of the problem. In short, to create an effective team learning process. In this process it is important to emphasize the whole rather than the individual parts and to pay attention to potential feedback processes underlying the problem, since humans tend to ignore them.

The remainder of this book will demonstrate that the system dynamics method is a powerful way to avoid some of the common drawbacks discussed in this chapter. As pointed out in the introduction to this book, system dynamics will be effective to the extent that one will be able to involve the client in the process of building the model, a process known as group model-building. In order to be able to use this method effectively one has to be familiar with (a) the system dynamics method, (b) the way to set up a group model-building project, and (c) the way to facilitate the group model-building process. Each of the topics will be discussed in more detail in the coming chapters. To begin with, the next couple of chapters will focus on system dynamics. Chapter 2 will discuss qualitative system dynamics, while Chapter 3 focuses on quantitative model-building and simulation.

Chapter 2

System Dynamics: Problem Identification and System Conceptualization

INTRODUCTION

As mentioned before, the aim of this book is to prepare the reader to conduct his or her own group model-building sessions in order to help organizations tackle strategic problems. In order to conduct these sessions in a smooth way it is important that one gains a detailed understanding of system dynamics and the process of constructing a system dynamics model. To provide the reader with the basics of the system dynamics methodology this and the next chapter are devoted to this topic. The current chapter concentrates on the theory underlying system dynamics and the first stages of model-building: problem identification and conceptualization.

In the introduction to this book it was pointed out that this is a 'how to do' book. To be in a position to conduct group model-building sessions one needs to develop model-building skills. These skills can only be acquired through extensive training. This chapter as well as the next contains a number of exercises which aim at developing basic model-building skills. For the sake of clarity I have to point out that this is not a handbook on how to build system dynamics models. This chapter just presents elementary topics. It provides basic guidelines and exercises to learn to build system dynamics models. The reader who is interested in learning more about system dynamics is referred to Appendix 1, which contains a short annotated bibliography.

The first section will give a short history of system dynamics and describe its underlying theoretical position. Next I will describe the way in which a system dynamics model is constructed and provide examples of the construction of causal loop diagrams as a first introduction to system dynamics thinking.

A BRIEF HISTORY

System dynamics was developed in the second half of the 1950s by Jay W. Forrester at the Alfred P. Sloan School of Management at the Massachusetts Institute of Technology. Forrester joined the Sloan Management School in 1956, the year of its foundation. The first year was devoted to a study of activities in operations research (alternatively called management science), a branch of science which aims to support managerial decision making through the use of scientific and mathematical methods. According to Forrester (1975) this study indicated that operations research (OR) was not effective in helping to solve the broad, strategic management problems. OR was too mathematically oriented and focused too much on optimization and analytical solutions. As a result it neglected nonlinear phenomena, could only tackle rather simple situations and focused on separate corporate functions rather than relationships between corporate functions. One of Forrester's major criticisms of OR was its open-loop approach of the decision making process. An open-loop approach to decision making implies that decisions are seen as unaffected by the decisions themselves (Forrester, 1975). Instead Forrester proposed that closed-loop thinking would be required. In closed-loop thinking decisions are seen as a means to affect the environment, and changes in the environment in turn provide input to decisions which aim to influence the environment. The closed-loop approach was considered as a more meaningful way to practice OR. As Forrester points out: 'The first year of exploration pointed toward the concepts of feedback systems as being much more general, more significant, and more applicable to social systems than had been commonly realized.' (Forrester, 1975, 134.)

As a result Forrester originally deliberately set out on a course to dissociate from the prevailing operations research paradigm (Lane, 1994a) and started to make connections between the field of (electrical) engineering and management. This led him to the study of (decision making in) social systems from the viewpoint of information feedback control systems. Interestingly, Lane (1994a) points out that by setting himself apart from hard OR, Forrester made system dynamics more useful and relevant to the study of managerial problems. However, over the last decades it seems that system dynamics has been caught up and probably passed by soft OR. (Although it must be pointed out that there are differences in the way system dynamicists use the methodology. In another article Lane (1994b) shows this variety of movements within (the history of) system dynamics.)

One problem, however, was that in Forrester's view social systems generally contained many nonlinear relationships between system elements. The latter implied that analytical solutions of the model's equations was unfeasible. As a result Forrester resorted to an experimental approach, i.e. simulation of social systems with the support of a digital computer. In order to accomplish this a special computer language (DYNAMO) was developed to carry out the model simulations. Forrester himself has clearly pointed out that simulation and the DYNAMO language are not the essence of system dynamics. The essence of system dynamics is that it is a body of theory dealing with information feedback systems. In other words it is claimed that social systems can productively be studied as information feedback control systems, i.e as systems in which a decision affects the environment which in turn affects the decision. Or in Forrester's words: 'A feedback control system exists whenever the environment causes a decision which in turn affects the original decision.' (Forrester, 1958, 39). In that respect simulation is just a technique, which becomes necessary in order to reveal the behaviour of the system (because analytical solutions are unfeasible).

His studies led Forrester to develop a method to study and simulate social systems as information feedback systems. The method was first applied to corporate problems and was called industrial dynamics. Industrial dynamics was first introduced to the management world in an article in the *Harvard Business Review* (Forrester, 1958). In this article Forrester stated that he was interested in the development of a professional approach to management. The primary tools of progress that he identified were the recent advances in the data processing industry, in military research and in research in the field of information feedback systems. The article in the *Harvard Business Review* demonstrated the applicability of the method to strategic decision making in industrial organizations. In a nutshell this article contains the most elementary ideas and building blocks which would basically remain unaltered over the next decades.

Three years later *Industrial Dynamics* was published (Forrester, 1961). This book contained a much more elaborate description of the ideas put forward in the 1958 article. In 1968, *Principles of Systems* was issued. This book outlines a number of principles of the behaviour of information feedback systems as a result of their structure. It is still one of the best introductions to the field. Gradually, over the years the method was applied to other than industrial problems, e.g. urban problems (Forrester, 1969), and even global problems (Forrester, 1973). The book on urban problems received much attention and criticism, primarily because it presented a number of counterintuitive and unpopular conclusions (see Bloomfield, 1986). The study on global problems can be considered as a precursor to the famous report for the Club of Rome (Meadows et al., 1974), which was discussed widely in the press and translated in over 20 different languages.

Over the decades following Forrester's initial publications, the method came to be applied to a large variety of problems and as a result its name evolved from industrial dynamics into the more general 'system dynamics'. Fields of applications include amongst others: commodity production cycles, research and development, inventory control, corporate policy studies, economic fluctuations, dynamics of ecosystems, energy, health care delivery, and project management to name just a few. Currently system dynamics is applied by both academic researchers and practitioners from all over the world. There is an International System Dynamics Society, holding an International System Dynamics Conference yearly and publishing the Society's journal (*The System Dynamics Review*). In addition there is a large, and fast growing, body of literature on the subject.

THE SYSTEM DYNAMICS APPROACH

According to Forrester, system dynamics is a theory of the structure and behaviour of complex systems. The structure has four hierarchical levels:

1. the closed boundary
2. the feedback loop as the basic system component
3. levels and rates
4. goals, observed conditions, discrepancy between goals and observed conditions, and desired action.

An important premise in system dynamics is that the behaviour of a system is primarily determined by the characteristics of the whole and not by the characteristics of its individual parts (Forrester, 1958). In other words, system dynamics takes as a starting point the idea of a closed boundary. As Forrester (1975, 112) points out: 'The boundary encloses the system of interest. It states that the modes of behavior under study are created by the interaction of the system components within the boundary. The boundary implies that no influences from outside of the boundary are necessary for generating the particular behavior being generated.' Some have taken this to mean that system dynamics harbours the notion of 'materially closed systems', i.e. systems having no exchanges with the environment. But Forrester has clearly pointed out that this is not what is meant by the concept of closed boundary. 'It does not mean that one believes that nothing crosses the boundary in the actual system between the part inside the boundary and that outside. Instead it means that what crosses the boundary is not essential in creating the causes and symptoms of the particular behavior being explored.' (Forrester, 1975, 142.)

In other words, system dynamics models are materially open: they exchange material with the environment. The idea of a closed boundary is supposed to imply a so-called 'causally closed' system, i.e. '. . . the closed boundary separates the dynamically significant inner workings of the system from the dynamically insignificant external environment.' (Richardson, 1991, 297). As a consequence, all the relationships between elements in the system which are considered important to explain the dynamic behaviour should be included in the system dynamics model. From a system dynamics point of view the behaviour of the system is determined by the structure of interacting feedback loops inside the closed boundary. As Richardson and Pugh (1981, 15) state: 'The system dynamics approach to complex problems focusses on feedback processes. It takes the philosophical position that feedback structures are responsible for the changes we experience over time. The premise is that *dynamic behavior is a consequence of system structure.*' Or to put it another way, system dynamicists tend to take an endogenous rather than an exogenous view: systems behave the way they do because of their internal structure rather than as a result of external factors.

This implies that decisions within a system are embedded in feedback loops. In the first chapter we have seen that a distinction is made between positive and negative loops. A positive loop creates action which increases a system state, which in turn leads to more action further increasing the system state. In other words a positive loop is self reinforcing. An example of a positive loop is the wage-price spiral. Higher wages lead to higher prices, which in turn increase the wages etc. A negative loop on the other hand is goal seeking. A negative loop thus leads to

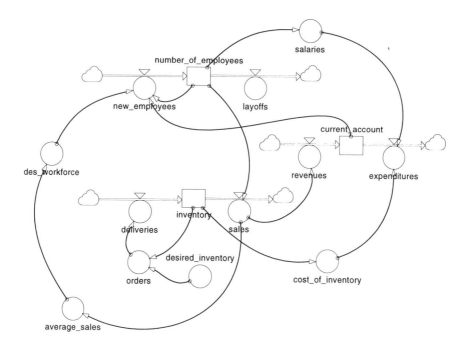

Figure 2.1 Example of Feedback Structure in System Dynamics

stabilizing behaviour. An example of negative feedback is the central heating system. It ascertains that the room temperature will remain within a certain range.

Any feedback loop in a system dynamics model contains at least one level and
one rate. Levels (or stocks) represent accumulations within the system, e.g. the
amount of inventory or the number of employees at a certain point in time. As can
be observed in Figure 2.1 stocks are represented by squares and the accompanying
flows by valves.

The flow diagram in Figure 2.1 contains three stocks (or levels) with accompanying flows. The stocks are: employees (people), current account (money), and inventory (for instance a number of books in a bookshop). Stocks represent the
(observed) state of the system in a system dynamics model and their value can only
be changed by flows. For instance, the inventory will be increased by deliveries
(which flow into inventory) and will be depleted by sales (which flow out of inventory). Hence, deliveries is the inflow, while sales is the outflow for inventory. Current account is increased by revenues and depleted by expenditures. Finally, the
number of employees is increased by new employees hired and decreased by
layoffs. The cloud symbols represent the boundaries of the system which is modelled: people, money and books arrive from the environment of the defined system
and are returned to the environment. Below I will discuss the diagram of Figure 2.1
in more detail. At this point it is not important to try to understand everything in
detail. The discussion is meant to give the reader a grasp of what a system dynamics

model looks like and how it should be 'read'. In the remainder of this and the next chapter a number of issues will be explained in more detail and exercises will be provided.

The flows in the model in Figure 2.1 are controlled by decision policies, which in turn are embedded in feedback loops. As a simple example take the inventory and orders. If desired inventory (an auxiliary variable) exceeds actual inventory (the stock) a decision will be made to place orders which will in turn be delivered and thus increase inventory. The result will be that the discrepancy between desired and actual inventory will be reduced. The smaller the discrepancy the less the number of orders, the lower the deliveries and thus the less inventory will be increased. The reader may have gathered that the process described here is an example of a balancing feedback loop: the larger the discrepancy between desired and actual inventory, the larger the orders, which decreases the discrepancy, which will decrease orders etc. Conversely, if the actual inventory exceeds the desired inventory, orders will most probably be reduced to zero until inventory drops below desired inventory. The latter is the result of the sales. Sales thus deplete inventory. Simultaneously, sales will generate revenues and will thus affect the money flow in the model. More specifically, they will increase the current account. The higher (lower) the sales, the higher (lower) the revenues. This is indicated by an arrow between sales and revenues.

The model also shows that there is a second arrow leaving sales. If sales change over time (grow or decline) this will show in the average sales over time which in turn affects the desired workforce: the higher the average sales the higher the desired workforce and the lower the average sales the smaller the desired workforce. As is the case with inventory and desired inventory, the desired workforce is compared with the actual workforce (indicated by the stock: number of employees), which leads to a decision to hire new employees (if desired workforce exceeds actual workforce) or not (if the reverse is the case). If new employees are hired this will in turn increase the number of employees and thus close the gap between desired and actual number of employees (a balancing loop, similar to the one controlling inventory).

On the other hand, the higher the number of employees the higher the amount of salaries to be paid (arrow running from number of employees to salaries), which constitute expenditures and decrease the current account. The lower the current account the smaller the chances that new employees will be hired, because money will be required to pay the salaries (hence, the arrow from current account to new employees).

If we assume that the larger the number of employees the more will be sold to potential customers who visit the bookshop, then more employees lead to more sales, which increases average sales and thus augments the desired workforce and the number of new employees hired. This process is an example of a reinforcing loop and this loop would dictate that once sales start rising they will keep on rising further and further, if there were no balancing loops to control this process. These may be formed by increasing costs through a rising workforce or inventory. But there will also be an upper limit formed by the number of customers who visit the shop. (Both are balancing loops and are not depicted in the diagram).

The reader will understand that in the foregoing paragraphs I have discussed a fictitious example of a bookshop. The model does not claim correctness nor completeness. The example merely serves the function to demonstrate the basic idea of interconnected feedback loops and how these are portrayed in a system dynamics flow diagram. As stated, it is no problem if the reader does not understand all of it at this point. Things will be explained in more detail in the coming sections and the next chapter. For now, let us return to our discussion of the basic elements of the system dynamics methodology.

As stated, any feedback loop will contain at least one stock or level variable. For instance in a negative feedback loop if an observed state of the system (e.g. number of employees) shows a discrepancy with a desired state (e.g. desired number of employees), this gives rise to a decision to close the gap between perceived and desired state (i.e. to hire new employees if the desired number is larger than the actual number of employees). Subsequently, the decision affects the inflow of new employees and thus alters the (observed) state of the system. The newly observed state of the system will again be compared to the desired state, which will lead to a new decision depending on the value of the discrepancy between desired and observed conditions. As the reader may have gathered in this case we have a negative or stabilizing loop. Once the number of employees matches the desired number, no new employees will be hired and the number of employees will stop rising (provided there are no lay-offs).

In system dynamics, social systems are seen as composed of a number of interlinked feedback loops. And as stated before, many relationships between variables in social systems are non-linear. The combination of feedback loops with delays and non-linear relationships gives rise to a wide variety of behavioural characteristics of these systems. Basically, the dynamic characteristics of a system are determined by the interaction between the system's positive and negative feedback loops. And exactly because of the fact that a system dynamics model contains non-linear feedback loops, shifts in the dominance of loops within the system can occur. For instance, a positive loop which at first has a relatively minor effect, might become dominant during the course of the simulation and radically change the system's behaviour. It is the combination of feedback with delays and non-linearities which can produce unexpected or counterintuitive model behaviour. As was pointed out in the first chapter, the human mind is ill-suited to derive the dynamic consequences of complex feedback systems. Hence the need for simulation, since an analytical solution of the model is unfeasible.

THE PROCESS OF BUILDING A SYSTEM DYNAMICS MODEL

System dynamics model-building is an effective tool in promoting systems thinking in an organization. In order to be in a position to employ that tool it is necessary that one at least understands the basic principles of system dynamics and the stages in model-building. In this and the following chapter I will outline the basic stages in system dynamics model-building. The chapters also contain a number of exercises for the reader who is unfamiliar with system dynamics. I do have to point out that working one's way through these chapters will provide a good first introduction to system dynamics. However, there are a large number of issues involved in system dynamics model-building, which cannot all be covered in the context of two chapters. I would advise the reader who has become interested after reading these chapters to consult one of the many high quality handbooks which are currently available. As stated, an annotated bibliography is contained in Appendix 1.

In my discussion of the model-building process I will largely follow Richardson and Pugh (1981). These authors distinguish seven stages in a system dynamics model-building process. These stages are:

1. Problem identification and model purpose
2. System conceptualization
3. Model formulation and parameter estimation
4. Analysis of model behaviour: testing and sensitivity analysis
5. Model evaluation: model validity
6. Policy analysis
7. Model use or implementation

As can be seen from these stages the primary purpose of system dynamics (and this goes for many simulation models) is to build a model of some system with which one can conduct experiments for the purpose of: (a) a better understanding of the system's structure and behaviour; and (b) designing robust policies to alleviate problems in the system. Of course, the advantage of building a simulation model derives from the fact that a large number of model experiments are possible, which would hardly be feasible in reality.

The process starts with the identification of a problem and ends with the implementation of a solution. One has to keep in mind that the process is not characterized by a linear progression but is highly iterative or cyclical in nature. There is considerable going back and forth between the various stages in model-building before an adequate policy to alleviate the problem is identified (Randers, 1980; Richardson and Pugh, 1981). This cyclical character is also an indication that the model-building process involves considerable learning. In the remainder of this chapter we will be concerned with the first two stages of model-building. Chapter 3 will discuss the remaining stages.

Problem Identification and Model Purpose

In order to build a model one needs a clear purpose and one needs to focus on a problem rather than a system. The latter might sound paradoxical given the fact that system dynamics focuses on systems. However, what is meant is that a clear purpose is needed to focus the study and to decide what to include in the model and what to leave out. In other words, the problem is taken as a starting point but it is studied from a systems point of view. The reader will recall the example in the first chapter on the health care insurance organization. The organization's objective was to reduce health care costs by reducing referral rates. Although this seemed to be a solid approach to the problem at first sight, it was shown that when viewed from a systems point of view, the adopted policy might lead to undesirable effects. In this case the problem of health care costs was the starting point, but it was studied from a systems point of view. In other words we did not want to model the (whole) health care system, but rather we included those elements which were deemed necessary to understand the problem of rising health care costs. In this case the model served the purpose of a better understanding of this problem.

In general, several purposes of model-building can be identified. In its most simple form the purpose is to understand a problem better and the potential effects of courses of action. The process starts with the identification of some problematic behaviour, e.g. increasing sickness leave (as opposed to a desired level of sickness leave which creates a problem). Other examples of problematic behaviour constitute a decrease in customer satisfaction, fall in sales, rising unemployment, increasing work pressure etc. The problematic and/or desired behaviour can be sketched over time in one or more graphs and is called the 'reference mode of behaviour'. An example is presented in Figure 2.2.

The notion of a 'reference mode of behaviour' is central to the whole model-building process. Note that the reference mode of behaviour can be derived from the perceived system's behaviour and represents its problematic behaviour. In turn, the model-builder will attempt to construct a simulation model which is capable of replicating this reference mode of behaviour in order to increase confidence in the model.

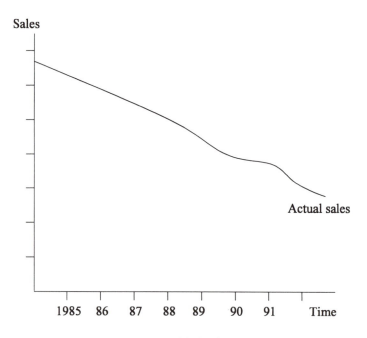

Figure 2.2 Example of a Reference Mode of Behaviour

One might however also encounter situations in which no reference mode of behaviour can be established, because the data are simply not available. This is generally the case if new systems have to be designed. A classic example of the use of system dynamics for systems design is Forrester's market growth model (Forrester, 1975). For another example the reader is referred to Chapter 7 of Wolstenholme's System Enquiry (Wolstenholme, 1990). In Chapter 7 I will present an example of a group model-building exercise in which a model was built for a number of housing corporations to explore future market policies. For a couple of years housing corporations in the Netherlands, who used to be subsidized by the Dutch government, had to operate independently on the housing market. This created a whole new situation and as a result there was no unambiguous (historic) reference mode of behaviour to guide our model-building efforts. In this case, however, the model-building process as well as the resulting system dynamics model could be used as a tool to explore the potential dynamics of the structure as identified by the participants.

In other cases, people employ system dynamics to construct social theories and test their dynamic implications (cf. Hanneman, 1988; Sterman, 1985; Wittenberg, 1992). Here too, a clear (historic) reference mode of behaviour may not be present and the model-builder will have to proceed without its guidance.

In cases where a reference mode of behaviour from the system might be lacking it is still useful to think of a clear purpose in terms of a dynamic process which will have to be simulated. Stated differently, one always needs to ask the question what kind of time series the model will have to generate and how this will be helpful in the study of the problem. For instance, in the case of the housing corporations discussed in Chapter 7, one of the purposes of the model was to explore the conditions under which survival of housing corporations on the free market could be accomplished. This gives the model-builder (and the group with which the model is built) a clear reference point with which to work: the model will have to be able to simulate variables which serve as indicators of the financial continuity of a corporation over time and the extent to which it accomplishes its social objectives. One such indicator could be the corporation's solvency.

A second important element in problem identification is the so-called time horizon. Although this might look strange at first sight, the time horizon affects the way the problem will be studied. If for instance one looks at increasing health care costs over a time period of say, 10 to 15 years one might safely assume that there might be an effect from the increase of average age on costs. Conversely, one does not expect the health care system to substantially affect the average life time within that time span. If, however, the time horizon is increased to say 100 years, there might be a significant effect of health care on average life time. Hence, at the point of identifying the reference mode of behaviour it is important to simultaneously think about the time horizon.

System Conceptualization

As mentioned previously, system dynamics harbours the notion of a causally closed boundary. An important step in conceptualizing a system for system dynamics model-building is to settle on the system boundary. The boundary determines what is considered to belong to the system and what is not. Given the purpose of the study the question is whether some element needs to be included in the model or not. Forrester (1975) points out that if an element can be omitted without destroying the purpose of the study or misrepresenting the problematic behaviour then that element can be left out and the system boundary can be drawn more narrowly. If an element cannot be left out, for instance because it causes a misrepresentation of the reference mode of behaviour, the model boundary has to be drawn more broadly. Needless to say that the boundary can be subject to change during the course of the process of model-building.

After the system boundary has (preliminarily) been defined, conceptualization of the system starts. Conceptualizing the system is generally accomplished in a visual way. Two types of diagrams have generally been employed: the causal loop diagram and the flow diagram. Above, I have discussed an example of a flow diagram. In the previous chapter I introduced some examples of causal loop diagrams. In the next section I will concentrate on the way causal loop diagrams are constructed and I will provide a number of exercises with which the reader (if inexperienced with system dynamics) can start to build his or her modelling skills.

Exercises in Causal Loop Diagramming

Causal loop diagrams constitute a powerful way to express concisely causal statements and to identify feedback processes. In a causal loop diagram a causal relationship between two variables is represented by means of an arrow. The variable at the tail is supposed to have a causal effect on the variable at the point. In addition, a distinction can be made between two types of causal relationships: positive and negative. A positive causal relationship implies that both variables will change in the same direction. The statement that more cars will lead to more air pollution can be represented as in the upper part of Figure 2.3. The upper part of the diagram can be read as follows: the higher the number of cars, the higher the amount of the air pollution. Or alternatively: the lower the number of cars, the lower the amount of the air pollution.

A negative relationship on the other hand implies that both variables change in opposite directions. An example is shown in the lower half of Figure 2.3. It can be read as: the higher the number of cars, the lower the number of travellers by train. Or as: the lower the number of cars, the higher the number of travellers by train.

A couple of remarks are in order. First, the primary question is whether the verbal statement and the diagram match. In other words, for now we disregard the question whether this statement is valid. Second, be aware that the polarity of the

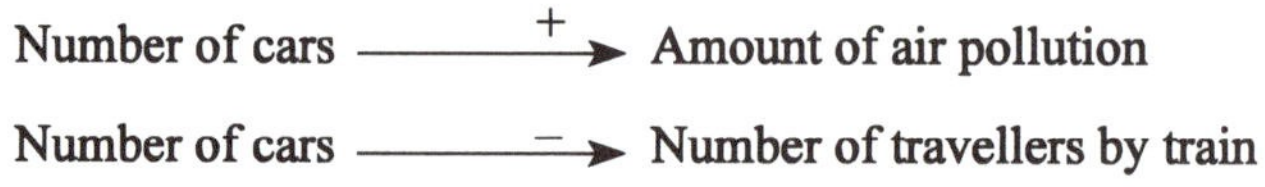

Number of cars ———— $+$ ⟶ Amount of air pollution

Number of cars ———— $-$ ⟶ Number of travellers by train

Figure 2.3 Example of Positive and Negative Causal Relationship

relationship (+ or –) is solely determined by the relationship between the two variables and does *not* depend on the fact whether the effect variable actually increases or decreases. The latter is a common mistake made by novices. Third, the arguments in the examples can only be considered valid under the assumption that all else in the system is held constant. So the number of travellers by train can (and will) be affected by other variables, which might for instance actually increase the number of travellers by train although the number of cars multiplies too. The latter would imply that new variables will have to be added to the diagram, e.g. the price of petrol relative to price of train tickets. Before discussing cases with more than two variables in more detail, let us first focus on the case of two variables. Below is an exercise in extracting causal representations from written text.

Relationships Between Two Variables

Let me provide a couple of guidelines before starting. First, from the sentences in Exercise 2.1 select the variables which are supposed to be related, but do not incorporate the value attached to the variables. For instance in the car example that I presented above the variable is not 'high number of cars' but just 'number of cars'. This is the variable which is supposed to increase or decrease. In other words adding the word 'high' implies adding a value of the variable in the name of the variable itself. The idea is to select variable names in such a way that they can take on high or low values. Hence the variable name 'number of cars', which can take on a high or low value or anything in between. Second, it is also wise to formulate variables in a positive rather than a negative way. For instance, 'political motivation' as a variable name rather than 'political demotivation'. This will make argumentations in causal diagrams easier to grasp. Third, it is generally helpful to try to think in terms of aggregated variables. For instance, 'average age of a group' rather than age of an individual. This is because most system dynamics models are at an aggregated level. Finally, although this is not obligatory, it helps if the names of variables are as terse as possible.

Exercise 2.1   Identifying Causal Relationships

As a first exercise the reader is invited to translate the sentences below into causal diagrams. Make a separate diagram for each sentence. Remember, do not worry if you consider these statements correct or not. The sole purpose is to learn to translate verbal statements into causal diagrams.

1. The higher the investments, the more employment.
2. If employment increases, unemployment will decrease.
3. The higher the motivation of the workforce in an organization, the higher each person's productivity.
4. Rising social security outlays will increase the government's budget deficit.
5. The more hours a student works the higher his/her grades.

6. The higher the number of people participating in politics, the lower the disinterest in politics.
7. The higher a product's quality, the better it will sell.
8. Higher taxes will increase the size of the black market.
9. The high unemployment rate is the consequence of the government policy.
10. The better a person's arguments in a discussion, the higher the chances he will win a discussion.

The reader can check the correctness of the solutions by consulting Appendix 2. It contains suggested solutions to the above exercise. It is particularly important to check whether the polarity of the relationships have been specified correctly. Mistakes with regard to the correct specification of the polarity derive in general from a confusion of the actual change in the effect variable with the polarity of the relationship. Let me explain this in some more detail.

A common mistake made by novices is to denote an influence as positive if the verbal statement specifies that the effect variable will increase. For instance, if the second sentence of the exercise is rephrased as: decreasing employment will lead to a rise in unemployment, some will then denote this as an influence of employment on unemployment with a positive polarity (because the rise of unemployment is taken to mean a positive relationship). But the polarity of a relationship is solely dependent on the fact whether an increase in the cause variable will produce an increase (i.e. positive polarity) or a decrease (negative polarity) in the effect variable. Or conversely, whether a decrease in the cause variable will produce an increase (i.e. negative polarity) or a decrease (i.e. positive polarity) in the effect variable. In the employment example above the polarity of the relationship between employment and unemployment is thus unrelated to whether one starts with an increase or a decrease in employment. The question is whether, if one starts with an increase in employment this will lead to either an increase (+ sign) or a decrease (– sign) in unemployment. If higher employment leads to lower unemployment then the relationship is negative (–). Conversely, if one starts with a decrease in employment and it is supposed that this will lead to an increase in unemployment again the relationship is negative (–).

Four additional remarks need to be made. First, as stated before the exercise, frame variables without their associated values. Hence, social security outlays as the variable in the fourth sentence rather than rising social security outlays. Second, note that a causal loop diagram can only contain variables which are at least of an ordinal level of measurement. The values of the variables are supposed to increase or decrease. This is not the case for variables at a nominal level, e.g. sex or denomination. These have to be translated into continuous variables. Sex can for instance be replaced by the percentage of women (or men) in the population and denomination for instance by the percentage of catholics or protestants, etc. Second, a concept like government policy (although it can be quite variable) is not a variable in the above sense. As can be seen in the ninth sentence of the exercise it is not quite clear what it was in the government policy that caused the high unemployment rate. Stated differently, the concept of government policy can be seen as a

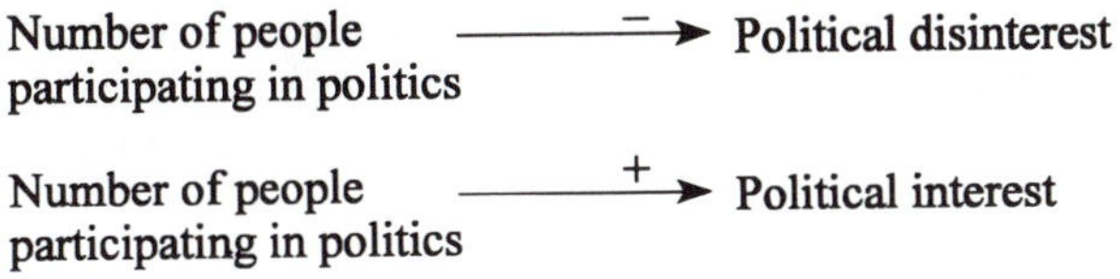

Number of people ⟶ Political disinterest
participating in politics

Number of people ⟶ $+$ Political interest
participating in politics

Figure 2.4 Example of Effect of Framing a Variable on Polarity of Relationship

bundle of underlying separate variables, including for instance government expenditures, investment premiums etc. One or more of these variables then have to be identified as the cause of the high unemployment rate. Third, although the polarity of a relationship is unrelated to whether one starts from an increase or a decrease in the cause variable, the polarity of the relationship does depend on the way the variables are framed. Statement six in the first exercise reads: the higher the number of people participating in politics, the lower the disinterest in politics. This can be represented as a negative relationship as can be seen in the upper part of Figure 2.4.

However, if one has chosen 'interest in politics' as the effect variable (rather than 'disinterest in politics') the polarity will change from negative to positive, as can be seen in the lower half of Figure 2.4. The argument is that the more people participate in politics, the lower the disinterest (–) or the higher the interest in politics (+).

It is important that one understands this type of argument correctly, because misspecification of a single relationship between two variables can also lead to a misspecification of the polarity of a feedback loop, since loops are composed of a chain of single relationships as we will see below.

Relationships Between More Than Two Variables

The previous exercise was rather straightforward and simple, because only two variables were involved at a time. In general, people tend to make many causal statements with regard to problems. The second exercise contains sentences which are composed of more than two variables.

Exercise 2.2   Relationships Between More Than Two Variables

Again make a separate diagram for each of the sentences below. For each causal diagram determine the polarity between the first and the last variable of the path. The reader will find my solutions to this exercise in Appendix 2.

1. Wage costs decrease and as a result profits will climb, which will positively affect investments which will increase employment.
2. The more wage costs will decrease, the higher investments will be, because profits improve.
3. If the number of sick people in an organization increases this will boost the work pressure, because the same amount of work has to be completed with fewer people.

4. The number of people admitted into hospital is not the primary cause for rising health care costs, the main cause is the length of stay in hospital of those admitted.
5. Family doctors who order many patients back, also refer many patients to medical specialists. This is because these doctors are uncertain with regard to their decisions.
6. The higher the employment, the lower unemployment, unless labour supply increases.
7. If social premiums increase, the premium pressure will increase unless the gross income rises.
8. The higher the number of students admitted to a university, the more staff will be hired. But typically, less staff will be hired than would be necessary to keep the staff/student ratio constant. As a result, the staff/student ratio will drop, which will negatively affect the quality of teaching and thus result in less well educated students.
9. The higher the number of people on a project, the more work can be done and the sooner a project will be completed. On the other hand the more people working on a project, the more difficult the coordination of individual activities, hence the more need for mutual communication which slows down the completion time of the project.
10. If the premium percentages increase, the wage costs will rise, the available income will decrease, and the amount of social premiums paid in a country will rise. The lower the available income, the lower the demand for goods and services, which will slow down investments and thus decrease employment. The higher the amount of social premiums paid, the higher the trust fund reserves, the less government subsidies to trust funds are needed and the higher the government expenditures which will raise the demand for goods and services. Higher wage costs will decrease investments and thus the production capacity. Given that the production capacity utilization factor will remain stable, a lower production capacity will mean less employment.

A number of sentences in the above exercise contain important insights. The first relates to the word 'because'. If we have an argument in the form of the second and third sentence then the 'because' part of the sentence generally elaborates the argument and thus forms an intermediating variable in the argument. So, the second sentence in essence states that lower wage costs will lead to higher investment, because profits improve which in turn will increase investments. This is important from the point of view of group model-building. Suppose that during a session someone points out that lower wage costs will increase investments, then the question why this is the case will generally lead to a 'because' type of response. And the variable which is mentioned in the 'because' part will in general intermediate between the two original variables of the statement. Note the subtle difference with the fifth sentence where number of back orders and number of referrals are juxtaposed and both are caused by the same variable, i.e. a doctor's uncertainty. In the second and third sentence, in contrast, the original two variables stand in a causal relationship with each other!

The second insight relates to the word 'unless'. The sixth and the eighth sentence contain the word unless. Generally the word unless refers to a situation in which there are two (opposing) cause variables. The sixth sentence in essence states that on the one hand an increase in employment will reduce unemployment (negative relationship), but at the same time an increase in labour supply will increase unemployment (positive relationship). A similar argument can be made for the eighth sentence.

The third sentence shows another typical characteristic of constructing system dynamics models. Alhough the sentence does not explicitly mention the number of employees, I have chosen to include this variable, because this gives a more accurate representation and shows the similarity with the amount of work. Although the sentence mentions 'the same amount of work', this can be seen as a variable (amount of work), which, if kept constant, will increase the work pressure when the number of employees drops. But, if simultaneously with a decrease in the number of available workers the amount of work decreases, then work pressure would remain stable or might even decrease, depending on which of the two (amount of work or availabale workforce) drops faster. There might even be a link between the amount of work done and the number of available people, in the sense that less available people might lead to a decrease in the amount of work and in that case work pressure might remain stable. A similar argument can be made with regard to the available number of employees which depends on number of sick people and total number of employees. A similar situation is encountered in the last sentence of number 10 with regard to the stability of the production capacity utilization factor.

The fourth and the eighth sentence may have confused some readers. In the fourth sentence two factors are identified which cause health care costs. Some people only include the main cause (i.e. length of stay), but the sentence mentions two causes and states that the second might be more important than the first with regard to costs. Hence, both will have to be included and the problem of which factor is most important will have to be addressed when the model is quantified. The issue of model formulation and quantification will be discussed in the next chapter. A similar case is encountered in the eighth sentence, which states that the growth in staff will lag behind the enrolment of students.

With regard to the polarity of the relationships, I again urge the reader to check these carefully. One point where mistakes might occur is, for instance, at the end of the ninth sentence where the increased need for mutual communication is supposed to slow down the completion time of the project. It is tempting to draw an arrow from 'need for mutual communication' to 'project completion time' with a negative polarity. But since the completion time is slowed down by increased communication the polarity of this relationships needs to be positive: more need for communication leads to a higher project completion time. This needs of course not be the case if variables have been framed differently by the reader (e.g. duration of project, or total project time. See also Figure 2.4.)

Finally, the last two sentences show examples of arguments in which more than one path leads from a cause variable (e.g. premium percentages) to an effect variable (employment), while these paths do not all have the same polarity. The situation is thus imbalanced as we have seen in the first chapter.

Feedback Loops

Thus far we have been concerned with one-way causality. As stated before, the purpose in system dynamics is to find the feedback loops underlying a problem. Two types of feedback loops are distinguished: positive and negative. The third exercise is meant to identify feedback loops. The reader is warned that in this case some of the exercises do not specify the whole argument. In other words the reader is invited to 'discover' (or develop) a potential feedback loop based on the text.

Exercise 2.3   Identifying Feedback Loops

For each sentence in the exercise below: (a) draw the causal loop diagram, and (b) identify the number of loops and determine for each loop whether it is positive or negative.

1. The wage-price spiral.
2. If the number of sick people in a company increases this will boost the work pressure, because the same amount of work has to be completed with fewer people. The higher the work pressure the more people will get sick.
3. In the beginning of this century, high unemployment led to a decrease in consumption. This in turn affected sales, which caused more unemployment. In order to stop this type of process social security benefits were created. (Two loops!)
4. General practitioners with a high workload tend to refer more patients to medical specialists, which decreases their workload temporarily. However, referred patients will again show up at a doctor's consultation hour after some time, because they will be referred back by the medical specialist.
5. When the number of rumours about a bank's insolvency increases, the likelihood increases that a self-fulfilling prophecy will occur.

The three exercises have given you an idea about how to construct causal loop diagrams. They show that written text is an excellent source to construct causal loop diagrams and to train your modelling skills. However, the above examples were still rather straightforward. In general, statements in documents are more ambiguous and more difficult to translate in causal loop diagrams. But still they provide an excellent opportunity to develop your diagramming skills further, because in group model-building sessions participants also talk equivocally and you will have to try to identify any causal arguments in their statements. So, as a fourth exercise I have included in this chapter a longer piece of text, which the reader can use. A couple of guidelines may be helpful. It is best to start by reading the entire text, in order to get a feel for the context. The next step is to reread the document sentence by sentence, and to identify causal relationships between variables and their direction. The reader who has taken the opportunity to do the previous exercises will have learned to recognize expressions like: 'leads to'; 'has as a consequence' as causal relationships between two variables. These relationships can be listed on a separate sheet of paper in the form of a causal loop diagram. Finally, the resulting causal diagram has to be checked with the original text in order to eliminate potential mistakes and to make sure it is the best accurate representation of it.

Exercise 2.4   Constructing a Causal Loop Diagram From a Document

In this policy note, which will describe some options to decrease the social security outlays, we will mainly concentrate on the reduction of unemployment. This is because unemployment outlays take a substantial part of the social security outlays and hence when the former drop this will also lead to a reduction of the total social security outlays, which will reduce the premium percentages for both employers and employees.

In order to arrive at a reduction of unemployment an important policy is to alter the percentages of social security premiums paid by employers and workers respectively. I propose to decrease the premium percentages for employers while increasing those for workers. In other words: workers should pay a larger percentage of the premiums. For employers this would result in a lower amount of premiums to be paid (the workers pay a larger share). This will result in higher employment in several ways. As a result of a lower amount of premiums to be paid by employers, labour will become cheaper and this will lead to higher profits and thus more opportunity for investment which will result in more jobs. Moreover, because of cheap labour, companies will be able to produce at a cheaper level, which leads to an improvement in their competitive level on the foreign markets, where more will be sold (exports will increase), which leads to more employment.

The disadvantage of the increased amount of premiums paid by workers is that it will result in a lower net wage level. In the short term this will result in a decrease of the purchasing power, which will lower the total demand, and thus affect the number of jobs negatively. Fortunately, because of the increased opportunity to export, demand will be kept up. In addition, as a result of lower costs, companies will lower prices, which leads to a slight increase of the purchasing power of workers in the longer run. On the other hand it is also known that workers, when confronted with higher premium percentages, will roll these off at employers. In other words, workers will demand higher gross wages to compensate for increased premiums and to keep net wages up. This will in turn increase the cost of labour. The result will be declining employment, more unemployment and unemployment outlays which closes the circle.

This exercise is still pretty basic because the text contains statements which can be translated rather easily into causal statements. The reader will however also have felt that sometimes the text leaves some ambiguity as to the exact meaning of a word. The author switches concepts and the reader will have to interpret whether two different concepts (e.g. employment, number of jobs) can be represented by one and the same variable. By necessity, the reader will have to make a choice as I have also done in the causal map that I have drawn from this text (see Appendix 2). Since this text is more ambiguous than previous exercises, the reader might disagree with my solution at a couple of points. The only way to find out what the best solution is, is to actually ask the author of the document, or, as in group model-building, have the participant explain his or her argument. Remember that in the context of group model-building the first step is to make an accurate representation of people's points of view.

Building Diagrams From Scratch

Thus far causal loop diagrams were created from written text. Although this is an excellent way to exercise one's modelling skills, building system dynamics models mostly involves the creation of a model from scratch.

In the next exercises the reader is provided with a short problem description and is invited to build a small causal loop diagram underlying the problem.

Exercise 2.5   Generating Feedback Loops

1. *Traffic jams and highway construction*   Constructing more highways will not solve the problem of traffic congestion. On the contrary it will create new traffic jams. (Think of short and long term effect: two opposing loops!)
2. *Pesticides*   Another example derives from the use of pesticides to decrease the number of insects which damage the crop. (Also, try to think of two opposing loops for short and long term.)
3. *Arms race*   Construct a causal loop diagram of an arms race between two countries: A and B. (Try to conceive of two interconnected loops, where the amount of arms of both countries are compared to each other, and which induces the process.)
4. *Inventory control*   In the beginning of this chapter I have pointed out that negative feedback loops are goal-seeking or balancing. A simple example is the problem of inventory control. Let us take a bookshop as an example and let us distinguish only one type of book. The goal can be seen as the desired level of books in store. Orders of new books will increase the inventory of books, sales deplete it. The first assignment is to compose a causal loop diagram in which inventory will be goal-seeking. For reasons of simplicity assume that sales are constant (and cannot be controlled by management). However, management can control the rate at which new books will be ordered.

Next, suppose that the higher the discrepancy between actual and desired inventory the larger the delivery delay of books to your customers. And in turn the larger the delivery delay at your bookstore the more customers will go to the competitor.

How many feedback loops does the diagram contain? What are their polarities? What behaviour might be expected from this?
5. *Market saturation*   Suppose you sell a new kind of TV set and you are the only supplier. You do not advertise, the product sells by word of mouth. This means that the more people have your product, the more people will buy it. On the other hand, the more people have your product the lower the number of potential buyers.

SYSTEMS ARCHETYPES

Over the years, a large number of system dynamics models have been built. Most system dynamicists have constructed case-specific models, i.e. models which apply to a particular case. As might be expected, several system dynamicists have asked themselves whether there might be so-called generic structures which apply to more than one particular situation (Forrester, 1975; Bell and Senge, 1980; Paich, 1985). If these were to be identified they might increase intellectual efficiency, because of their transferability to multiple situations. The discussion on generic structures, however, is quite confusing. As Paich (1985) pointed out it is questionable whether two system dynamicists discussing the concept would be discussing the same thing. Lane and Smart (1994) have reviewed the literature on generic structures and have come up with three different views on the concept. They call the first canonical situation models. These can be seen as case-specific models reduced to their essentials and hence applicable to more than one case. An example of a canonical situation model is Forrester's urban dynamics and his market growth model (Forrester, 1975), which may be applied to a specific case. The second class is those of the abstracted micro-structures. These are combinations of system dynamics components which generate particular behaviour modes. An example is a level and a rate which together produce exponential growth. We will see examples of this in the next chapter. Finally, the authors distinguish so-called archetypes. In this case generic structure has the meaning of '. . . recurrent patterns of structure which are associated with a distinctive behaviour mode and exhibit one of the characteristics of complex systems, a system insight.' (Lane and Smart, 1994, 73.) Archetypes serve the purpose of behavioural insight. They have become popular through Senge's *The Fifth Discipline* where they are discussed with the aid of causal loop diagrams. To introduce the reader to the phenomenon of archetypes I will present a couple of examples below. More examples can be found in Senge (1990).

Fixes That Fail

In this archetype a solution to a problem is designed, but this solution although effective in the short run, proves to have unintended and undesirable consequences in the longer run. This archetype can be observed frequently: a solution to a problem is designed which in turn creates a new problem in the long run. Actually the reader has already identified a potential example of such an archetype in the first sentence of Exercise 2.5. The decision to build more highways solves the problem of traffic congestion in the short run. But in the longer run this may create a high quality traffic infrastructure which in turn may seduce people to take the car rather than other means of transportation. The exercise on the pesticides is similar to this one.

Typically, these situations may arise because long term effects are disregarded either out of ignorance (e.g. lack of thinking in dynamic terms) or because a decision was forced by a powerful group or lobby which deliberately ignored the long term effects.

Delayed Balancing Process

A second archetype is a negative feedback loop (or balancing process) with a delay. In behavioural terms this archetype frequently gives rise to overshoot. A lively example is the so-called sluggish shower. The model is presented in Figure 2.5.

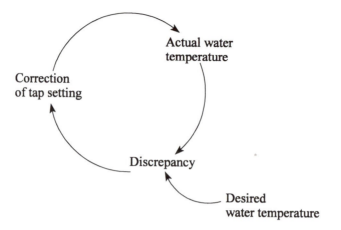

Figure 2.5 Balancing Process With Delay: The Sluggish Shower

The discrepancy between the actual water temperature and the desired temperature leads to corrective action. (In this case it would make no sense to add + and— signs to the arrows. More aggressive correction of the tap setting may lead to a higher or a lower water temperature.) However, if the system does not respond quickly enough and one reacts a little aggressively, the temperature might easily never reach the desired value. The trick is to be patient or decrease the system's sluggishness. Any system containing a negative loop may exhibit unstable behaviour (i.e. the system never reaches an equilibrium nor will it remain within an acceptable range). In Exercise 2.5 I introduced an inventory control model. Since it contains one negative loop it may also give rise to unstable behaviour if ordering policies are aggressive and there is a large delay between orders and deliveries. Many production distribution systems have similar characteristics. This is most vividly demonstrated in the so-called beer game. (For a vivid description of the beer game, see Senge (1990). The beer game can be purchased from The International System Dynamics Society, 49 Bedford Road, Lincoln MA 01773, USA.) In this simulation game there are four roles: brewer, wholesaler, distributor and retailer. The demand for beer at the start of the simulation game is four cases of beer at the retailer's outlet. In turn the retailer orders four cases of beer from the distributors, who orders from the wholesaler and so on. In other words initially the system is in equilibrium. However, after a couple of weeks the demand for beer rises to eight cases at the retailer. Since the retailer's inventory starts to drop, he will increase orders for beer. With some delay the same happens for the distributor, the wholesaler and the brewer. Since the production distribution system contains delays it takes some time before the original orders placed by the retailer will be received. But in the meantime the retailer's inventory might have dropped to zero and he might even have built up a substantial backlog. Most players in the retailer's role counteract these developments by ordering more and more beer, which does indeed start to arrive after some time. Since demand is still constant at eight cases, the retailer's inventory then starts to rise quickly. As a result the retailer starts to decrease the new orders sharply. The attentive reader may have noticed the similarity with the sluggish shower. But in this case matters are somewhat more complicated. The retailer's decisions reverberate throughout the whole production distribution chain as the reader may imagine. As a result the whole system starts to become instable and fluctuations in inventories and orders become wider and wider. This destabilizing result is typically produced by the decisions of the players in the game, who become impatient and may even start to panic when their inventory drops.

Escalation

A third archetype is escalation, which is caused by two interlocked balancing feedback loops. The classic example is the arms race between two countries, which was included as an exercise above. The higher the amount of arms in country A, the better its relative position to country B. This will slow down A's production. On the other hand it will increase B's production, which will increase the amount of arms in country B, which decreases the relative position of A, which then leads to more production in country A, etc. Typically, the growth curve of such a situation will be exponential.

A similar example that I encountered in one of the projects that I did with a couple of colleagues related to the growth process of a multinational company. This company had a highly decentralized structure, with a number of regional autonomous business units. The founder's philosophy included the idea that the size of the business units should be kept limited in order to keep employees motivated. In other words, each time a unit passed the 50 person limit it was split into two units each covering their own region. This had worked well in the past and had ensured rapid growth, primarily because the continuous division and creation of new units created fast career opportunities for employees. The process is depicted in Figure 2.6.

A situation of sustained growth of the company (which had been the case in the past) increases the number of business units. This results in a stabilizing ('BU split-up') loop. The number of employees per business unit is stabilized at its desired value. Small units are effective in generating projects, because they create a highly motivated workforce, foster team spirit and boost career opportunities. This in turn increases business performance and the number of projects. More projects result in more people being employed, thus closing the second ('motivation') negative loop, which in turn sets the first loop in motion (more employees leading to more divisions). The two negative loops together seemed to have caused a rapid growth in the number of business units in the company (Vennix, Akkermans and Rouwette, 1996).

Limits to Growth

Another archetype is called 'limits to growth'. Its behaviour is characterized by the typical growth curve exhibited in Figure 2.7.

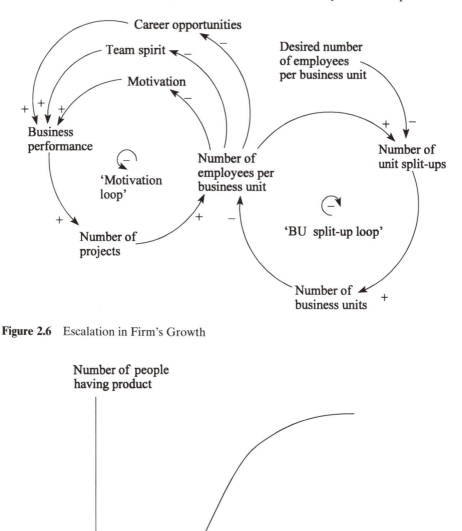

Figure 2.6 Escalation in Firm's Growth

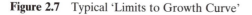

Figure 2.7 Typical 'Limits to Growth Curve'

As can be seen from the curve, the process starts out gradually, then quickly accelerates and finally growth declines and comes to a halt. This behaviour results from a combined positive and negative feedback loop. A typical example of limits to growth was the market saturation example in Exercise 2.5. Another typical example is a situation of growth (for instance in animal population) in which a certain carrying capacity halts the growth. The reader is invited to draw the causal loop diagram (with a balancing and a reinforcing loop) involved in such a situation.

Success to the Successful

Another archetype is called 'success to the successful'. The characteristic mechanism is two positive feedback loops describing two activities which compete for limited resources. The more one invests in one the less the other gets. As a result one activity will flourish at the expense of the other. This is depicted in Figure 2.8.

In the project that I described under escalation we also identified this archetype. The management style in the business units was entrepreneurial and was perhaps best typified as 'healthy egoism'. In this structure, each BU tried to serve as best as it could its own particular market. This structure had provided the company with a highly flexible and dedicated workforce close to the customer base. This clearly was an asset for the 'old business'. However, at the time we intervened the market appeared to be changing. A trend could be distinguished toward what might be called the 'new business'. The primary difference with the old market was the increasing international orientation. The autonomous organizational structure with small business units seemed less well suited to serve the international market optimally. In the 'new business' units would need to collaborate closely if the company as a whole was to remain competitive. Clearly, the ruling attitude of most BU management teams would have to change from one of 'healthy egoism' to a

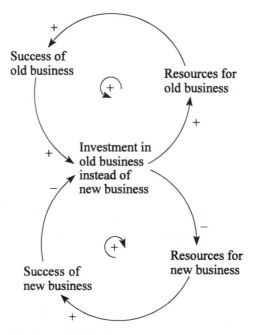

Figure 2.8 Success to the Successful Archetype

more collaborative attitude. However, the autonomy of business units prevented the company from further developing a 'new business' infrastructure. Typically the success of the 'old business' created a tendency to allocate resources (financial and managerial) to this market. The performance in the new market thus seems to suffer from the 'success to the successful' archetype. Supporting the old business was seriously withdrawing resources from entering the new market successfully (Vennix, Akkermans and Rouwettte, 1996).

LIMITATIONS OF CAUSAL LOOP DIAGRAMS AND ARCHETYPES

Thus far we have only been concerned with causal loop diagrams as a way of conceptualizing system structure. Experienced system dynamicists generally warn against the use of causal loop diagrams and point out that it is best to start the conceptualization process by identifying the stocks and flows in the system. The reason for this is the notion of accumulation in systems. In order to explain this, take a look at a simple population model in Figure 2.9.

Now, assuming for the moment that there are no deaths, let us trace the loop from number of births through population to births, starting with an increase in the number of births: when the number of births increases population will grow. The higher the population, the higher the number of births. Now, before proceeding to read, the reader is invited to do the same, starting with a decreasing number of births rather than an increase.

As you will notice, the argument does not hold anymore. When the number of births decreases, population will not decline but it will still increase. The lower limit for the number of births is zero, in which case the level of the population stops growing. The reader should not be misled by the fact that population can decline as a result of deaths. In the example, the number of deaths is considered to be zero and in this situation it is clear that the argument is incorrect when starting from a declining number of births. The example shows that causal diagrams can easily be misleading when attempting to derive dynamic consequences from them

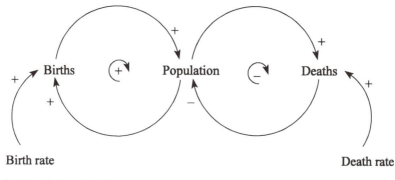

Figure 2.9 Population Model

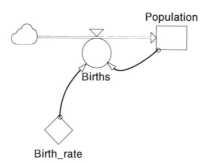

Figure 2.10 Flow Diagram of Population Model Without Deaths

(Richardson, 1986). The reason is that a causal diagram does not contain levels (or stocks) which serve as integrators. If the population is seen as a stock and births as the inflow (disregarding deaths for the moment), the above problem disappears. Figure 2.10 contains the flow model for births and population.

As can be seen in the above exhibit, there is one stock, which contains the level of the population at some point in time. To the left of the stock there is an inflow (i.e. births) which represents the number of births in a given period. The level of the stock is defined as the level at some previous point in time (e.g. one month ago) to which the number of births in the preceding month is added. This flow diagram clearly shows that population could never decrease no matter how small the number of births. The most extreme situation would be no births which would lead to a constant population. In the next chapter on quantitative system dynamics I will discuss these issues in more detail. The reader may think of similar examples in which a causal diagram can lead to misleading dynamic conclusions.

Apart from the problems involved in the use of causal diagrams, I would also like to point out that the use of systems archetypes contains an additional danger. That is, the risk of premature recognition. If applied thoughtlessly one might label a problem as a certain archetype, while in fact a closer look would have revealed that it is not. Needless to say that if policy conclusions are based on an erroneous archetype, the policy results will be ineffective at best, and disastrous at worst. Archetypes should be applied with care and with a more fundamental understanding of the relationship between structure and dynamics, to which we will turn our attention in the next chapter.

SUMMARY

This chapter has discussed the system dynamics methodology and the first stages in model construction. Important elements of the method are: the idea of the closed boundary, the feedback loop, levels and rates and discrepancies between (observed) conditions in a system and desired conditions. Next, I have discussed the first two steps in constructing a system dynamics model: problem identification and conceptualization. As an introduction to thinking in system dynamics terms I have presented and discussed a number of exercises in causal loop diagramming. Although extremely important and a useful way to analyse problems I have also pointed out that causal loop diagrams do not allow rigorous conclusions to be drawn regarding behaviour. They can even lead to misleading inferences. In order to be in a position to derive valid dynamic insights, one will have to formalize and quantify the model. This issue will be the topic of the next chapter.

Chapter 3

System Dynamics: Model Formulation and Analysis

INTRODUCTION

In the previous chapter I have discussed problem identification and system conceptualization, sometimes labelled qualitative system dynamics. This chapter is concerned with quantitative system dynamics. It follows that this chapter will focus on the remaining stages in model construction: (a) model formulation and calibration (i.e. parameter estimation), (b) analysis of model behaviour (i.e testing and sensitivity analysis), (c) model evaluation, (d) policy analysis, and (e) model use or implementation. I will start with the flow diagram and some basic equations in system dynamics models.

FLOW DIAGRAMS AND BASIC EQUATIONS

As stated in the previous chapter, two types of flows can be distinguished in system dynamics models: material and information flows. I will first discuss characteristics of material flows.

Material Flows and Delays

In the previous chapter I have introduced the population model as a flow diagram. In Figure 3.1 I have reproduced this flow diagram.

The corresponding mathematical equation for the population is:

$$POP_t = POP_{t-1} + DT \, (births_{dt} - deaths_{dt})$$

Stated verbally: the level of the population at time t equals the level at time t–1, to which the number of births in the time interval between t and t–1 (i.e. DT) is added

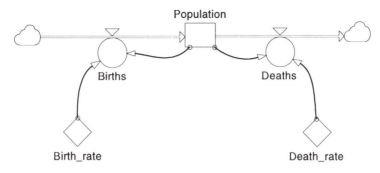

Figure 3.1 Flow Diagram of Population Model

while the number of deaths is substracted. Basically this is the standard equation for any stock in a system dynamics model, regardless of whether the stock contains people, money, goods or something else. (I will use the terms 'stock' and 'level' interchangeably, although strictly speaking stock is the correct term and level refers to the value of the stock.) Stocks in the system can be identified by imagining that the flow processes in a system are stopped as if a picture of the system were taken. What can be seen in this 'static picture' are the stocks of the system. If, for instance, in the population example the process was halted, I would still be in a position to measure the number of people in the population. The latter would not hold for births or deaths. These are measured over some time interval.

The reader will have noticed that every stock thus functions as an integrator, that is, it accumulates the inflows. Every stock equation also contains the time increment of the simulation, i.e. DT. A clear distinction has to be made between (a) the simulation time, (b) the time interval of the model, and (c) the time increment DT. The simulation time or time horizon is the total time period over which the model is simulated. The time interval in the model is specified by the model-builder. In the above example of the population model this time interval could be specified as years, months, weeks, days etc. The selection of the time interval of the model has to be in accordance with the type of process one is simulating. In the population model it would not make much sense to simulate the model in intervals of minutes or seconds. However, in a model in which one simulates the cooling of a cup of coffee from the time when it is poured to the time when it reaches the room temperature, it would be senseless to specify the time interval in weeks or days or even hours. This is because the whole cooling process might have been completed within that one time interval and hence no behaviour of the model could be observed, only its initial temperature and the final room temperature. In this case, it would make more sense to think in min-utes as the appropriate time interval.

Finally, the time increment specifies the number of computation cycles in be-tween one time interval in the model. If DT is fixed at 1.0, and the model's time interval is months this implies that every DT cycle equals one month. If DT is set at 0.5 then this means that two computation cycles with the model represent one month of elapsed time. If, on the other hand, DT is set at 2.0 then each computational cycle equals two months. The general rule is that the smaller the DT, the more the simulation process will approach a continuous process. On the other hand the smaller the DT the larger the number of computation cycles which have to be made. If DT equals 1.0, the time interval is months and the total simulation time for instance equals 10 years, then there will be 120 simulation cycles. If in this case DT is set at 0.5 there will be 240 cycles and so on.

The selection of DT is not an arbitrary choice. If DT is set inappropriately this might cause the model to produce so-called artefacts, i.e. the simulation results are an artefact of the model. This can easily be shown with a simple example. Suppose for instance that we have a stock which contains unemployed people and the average unemployment time equals 2 months. The rate equation for the persons who find a job would then be formulated as follows:

persons finding work = number of unemployed persons ÷ average time of unemployment

If average unemployment time equals two months then each month half of the unemployed will leave the stock. The accompanying stock equation looks as follows:

$$UNEMPL_t = UNEMPL_{t-1} + DT \, (NEW\text{--}UNEMPL_{dt} - FIND\text{--}WORK_{dt})$$

Let us suppose that the number of unemployed equals 1000. The number of people finding a job each month would then equal 500, provided that DT equals 1.0. But for the sake of demonstration let us suppose that during the simulation the average unemployment time decreases due to economic growth and reaches a value of two weeks, i.e. half a month, rather than two months. In this case with a value of 1.0 for DT, things could easily go wrong. The number of people finding work in one month would be calculated as: number of unemployed ÷ 0.5. This would mean that twice the number of unemployed would leave the stock, and this stock would then take on a negative value. If unemployed is 1000, then 2000 people would find a job and the number of unemployed would become –1000. In the next simulation run this would imply that –1000 ÷ 0.5 = –2000 would flow out which would be equal to an inflow of 1000. So, to be on the safe side it is best to take DT as small as possible. The general rule is to set the value of DT between ½ and ⅕ of the smallest time constant in the model.

Rate equations do not have a standard structure like stock equations. However, in this population model the equations for the number of births and deaths are quite straightforward. For the sake of simplicity, we have assumed that the number of births depends on the level of the population and the birth rate. Stated mathematically: the number of births = level of the population × birth rate. Since the birth rate is assumed to be constant it is depicted as a rhombus in Powersim. A similar argument can be presented for the death flow. Death flow = level of the population × death rate. In system dynamics models an outflow rate is often formulated as its

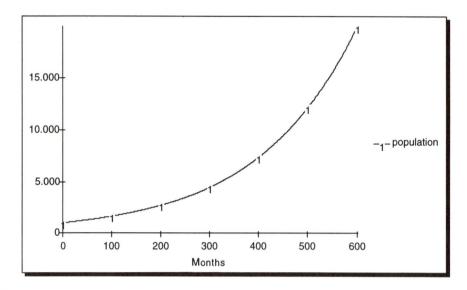

Figure 3.2 Behaviour of Positive Population Loop

inverse: the average time that elements remain in the level, in this case average life time. If, for instance, the average life time is 50 years, then the average death rate is $1 \div 50 = 0.02$, i.e. 2% per year. Hence, death flow = level of the population ÷ average life time.

For purposes of illustration let us next take a look at the behaviour of positive (or reinforcing) and negative (or balancing) loops. Suppose that at the beginning of the simulation the population is 1000 persons and the birth rate is 0.5% of the population, while there are no deaths. If simulated the model will behave as in Figure 3.2.

The horizontal axis represents the elapsed time in months, while the vertical axis represents the level of the population. The initial value of the population (which must be specified by the modeller) is set at 1000. The figure shows that over time population will increase at an ever faster rate. This is the result of the positive feedback loop between births and population: even with a constant birth rate, when population increases, the number of births will increase, which in turn makes population grow, which then augments the number of births etc. The result is not linear, but exponential growth. In other words, positive (or reinforcing) feedback loops produce exponential growth. Note that while the speed with which population rises does depend on the actual birth rate the shape of the curve (i.e. its exponential character) is independent from the birth rate (unless the birth rate becomes zero, in which case population ceases to grow).

On the other hand, there is the negative (or balancing) feedback loop. Suppose that we have a constant number of births per year (i.e. 25) and the average life time is 75 years. This produces a negative feedback loop in the model: if the population level rises, so will the number of deaths, which results in a decrease of the

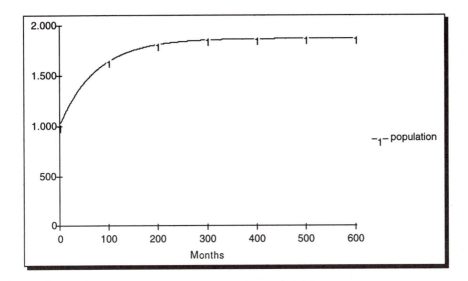

Figure 3.3 Behaviour of Negative Loop with Constant Births

population. However, a fall in the population will in turn give rise to a fall in the number of deaths too. A negative feedback loop thus produces stabilizing behaviour in a system, it corrects deviations in the opposite direction of the original deviation. In this particular case it will produce the curve in Figure 3.3.

Again, the initial value of the population is set at 1000. It is increased with 25 births per year. The deaths initially take on a value of 1000 ÷ 75, which equals 13.33, thus the population starts to rise because the number of births exceeds the number of deaths. As the population rises, however, so does the number of deaths. Ultimately an equilibrium value is reached at a level of 1875 people. At this point the inflow (25 births) exactly matches the outflow (1875 ÷ 75 = 25).

As I have indicated in the previous chapter, system dynamics models are built up on the basis of a variety of flows. Forrester (1961) makes a distinction between six kinds of flows in a system: people, money, goods, orders, capital goods and information flows. With the exception of information, these are all material flows. This also implies that a stock will contain one of the above variety of things. Whatever stuff a stock contains, it is quite irrelevant to its behaviour. Each stock represents a conservation of the flow and thus represents a delay. This means that stuff which is going in will take some time (at least one time increment DT) before it will get out. Although some software packages recognize a variety of types of stocks, for reasons of simplicity I will only discuss two here. The reader is referred to the user's guides which go with these packages for information on other types of stocks.

The two types of stocks I will discuss are continuous and discrete stocks. Two simple examples of both types are: a stock representing unemployed people (continuous) and a stock containing pupils at school (discrete). The basic difference between the two is that in the first case the time that elements remain in the stock differs for various elements. For instance, some people might easily and quickly

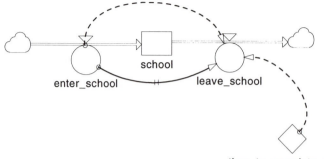

Figure 3.4 Example of Discrete Stock: School Model

find a new job while for others it might take considerable time. Stated differently, some people would remain in the stock for a short and others for a long time. Hence, the term *average time of unemployment* in these cases. In the school situation on the other hand, basically every pupil will remain in the school for the same period of time (e.g. five years) and pupils who have gone in first will generally come out first. This difference also shows up if different types of levels are employed. Let us first take a look at a discrete stock of pupils in a school. The corresponding figure is presented in Figure 3.4.

The arrows from the inflow of the stock (enter–school) to the outflow (leave–school) indicates that the outflow depends on the inflow, with a specific delay time. This is indicated by two arrows: one with two small lines, indicating the delay, and one broken arrow, indicating that at the start of the simulation, the variable leave–school will take on the value of enter–school. For the sake of simplicity let us assume that the school initially has 1000 pupils, five grades (time–to–complete–school equals five years) and that each year 200 new pupils enter while 200 pupils leave the school. (In order to avoid misunderstandings for the novice model-builder it might be useful to explain, that we are not interested in the actual daily process of children entering and leaving the school. What we are concerned with is that people have a characteristic (i.e. a person is in the second grade) and it is this characteristic which determines whether they belong to a certain stock or not. For reasons of simplicity we have ignored the phenomena of repetition and drop out.) At the start of the simulation each grade contains 200 pupils adding up to 1000 pupils for the whole school. This means the model is in steady state because the inflow equals the outflow and the level of the stock remains unaltered. In order to study the effect of this type of stock in the flow of pupils, one may deliberately change the inflow of the number of pupils from say 200 to 250 for one particular year (e.g. year 10). This is accomplished by a so-called PULSE function. All software packages contain so-called built-in functions and can easily be invoked by the user. Examples of these functions are PULSE and STEP, but most system dynamics software packages contain a large variety of other functions including stochastic functions. The effect of such a PULSE input at time 10 is shown in Figure 3.5.

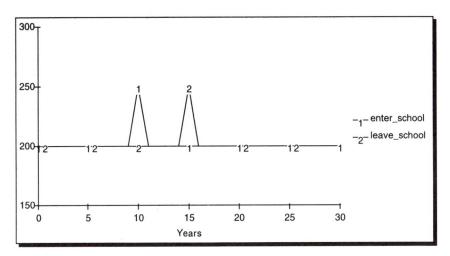

Figure 3.5 Reaction of Outflow (Leave School) to a One Time Change in Inflow (Enter School): discrete case

In the case of the PULSE of 50 extra pupils in year 10 (see curve labelled -1-) the outflow reacts with 50 extra pupils exactly five years after the PULSE was initiated (see curve labelled -2-). (The figure is somewhat misleading. It looks as if the pulse starts at time 9 and ends at time 11. This is not what happens in the calculations of the model, there is a single pulse at time 10.) This corresponds to the way we understand these discrete systems. It works like a FIFO (First In First Out system). Let us next take a look at the continuous case and use the number of unemployed people as an example (Figure 3.6).

Suppose the number of unemployed people equals 1000. For reasons of simplicity we assume in this case that each month 100 people will lose their jobs and will register as unemployed persons (new–unempl). We also assume that the average time of unemployment (av–unempl–time) equals 10 months, which sets the outflow (find–work) at 1000 ÷ 10, which is equal to the inflow. This means that the model is in steady state, i.e. the inflow equals the outflow and as a result the value of

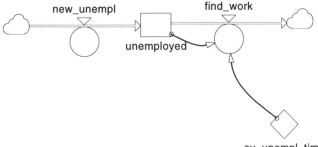

Figure 3.6 Example of Continuous Stock: Unemployment

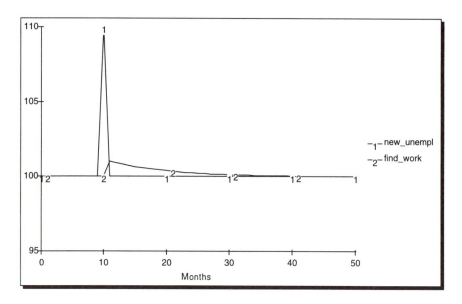

Figure 3.7 Reaction of Outflow to a One Time Change of Inflow: Continuous Case

the stock remains at the same level. In order to study the effect of the stock in the flow of unemployed people we deliberately change the inflow from 100 to 110 in the fifth month by means of a PULSE function. The resulting behaviour is shown in Figure 3.7.

As opposed to the previous case, the outflow in this model does not 'wait' five periods but immediately reacts to a change of the inflow. This is because some of the new unemployed will find a new job quickly, while for others it will take considerable time. Of course, as might be expected, if one increases the average time of unemployment, the slower the model will react to the change in input, but the form of the curve remains unaltered.

Thus far we have looked at the results of a one time change in the inflow of a stock on its outflow. In order to understand how system dynamics models behave it is also useful to take a look at the behaviour of a model with a continuous change in an inflow. This can be accomplished by a so-called STEP function. Figure 3.8 shows the results of a permanent change in the inflow of unemployed from 100 to 110 starting in the tenth month.

In the case of the STEP the curve of the outflow (curve -2-) will gradually move towards the new level of the inflow (curve -1-). In other words the outflow reacts almost immediately to a change in the inflow. This is in line with the notion that an increased inflow in the number of unemployed may contain people who will quickly find a new job. If we would have simulated a STEP input in the school model then the reaction of the outflow would not have occurred until after five years, because in this case we have a discrete stock. In both the discrete and the continuous case the stock in the flow produces a delay in the reaction of the outflow to a change in

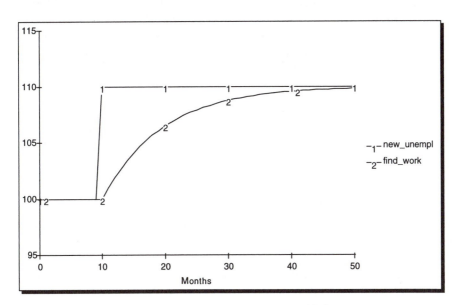

Figure 3.8 Reaction of Outflow to a Permanent Change of Inflow

the inflow. Even in the continuous case it takes at least one time interval before the outflow will react to a change in the inflow.

Thus far I have discussed cases in which there is a flow which contains one level. One might easily imagine situations in which a flow consists of more than one level. Suppose, for instance, that in a model of a consultancy company we take the flow of personnel. If one wants to make a distinction between junior, senior and principal consultants, this can be depicted as in Figure 3.9.

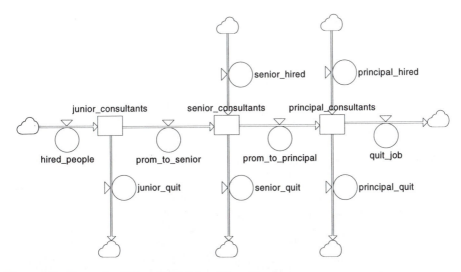

Figure 3.9 Example of Flow Containing Three Stocks

People are hired by the company and start as a junior. After a couple of years of experience they will be promoted to senior consultant and finally they may become principal consultant. Of course, each of these stocks can be depleted when people quit their jobs or increased when seniors and principals are directly hired.

Information Flows and Delays

Thus far we have discussed material flows and delays. One special type of flow in system dynamics models is the flow of information. Information links the various flows in a model. Information from some point in the system is used to produce a decision somewhere else in the model. Stated differently, the state of elements in one flow (e.g. sales of goods) provides information which forms the basis for decisions with regard to the same or other flows (e.g. personnel) in the system, which in turn might affect the original flow thus forming an information feedback system, as we have seen in the first part of Chapter 2. In that sense flows are the result of policies (decisions) within the system to control the system. More specifically, rate equations represent policies within the system. A rate consists of four elements: a goal (or desired system state), an observed state of the system, a discrepancy (defined as the difference between desired and observed system state) and a desired action based on the discrepancy. One example of such a policy is the difference between desired and actual inventory which we have discussed in the previous chapter. Figure 3.10 shows the inventory control model in the form of a flow diagram.

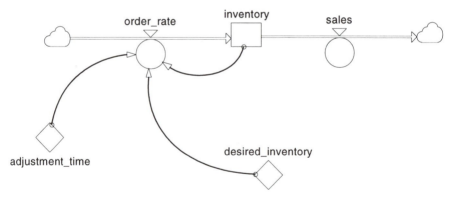

Figure 3.10   Inventory Control Model

In this model inventory is depleted through sales. Let us assume that sales are 100 items each week. The decision to order goods is defined as the discrepancy between the desired inventory minus the actual level of inventory. Hence, if inventory equals desired inventory no items will be ordered. But if 100 items per week are sold then inventory will start to drop and as a result orders will be placed to keep inventory up to the desired level. In the model this is accomplished by defining the order rate as:

order rate = (desired inventory – inventory) ÷ adjustment time

The equation shows that if desired inventory equals inventory, orders will necessarily be zero. So, if we start the simulation under these conditions no orders will be placed in the first week. But at the same time in the first week 100 items will be sold. So by the end of the first week inventory will have dropped to 900 items. As a result in the second week orders will be placed. These will equal 1000 (desired inventory) – 900 (actual inventory) = 100 items. Now, if we place all orders in the same week, the adjustment time would be 1 and if we assume that there is no delay between the orders and the deliveries, the order rate would be 100 items. Let us however assume that the adjustment time equals two weeks, indicating that if there were no sales we would like inventory to catch up with desired inventory in two weeks. This then implies that half of the ordered items (i.e. 50 items) will be delivered in one week. So by the end of the second week the level of inventory would equal: 900 items (level at end of first week) minus 100 (items sold in week 2) plus 50 (order rate) = 850 items. These 850 items constitute the value of inventory at the end of the second and the start of the third week. In the third week again 100 items will be sold. The order rate is again calculated with the formula: (desired inventory – inventory) ÷ adjustment time. This will result in: (1000 – 850) ÷ 2 = 75 items. The net result is that by the end of the third week the level of inventory equals: 850 (value at start of third week) – 100 (sales) + 75 (order rate) = 825 items. In the fourth week orders will be (1000 – 825) ÷ 2 = 87.5. Sales will again be 100 and the level of inventory at the end of the third week will be: 825 – 100 + 87.5 = 812.5. The results of these calculations can be seen in Table 3.1.

Table 3.1 Behaviour of Inventory Model Towards Equilibrium Value

Time	Desired-inventory	Inventory	Order-rate	Sales
0	1.000,000	1.000,00	0,00	100,00
1	1.000,000	900,00	50,00	100,00
2	1.000,000	850,00	75,00	100,00
3	1.000,000	825,00	87,50	100,00
4	1.000,000	812,50	93,75	100,00
5	1.000,000	806,25	96,88	100,00
6	1.000,000	803,13	98,44	100,00
7	1.000,000	801,56	99,22	100,00
8	1.000,000	800,78	99,61	100,00
9	1.000,000	800,39	99,80	100,00
10	1.000,000	800,20	99,90	100,00
11	1.000,000	800,10	99,95	100,00
12	1.000,000	800,05	99,98	100,00
13	1.000,000	800,02	99,99	100,00
14	1.000,000	800,01	99,99	100,00
15	1.000,000	800,01	100,00	100,00
16	1.000,000	800,00	100,00	100,00
17	1.000,000	800,00	100,00	100,00
18	1.000,000	800,00	100,00	100,00

Gradually over time the level of inventory will move towards 800 items, which is its equilibrium value. This can easily be seen since in that case deliveries (inflow) will equal sales (outflow) and as a result the level of inventory will remain constant. When inventory equals 800 items then deliveries will equal: $(1000 - 800) \div 2 = 100$ items which is exactly equal to sales.

In this case we have assumed that the level of inventory is perceived correctly by management. As I have indicated before, Forrester (1961) points out that information can be distorted or outdated. Hence, policies are designed on the basis of perceived conditions rather than 'the actual' conditions. In this case management might have incorrect information about the exact level of inventory. There might for instance be an information delay. The policy is then based on the perceived inventory rather than actual inventory. The resulting model is shown in Figure 3.11.

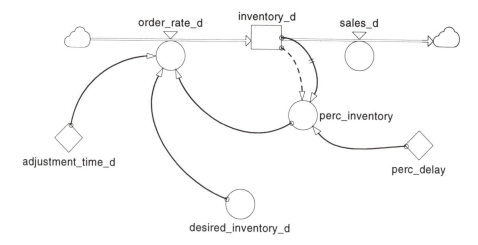

Figure 3.11   Inventory Control Model with a Delay in Perception

In Figure 3.11 the delay in perceiving changes in inventory is represented by perc–delay (i.e. two weeks) and the perceived inventory (perc–inventory). In other words the discrepancy is now modelled as the difference between desired inventory and perceived inventory. The perceived inventory is a delayed function of the actual inventory. Thus, if the actual inventory changes it will take on average two weeks before the changes are perceived by management. As a result it will take more time before management reacts to a discrepancy between desired and actual inventory. The latter affects the behaviour of the system. This can best be seen if the two situations (i.e. with and without a perception delay) are compared with each other. In Figure 3.12 the reaction of the inventory for the two models is compared for a STEP input to the sales. The variables in the model with the perception delay are indicated with an additional –d. It must be pointed out to the reader that in this case the initial value of inventory was set at 800 items, so that the model starts in equilibrium.

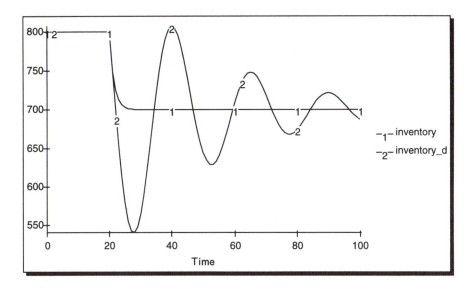

Figure 3.12 Reaction of Inventory to STEP Input in Sales Without -1- and With -2- Perception Delay

In this case we have simulated a step input to the sales, i.e. sales rise from 100 to 150 starting in week 20. As can be seen there is a clear difference in response in the case with and without an information delay. In the original situation, before the step input is applied, the level of the inventory equals 800 items. The desired level of inventory is 1000. The difference between the two is the part which is being shipped and will be delivered after two weeks on average. After the step input becomes effective in week 20, sales rise from 100 to 150 which makes inventory drop to 700 in the case of no delay in perception of the level of inventory. The drop in inventory to 700 is understandable because now there will be 300 pieces in the process of ordering and shipment rather than 200. The drop of inventory to 700 pieces is quite smooth. This is in contrast with the situation when there is a delay in perception. In this situation the level of inventory starts fluctuating. It first drops to below 600, then overshoots the final equilibrium value of 700 and through a number of cycles gradually starts working its way to the new equilibrium value. The difference in behaviour between the two models can only have been caused by the delay in perception, because this is the only distinction between them. In the case of a delay in perception the drop in inventory is recognized later than in the no delay situation. This allows the inventory to drop to a lower level before action is taken to restore inventory. But, eventually as a result of the fact that the sales stabilize at a new level, inventory also reaches the level of 700 in the case where there is a perception delay.

This simple inventory control model should provide the reader with a flavour of system dynamics models and the way in which information feedback plays a role to produce decisions which result in a specific model behaviour. To clarify, the above two situations must be considered as policies to control inventory, i.e. they represent the decision rules which are employed by someone in an organization to control the level of inventory.

The best way to get acquainted with system dynamics and to see if you understand what was explained above, the reader is invited to take a look at exercise 3.1. The exercise can be done with paper and pencil. Readers who have access to one of the suitable software packages mentioned at the end of the introduction may build the models in the exercises of this chapter on their computer. But, I would advise that the exercise is first done on paper and then checked with the help of the computer.

Exercise 3.1

The reader is invited to construct a personnel model which is similar to the book-shop model. In other words, the model should consist of a stock (number of employees with an initial value of 500), a desired number of employees (600), an inflow of new employees (which is triggered by the difference between desired and actual workforce and an adjustment time) and an outflow. For the outflow assume that the average length of stay of an employee equals 60 months.

How would you expect the actual number of employees to behave over time given an adjustment time of (a) two months, (b) four months, and (c) eight months? Sketch the graphs over time and check with computer output.

MODEL FORMULATION

In the previous section I have shown a couple of examples of simple system dynamics models and their behaviour. An important step in the model-building process is to specify mathematical equations for each of the relationships in the model and to quantify the model's parameters. Let us first take a look at the way equations are formulated and how their consistency can be checked.

Equation Formulation and Consistency Checks

As we have seen, the structure of the equation for a stock is rather straightforward and similar for all stocks. Software packages like Ithink, Stella, Powersim and Vensim automatically produce the equations while the flow diagram is constructed on the computer screen. Equations for the flows and auxiliary variables are not always straightforward. A couple of examples will provide the reader with a basic idea of what this type of equation might look like.

Let us first take a look at the inventory control model without the delay. The equation for orders looks as follows:

$$orders = (desired\ inventory - inventory) \div adjustment\ time$$

Stated verbally, the number of orders is equal to the discrepancy (between desired and actual inventory) divided by the adjustment time. If the adjustment time is two weeks and the discrepancy amounts to 200 items then the deliveries will be 100 items. Normally, if inventory exceeds desired inventory this would imply that orders become negative. This can be prevented by including a MAX statement in the equation. Hence: orders = MAX (0, ((desired inv – inv) ÷ delivery time)).

An important check on the internal consistency of a system dynamics model is the so-called 'dimensional consistency check'. The check entails that for each equation in the model the dimensions on the left hand side and the right hand side need to match. Let us next take a look at the dimensions in the equation, where discrepancy is measured as a number of items [I] and time is weeks [W]:

Items per Week (ordered) = (desired number of) Items – (actual number of)
Items ÷ Weeks (adjustment time); or:
Items per Week = Items ÷ Weeks; or:
$[I÷W] = ([I] - [I]) ÷ [W]$
$[I÷W] = [I] ÷ [W]$
$[I÷W] = [I÷W]$

The number of items per week (orders) equals a number of items (discrepancy) divided by the number of weeks (adjustment time). This substitution exercise indicates that the equation is consistent.

Slightly more complicated is the population model. In the population model the number of births was formulated as:

births = birth rate × population

The number of births is equal to the level of the population multiplied by the birth rate. In the above equation the dimension for the number of births per month is persons ÷ month or [P ÷ M]; the dimension for population is persons or [P]; and the dimension for birth rate is the proportion of persons (i.e. persons born relative to persons in the population) per month or [P ÷ P ÷ M]. This produces the following dimensional consistency check:

births = birth rate × population, or:
$[P ÷ M] = [P ÷ P ÷ M] × [P]$, which is equivalent to:
$[P ÷ M] = [1 ÷ M] × [P]$, and to:
$[P ÷ M] = [P ÷ M]$

As this substitution exercise demonstrates the dimensions of the variables on both sides of the equals sign match. Now let us see whether this is also true for the corresponding stock equation. The reader will recall that the equation looked as follows:

$POP_t = POP_{t-1} + DT (births_{dt} - deaths_{dt})$

The corresponding dimensions are:

$[P] = [P] + [M] \times ([P \div M] - [P \div M])$, which is equal to:
$[P] = [P] + [M] \times ([P \div M])$, and to:
$[P] = [P] + [P]$

Hence, in this equation dimensions on both sides match too.

A more complicated example of an equation concerns a doctor's workload. The workload is determined by the number of patients in his practice, the average frequency with which patients visit their doctor each month and the average time each visit takes. The resulting equation is:

workload = number of patients × frequency of visit × time per visit

If a doctor has for instance 2000 patients, which visit him once every two months, and each visit takes on average 10 minutes then the workload is 166.67 hours per month. The corresponding dimensions of the variables are:

workload = hours per month or $[H \div M]$
number of patients = patients or $[P]$
frequency of visits = visits per patient per month or $[V \div P \div M]$
time needed per visit = time (hours) per visit or $[H \div V]$

Substituting these dimensions in the above equation yields:
$[H \div M] = [P] \times [V \div P \div M] \times [H \div V]$
$[H \div M] = [V \div M] \times [H \div V]$
$[H \div M] = [H \div M]$

which demonstrates that the equation is consistent.

When constructing a system dynamics model this dimensional consistency check has to be conducted for every equation in the model, and needless to say a variable can only have one dimension throughout the model. In other words if the workload appears elsewhere in the model as an independent variable it still has the dimension hours per month $[H \div M]$. Only, and only if, all equations in the model are checked and the model is shown to be internally consistent can it be used for further analyses. In addition, the dimensions for each variable have to make sense. To measure workload as time per month for instance makes sense, because the more hours one works the higher the workload.

Exercise 3.2

Take the personnel model from Exercise 3.1 and:

1. determine the dimensions for each variable and constant in the model,
2. substitute these dimensions in each of the equations of the model, and
3. check by means of substitution whether all equations in the model are consistent.

Parameter Estimation

Thus far we have been concerned with writing simple equations and checking the consistency of equations. Before a model can be run on a computer it has to be calibrated: the parameters in the model have to be provided with a numerical value. This is known as parameter estimation, because the *exact* numerical value of the parameters is rarely known.

Each of the models presented in the previous sections contain one or more parameters. One set of parameters are the initial values for the stocks. For instance population, inventory, and books on order. Another set is the constants in the model. For instance: desired inventory, adjustment time, birth rate, average life time, and perception delay.

In the example of the inventory control model with the delay in perception (Figure 3.11) there are four parameters which have to be estimated: the initial level of the inventory, the delay in perception of inventory, the level of the desired inventory, and the adjustment time. (In this simple model, sales is a constant which will have to be provided with a value. Normally sales will be variable and depend on such factors as (potential) customer base and price.) In the example of the doctor's workload for instance, the number of patients might be one of the other variables in the model, while time needed per visit and visits per patient could for instance be constants. When they are constants these too will have to be provided with a numerical value.

There are several ways to determine parameter values in system dynamics models (Graham, 1980; Richardson and Pugh, 1981). The most straightforward way is from firsthand knowledge of the process. For instance the number of patients in a doctor's practice can be found in a doctor's database. To provide another example, the number of houses in stock by a housing corporation is generally also known directly. Sometimes data can be found in statistical yearbooks, e.g. the birth rate. Richardson and Pugh (1981) point out that care must be taken that the data gathered have the same meaning as the model parameter, e.g. is the birth rate in the model specified as number of births per person, per adult, per female or per woman of child-bearing age and do the data gathered match this meaning of the parameter?

There are other simple ways of parameter estimation if the above situation does not apply. For instance, if the average number of visits per patient is not known directly, it can be calculated by dividing the total number of visits per month (or year) by the number of patients in a doctor's practice. A similar procedure could be followed for the time needed per visit. Divide the total time of consultation by the number of visits. Or to provide another example, if the average wage level is unknown this can simply be calculated by dividing the total wage costs by the number of employees.

However, matters can become complicated if data are not available and parameters have to be estimated from the process and behaviour. Then parameter estimation procedures become more complex and it may require quite some statistical insight and experience to produce a valid estimate for a parameter. It is not within the scope of this book to deal with these more difficult parameter estimation procedures nor with statistical procedures for model calibration. For this the reader is referred to Richardson and Pugh (1981), Graham (1980), and Peterson (1980).

There are two more points I would like to emphasize. First, each parameter in the model also needs to be expressed in dimensional units which need to make sense if compared with the system under study. Parameters should not be entered into the model simply to accommodate a mathematical formulation, but should be observable in the 'real' system. The second point relates to the accuracy of the estimates. With regard to the accuracy, again the purpose of the model is important. As Richardson and Pugh (1981, 231) point out: 'But in the last analysis, the purpose of most system dynamics studies is policy analysis. *If the policy implications of a model do not change when its parameters are varied plus or minus some percent, then from the modeler's point of view the parameters do not need to be estimated any more accurately than that*' (emphasis as in original). One of the goals of testing the model by means of a number of sensitivity analyses, which will be discussed in the next section, is to find out which parameter changes have a significant effect on model behaviour and thus need to be estimated as accurately as possible.

MODEL TESTING AND SENSITIVITY ANALYSIS

Another important step in system dynamics model-building is testing the model. Its primary goal is increased understanding of model behaviour and more insight in the system under study. Simulation models are powerful devices to carry out such repeated tests, which can increase understanding. Let us take a look at a simple sensitivity analysis of the inventory control model with the delay in information. In the original model it is assumed that the average delay in perception equals four weeks. In Figure 3.13 the results of three simulations can be seen in which the delay is increased from four (curve 1) to six (curve 2) and then to eight weeks (curve 3).

As can be seen (and might be expected) the longer the delay the later the discrepancy between actual and desired inventory is signalled. As a result, inventory drops to a lower level after the first step input, it shows wider fluctuations, and it takes a longer time before the equilibrium value of 700 is reached. But in all cases (and this might not have been anticipated), the inventory eventually settles at 700. Stated differently, a doubling of the perception time does not affect the eventual level of inventory.

Other sensitivity tests with this model might include a variation of the initial inventory level, the adjustment time or the desired inventory. For these tests to be effective, however, it is important to conduct them in a structured manner. Some guidelines will be helpful. A first suggestion is to design a list of tests that one wants to perform. The wrong way to proceed would be to just conduct a number of arbitrary tests. The correct way is to make a list of tests with an accompanying discussion of why these tests are selected. The second guideline holds when a model becomes larger. In those cases a good practice is to test the model in sections before testing the whole model. A third recommendation concerns predicting the effect of

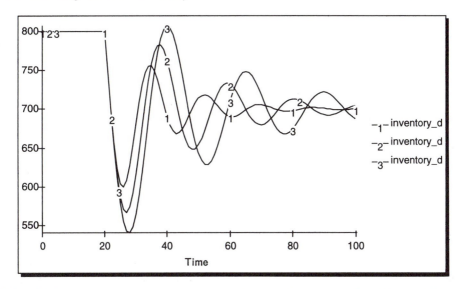

Figure 3.13   Sensitivity Analysis for Perception Delay of Four -1-, Six -2- and Eight -3- Weeks

a test before actually running the model. Conducting a test without previous estimation of what will happen is almost useless, because in retrospect the outcome is quite logical and of course one 'knew all along' that this behaviour would result (Hogarth, 1987). Remember the 'hindsight bias' phenomenon described in the first chapter. Explanations after the fact are easy and will prevent you to learn from the exercise.

Tests with the simulation model are conducted by first establishing a base or standard run. This is a run with the model in its standard form, preferably, but not necessarily, the run which replicates the reference mode of behaviour as perceived in the system. A standard run is needed as a base of comparison. In the example presented in Figure 3.13 the standard run is the situation of steady state in which the perception delay is four weeks and there is a step input to sales. (Note that the step input is required because no change takes place in the case where the model is in a steady state and the perception delay is changed. This makes sense because if desired inventory equals the sum of inventory + orders in the pipeline a longer perception delay will not affect this process. This will only happen when the model is put out of equilibrium, for instance by means of a step input.) The two runs which are added change the perception delay to six and eight weeks. The differences in the behaviour of the model can then be compared with the situation in which the perception delay had the 'standard' value of four weeks. In other words one first needs a standard run with standard values for parameters. Next runs are conducted by changing one thing at a time and studying the result of changes in the structure on the behaviour of the model by comparing the outcome with the base run.

As might be expected, the most important tests are those in which one or more feedback loops are deactivated. Comparison of the base run with this type of run shows the exact effect of a feedback loop on model behaviour. In Chapter 7 we will show some examples of this type of analysis.

Sensitivity analyses serve two important functions. First they are useful to better understand the model. Hence, the guideline to try to predict model behaviour before conducting the sensitivity analysis on the computer. Second, through sensitivity analysis the model-builder attempts to locate sensitive parameters in the model. The question in this case is: how sensitive is the model behaviour to changes in parameter values. In general many parameters in system dynamics models are rather insensitive if changed within reasonable limits. The first reason for this is that one might have altered a parameter which is not contained in a dominant loop, hence the small effect. The second reason is that feedback loops might compensate each other. Varying a parameter in a positive loop, which is linked with a negative loop, might cause the negative loop to compensate for this change.

If a sensitive parameter is located, one can respond to this in three ways (Richardson and Pugh, 1981, 291–292). First, one might decide to estimate the parameter as carefully as possible, because it obviously has a large effect on the model's behaviour. Second, one might decide to refine the model in order to capture the aggregate process, of which the parameter was the expression, in some more detail. Third, if parameter sensitivity corresponds to sensitivity in the real system, one might have located a leverage point in the system, i.e. a point with which to drastically affect the system's behaviour.

Thus far we have discussed sensitivity analyses which are based on the modeller's intuition and judgement of the outcome. There are more formal procedures to conduct and evaluate sensitivity analyses and to optimize system dynamics models. Fortunately the novice model-builder will generally not need these procedures, because these can become quite technical. These more technical approaches to sensitivity analysis and optimization are not within the scope of this book. For more information on sensitivity analysis the interested reader is referred to Tank-Nielsen (1980) and for optimization to Wolstenholme (1990), Wolstenholme and Al-Alusi (1987), and Kleijnen (1995).

Exercise 3.3

Consider the model you have built in Exercise 3.1. Now make a list of all the parameters in the model. Start from the assumption that the model is in a steady state (number of employees equals desired number of employees, i.e. 600). The first sensitivity analysis is a change in the parameter value for the adjustment time. In the standard run the adjustment time equals two weeks. Now imagine two situations. In the first the adjustment time suddenly rises to four weeks (at time 10) and in the second it suddenly drops to one week (at time 10). Now try to draw the corresponding behaviour of personnel over time. It will start at 600 and will stay there until time 10.

1. After you have drawn the corresponding graphs take the computer model and conduct the above sensitivity analysis. Compare the graphs produced by the computer with your own graphs. Explain any discrepancies.
2. Next, select another parameter and conduct an exercise similar to the one above.

MODEL EVALUATION

The stages discussed so far were concerned with the construction of the model. An important question relates to the adequacy of the model. Most textbooks on system dynamics discuss the adequacy of the model in relation to the representation of the system. The question framed is how accurate is the model representing the system under study? System dynamicists refer to this as the model's validity. As Lane (1995) points out, validation can be studied at different levels. On the 'macro' level the issues concern epistemological questions. On the 'micro' level, the focus is on actual tests of model validity. Validation of a simulation model is a widely debated topic and there is much disagreement about it. For a number of model-builders the ultimate test of model validity is whether the model is capable of replicating the reference mode of behaviour. This looks rather straightforward. However, matters are a bit more complicated. Before discussing this topic in more detail let me first formulate a couple of premises. The first is that absolutely valid models (i.e. models which perfectly represent a system under study) do not exist. However complex the model is, it is always a simplified representation of some system. What is needed is a so-called requisite decision model. A requisite decision model is a model '. . . whose form and content are just sufficient to solve a problem.' (Phillips, 1989, 108). This implies that a model is built with a specific purpose in mind. The model should generate insights with which a problem can be solved. This brings us to the second premise. Given that we are unable to build perfectly valid models a model's validity can only be judged in the light of its purpose (Shannon, 1975). The point is well made by Richardson and Pugh: 'The ultimate test of a policy-oriented model would be whether policies implemented in the real system consistently produce the results predicted by the model.' (Richardson and Pugh, 1981, 313.) However it is difficult to check whether a model meets this 'ultimate test', because in this case one would have to alter both the system and the model simultaneously for every test. Hence, modellers employ a number of other tests to determine the model's validity, to which I will turn shortly. The third point we have to keep in mind is that a distinction must be made between a model's validity and its utility. A perfectly valid model is not necessarily more useful. In general, the more money and time is invested in the model the more valid it might become. At the same time it will also become more complex and thus be more difficult to understand, a situation known as the Bonini paradox. If the model becomes overly complex it loses its utility. Given limited time and budget, this means that there is always a trade-off to be made between validity and utility and a decision has to be made at what point to stop the model-building process. The fourth premise is that since the exact validity of a model can never be established, in practice validity boils down to the degree of confidence that the model-builders and the client have in the model. The point is well put by Forrester and Senge:

> For the public and political leaders, a useful model should explain causes of important problems and providing bases for designing policies that can improve behavior in the future.. . . The notion of validity as equivalent to confidence conflicts with the view

many seem to hold which equates validity with absolute truth. We believe confidence is the proper criterion because there can be no proof of the absolute correctness with which a model represents reality. Einstein's theory of relativity has not been proven correct; it stands because it has not been disproven, and because there is shared confidence in its usefulness. Likewise one tests a system dynamics model against a diversity of empirical evidence, seeks disproofs, and develops confidence as the model withstands tests (Forrester and Senge, 1980, 211).

As will be clear from the above quote, Forrester and Senge also reject the notion of validation as a one time event. Rather they consider validation as a *process* of building confidence in the model, not as something which takes place after the model is 'finished'. Hence their conclusion: 'Validation is the process of establishing confidence in the soundness and usefulness of a model.' (Forrester and Senge, 1980, 210.)

In order to build confidence the model is subjected to a number of tests. The more tests a model withstands the higher the level of confidence in it. In their paper Forrester and Senge discuss no less than 17 different tests for model validation. We refer the interested reader to their paper or the discussion in Richardson and Pugh (1981). Below we will discuss some of the most well-known and most important of these tests.

The first two tests concern the structure of the model. One test that we have already discussed is the dimensional consistency check. If a model does not pass this test is must be considered useless, because it is not clear what the meaning of the output is. In addition, all parameters in the model need to have a '. . . meaningful real world interpretation and are not to be invoked merely to fix dimensional inconsistencies.' (Richardson and Pugh, 1981, 313). Another test is the model's face validity. Here the question is whether experts on the system agree that the model's structure is an adequate representation of the system. In group model-building a number of experts will automatically be present in the group. In other words, it will basically be the group who determines the model's adequacy. However, it is always useful at some point in time to ask outside experts their opinion of the model in order to have an external check.

Other tests focus on the behaviour of the model. For instance, sensitivity analyses can be employed to find out whether the model is not too sensitive to small changes in parameters. We have seen an example of a sensitivity test in the previous section. A test which is closely related to sensitivity analyses is the extreme conditions test. In this case the model is subjected to extreme conditions (even those which are not likely to happen in the system) to see whether it behaves in a reasonable way. Let us for instance suppose that in the inventory control model the sales quintuple from the twentieth week, a situation which may be considered relatively unlikely. The result of this test is shown in Figure 3.14.

As can be seen from the output of the simulation the level of inventory drops below zero. Although orders are increased, the perception delay and the adjustment time are responsible for the fact that inventory is depleted more rapidly than it is replenished. This extreme conditions test (but this could also happen during sensitivity tests) reveals a flaw in the model. It is impossible to deliver goods when

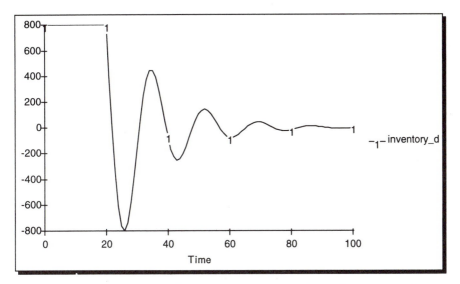

Figure 3.14 Extreme Conditions Test with the Inventory Model: Quintupling of Sales

inventory has become zero. In this case such a test may give rise to alteration of the structure of the model, which by the way nicely demonstrates the iterative character of model-building. In this case there are several options to adapt the model in such a way that unrealistic behaviour is prevented. The first is to specify a so-called MIN function in the sales equation. In order to accomplish this, one could specify an additional auxiliary equation, called normal sales, and make the sales depend on both inventory and normal sales:

sales = MIN (inventory, normal sales)

In this case the actual sales will either equal normal sales or inventory depending on which of the two is lower. So, if inventory is larger than normal sales, sales will equal normal sales. If, on the other hand, inventory is lower than normal sales, no more than what is available in inventory will be sold. However, as Richardson and Pugh (1981) point out, this solution might not be very valid or elegant. Normally, one might expect that if inventory becomes extremely low a pressure will build up to lower deliveries to customers to keep up inventory. Such an idea could be built into the existing model by specifying a variable normal sales and by including an effect from the level of inventory on the actual sales. This is depicted in Figure 3.15.

In this case the actual sales in the model are determined by the normal sales (exogenous) which are multiplied by an effect from the level of inventory on normal sales (eff–inv–on–sales). What the model-builder would like to accomplish is that if inventory falls, a pressure builds up which will decrease deliveries to customers (and hence sales) in order to keep up the inventory level. On the other hand, if inventory is sufficiently high all deliveries will be made. This can be accomplished by means of a GRAPH function, which specifies the relationship between

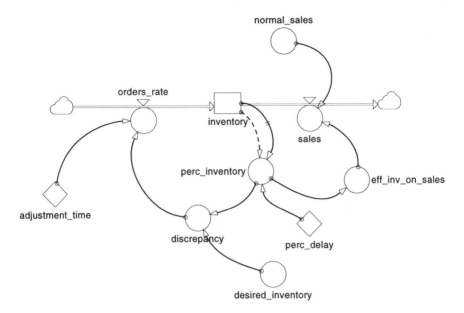

Figure 3.15 Revised Inventory Control Model after Extreme Conditions Test

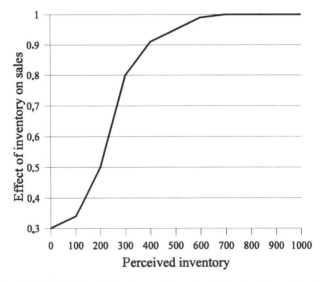

Figure 3.16 Graphical Relationship between 'Perceived Level of Inventory' and its 'Effect on Sales'

the level of inventory and the effect of this level on the amount of sales. This graphical relationship is depicted in Figure 3.16.

The figure shows that when perceived inventory gets lower, the effect of inventory on sales will also take on a lower value and as a result the actual number of sales

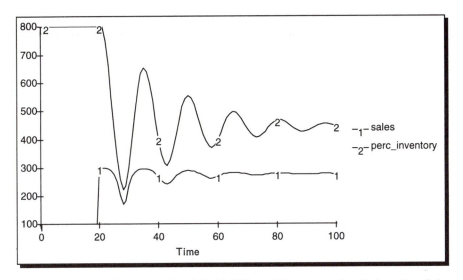

Figure 3.17 Adapted Inventory Model with Effect of Inventory after Quintupling Sales

will decrease. However, let us assume that there is a lower limit: no less than 30% of the sales will be delivered. On the other hand, if inventory is sufficiently high the effect takes on the value of 1.0 and as a result the actual sales will equal the normal sales. If this relationship is built into the model and we conduct the same extreme conditions test as above, one can see that now inventory will not drop below 200 and a new equilibrium value is found at around 400 (Figure 3.17).

The above thus not only demonstrates the use of model tests, it also shows that testing the model can lead to considerable adaptations in order to remove unrealistic model behaviour and thus increase confidence in the model.

Finally, of course, there is the test of the replication of the reference mode of behaviour, which we have discussed previously. In this case the model-builder systematically compares the time series for a particular variable which is produced by the model with a time series perceived in the system. For instance, the behaviour of inventory is compared to actual figures of inventory over the last year. The central question is whether the time series produced by the model matches the one from the real system. As stated, no model will exactly replicate the time series from the system. The question then becomes when the model is considered 'valid'. It is important to keep in mind that system dynamics models aim at identifying behaviour patterns rather than attempt to make exact predictions. Typical patterns are sustained growth or decline, and sudden changes from growth to decline or the other way around. Others include damped or expanding oscillation. It follows, that the focus must be on patterns of behaviour and the model should be able to replicate these patterns.

To conclude this section let me again emphasize that validity eventually boils down to confidence in the model. Some people are overly concerned with the replication test and tend to forget other tests. Only when the model passes a number of the tests satisfactorily will the model-builder (and the client) have sufficient confidence in the model and can it be used as a basis for policy experiments.

Exercise 3.4

1. Take the model of the first exercise and conduct an extreme conditions test. If the model behaves in an unrealistic way adapt the model in such a way that this behaviour will be removed.

POLICY ANALYSIS

As mentioned earlier, an important reason to build a system dynamics model is to test a variety of policies to improve system performance. In the context of group model-building the purpose of these simulation experiments is to foster debate and learning about potential courses of action. From these tests the policy which produces the best results is selected for implementation in the system. Policy analyses focus on changes of decision points in the model and their effects on certain outcome variables. Changes in decision functions can involve parameter changes and structural changes. In the first case, conducting the policy analysis simply involves changing the numerical value of a parameter. For instance, in the inventory model more accurate and timely information gathering on the actual inventory level might be simulated by reducing the perception delay in the model. As might be anticipated from the sensitivity analyses which we carried out previously, this would improve the system's response to sudden changes in sales.

More complex policy experiments involve structural changes in the model. Suppose for instance in our inventory model that one would like to make the desired inventory level dependent on what happens on the market rather than keeping it constant. Suppose one would contemplate a policy in which the desired inventory would follow the trend in sales (perc–sales). Further suppose, that one would like to have an inventory coverage of say 10 weeks. The latter implies that one would like to be capable of selling goods from inventory for 10 weeks even if no new orders would be delivered. The above policy has been built into the model as the reader can see in Figure 3.18.

Next, one might again run the model with the step input which was used in the first simulations. And one might also run the model under the extreme condition which was discussed previously. The result of the first simulation shows that rather than decreasing, inventory will now rise as a consequence of the fact that sales have increased from 100 to 150 from the tenth week (see Figure 3.19). Initially from the twentieth week the inventory shows a small decline, but after that it rapidly increases as a result of the fact that desired inventory is now linked to perceived sales. Since sales increase, perceived sales will rise and next desired inventory rises. Since the perception of the increase in sales is averaged, the model does not react immediately to a change in sales. Hence the initial small drop in inventory (curve 2).

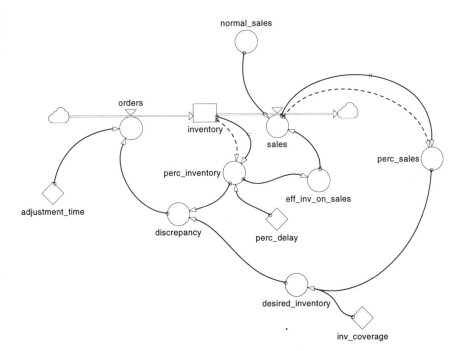

Figure 3.18 Inventory Control Model After Change of Policy

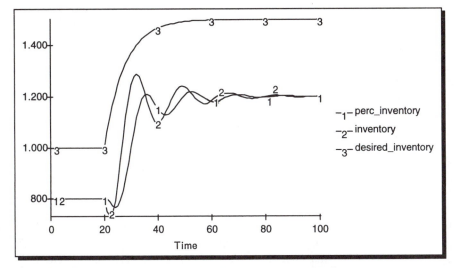

Figure 3.19 Behaviour of Inventory Model After Change of Policy

The reader may additionally design his or her own exercises with the model. The reader should not be misled by the fact that the model we have discussed so far looks quite simple, particularly compared with real life organizations. When seen from a mathematical and analytical perspective this model is already quite complex

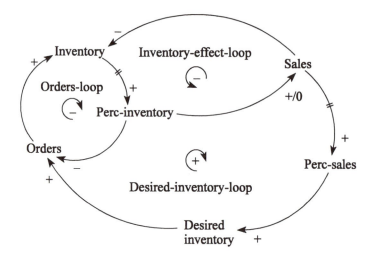

Figure 3.20 Causal Loop Diagram of Inventory Model

and provides a variety of possibilities for analyses. It is important to understand that this model contains three feedback loops, two first order information delays and one nonlinear relationship (effect of inventory on sales) as shown in Figure 3.20.

Two of the three feedback loops are negative, while one is positive. The first negative loop is the 'orders–loop'. If orders increase, inventory and perceived inventory will rise which will decrease the number of orders. This loop will tend to stabilize model behaviour. The second stabilizing is the 'inventory–effect–loop'. The lower the perceived inventory, the higher the decreasing pressure on sales and the more the inventory will be stabilized. However, this loop is only active when the perceived inventory drops below a certain threshold level. Above this level the loop is actually deactivated, because even if inventory increases further sales will not rise, because sales do then not depend on the level of inventory. Hence, the +/0 sign. Finally, the positive (desired inventory) loop runs from inventory, through perceived inventory, sales, perceived sales, desired inventory, orders to inventory again. This loop also contains the relationship between perceived inventory and sales. Hence, the loop will only be active when inventory drops below a threshold level. It will be clear that the causal loop diagram might aid in understanding model behaviour, but it would be hard to predict model behaviour from this diagram.

Let us return to the topic of this section: policy experiments with the model. When it comes to policy analysis, the final objective is to find robust policies.

In the system dynamics perspective a policy recommendation is robust only if it remains a good choice in spite of variations in model parameters, different external (exogeneous) conditions, and reasonable alternatives in model formulation. A policy that is sensitive to such variations is suspect. Policy robustness is vital because no model, mental or quantitative, is identical to the real system. The real problem will always have aspects that are not captured by a model. Consequently, to have effects in the system similar to its effects in the model, a policy must, by definition, be robust. The judgment is necessarily relative. The best we can do is to seek policies that tend to be more robust, less sensitive, than others. (Richardson and Pugh, 1981, 350–351.)

In other words, since no model is perfectly valid, a policy needs to be relatively insensitive to changes in the model. If a policy is sensitive it is suspect, because it is not known whether it will produce the effects as predicted by the model. The goal is to find an optimal policy aimed at alleviating the problem which formed the starting point for the model-building process.

MODEL USE OR IMPLEMENTATION

Thus far, we have just been concerned with the construction and analysis of a system dynamics model. But system dynamics models are created for the purpose of 'improving system performance'. This brings us to the topic of implementation of model results. If the model has revealed that a particular policy produces significant improvement and the policy itself is robust then the logical next step would be to implement this policy. The sequence of steps seems logical. A problem is studied by constructing a system dynamics model. The study produces one or more robust policy options, so nothing seems more logical than to implement the policy in question. However logical this may seem, it is naïve to assume that implementation will follow automatically if a good model is produced. The history of model-building and its impact on decision making just shows too many counterexamples (Vennix, 1990). Consider for instance Watt's experience who, in 1977, had been involved for over eight years in developing large-scale computer simulation policy models. He concluded: 'A primary goal of the project has been and is to influence decision-makers, a goal which we pursued aggressively. But by any objective standards, all of our efforts have had no impact whatsoever on public policy.' (Watt, 1977, 1.)

However, that was 1977. Haven't things changed since then, the reader might ask? If we may believe recent articles in *OR/MS Today* the problem still persists. Reminiscing about TIMS/ORSA conferences Gehani for instance asks himself: 'For whom do we really produce all these models? How many of these models are actually ever used by somebody other than the authors themselves or their graduate students. And if they aren't used, shouldn't we professors, who consume enormous society resources, be held accountable?' (Gehani, 1993, 9.) In other words, far from being solved the problem of implementation of model results still lingers.

This is not to say that nothing has changed in the last couple of decades. The most critical development has been the 'modelling as learning' approach within the system dynamics community. Two sources of information have spawned the modelling as learning approach. The first is systematic research in the area of models in the policy process. This research has revealed two important conclusions. First, that most of the insights gained from models are conceptual rather than instrumental. For instance Meadows and Robinson (1985) reviewed the implementation records of nine different mathematical policy models. With respect to the type of impact an important conclusion is that the '. . . main impact was on a vital but unmeasurable part of the system: the world of ideas.' (Meadows and Robinson, 1985, 382.) The second important conclusion is that most insights are gained *during* rather than after the model-building process. Hence, the persons who build the models will learn most. As Greenberger, Crenson and Crissey (1976) state it: 'Most [computer models] fall short of their potential as instruments for the clarification of policy issues and the enlightenment of policy makers. There is considerable evidence indicating that modeling is indeed effective in educating policy *modelers*.' (Greenberger, Crenson and Crissey, 1976, 321.)

Apart from systematic assessment research on the impact of computer models another source of information is the actual experience of consultants using system dynamics in applied consultancy projects. As early as 1972 Roberts explicitly addressed the question of implementation of model results (Roberts, 1978). He rejects the notion that implementation is a separate stage which follows the model-building process. Instead he suggests that an implementation orientation should be held from the outset and permeate the whole process. As he points out: 'But the implementation stage seldom occurs. Indeed, to produce implementation or change the needed perspective is that implementation requires a continuous process point of view that affects all stages of modeling.' (Roberts, 1978, 78). From 15 years of experience in working with system dynamics models in business consulting Roberts derived a number of guidelines for effective implementation. One of these guidelines is that the consultant should solve a problem (or realize an opportunity), which is important to the client. This implies that model-builders have to communicate extensively with the client in order to make sure that they understand what the problem is. Another important insight, which partly follows from the first, is that the client should be involved in the model-building process as much as possible. One important reason for this is model ownership. In order for the model results to be used, the client will have to own the model. This can hardly be accomplished without client involvement in the model-building process.

Weil (1980) made a comparable argument. He compared three case studies in which system dynamics modelling was used as a consulting tool in business spread over a period of 10 years. In the early projects, the emphasis was on the model, the modellers worked more or less independently of the client and interaction was mostly with the staff. The end product of the project generally was a report. In contrast, in the most recent projects, which now consist of line managers rather than staff, the client was actively involved in the model-building process. In addition the project is not concluded with a report but followed-up by transfer of know-how to create an 'ongoing analytical capability' in the client organization.

Over the decades several system dynamics model-builders have been experimenting with approaches to involve the client in the model-building process. Some have designed more or less standard procedures to accomplish this. Examples include the Reference Group approach (Randers, 1977) and the Strategic Forum (Richmond, 1987).

These experiences have given rise to the idea of models as transitional objects or microworlds (de Geus, 1988; Morecroft, 1988) and to the so-called modelling as learning approach (Lane, 1992). As stated the client in the modelling as learning approach is deeply involved in all stages of the model-building process. As was pointed out previously the primary reason is that the learning takes place during the model-building process. And this blurs the whole notion of implementation of model results. Modelling as learning defies the notion of a neat model-building process which is conducted before results can be implemented. If modelling as learning is taken seriously the whole concept of implementation becomes elusive. What one tries to accomplish in modelling as learning is that the model-building process significantly affects the client's thinking about the problem. This is most succinctly put by Eden:

> Problems are not entities outside the persons who define them, and people think and work on their problems so that they change. We hope they will do this as a consequence of our working with them. Quite often people have a nasty habit of changing the problems they are working on to such an extent that any work done by an analyst on the original problem produces polite disinterest from the client. While we are away from the client collecting data, building our model, and so on, the client talks with colleagues and events occur so that a satisfactory agenda for action may be developed; when we report back we are met with galloping apathy from our client. The more notice we take of the terms of reference and the more we have to leave the client while we conduct 'back-room' work, the more likely it will be that our work is not relevant to the problem the client is interested in when we report back. (Eden, 1982, 54.)

The inevitable conclusion is that implementation becomes evasive. At the outset of the project it cannot simply be predicted what the client will learn from the model-building exercise. Rather a variety of results can be anticipated. As Rosenhead points out in the introduction of his book on problem structuring methods for messy problems: 'Effective participation in the process of formulation, debate, and refocusing can take many forms. There can be both visible and invisible products . . . plans, designs, and recommendations, but also changes in understanding and in relationships.' (Rosenhead, 1989, 16.) In other words, the results and products of the model-building process cannot easily be anticipated and in retrospect they can take on a variety of forms. The reader may recall that in the first chapter I introduced the example of the health care insurance organization who wanted to reduce referral rates of family doctors. One important result of the model-building process was that the original policy to reduce referral rates was abandoned. This was partially a result of insight in feedback processes in the health care system. Another important result was that the organization started addressing the issue of patients being ordered back, an issue which had largely been neglected in the past. The model-building process showed the interrelationship of this phenomenon with other phenomena in which the client was interested. In Chapter 6 I will discuss a couple of other group model-building projects which produced quite unexpected results. Before the projects started none of these results could have been anticipated, nor by the facilitator, nor by the team participants. And this is exactly what group model-building is all about. Both the client and the facilitator embark on an inquiry process into a problem, a team learning process, aimed at increasing insight and, hopefully, finding a consensual decision to solve the problem. If conducted properly involving the client in the model-building process will increase the effectiveness of the model for the client organization. The next chapter will focus on a number of issues related to designing a group model-building project.

SUMMARY

In this chapter I have introduced the basics in the construction of a quantitative system dynamics model. I discussed the construction of mathematical equations, the topic of parameter estimation, the purposes of and methods to test the model and policy analysis. In the section on implementation of model results I have concluded that it is naïve to assume that an expert model-builder can take a client's problem, construct a model and deliver a number of recommendations based on the system dynamics model. Client involvement in the process of building the model is a necessary requirement to make model-building effective and to get results implemented. This belief has produced the modelling as learning approach and group model-building as a way of client involvement.

As might be anticipated, involving the client in model-building will drastically complicate the process. The question might be raised if effective procedures can be designed which involve the client in the process and at the same time keep the model-building process manageable. This issue will be taken up in more depth in the next chapter.

Chapter 4

Designing Group Model-building Projects

INTRODUCTION

In the two foregoing chapters we have been concerned with the construction of a system dynamics model. In the last section of the previous chapter I discussed the issue of implementation of model results and concluded that client involvement in the process of model-building is a prerequisite to increase the effectiveness of the model. As stated before, group model-building is an approach which involves the client deeply into the model-building process in order to enhance team learning, foster consensus and create commitment with the outcomes. But as the reader might anticipate, involving the client considerably complicates the model-building process. Careful preparation of a group model-building project may assist in its success.

This chapter discusses a number of issues in designing a group model-building project. A couple of important questions need to be addressed. Starting from an initial contact with a potential client organization the first question which needs to be answered is whether system dynamics is suitable to the problem in question. If not, the project should either be abandoned or one should look for an alternative methodology. If the answer is affirmative, a number of questions with regard to the design of the project need to be addressed. The first relates to the distinction between qualitative and quantitative system dynamics. Which of the two approaches will be most appropriate given the problem? The second question relates to participant selection: how many people to involve in the group model-building sessions and who? This question becomes important, because it may significantly affect the effectiveness of the project. Moreover, the answer to the second question is important because it is one of the factors which determines how the group model-building project will be designed. Some projects for instance, may require a large number of persons to participate, while in others only a small group will be involved. In addition, there are other factors which affect the design of the project. In some situations managers may have very limited time to participate in the process, while in other situations this is less of a problem. In some cases the problem may be politically sensitive, while in other situations the problem has a non-threatening character to the participants. In short, no two projects are alike and it is useful to be familiar with more than one approach to group model-building in order to be in a position to design a tailor-made project. It will greatly increase your flexibility to meet the requirements of the situation. (In the system dynamics literature there are also examples of group model-building approaches which follow a more or less standard approach (see for instance Richmond, (1987); Randers, (1977); Richardson and Andersen, (1995); and Vennix, Richardson and Andersen, (forthcoming). Although these approaches have their advantages, they will also limit the model-builder's flexibility to adapt to the specific situations which may arise in the case of messy problems.)

On the downside, it implies that matters may become slightly more complicated, because there is no standard procedure and no fixed set of steps to be executed. Rather, the project team will have to decide on the best design given a number of approaches and methods and techniques to be employed in group model-building. One of the purposes of this chapter is to discuss important issues, indicate viable alternatives and to formulate criteria with which to make appropriate selections. The third question, which may have far reaching consequences for the design of the project, is whether one starts from scratch with the group or whether the model-builder first constructs a preliminary model which serves as a starting point for the group model-building sessions. When starting from scratch the system dynamics model is constructed with the group at the spot. The model-building process starts during the first session. In this case no preparatory interviews are conducted, at least not with the explicit purpose to elicit viewpoints to build a preliminary model. (The model-builder may decide, however, to conduct a number of interviews in order to get acquainted with group members and to get a better understanding of the problem at hand. The latter might be particularly useful if no written material is available with which to prepare for the project.) When starting with a preliminary model the model-builder (or project group for that matter) first creates a preliminary system dynamics model which is subsequently presented to group members in the first group session. The group is invited to adapt this model as they see fit. Many system dynamics model-builders use preliminary models as a way to speed up the group model-building process.

Basically, there are two ways to construct preliminary models. The first is by means of individual interviews of participants. During the interviews information is gathered from the participants with which the model-builder constructs a preliminary model. This model is used as a point of departure in the first group session. The second way to construct a preliminary model is on the basis of research reports or policy documents. In this case the project team examines a number of relevant reports and extracts a preliminary model from it. The latter implies the use of content analysis as a research technique. If constructed from documents this preliminary model can also be presented in the first group session as a starting point for the discussion. Alternatively it can also be used to have individuals comment on it

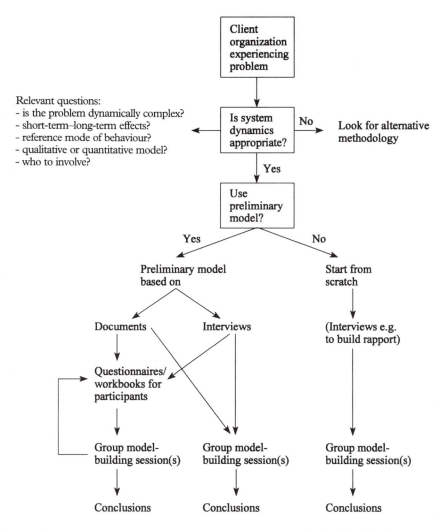

Figure 4.1 Choices to be made in the Design of Group Model-building Projects

before the first group session, for instance by means of questionnaires or so-called workbooks. Comments of individuals are used to further adapt and refine the model before it is presented in a group session. I have summarized the previous questions and accompanying choices in Figure 4.1.

In this chapter I will discuss these questions and issues in more detail, starting with the initiation of a system dynamics group model-building project. Next, I will focus on the questions relating to qualitative and quantitative system dynamics as well as the question, who should be involved. A large part of the chapter will then be devoted to the choice between starting from scratch or employing a preliminary model as the basis for group model-building. In that respect techniques like interviewing, document analysis and questionnaires will be discussed in relation to group model-building. Finally, a number of practical issues will be discussed with regard to the preparation of group model-building sessions.

Before discussing these issues in the coming sections let me point out that in most projects the model-builder will not be working in isolation. Sometimes a project group is created to design and guide the group model-building process. The project team may, for instance, consist of one or more model-builders, a group facilitator and one or more persons from the client organization. In the text of this chapter I will generally use the term project group (or team) when it comes to preparing the group model-building project. The project group is thus not to be confused with the group of persons from the client organization who will actually participate in the group sessions. In the final part of this chapter I will also discuss the various roles of people in a project group.

INITIATION OF A PROJECT: THE SUITABILITY OF SYSTEM DYNAMICS

In general, the initiation of model-building projects can be client driven or modeller driven. In the first case a potential client contacts you with the request to conduct a system dynamics project for his or her organization. In the second case the model-builder deliberately initiates contact with potential clients to offer his or her model-building services. Whichever way the project originates in retrospect origination of a group model-building project frequently looks quite accidental.

One of the first issues to be discussed between the client and the model-builder will be the suitability of system dynamics for the problem the client organization faces. Even when a client contacts you with the specific request to construct a model, this is no guarantee that a system dynamics project is the best approach to their problem. In my experience it is rare that the client has a thorough understanding of what system dynamics is and for what type of problems and under which circumstances it is most suited.

One of the most difficult questions to be asked, even to experienced model-builders, is when to use system dynamics or when to rely on other methodologies to help a client organization tackle a strategic problem. Although most of us are aware of Linstone's adage to 'suit the method to the problem, and not the problem to the method' (Linstone, 1978, 275), it may prove difficult to put this maxim into practise for various reasons.

The first is that we may be familiar with only one particular method. This situation may give rise to the 'child with the hammer' syndrome: give a child a hammer and it will start seeing nails everywhere. If I am only familiar with system dynamics there is a danger that in practice I will translate any problem into a system dynamics problem. And if I am not familiar with let us say Soft Systems Methodology (SSM), the idea to apply it to a certain problem could hardly pop up in my mind. Hence it may pay to be familiar with more than just one method to tackle messy problems. As Lane points out: 'Nevertheless, it is surely a fallacy to propose, implicitly or explicitly, that any single tool or approach can be used in all cases. The notion that any tool might be a panacea is chimerical. Since clients do not wish to be sold tools, but rather have problems studied, they are surely better served by flexibility.' (Lane, 1993, 261.) Others have argued that methods should be combined in order to overcome inherent weaknesses of each separate method. Although attempts in that direction have been made, blending methods in order to overcome inherent weaknesses of one particular method, is inhibited by the fact that each method has a different underlying theory (Eden and Radford, 1990). For instance Lane and Oliva (1994) have made an attempt to combine SSM and system dynamics, while Eden (1994) has argued that cognitive mapping can be employed as a pre-stage to system dynamics model-building. However, these attempts have not yet been tested in applied projects and the suitability of combined methods still awaits further investigation.

A second reason for the inability to suit the method to the problem is formed by the fact that problems are generally ill-defined and may thus be defined in various ways. As a result although one may expect that the type of problem determines the kind of method to be used, the situation is complicated by the fact that the same problem can be formulated in various ways, to fit in with different methodologies. It may be difficult then to practise Linstone's maxim because of our inability to carefully listen to what the client tells us. Remember the phenomenon of selective perception which was discussed in the first chapter. We may actually hear what we would like to hear, rather than what the client means. Hence, it is critical to listen carefully to the client's message. Try not to draw premature conclusions, or to hear what you want to hear. An effective way to accomplish this is by asking clarifying questions and by reflective listening, a skill which will be discussed in more detail in the next chapter on group facilitation. This does not however mean that you just listen and absorb. It is of critical importance that you ask questions to challenge the client's problem perception. The reader may recall that this is exactly what we did in the case of the health care insurance organization, which was introduced in the first chapter. It is no problem to ask critical questions, provided that the client sees this as useful and that it is the client who may ultimately decide what approach will be employed. Finally, it pays to be thoroughly familiar with the potentials and limitations of system dynamics (and possibly other methods) in order to be able to evaluate its suitability in a particular situation. Let us take a closer look at this and try to provide some guidelines on when to use system dynamics and when not.

A first criterion is that the problem needs to be dynamically complex, because of potential underlying feedback processes. In other words, decisions will provoke intended and potentially unintended consequences, which cannot be easily foreseen without the help of a computer model. This excludes all kinds of 'static' problems, i.e. questions which aim at identifying an existing situation at some point in time. In reality, it may be difficult to employ this as a criterion. Let us take the example of a company which goes through a selection process for a new site, or a government which attempts to decide on a site for a waste disposal unit. The question is to determine the best site given a number of criteria to include in the decision process. Typically, a problem like this can be tackled with the aid of techniques from the realm of Multi Attribute Utility

Decision making or MAUD (see for instance von Winterfeldt and Edwards (1986)). The process leads to an optimal choice given a number of criteria (e.g. cost, parking space, available room, attractiveness). The same problem however, could also be tackled from the point of view of system dynamics, if one is interested in the potential effects a particular decision might produce. For instance, selecting a particular site will produce all kinds of (un)intended consequences, which could only be established with the aid of a dynamic (computer) model.

To provide another example, let us take the problem of sickleave in an organization. The question might be what can be done about the high rate of sickleave. This question may lead to two different kinds of approaches. The first is to apply some kind of ideation technique (e.g. brainstorming) in order to generate a large number of potential solutions to the problem. Next, one might select one of these alternatives based on such criteria as implementability, expected succes etc. In other words, the problem is taken for granted and one immediately focuses on potential solutions. Although this method is rather quick and relatively cheap, it entails the danger of fighting symptoms rather than causes. A system dynamics approach on the other hand would focus on the identification of potential causes and feedback loops underlying the problem. Rather than just fighting symptoms a careful analysis might reveal underlying causes which have to be eliminated to solve the problem. The system dynamics model would be used to identify and evaluate robust and effective policies.

Closely related to the first criterion of dynamic complexity is the time horizon. System dynamics models frequently show that a particular policy works well in the short term, but might prove ineffective in the long term and vice versa. Typically, system dynamics addresses long term problems, frequently those problems which have been tackled unsuccesfully in the past. The latter might be an indication that attempted policies have failed, because of systemic compensation. In other words, feedback processes within the system counteract the assumed effectiveness of the policy. System dynamics aims at identifying policies, which prove effective in the longer run. In short, system dynamics is appropriate in situations where (a) the problem is dynamically complex because of underlying feedback processes, and (b) one looks for robust long term solutions.

These directions still leave considerable room and may be difficult to apply in a concrete situation. Fortunately, there is a more tangible guideline to be applied. The best practical approach is to check whether it is possible to generate a reference mode of behaviour which may represent a problem. If this cannot be accomplished one needs to be particularly careful. As an example let us take the following two problem formulations:

1. How can the decreasing trend in the number of ships flying the Dutch flag be reversed?
2. How could this organization best be designed?

In the first case, I am easily able to produce a reference mode of behaviour, while in the second this is virtually impossible. Problems like the second should thus be treated with caution when system dynamics is concerned.

As pointed out in Chapter 2, there does not necessarily need to be an empirical (historical) reference mode of behaviour. A hypothetical reference mode may well suffice. In Chapter 7 for instance, I will present the problem of the Dutch housing corporations. As explained in the Chapter 2, their primary objective is to build sufficient low cost housing (i.e. the social goal). Until the beginning of the 1990s these corporations did not have to worry about money, they were heavily sub-sidized by the Dutch government. Recently, however, the government decided that housing corporations would have to operate on the open market. This created a completely new situation, in which the corporation's survival was no longer guaran-teed by government support. The question then was whether, and under what conditions, the social goal could be accomplished, while simultaneously ensuring financial continuity. In this case there was no real reference mode of behaviour to guide the model-building process, but still a system dynamics approach proved to be useful, because one might construct a hypothetical reference mode in the form of a couple of time series. One of these time series would represent the social goal (will we build enough low cost housing) while the other would represent the finan-cial continuity. Typically, time series like these can be generated by a system dynamics model, which may be an indication that system dynamics will be an appropriate method. Stated somewhat bluntly, a system dynamics model will pro-duce time series for variables in the model. If one gathers that these time series will be able to provide answers to the problem, then system dynamics is a likely candi-date to tackle the problem. Take the example from the project for the Royal Dutch Medical Association (RDMA), mentioned in Chapter 1. One of their questions was related to the decreasing membership level. This question may typically point towards system dynamics. However, another question was related to the status of the so-called 'scientific associations' with the RDMA namely, how to best incorpor-ate these into the structure of the RDMA. The latter question generally does not point towards system dynamics as a problem solving methodology, it is related to such subjects as legal rights, design of organizations, etc.

Another practical guideline is to check whether the problem description gives rise to thinking in terms of flow processes. In Chapter 1 I introduced the case of the health care insurance organization that was looking for ways to decrease health care costs. Basically, what one attempted to accomplish was a change in the flow from patients at the family doctor to the medical specialist. This is also an indication that system dynamics might be appropriate.

From the previous discussion the reader may have gathered that system dynamics is primarily a diagnostic and impact assessment method: finding out what the prob-lem is, what structural causes are responsible for it, and which policies prove robust to tackle the problem. In other words, the first discussion with a client should attempt to establish if the above applies to their situation. This might be done by asking critical questions from a systemic and dynamic perspective. Remember the questions we asked the regional health care insurance organization, when they requested us to statistically correct the raw referral rates. Our questions typically aimed at potential dynamic consequences of reducing referral rates in the health care system (i.e. what do you think will happen if your policy will be successful?).

If the result of this first discussion with the client is that system dynamics is not a suitable candidate, then there might be other methods which might be useful. I refer the reader to Rosenhead (1989) and Eden and Radford (1990) for an overview of other soft OR methods. If on the other hand the discussion reveals that system dynamics is suitable a number of other questions still have to be answered. These are related to the design of the project and will be discussed in the next section.

THE DESIGN OF A SYSTEM DYNAMICS GROUP MODEL-BUILDING PROJECT

If system dynamics is considered appropriate at least three questions need to be answered. The first question is whether to apply qualitative or quantitative system dynamics. The second is who to involve in the sessions. The third is whether to employ a preliminary model and how to generate the information on the basis of which such a preliminary model can be constructed.

Qualitative or Quantitative System Dynamics?

In the previous chapters I have discussed the system dynamics methodology. Chapter 2 focused on problem identification and conceptualization. The result is a visual representation of the problem in the form of a causal loop diagram or a flow diagram. Chapter 3 discussed model formulation, quantification and analysis. Most system dynamicists hold the opinion that only a full-blown, quantified model deserves the label 'system dynamics model'. Some are of the opinion that it is unwise to limit system dynamics to quantified models. They argue that the conceptualization stage has its own value as a way of describing and analysing a problem. In a number of cases proper conceptualization will suffice to help solve a messy problem. In this respect a distinction is made by some authors between qualitative and quantitative system dynamics (Wolstenholme, 1982; Wolstenholme and Coyle, 1983; Wolstenholme, 1990). Qualitative system dynamics refers to the stages of problem identification and conceptualization. Quantitative system dynamics involves building a full-blown system dynamics model including its simulation. In both cases, however, the model aims at identifying the feedback processes causing the system's problems and thus looks for the dynamic structure underlying the system's behaviour.

Many system dynamicists argue that qualitative system dynamics is at best dangerous and at worst misleading. As I have already pointed out earlier the reason for this is that the human mind is not capable of inferring the dynamic characteristics of a complex structure involving delays, nonlinear relationships and feedback loops (Forrester, 1961; 1968; 1987; Sterman, 1989a and b). Only when a model is quantified and simulated on a computer can we learn to understand its dynamics. This argument can hardly be disputed. There is simply too much empirical evidence demonstrating its accuracy. Human beings have for instance difficulty in extrapolating growth processes when these have an exponential character (Wage-naar and Sagaria, 1975; Wagenaar and Timmers, 1978; 1979). Other experiments have clearly demonstrated that people perform poorly in even the simplest of feedback systems. (Empirical evidence can, for instance, be found in: Brehmer (1987; 1989), Kleinmuntz (1993), Sterman (1989 a and b), Paich and Sterman (1993), Morecroft (1983), and Diehl and Sterman (1995).) In other words, there is ample evidence that system dynamicists are correct when they assume that people cannot correctly infer the dynamics from a qualitative model which includes feed-back loops.

However, in the argument above the baseline from which one starts is the 'full' understanding of the system's behaviour. From that point of view the argument looks correct. However, in many situations in which one wants to help a client, it is not always necessary to have this full understanding. This depends in large part on the nature of the client's problem and on the goals one wants to accomplish. Given what was said in Chapter 1 on the nature of messy problems, understanding the relationship between structure and dynamics is only one of the many possible goals. Other goals might be to change perceptions, to create a shared language for mutual understanding, or to foster consensus and commitment with the decision etc. In these cases, practice frequently demonstrates that building a qualitative model is sufficient. I agree with Checkland and Scholes when they state:

> ... what is probably more important (but usually escapes the files) is the *change in perceptions* which take place in the heads of the users of SSM as the methodology is used. The cycle from perceptions to relevant systems, to models, to new perceptions is an organized way of thinking one's way to clearer, or new, perceptions. In terms of ultimately taking purposeful action to improve a problematical situation, it is the original perceptions and the new perceptions which are crucial, not the models. And it is the difference between the two sets of perceptions which stimulates the debate about change. The importance of the methodological skeleton is that it makes the thinking process coherent and capable of being *shared*. (Checkland and Scholes, 1990, 67.)

This view is also perfectly compatible with the goals of group model-building. The process of assembling a model is a way of eliciting mental constructs, ideas about how things work in order to clarify and structure debate about a situation which is seen as problematic. In other words, from the point of view of problem solving, it is unwise to limit the application of system dynamics to quantitive simulation only. It severely underestimates the strength of building conceptual models to aid a client in solving a problem.

As stated, part of the discussion on qualitative versus quantitative system dy-namics derives from what is taken as the baseline of comparison. If the baseline is that systems must be understood fully and that this can only be accomplished through rigorous modelling and simulation, then qualitative modelling makes little sense. If, however, one takes as a base of comparison the way decisions are nor-mally made (i.e. without any formal aids), things look different. In this situation anything that is added to this baseline might improve the quality of the decision, not only the quantified model and the simulations. Remember, for instance, that many studies have demonstrated that people in general ignore feedback processes, which must be considered a high risk habit. And although *awareness* of feedback processes (which might come through qualitative modelling) does not imply that one understands its dynamic consequences, it is probably still better to be aware of them than to ignore them entirely. In the examples in Chapter 1, I have demonstrated that awareness of feedback processes can significantly alter people's perception of the problem and the resulting decisions. This position seems to be acknowledged implicitly by other system dynamicists. For instance, Richardson and Pugh (1981) emphasize that any of the model-building phases aids to understand the system, which in turn might give rise to policy implementation. Also Peter Senge's *The Fifth Discipline*, primarily shows qualitative models, although this is not to say that these are not grounded in a thorough knowledge of quantitative model-building and analysis.

Wolstenholme is one of the few system dynamicists who has repeatedly emphasized the usefulness of qualitative as opposed to quantitative system dynamics. As he points out:

> Indeed many traditional system dynamics practitioners would find it incongruous to separate the methodology into the distinctive phases suggested here and argue that influence diagrams are drawn with the relationships and dimensions of quantified analysis in mind. However, whilst this statement is true, it is important to realise that the argument only tends to reinforce the perception of system dynamics as just a technique for simulation analysis. In general system enquiry terms it is much more, and the simulation phase of system dynamics can alternatively be viewed as just in-depth expansion of the analysis phase of the methodology—that is the technique *within* the overall methodology. (Wolstenholme, 1982, 554.)

In other words, Wolstenholme considers system dynamics as more than just a simulation tool: it is also a more general method for system description and analysis. (Note the similarity in argument between Wolstenholme and Forrester when they emphasize that system dynamics is not just a simulation tool.) Although Wolstenholme (1982) is quite aware of the fact that the dynamics of a system can only be derived through simulation of the model he also points out: 'It is important to note that the qualitative analysis facilitated by this description phase of applying system dynamics is often sufficient in itself to generate problem understanding and ideas for change' (Wolstenholme (1982, 549). In other words, building a conceptual model can aid in improved understanding of the system, facilitate communication and reaching consensus between different decision makers. I agree with Wolstenholme that qualitative system dynamics has a lot to offer when one has to deal with messy problems.

For those readers who have never actually built a full-blown system dynamics model, the above might easily lead to the wrong impression that quantitative analysis does not have anything to offer and conclusions can easily be drawn on the basis of a conceptual model. System dynamicists correctly argue that this practice may easily give rise to faulty conclusions and wrong decisions. As stated, trying to derive the dynamic behaviour of the system from a conceptual model (be it a stocks and flow diagram or a causal diagram) is at best dangerous and at worst misleading. If one is serious about studying the dynamics of the system there is no other reliable way than to build a quantified mathematical model and to test it thoroughly.

As a result, the question whether to apply qualitative or quantitative system dynamics depends on a number of criteria. The first is the level of system understanding. System understanding is increased with every stage in the model-building process. In that sense quantification can add significant understanding of the system's behaviour not provided by the qualitative model. The second criterion is that quantification also requires relatively more time and effort when compared with the qualitative stage, and hence: '. . . qualitative analysis can often provide a significant level of understanding for a minimum investment of time and effort and is clearly appropriate when these resources are limited' (Wolstenholme, 1990, 6). In other words, a trade-off will have to be made between system understanding and the time and cost involved in building a quantified system dynamics model. The less time and money available the less likely that quantification can be accomplished.

A third criterion relates to the fact that quantification cannot always be accomplished. There are problems which defy formalization and quantification, at least within a reasonable time limit. Some problems are even hard to conceptualize, let alone to express them in mathematical formulae or to build a quantified model. On the other hand I do have to point out that this argument is sometimes quickly used as a legitimation *not* to quantify. Although it may be difficult to quantify, the simple attempt to do so may add considerably to one's understanding of the system. Quantification does not necessarily make our qualitative expressions more reliable or valid, but they do provide a clearer base for communication (Forrester, 1992). In other words, one should not prematurely decide that in a specific case quantification will not be attainable, just to escape the burden of quantification.

Fortunately, in a number of cases the decision to build a qualitative or a quantitative model does not have to be made at the start of the project. As the reader may have gathered from the stages in the model-building process one might start with a qualitative model and postpone the decision on whether to build a quantitative model until after the qualitative model has been finished. Obviously when the qualitative model does not provide enough confidence as to which policy is best one can take the decision to quantify the model.

Who to Involve in the Model-building Sessions?

An important question is who to involve in the group model-building sessions. What criteria should be employed to decide on group size and on who to involve in the process. There are a couple of guidelines which might be of help.

If the project aims at bringing about particular decisions one important point to keep in mind when selecting participants, is to have those present who have the power to act, i.e. those who can implement a decision. Excluding these persons from the process may easily render the whole project useless. Another important criterion relates to the acceptance of the results of the group model-building process. Excluding certain persons from the process (in order to keep the group sufficiently small) may create the risk of lack of commitment with the final decision. As a result I generally apply the rule: better one person too many than one too few, since people who feel excluded from the process may easily resist the resulting conclusions. In this respect I would like to remind the reader of the formula on the effectiveness of a decision presented in the first chapter.

But the latter rule may easily increase the group's size, which is not without consequences. Research in the realm of small groups confirms our everyday notion that the larger the group the fewer people participate in the discussion. In larger groups discussions tend to be dominated by a few group members (Bales et al., 1951; Stephan, 1952). As a result, regardless of the task which the group has to perform, group members in larger groups show less satisfaction with the amount of time for discussion, the opportunity to participate, and the resulting decision (Thomas and Fink, 1963). When it comes to satisfaction, a group of five seems to be optimal (Slater 1958; Hackman and Vidmar, 1970). However, research on the relationship between group size and group *performance* has produced inconsistent results. Research has shown that a larger group does not always outperform a smaller group, although there are counterexamples. In some cases larger groups produce better results, while in other situations they perform worse than smaller groups. (Evidence of the fact that larger groups do not outperform smaller ones can be found in Bray, Kerr and Atkin (1978), Lorge and Solomon (1959), Taylor and Faust (1952), and Thomas and Fink (1963). Counterexamples can be found in Littlepage and Silbiger (1992).) The outcomes suggest that other factors than group size (e.g. type of task) determine performance of the group. A number of these will be discussed in the next chapter on group facilitation.

To complicate matters, experienced model-builders advise that the selection of group members should incorporate a wide variety of viewpoints in order to ensure that the model constructed will not become overly idiosyncratic (Forrester, 1980; Morecroft and Sterman, 1994; Phillips, 1984). However, increasing diversity produces two opposing forces in the group. On the one hand, it may increase performance (in terms of resulting model quality) because more viewpoints will be present. On the other hand, the larger the diversity the higher the difficulty of building interpersonal relationships, which may decrease group performance (Collins and Guetzkow, 1964). As a result, empirical studies on the effect of group composition on performance have also produced mixed results. Some studies indicate that heterogeneous groups perform better, while others show the opposite. Hoffman (1959) for instance found that groups composed of heterogeneous personalities performed better than homogeneous groups both on intellective and decision making tasks. For similar results in the domain of brainstorming see Stroebe and Diehl (1994). Other studies have revealed the opposite, i.e. homogeneous groups perform better (Schutz, 1955). Status differences can also play a role in group performance. In particular status incongruity (i.e. high status on one dimension, e.g. education and low status on another, e.g. official rank) increases interpersonal conflict and decreases group performance (Exline and Ziller, 1959). It is clear that when selecting participants the model-builder is faced with a couple of dilemmas:

1. Increasing the group size will be beneficial to create a larger organizational platform for change and commitment with a decision, but it simultaneously decreases participation and satisfaction of group members.
2. Increasing a group's diversity will be advantageous with regard to the model's quality, but it might at the same time create more tension within the group, which in turn reduces group performance.

Hence, a smaller group might be easier to work with, but it might go at the cost of model quality and acceptance of the results of the group model-building process. As stated before, I generally follow the rule that it is better to have one participant too many than one too few. When this leads to larger groups (say, larger than about 10 to 12) the potential negative side-effects of such a large group (or a heterogeneous group) must be dealt with in some way. As we will see in the next chapter, one way to accomplish this is to introduce more structure in the group interaction process. Solutions to this problem can also be found in the way the group model-building project is designed, for instance by employing a preliminary model. This will be the topic of the next section.

Employing a Preliminary Model

In the introduction to this chapter I have pointed out that one critical choice is whether or not to work with preliminary models. Let us first focus on the situation in which a preliminary model is employed. In this situation the model-builder (or the project team for that matter) develops a system dynamics model, which is used as a starting point for the process. Two questions need to be addressed: (a) what are the potential (dis)advantages of using preliminary models, and (b) in what ways can they be constructed?

With regard to the first question, using preliminary models has both advantages and disadvantages. Starting with a preliminary model may speed up the model-building process in the group considerably, and may thus significantly cut into the participants' time investment. This approach will thus be especially useful when participants' time is severely limited. Another advantage might be that it is easier to start the group discussion when a preliminary model is available. This is particularly useful for the non-experienced modeller. On the downside however, the use of a preliminary model might infringe on the degree of ownership over the model as experienced by the group. Since the model is not created by the group the model might not be recognized by the group and the feeling of ownership could be quite low. Low ownership in turn leads to low commitment (Akkermans, 1995). In order to prevent low ownership in the case of a preliminary model, it is essential not to be defensive about it, but to consider it as a sort of 'straw man' or 'kick-off' model, where the group is strongly invited to adapt the model as they see fit. Apart from not being defensive, another way to ensure that ownership can be created is to build a model which provides ample opportunity for adaptations (Richardson and Andersen, 1995; Vennix et al. 1990). Stated differently, the more effort is put into the preliminary model the more difficult it might become for the group to discover flaws in it, and the higher the likelihood that the model-builder will become defensive about the model. Both factors will jeopardize model ownership felt by the group. In addition, it might be that all your preparatory efforts will be in vain since the client group may decide that other issues need to be modelled than the ones you have selected (Lane, 1993).

With regard to the second question, how to build preliminary models, I have identified two ways of constructing preliminary models. Preliminary models can either be based on documents or on interviews (or both). If they are based on documents, the project group will have to apply document analysis (or more generally content analysis) to construct a preliminary model. As stated, this preliminary model can be used as input for the first group session. Alternatively, the first session might also be preceded by questionnaires and so-called workbooks in order to gather comments and suggestions for adaptation from individual participants. The model can then first be adapted before it will be presented to the group in the group session. An elaborate example of this sequence of activities (i.e. preliminary model, questionnaires, workbooks, group session) will be presented in Chapter 6.

On the other hand, if the preliminary model is primarily based on the participants' mental models then interviews will be applied. From these a preliminary model will be produced and presented in the first group session. Preliminary models have been used in a couple of standard model-building procedures in system dynamics. The first is the 'Reference group' approach (Randers, 1977). Characteristic for the 'Reference group' approach is that (a) the product is a process of learning rather than a statement of fact, hence the model becomes a tool to improve discussion rather than to make predictions; and (b) the user becomes a tangible group (eight to ten persons) encountered in frequent discussions (every two to four weeks), hence a continuous interaction between users and model-builders.

The 'reference group' approach consists of a number of stages (see also Stenberg, 1980):

1. initiation of the study;
2. establishment of reference groups;
3. initial meetings with reference group to define problem;
4. construction of the initial (simple) model based on discussions with the reference group;
5. model improvement through scenario discussions (based on a model run) with the reference group;
6. reporting;
7. strategy discussions with interest groups to further enhance the diffusion of the results of the model study.

In this approach, the preliminary initial model and model improvements are made by a small project team. The reference group is primarily used as a critic while at the same time the computer model is employed as a structured discussion and scenario tool. A scenario discussion typically runs as follows. A model run is described and explained by the analysts. The reference group is asked whether they think something like this could happen in reality. If the answer is no (which is the case most of the times), the next question is why not. This question gives rise to various answers which usually fall in one of three categories. First, the group refers to relations already in the model. The discussion then focuses on the question why the model behaves the (unexpected) way it does. If relations are suggested which are not in the model, these are then built into the model and two situations can arise. The model behaves the way it is expected by the group. This means that the computer model is improved. Or the model does not behave in an expected manner. In this case the focus of discussion is again, why not.

From this description it becomes clear that the model is a means to support the thinking process and discussion within the reference group. The model and its behaviour is continuously checked against the way human beings think the problem would behave.

Another example of the use of a preliminary model is the Strategic Forum (Richmond, 1987). The Strategic Forum consists of eight steps. The first two steps are conducted before the actual forum meeting. The first step involves a number of interviews (prepared by a small questionnaire). These interviews aim at:

- identifying people's current mental models of their business;
- a statement of the vision, strategic objectives and specific strategies; and
- obtaining a 'signoff' on a preliminary operating map of the business.

This preliminary map and accompanying computer model is constructed on the basis of the interviews by the modeller and is used in the forum to conduct the simulations. In the second step, a number of small group exercises to be used during the forum are designed by the project team. The exercises, consisting of a couple of typewritten pages, are discovery oriented and basically are similar to the scenario discussions in the approach described by Randers (1977). The most important difference being that before any simulation run people have to 'put a stake in the ground', e.g. they have to make a prediction of model behaviour before a simulation run is actually carried out.

The next steps in the procedure make up the Strategic Forum. After an intro and a big picture discussion, the heart of the session consists of exercises aimed at internal consistency checks (is the group's mental model consistent with the computer model?) and policy design (what are potential consequences of strategic policies and in how far are they capable of realizing the strategic objectives?). The Strategic Forum concludes with a wrap-up discussion and some follow-up activities.

In summary, when a preliminary model is constructed the project team will have to gather information from one or more different sources: (a) conduct interviews with individuals, (b) employ documents and content analysis, or (c) design questionnaires or workbooks which have to completed by individuals. Each of these techniques will be discussed in the following sections in the light of their applicability in group model-building projects.

Preparatory Interviews

Interviews are widely used in a variety of settings and by a variety of people, e.g. doctors, lawyers, survey researchers, management scientists, and consultants. Many system dynamicists also routinely employ interviews to prepare group model-building sessions (see Richmond, 1987; Morecroft and Sterman, 1994; Akkermans, 1995).

One can conceive of at least three different reasons why interviews might be useful. The first is to gather information to prepare for the group model-building sessions by building a preliminary model. Second, it will provide the modeller with a chance to become familiar with the topic as well as the players, without the simultaneous burden of the group process. The third, if conducted in an appropriate manner will build rapport with the participants, which might prove useful during subsequent sessions, particularly if the subject is politically sensitive or threatening to participants. The reader may recall the example of the Dutch commercial fleet, which was introduced in the opening chapter of the book. In that project there was no time to conduct preparatory interviews with participants. As a result a situation arose in the first session which came as a surprise to the facilitator. Preparatory interviews would probably have revealed that there were sharp differences of opinion on the necessity to support the Dutch commercial fleet. This might have helped to prepare for such a situation, and the facilitator might not have been caught by surprise. But the example also reveals that even in politically sensitive situations, group model-building sessions without preparatory interviews can be successful. This situation however places a heavy burden on the group facilitator, an issue to be discussed in more detail in the next chapter.

In addition to reflecting on the necessity for interviews, it is also useful to be aware of different types of interviews. Patton (1980) distinguishes four different types of interviews. They differ in the degree of structure, which is introduced by the interviewer. The least structured is the informal conversational interview, where questions are not predetermined in advance but arise more or less naturally during the course of the interview. The interview guide approach employs a list of predetermined topics, but the interviewer is free in determining the sequence of topics and the wording of questions. In the standardized open-ended interview the wording and sequence of the questions is determined in advance, but the questions are phrased in an open-ended format. Finally, the closed, fixed field response interview not only employs standardized questions, but also fixed response categories from which the interviewee has to choose.

Interviews for the purpose of model-building will generally be of the first or second type: an informal conversation or an interview guide approach. The greatest disadvantage of the informal conversational interview is that it might elicit quite different information from different respondents, particularly if more than one interviewer is involved. It seems that this approach is particularly suited when the model builder wants to get acquainted with the players or when he wants to build rapport. If the focus is to build a preliminary model it seems that the guided interview is more appropriate. A list of discussion topics will help to prevent different people providing widely different information, which may be difficult to relate. A standardized open-ended interview is only required if the wording of the questions has to be *exactly* the same for all respondents. This is generally not useful as a preparation for group model-building, since it would unnecessarily restrict the free flow of discussion.

Determining Objectives of the Interview

Before starting interviews it is useful to think about their purpose and what kind of questions to ask. Kahn and Cannell (1957) suggest the following sequence. First state the general purpose of the interviews, next specify the objectives and only then start designing questions. In the context of model-building the purpose of interviews frequently is to elicit relevant information to construct a preliminary model. The purpose of the interviews will have to be aligned with the overall goals of the model-building project. If the overall goal of the model-building project is to resolve a strategic problem then interviews are only one single stage in the whole process, aimed at generating relevant information for the model construction process. Specific objectives for the interviews will define what kind of information will have to be obtained. Depending on the specific project these can range from general knowledge about the problem to be modelled to specific variables to complete 'cause maps' representing the respondent's view on the problem. I have discussed the construction of cause maps from documents in the second chapter as a means to develop one's model-building skills. If cause maps are produced during interviews, these can be used to build a preliminary, qualitative system dynamics model. (A comparable procedure is followed in cognitive mapping (Eden, Jones and Sims, 1983; Eden and Radford, 1990). The primary difference with system dynamics is that cognitive mapping is based on Kelley's personal construct theory, which focuses on the meaning people attach to concepts. In contrast, cause maps for system dynamics primarily focus on variables and causal relationships as a basis for either a qualitative or a quantitative model.)

Clearly defined objectives of the interview also have the obvious advantage that they can be used as an introduction to the interview. Kahn and Cannell (1957) point out that in order to motivate respondents it is important that the interviewer makes clear at the outset what the exact purpose of the interview is and how the results will be used. Although one might think the interviewee is informed about the project, it almost never hurts to repeat the objectives at the beginning of the interview. Another reason why thinking about objectives is important is also related to the respondent's motivation. The better the interviewee understands the relationship between the questions and the purpose of the interview the more motivated he/she will be to continue the interview. Last but not least, clear objectives will be helpful in designing the topics and questions for the interview.

Interview Questions

In the interview guide approach, wording of questions and sequencing are left to the interviewer's judgement. Since the actual wording of the questions is not written out, the interviewer will have to formulate the questions during the interview. This makes the interviewer's job difficult because the wording of the questions strongly affects the nature and quality of the responses (Patton, 1980). Patton makes a distinction between several types of questions, e.g. questions about feelings, opinions/values, behaviour, and knowledge. For model-building questions about opinions/values and knowledge are most relevant. Opinion questions are concerned with understanding the cognitive and interpretive processes. Knowledge questions are concerned with factual knowledge.

Kahn and Cannell (1957) and Patton (1980) argue that questions should be open-ended, neutral, singular and clear. Formulating open-ended questions is more difficult than might look at first sight. Consider the following question: 'what in your opinion constitutes the most important aspects with regard to problem x?'. This looks like an open-ended question, but in fact it presupposes that the respondent considers any aspect important, not to mention the fact that the individual might consider the whole problem irrelevant. Hence, the latter question should be preceded by at least one other question. For instance: 'what aspects can be distinguished about this problem', provided that there is agreement on the nature of the problem.

Apart from being open-ended, questions should be neutral. In other words, the modeller should not frame any leading questions or make any presuppositions with regard to the respondent's answer. Asking neutral questions will be easier if the interviewer's opinions on the subject matter are less strong. Neutrality also helps to prevent premature evaluation of the answers by the interviewee, and is particularly helpful to build rapport. Questions should also be singular, i.e. only one question at a time. Multiple questions will create tension in the respondent and decrease his or her motivation to continue the interview. In addition, answers to multiple questions are difficult to interpret. Finally, questions should be as clear as possible. An approach which helps in this respect is to formulate the question in different ways. For instance, a question for the causes of the problem could also be phrased as why this problem still persists, since this will elicit a 'because' type of response, indicating potential causes.

Patton strongly argues against 'why' questions in qualitative interviewing. Answers to this type of questions are difficult to analyse. If, for instance, an interviewer asks a respondent why he joined a certain government programme, the interviewee might provide a host of reasons and different respondents obviously respond to different questions. This might indeed be troublesome with regard to context in which Patton predominantly operates (i.e. qualitative interviewing in programme evaluation). However, in the context of model-building 'why' questions are one of the most important type of questions, because they will elicit causal argumentations from the respondents. If, for instance, a manager argues that having offices in the primary business centres of the world will generate more revenues, then a 'why' question will elicit hidden causal argumentations underlying this statement. If the interviewer asks the manager why he thinks this is the case, the normal response would be something like: '. . . because having an office there will provide easier access to top decision makers'. The original causal relationship is then elaborated and contains three rather than two concepts in a causal chain: offices in large business centres lead to easier access to top decision makers, which in turn will generate projects and thus revenues. Hence, for the purpose of building causal models 'why' questions are extremely important and useful. In cases when an interviewee is not able to answer the 'why' question, it will reveal unwarranted assumptions in his or her mental model, which might also be useful, provided that the interviewer takes care that the interviewee does not interpret this as loss of face. One way to accomplish this is by pointing out that several of the questions you ask might prove difficult and that it is no shame if the respondent does not have all the answers.

Apart from the particular wording of questions the interviewer will also have to think about a proper sequence. Two types of sequence must be distinguished. The overall sequence of the interview and the particular sequence of questions. In general, it seems wise to start interviews with noncontroversial topics in order to get acquainted and to build rapport. Once this is accomplished more complicated opinion and knowledge questions can be introduced. Sequencing of more specific questions for model-building will largely depend on the actual stage in the model-building process. Suppose for instance that the interviewer attempts to actually build a cause map during the interview. After having discussed the problem with the interviewee, one way to start would be to elicit a list of potentially relevant variables which, in the respondent's view, may be related to the problem. After identifying the 'problem variable' (for instance the increasing number of sick people, or declining sales) one might ask the respondent to identify, from the list of variables generated previously, those variables which may be seen as the causes of a problem situation and try to interrelate these. In a subsequent step one would identify consequences of the problem. In other words, in this step the 'problem variable' is taken as a starting point and the question becomes what kind of effects might be expected when this variable increases or decreases. Finally, one would look for potential feedback loops in the map by linking consequences to causes. Basically, the approach is as shown in Figure 4.2. in four distinct steps.

The first step involves the identification of a problem variable. In the second step cause variables are selected from the list of generated variables. In the third step effect or consequence variables of the problem variable are included. Finally, feedback loops are established. The final step can prove difficult. There are two ways to proceed. The first is to check all variables with incoming arrows but no outgoing arrows. These are most likely to be found on the 'consequence' side and might open up the opportunity to find connections with other variables in the diagram. Alternatively, one might concentrate on variables with no incoming arrows but solely outgoing arrows. These are most likely to be found on the 'causes' side of the diagram.

Another good way to proceed is to have people think about a constant but persistent increase (or decrease) in values of variables, and ask what would be the effect. This may lead to the identification of potentially balancing loops. For instance, if one assumes that sickleave is gradually increasing, one consequence may be an increasing workload, which in turn may increase sickleave (a reinforcing

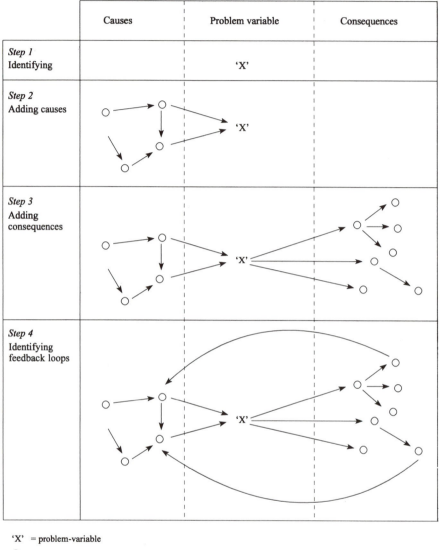

'X' = problem-variable

◯ = other variables

Figure 4.2 Building a Causal Loop Diagram in an Interview

loop), but this assumption might also lead to hiring more people to get the work done and thus to lower work pressure (a balancing loop).

The approach to building a causal loop diagram, during an interview, was used in the case of the Dutch commercial fleet project in the first group session. In Chapter 6 the methodological aspects of this project will be discussed and I will show in more detail how the approach works.

Whatever approach is employed, it is important to explain clearly to the respondent at the outset what you are going to do and how you will try to accomplish this. Clearly state the steps that will be taken and announce transitions from one step to the next.

The Interviewer Role

Thus far I have discussed types of interview, objectives for the interview and interview questions. All of these are necessary ingredients of knowledge for a group model-builder. But, probably the most important factor in interviewing is the role of the interviewer itself and the way he or she looks at the interview. From the point of view of eliciting information it might look to some practitioners that interviewing is a one way process in which the interviewer is supposed to extract information from the interviewee. As Kahn and Cannell point out:

> There are, of course, many ways of looking at the interview. The most common approach implies that it is a sort of battle of wits between the respondent and the interviewer. The respondent has somewhere inside him information which the interviewer wants, and the interviewing techniques are designed to force, trick, or cajole the respondent into releasing the information. The literature on research into the interview process and the firsthand experience of interviewers indicate that this conception is misleading and inaccurate. Rather, the interview is an interaction between the interviewer and respondent in which both participants share. (Kahn and Cannell, 1957, vi.)

In other words interviewing is a two way process, it is an interaction in which both interviewer and interviewee contribute to the results. To a large extent the quality of the interaction will determine the quality of the information elicited from the respondent. And in turn it is the interviewer (and not the interviewee) who is responsible for creating a high quality interaction process and an open communication climate (Patton, 1980). This places a large burden on the interviewer and raises the question how an interviewer can increase the quality of the interview.

There are several things an interviewer can do to ensure high quality communication and keep a respondent motivated. The first is, as we have seen, to clearly explain the purpose of the interview, the way the information will be used and the steps being followed. In addition, the interviewer should make sure that the respondent understands what will be expected of him or her as well as the relevance of each of the questions. Interviewing is a dynamic interaction process and the interviewer has to try to positively effect this process. As Patton points out: 'The interviewer must maintain awareness of how the interview is flowing, how the interviewee is reacting to the questions, and what kinds of feedback are appropriate and helpful to maintain the flow of communication' (Patton, 1980, 330).

Two important aspects in effective communication are the right attitude and the right skills. As with the group facilitator role (which will be treated in more detail in Chapter 5) the attitude is most important because the skills will only become effective if these are embedded in the right attitude. Since I will discuss group facilitator attitudes and skills in more detail in the next chapter, and since these do show considerable overlap with those of an effective interviewer, we will be brief about it here.

One important attitude is to be neutral with regard to the content. Most people have the tendency to immediately evaluate what other people say. According to Rogers this constitutes the major problem in communication (Rogers and Roethlisberger, 1988). Hence, it is important that the interviewer does not place any value on what a respondent says, positive or negative. As stated before, neutrality will help to build rapport and will elicit information in an unobtrusive way. Another important attitude is to be genuinely interested in other people's ideas and opinions. In other words, it is important that you are concerned about how other people feel and think about things. If you are not really interested, this will probably show in your behaviour. In turn the interviewee will not be as motivated as he or she might have been.

The most important skill is listening. This is also one of the most difficult skills to learn. The interviewer has to make sure that he or she understands what is said by the respondent. The best way to ensure this is by what is called reflective listening, i.e. reflecting back what you think you have heard the other person say. Reflecting back will help to prevent miscommunication. (Reflective listening will be discussed in more detail in the chapter on group facilitation.)

Another important skill is to provide appropriate feedback or reinforcement to the respondent. Providing positive reinforcement can be accomplished by an attentive posture, by looking at the interviewee (rather than taking notes) and by cues like gentle head nodding (showing that you are interested and understand what is said). Here in particular, if this skill is used as a trick and if it is not embedded in the corresponding attitude of genuine interest, the other person may infer that you are just being polite. The latter is not enough to motivate the other to really talk about the problem which has to be addressed. Apart from providing positive feedback the interviewer can also use negative feedback in order to show that the respondent does not reveal relevant information. Negative feedback is shown by withholding the above cues.

Recording and Reporting

Making extensive notes during an interview will generally disturb the flow of communication. Unless the interview is conducted by two people, it is wise to employ a tape recorder and have the contents of the interview transcribed. The resulting documents can be content analysed as we have seen in a previous section. Even if the interviewer actually constructs a map during the interview and thus makes the interview more or less self recording, it is still wise to employ a tape recorder. For instance, the cause map might contain relationships of which the exact argumentations might be forgotten by the modeller. A tape recorder will prove useful in these cases. If you do employ a tape recorder always ask the respondent if he or she agrees and provide the opportunity to have the interviewee stop the tape whenever he or she feels like it. Make sure that the tape recorder is in good order and check at the beginning of the interview if it records well (by replaying a couple of minutes). After the interview, always check if the tape has functioned properly and if not make extensive notes of what you recall as soon as possible (see also Patton, 1980).

After all interviews have been conducted, the project team will have to summarize the findings in order to be able to report back in the group session. The kind of report which is presented depends on the type of information which has been collected during the interviews and may differ from one situation to the next. If, for instance, the interviewer has been talking to find out what kind of problems should be addressed, the report will be different than in the case of the interviewer who has actually constructed cause maps with the managers during the interviews. In the former case, the various problem definitions will be presented. In the latter case, the project team may design a preliminary model based on the cause maps constructed during the interviews. Generally, this is not just a matter of putting the maps together. (For problems involved in putting cognitive maps together, the reader is referred to Eden, Jones and Sims (1983), Eden and Simpson (1989), and Eden and Radford (1990).) There will be similarities as well as dissimilarities in the individual maps. In addition, when starting to build a causal loop diagram from the individual maps the project team may find that information is missing or different maps may contain contradictory information. Finally, some people might have generated information which cannot be incorporated in the preliminary model. The project team has to keep track of these distinct possibilities and will have to report back to the group how they handled these situations and what questions are still left unanswered after his or her attempt to piece the maps together. These questions and the differences and similarities between the individual maps will provide the starting point for the discussion. In Chapter 6 we will present a detailed case description of how information which is gathered in a previous round can be reported back in a group model-building session.

Content Analysis of Documents to Construct a Preliminary Model

In the previous sections I have discussed the role of interviews in the construction of a preliminary model. As mentioned previously, the second way to construct preliminary models is on the basis of documents. When analysing documents the analysis can generally not be directly checked as is the case during an interview. Making valid inferences from the text is more problematic in this case. A technique which is specifically oriented toward analysis of documents is content analysis. Content analysis as a research method can be applied to any documentary evidence and can be employed with a variety of theoretical research questions. It has been used extensively and systematically since the beginning of this century. Applications can be found in quantitative newspaper analysis, propaganda analysis, as well as analysing verbal records in psychological research and open-ended interviews (Krippendorff, 1981). When applied in the context of conceptual model-building, content analysis frequently implies deriving cause maps or causal loop diagrams from written documents. This approach was employed in the exercises presented in Chapter 2.

Those who are experienced in conducting content analyses have emphasized that producing valid inferences should not be underestimated because '. . . language is complex and even the trained analyst with keen insight may find it difficult to make maximum use of his data unless he uses systematic methods.' (Holsti, 1969, 19). Any content analysis will involve considerable interpretation from the part of the analyst. The latter is for instance clearly demonstrated by such procedures as inter-coder reliability. Intercoder reliability refers to the degree of agreement between two or more persons coding the same text. Experience and research demonstrates that the same text can be interpreted in quite dissimilar ways by different persons, even after these persons have had extensive training in applying a systematic coding procedure (Vennix, 1990; Verburgh, 1994; Kenis, 1995). Without applying systematic procedures one might speculate that results become even more unreliable. In that sense content analysis is defined by Holsti as: '. . . any technique for making inferences by objectively and systematically identifying specified characteristics of messages.' (Holsti, 1969, 14). Two words in this definition are critical: objective and systematic. Objective implies that there are rules and procedures which serve as a basis for each step in the process. These rules need to be as explicit as possible, so that others can check on how a particular person came to certain conclusions or interpretations. Systematic in the definition of content analysis implies that rules are consistently applied in the coding process. The latter may be difficult, because generally coders are provided with a variety of rules some of which might contradict each other. For example, in research that I have conducted into the coding of cause maps from written texts, there was one step in the coding process in which coders had to extract variables from the text. One rule was that coders had to stay close to the original text, i.e. they had to employ the concepts used by the authors of the text. However, authors have the tendency to produce variety in their text. They employ different words which obviously refer to the same variable. That is why there was another rule which dictated that variables had to be 'translated' to variables which had been used previously in the text. This rule had to ensure that the cause map which was produced would not contain different concepts with the same meaning. Obviously the two rules may contradict each other in certain cases, and the problem is left to the coder who has to make a decision based on his interpretation from the text. If not carried out very carefully a coder may apply the first rule in a specific instance and the second in a similar case. The coding rules are then not applied in a systematic manner. Hence, the need to be explicit about the application of the rules. (There is almost no way to ensure that coding rules won't contradict nor that they will be applied consistently by coders. For those readers in doubt, employ the fourth exercise provided in Chapter 2 and produce a cause map. Next, find another person to produce a cause map from the same text, without him or her seeing your own map. Then compare both cause maps.)

Axelrod (1976) describes methodological rules to identify concepts and causal relationships from documents. Basically his method consists of close reading of every sentence in a policy document and trying to rephrase it in a statement which expresses a causal relationship between two concepts. The author uses a number of rules to determine, whether certain statements can be coded as relationships between concepts. When the list of coded statements is put together cause maps, strongly resembling causal loop diagrams, result. (Cause maps should be distinguished from cognitive maps. Cognitive maps can take on a variety of forms (Huff, 1990), from simple category systems to maps focusing on the meaning people attach to concepts as for instance employed by Eden (Eden, Jones and Sims, 1983). Cause maps are representations with variables where arrows indicate causal relationships between these variables.) Building a cause map or a causal diagram from a written document can be accomplished by completing the following steps. First, one should read the document entirely. Second, reread the document sentence by sentence and record relationships between variables on a separate sheet of paper in the form of a diagram. Finally, check the resulting causal loop diagram with the text of the document.

Generally, the type of map constructed in this manner will show a number of white spots, because documents have normally not been written for the purpose of building system dynamics models. In other words, the information retrieved from documents will generally have to be completed by the project team or one or more persons from the client organization. Remember, that it is just a preliminary model and it should put people in a position to criticize and adapt it. How this can be achieved will be demonstrated in Chapter 6 by means of an example of a model-building project in the Dutch health care system.

Questionnaires in the Context of Group Model-building

Interviews are known to most group model-builders as a means to elicit information and to prepare the group model-building sessions. It is less well known that mailed questionnaires can also be fruitfully applied in the context of group model-building, particularly when working with a preliminary model. Mailed questionnaires are particularly advantageous if participants are geographically dispersed, or if the group is large in which case interviews are too time consuming and expensive. The most important danger in employing mailed questionnaires is the low response rate. If it is decided to use mailed questionnaires one has to make sure that participants will fill them out, either because they are highly motivated or because they are, for instance, compelled by their superior.

When conducting interviews, it is extremely important to be specific about the overall purpose and the specific objectives of the interviews. This becomes even more important when employing mailed questionnaires. An important difference between interviews and questionnaires is that in the latter case there is no face to face communication between interviewer and interviewee. There is no chance for the interviewer to explain questions which might be unclear to the respondent. Hence, more preparation should go into questionnaire design and testing. The best way to find out whether the questionnaire works is to pretest it at least once with an audience similar to the participating group.

To keep the respondent motivated, questions should be formulated in such a way that the respondent can answer them briefly. Most people are reluctant to produce a lot of text. As a consequence, research has shown that in general answers in mailed questionnaires are more to the point than in interviews (Van Dijk, 1990).

Kahn and Cannell (1957) point out that the sequence of topics and questions should follow the logic of the respondent. In addition, they advise that opening questions should be simple and easy to answer for the respondent. More difficult questions should be saved for later. Also in transition from one topic to another introductory remarks should prepare the participant for this switch of topics.

An important point concerns the actual formulation of questions and the use of open-ended and closed questions. As was the case with interview questions the formulation of questions needs to be strictly neutral, singular and one-dimensional. The question of the appropriateness of open and closed questions must be related to the purpose of the questionnaire and a number of situational factors (Lazarsfeld, 1944). For model-building purposes both open-ended and closed questions can be relevant. If, for instance, the objective of the question-naire is to find out whether there is consensus in a group about the model, then closed questions might be very relevant. If, on the other hand, the purpose is to learn something from the respondent open questions will be more appropriate. The latter is also true when the model-builder expects the respondent not to have clearly formulated ideas or opinions or when the model-builder is not very well informed about the participants' opinions. This type of situation will generally predominate in model-building since the researcher is interested in eliciting causal argumentations from the mental model of the participant. As a result, open-ended questions will have to be used frequently in extracting information for model-building. There is a trade-off however, since open questions will be more demanding for the respondent and a high motivation level will be needed. In addition, analysing the answers to open-ended questions is more complicated and more time consuming.

Vennix et al. (1990) employed a mailed questionnaire to invite participants in a health care region to review a preliminary model of the health care system. This model was constructed by a small project group on the basis of a literature survey and content analysis of documents. It was divided into four sectors (e.g. general practitioner sector, hospital sector, etc). The questionnaire was accom-panied by a letter from the health care insurance organization's CEO. It intro-duced the project by a short explanation and the specific purpose of the questionnaire as well as the expected role of the participants. Participants were asked a number of questions within each of the sections of the model. The most important of these consisted of a combination of a closed and an open-ended question. The questions were based on the causal relationships contained in the preliminary conceptual model, which was constructed by the project group. As we have seen in Chapter 2, each causal relationship in a causal loop diagram can be formulated in a verbal way. This verbal statement can be used to ask particip-ants whether they agree or disagree with it. Combined with an open question why people (dis)agree will elicit causal argumentations. This can be demon-strated by means of the following example. In the preliminary model there was a causal relationship between the general practitioner's workload and the number of prescriptions. This relationship was put in the questionnaire in the form of a verbal statement.

Statement: 'the higher the workload of a general practitioner, the higher the number of prescriptions'.

- strongly agree
- agree
- agree nor disagree
- disagree
- strongly disagree

because ....

The statement is followed by a closed and an open question. The closed question asks to what degree the respondent (dis)agrees. The open question (because ....) aims to elicit causal argumentations as to why a person agrees or disagrees. A participant might, for instance, answer this question by indicating that he agrees, because as a result of a high workload a general practitioner will use a prescription as a means to end a consultation with a patient. The reader may recall that in Chapter 2 I have indicated that a 'because' type of answer will generally provide new variables which intermediate between the original two variables. In this case: a higher workload leads to prescriptions as a means to stop the consultation discussion, and as a result the number of prescriptions rises.

As this example demonstrates, the answers to the first part of the question indicate the degree of consensus within the group on the above statement. I have to point out however, that people might agree for different reasons. This can be seen from the arguments presented by the respondents in the 'because section' of the statement. Statements about which there is a lot of disagreement (either because some agree while others disagree or because different explanations are provided) will definitely have to be discussed in the group. Answers to the second part of the question can be content analysed and may give rise to interesting conclusions. Since in the above example there was a high level of disagreement among the 60 respondents the project team clustered arguments into two categories, i.e. arguments presented by proponents and adversaries of the above statement. Careful content analysis revealed that both groups employed a different kind of 'workload' concept in answering the question. One group obviously had 'temporary workload' in mind when answering the question, while the other employed a concept like 'structural workload'. In the second cycle of the process a workbook was employed in which the group was asked whether they agreed with this distinction or not (see also Chapter 6).

Open questions can also be used to simply elicit variables which will have to be included in the model. This can be accomplished by asking respondents which variables play a role in the problem to be modelled. In the health care case for instance, the project team asked respondents whether they were aware of any other factors (apart from the ones already introduced in the questionnaire) which would affect the number of prescriptions.

Finally, open questions can be employed to have the participants rank order the 'independent' variables in order of importance. In general if individuals are asked to generate variables this may produce a long list. In order to have some guidance on what to include in the model and what not, the modellers in the above case asked respondents to indicate the three most important factors affecting the number of prescriptions. This reduced the list considerably as we will see in Chapter 6, where this project is discussed in more detail.

Workbooks for Group Model-building

Sometimes the traditional questionnaire format is too rigid in the context of group model-building. A workbook can be considered an alternative for a questionnaire. Its format allows more flexibility in presenting materials and asking questions. Workbooks contain text as well as diagrams which are interspersed with questions for the participant. Participants are also invited to adapt diagrams contained in the workbook. The answers and comments in the workbooks are used in a subsequent session to start the discussion. Workbooks have been used in a variety of settings in particular in the context of so-called policy exercises (Underwood, 1984). They are particularly useful when employed in between sessions to summarize the discussions of the foregoing session and to prepare for the next. This then leads to an alternating sequence of sessions and workbooks as can be seen in Figure 4.3.

Let us assume that the project was started by a preliminary model designed by the modeller or the project group. This model may be discussed during a first group session. In particular when the group is large or opinions diverge widely, a host of information will be generated, which needs to be analysed by the model-builder or project group after the session. The results of this analysis are presented in a workbook, which contains a number of questions for the participants. Answers to these questions are again analysed by the project team as a preparation to the second session. These are reported back in the second session and the cycle starts again, until a satisfactory model is obtained. Workbooks are extremely useful if it is difficult to keep the model-building project on track, for instance because of a large number of participants or because of the complexity of the model.

In order to design a workbook, the best way is to conceive of it as a research report on a system dynamics study. The main difference lies in the fact that one does not solely report the model, but every now and then formulates one or more questions, which have to be answered by the participant(s). The construction and use of workbooks will also be described in detail in Chapter 6.

Group Model-building: Starting from Scratch

Thus far we have been concerned with group model-building approaches in which a preliminary model is constructed by the project team as a start of the group model-building sessions. There are also situations in which a preliminary model cannot be constructed or even preliminary interviews prove unfeasible. In the first chapter I introduced the example of the Dutch commercial fleet. The reader may remember that in this case the group model-building session was started after two short discussions with two persons from the client agency. In other words, no interviews,

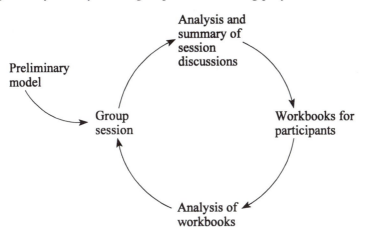

Figure 4.3   Alternating Sequence of Sessions and Workbooks

questionnaires or documents were employed and no preliminary model was constructed. This approach can be very effective from the point of view of time investment and cost. There are, however, some potential drawbacks which I would like to
share with the reader. The first is that this approach requires extensive experience
with group model-building, particularly when a quantified model is to built. The
model-builder needs to be very skilled in translating ideas from the discussion into a
model, a skill which requires extensive training. In that sense a safer way is to
prepare sessions with a preliminary model and to intersperse sessions with workbooks. Closely related to this is the question whether the group model-building
sessions are extended over some period of time or whether the whole session is
completed within one or two days as is for instance done by Richardson and
Andersen (1995) and Richmond (1987). Again, the latter case is most difficult to
handle. Sessions which are extended over time provide the opportunity to let things
boil down and provide ample opportunity to think things over within the project
team. The inexperienced model-builder is advised (a) to use a preliminary model,
(b) to conduct more than one session, and (c) to intersperse sessions with workbooks (or interviews for that matter).

The second point is that starting from scratch without having met the group
members may be dangerous, because the model-builder may be caught by surprise.
The case description with which I opened the first chapter provides a case in point.
Because there was no time for preparatory interviews, I was largely unaware of the
political sensitivity of the subject. Again the unexperienced group model-builder is
advised to meet people individually before the first session.

If a group model-builder feels sufficiently confident to start from scratch, the
question can be raised how the group model-building process could best be started
in the first session. There are several approaches. One approach that I frequently
use is a modified version of the Nominal Group Technique (Delbecq, Van de Ven
and Gustafson, 1975). First, the group silently writes down a number of variables
which people consider to be related to the problem. Next, individuals in turn are

allowed to read one variable from their list. These variables are put on a flip-chart. (In the next chapter I will demonstrate the use of this approach with the use of so-called hexagons. This allows more flexible transportation of variables from the brainstorming list into the model. The difference with a flip-chart however, is not essential.) In the next step these variables are used to construct a causal loop diagram, much like the sequence of steps that I described in the construction of cause maps during interviews (see Figure 4.2).

The reader may wonder why I do not start immediately with the construction of a causal loop diagram. The primary reason why I start with the generation of variables is to motivate the group. Generating variables is a relatively easy cognitive task for people to handle. Generally, a large list of variables can be generated within half an hour. This will provide the group with a sense of accomplishment and motivate group members to continue. In addition, NGT allows each individual early in the process to contribute to the process, which eases later contributions. On the other hand, starting immediately with the construction of a causal loop diagram might prove more cumbersome than was expected. If not succesful within, let us say, an hour, group members might start wondering if this is an appropriate approach and whether group model-building is not a waste of time and money; hence, the first more simple step of brainstorming variables. The idea is not to produce the ultimate list of variables with which the model can be constructed. You will find that during this brainstorming a number of variables will be produced which will never end up in the model. Alternatively, during the construction of the causal loop diagram variables will be required which were not generated in the first step. These will then have to be identified and included in the model. The basic idea is to speed up the first step of the model-building process, because this step generally proves to be most difficult. Chapter 6 will demonstrate this NGT approach by discussing the methodological details of the Dutch fleet case.

When to Use Which Approach?

In the previous sections I have discussed several approaches to design a group model-building project. The reader may be left with the question of which approach to use in group model-building. There are no unambiguous criteria with which to decide which approach is optimally suited to what situation. However, a number of guidelines can be provided. Let us first take a look at the decision to use a preliminary model or to start from scratch. As I have indicated in the previous section, starting from scratch:

1. is generally very time effective in terms of project completion time, because no preliminary model is required, no interviews have to be scheduled etc.;
2. may be ineffective in terms of time investment from participants;
3. presupposes considerable prior experience with group model-building and system dynamics; this is particularly the case if (a) a quantified model is required, and (b) the group model-building session needs to be completed within one or two days;
4. entails certain dangers, because one might not be aware of the specific circumstances surrounding the project.

It follows that, unless one is very experienced, it is wise to start with a preliminary model, spread the model-building over more than one session, start with a qualitative model, and do most of the quantification through backroom work.

The next question then is how to produce a preliminary model and how to present it to the group. I have made a distinction between the two ways of constructing a preliminary model. Interviews are particulary useful, because one gets acquainted with group members and their opinions on the problem. Large discrepancies of opinion within the group may be discovered early on and can be anticipated. In addition, the resulting model is designed on the basis of information from group members. Interviews can become extremely time consuming if the group becomes large or group members are geographically dispersed. Other approaches may be required in these situations.

One way to proceed is to construct a preliminary model on the basis of available documents and have this model criticized by the group. If the group is large and people are geographically scattered, questionnaires and workbooks become useful. The latter is also the case when participants have limited time available. The less time participants have available for active participation in the modelling effort, the more the process will have to be carefully structured and prepared.

With regard to the group sessions, one may conclude that if the group is small (less than five members) less structure is needed and the model-builder may rely on unrestricted interaction unless this leads to undesirable consequences. If the group is larger more structure needs to be introduced. Structure can relate to the tasks and to the communication process. An example of simplifying tasks was discussed under the NGT approach in the previous section. Rather than starting with the causal loop diagram one starts with the more simple task of generating variables. NGT also provides an illustration of structuring the communication process within the group. Another example of restricting communication within a group is Delphi, the use of which will be illustrated in Chapter 6.

To help the reader make effective choices, I have summarized the discussion so far in Table 4.1. The left hand column in the table indicates particular circumstances or problems which are important in designing a group model-building project. The right hand column presents suggestions on how to handle these circumstances.

It is useful to point out a few of the potential drawbacks in following some of the suggestions in the table. Using a preliminary model must be done with care in order to avoid low ownership by the group. Ownership of the model may also be endangered if applying questionnaires and workbooks. Be aware that questionnaires and workbooks may be unsatisfying for participants, so combine it with at least one or two face to face sessions (see also Chapter 6 for an example). If using multiple sessions make sure that time in between sessions is not too long (generally no more than one or two weeks). Finally, if the client wants robust policies which have been tested with the aid of the model, while resources are limited you might consider not to conduct the project, because the model cannot be quantified.

Group model-building will always involve one or more meetings with a client group. In the remainder of this chapter I will focus on a number of issues which

Table 4.1 Choices to be Made in the Design of Group Model-building Projects and Potential Consequences

Indicator/circumstance	Suggestions
Large group for model-building sessions	Introduce structure in: • Communication pattern (e.g. NGT; Delphi; workbooks) and/or • Tasks (e.g. split up generating, assembling and evaluating information)
Facilitator has low experience in group model-building	• Use multiple sessions • Use preliminary model • Conduct preparatory interviews
Subject is politically sensitive	• Use preparatory interviews • Avoid politicking and concentrate group on task (see Chapter 5)
Participants have little time available	• Use preliminary model • Use workbooks to prepare meetings
Group members are geographically dispersed or meetings are difficult to schedule	• Use preliminary model • Use questionnaire and/or workbooks
Sessions have to start from scratch	• Split up steps (e.g. brainstorming variables and assembling causal loop diagram) • Use NGT to start process
Quantitative model sessions	• More persons needed to guide process • Use model coach (see next section) • Conduct part of model-building in back-room if unexperienced with system dynamics
Resources are limited	• Skip interviews • Restrict to qualitative model or decide not to conduct the project

relate to the preparation of meetings, procedures in group model-building sessions, work in between sessions and the conclusion of the project.

PREPARING SESSIONS

A couple of topics need to be discussed as a preparation to the actual group model-building sessions: determining roles played by members of the project team, deciding on the agenda, selecting a location and paying attention to room layout and equipment.

Roles of Project Group Members

Recent publications in the system dynamics literature have emphasized the importance of group facilitation (Lane, 1992; Richardson and Andersen, 1995; Vennix et
al., 1993). An effective facilitator will contribute a great deal to the effectiveness of
the group. But in general, group model-building is quite complicated, particularly
when working with quantified models. As a result, more than one person generally
helps to turn the process into a succes. Richardson and Andersen (1995), for
instance, make a distinction between five different roles: the facilitator, the content
coach, the process coach, the recorder, and the gatekeeper. The facilitator is the
person who actually guides the group process and who elicits the participants'
points of view on the problem in order to construct the system dynamics model.
The facilitator role is not only the most conspicuous, but also the most crucial role.
In effect, the behaviour of the facilitator will either turn the project into a success or
into an utter failure. This is *a fortiori* the case when the subject is politically
sensitive and the management team shows ineffective communication patterns.
Since the facilitator role is so crucial the next chapter will be entirely devoted to
group facilitation in the context of group model-building. For now let us return to
the other four roles, discussed by Richardson and Andersen.

Another important role which can hardly be ignored or left out is the recorder.
The recorder can be considered the right hand of the facilitator. It is of the utmost
importance that both work together effectively. The facilitator and recorder must
work together as a team or else they will be in each other's way half of the time.
This also means that both need to understand the philosophy underlying system
dynamics and group model-building and have sufficient understanding of group
processes. In general, the qualitative side of model-building is relatively easy to
handle, particularly if the process is divided into a number of simple steps as I
have indicated in the previous chapter. Here the facilitator might easily handle
the discussion as well as record the variables and the causal diagrams on a white
board. As I have indicated in the first chapter, short-term memory of people is
limited. The facilitator's task is to create a so-called group memory on the flip
chart or white board. This group memory helps to keep the group on track (it can
easily be seen if something has been discussed before) and creates a common
focus point for the discussion. This will also be helpful to detach ideas from
people and to prevent disruptive mechanisms like face saving and personal conflict. If the group facilitator records input on the group memory the recorder
should make notes which can be used to (a) keep the discussion on track, (b)
construct the workbooks, and (c) make the final report. If the group becomes
larger the recorder may also participate more actively in the process by recording
input on the white board or flip-chart. The facilitator can then concentrate more
fully on the group process. In this case the recorder will have to adhere to the
same rules as the facilitator. The person who records ideas onto the group memory, be it the facilitator or the recorder, should be capable of listening very
carefully and translate people's ideas into brief key phrases or words. In other
words, first listen, then paraphrase, next write.

It is important to point out that both the facilitator and recorder need to be experienced system dynamicists, in order to draw relevant knowledge out of the group and to know what to record. If the facilitator (and recorder) are not fully aware of where they are heading the group will get lost in no time.

The third role discussed by Richardson and Andersen is the process coach. The process coach primarily focuses on group process and group dynamics. In general the process coach does not interact with the group, it is more of a silent observer role. The process coach may reflect his or her observations back to the facilitator during breaks and helps the facilitator to identify strategies to keep the group effective.

The fourth role is called the modeller or reflector role. This person needs to be particularly experienced in system dynamics modelling. In addition it may help if the reflector is also knowledgeable about the subject matter. This may help to prevent the group from developing a one-sided view of the problem.

Finally, the gatekeeper is generally a person from the client organization, who is responsible for the project. The gatekeeper is a sort of liaison person between the model-builders and relevant persons form the client organization. To increase the chances of success of a group model-building project the gatekeeper can prove to be critical, for instance because he or she can motivate people in the client organization to participate.

As Richardson and Andersen (1995) point out the five roles will always be present, but they do not necessarily have to be performed by five different people. If there are less than five persons who guide the process, then generally one person combines more than one role. The project team may for instance lack a process coach and the facilitator will then have to combine two roles. Or in other cases a reflector might be lacking leaving this role to be distributed among the other persons guiding the process. In some cases the gatekeeper will also be the recorder etc.

The question may be raised, under what circumstances these five roles have to be performed by five different individuals. As a minimum, two people should guide the process: facilitator and recorder (which in this case might also be the gatekeeper). But when to use five people? An important circumstance is the size of the client group. If this group is very small it will come as a surprise if there are more coaches than participants from the client organization. As a general rule, more people will be needed to perform these roles if (a) the client group becomes larger (more than 12), (b) a quantitative model will be constructed, and (c) if group dynamics become complicated because the client group shows ineffective communication patterns.

The more coaches present, the more tasks can be divided and the more each person can concentrate on his specific task. On the downside however, this simultaneously creates a coordination problem. If the persons guiding the group model-building process do not work as a high performing team this will counteract or even cancel out the advantages of the division of labour. As a general rule, it seems best to have one captain on board during the session. It is almost impossible to facilitate the process with more than one person unless both persons have extensively worked together so that one will not derail the other's efforts. If two persons do not share this experience it is best to have the facilitator guide the process. The facilitator in turn will have to provide the chances for the other roles to become active during the session or during breaks. At some point during the process the facilitator may, for instance, invite the reflector to share his or her comments with the group, or he/she may ask the recorder to summarize the flow of discussion etc. This, by the way, simultaneously creates a little break for the facilitator, which may become necessary every once in a while, because the facilitator role may prove quite exhausting.

After having described the various roles of project team members let us next take a look at the preparation of the session(s) and the way these are guided.

The Agenda: Purpose and Outcome of the Session

The actual agenda of the meeting largely depends on the way the project was designed. If preparatory interviews were conducted it becomes necessary to report these back. If a preliminary model was constructed this could serve as a starting point for the discussion. If the session starts from scratch the first step is to discuss the problem to be modelled. If it is the first session an introduction to system dynamics might be needed for the group etc.

It is important to think about the purpose of the meeting and what its outcome should be in advance of the session. The purpose and agenda should be extensively discussed with the project team, so that everyone is well aware of what is going to be done. Some group model-builders follow a script of the meeting in detail (Richardson and Andersen, 1995). Although this is very useful it entails the danger that the facilitator might adhere too strictly to it and thus will not be flexible enough to meet the group's needs. In general, I employ a rough three or four step plan, which is discussed within the project team in terms of 'what if' analyses. We raise questions like: 'Suppose the group will react this way, how would we then best proceed'. By discussing a number of potential contingencies our minds are made more flexible and we may productively improvise during the meeting.

In one of the next sections I will provide a number of topics which need to be addressed in most sessions. In addition, the next chapter will discuss a couple of projects and sessions within projects in more detail. These will be helpful to think about an agenda for a group model-building session.

Location, Room Layout and Equipment

A frequently neglected aspect of facilitating group model-building (and meetings in general) is the selection of the meeting room and its layout. Practice proves that being in the 'wrong' room can be quite cumbersome and infringe on the project's success (see for instance Eden, 1985). The best place to conduct group model-building sessions is outside of the client's office. This will prevent people from leaving the meeting to contact a colleague or being called away for a phone call. However, finding a location outside of the client's office will not always be feasible.

In that case do not hesitate to use one of the rooms in the client's office, but try to arrange that disturbances will be kept to a minimum. In any case check the location if you are not familiar with it, in order to prevent surprises. Make sure it is large enough for the group and not too large. In addition check whether white boards or flip charts are available, or any other equipment that you might need. If you are unfamiliar with the location also check if food and beverages are available in the building or nearby.

An important element of a successful session, which is often overlooked or neglected is related to the layout of the room and the seating arrangements of group members. Hickling (1990) suggests having a large enough room with easy access to alternative spaces. The room needs to have enough uninterrupted wall space to accommodate flip chart sheets. Always make sure that people are arranged in a semicircle with the opening to the wall where the group memory, i.e. the white board or the projection screen is situated (Doyle and Straus, 1976; Hickling, 1990; Andersen and Richardson, 1994). If working with a computer make sure it is not in the way of group members and the person working with the computer, i.e. the model-builder. In this respect, it is important to make sure that you have all the necessary equipment. These include the following:

- portable computer(s) including a LCD screen; always check the computer and the computer model, before going to the session;
- overhead projector (maybe a slide projector); overhead projector is also needed for LCD screen;
- metal white boards (if working with magnetic hexagons); if there is only one white board make sure it is at least 1×2 m. However, it is always better to have two white boards. One can be used to brainstorm the variables, the other to construct the model;
- flip chart(s) to record problem definitions and preliminary conclusions;
- pencils both for white boards and flip charts (and keep these separate!);
- a tape recorder to tape discussions.

During the Session

Make sure that your team is at the location far ahead of time to install and check equipment. The first stage during the session is the introduction. First, introduce yourself and helpers and explain your role and those of your colleagues (facilitator, recorder, content, coach etc.). If required, have group members introduce themselves. It helps a great deal if you can refer to people during the group discussion by their first names (if this is appropriate within your culture) and participants can also call you by your first name. If you are bad at remembering names make it a habit to start the session by having everyone write down his or her name on a name-plate which is placed in front of each person so that you can see them.

The next step is to explain to the group what you are going to do: discuss the agenda. As stated, the actual agenda depends on the stage of the process and the way the project was designed. A number of general hints may be useful.

1. Check whether the group is familiar with system dynamics. If not, provide a short introduction. This introduction needs to take as little time as possible, because the group needs to start working as soon as possible. The project is not a course in system dynamics but is meant to solve a problem. I have found that explaining the basics of causal loop diagrams, flows (stocks and rates) and examples of information feedback structure are sufficient to provide the group with the necessary information. I leave other things to be explained during the meeting if the need arises.
2. Test whether there is consensus in the group on what problem to model. Formulate the problem by identifying a reference mode of behaviour of one or more variables. This will prevent potential miscommunication about the problem and provide a good start for the discussion. Further, record the problem definition in a place where it can be seen by everybody.
3. If it is not the first session, report results from previous rounds (e.g. interviews, previous session, workbooks etc.).
4. Indicate clearly what is expected from the group in this session and what outcome is anticipated.
5. Make sure that there is a group memory. If a qualitative model is built, this can be done on a white board. Building a quantitative model is best done on the white board first. Building models directly on the computer and projecting these via an overhead projector is quite difficult. The best way to proceed would be to construct the model on the white board and have someone else simultaneously build it on the computer (see Richardson and Andersen, 1995).
   Of course, the group needs to provide the input for the model construction process. As a general rule, do not write anything on the flip-chart or white board before testing whether the group agrees on it. If there is severe disagreement write the distinct possibilities on a flip-chart.
6. Have the group cycle back and forth between the problem and the model. Every once in a while stop the construction process, summarize what is modelled and take the group back to the problem and have them reflect whether the model-building excercise is on the right track. (This also means that there can be silences in a meeting in which persons can silently reflect on what has been accomplished thus far and how the group ought to proceed.)
7. Do not forget to plan breaks. Model-building is difficult for most people. If the discussion threatens to break down, or if there is an issue which does not lead to consensus, or is too difficult to model, then it is useful to have the group take a break. Frequently, when the group returns the problem is solved in no time.
8. Finally, it is important to record preliminary and final conclusions and insights. These conclusions should be formulated as clearly and as terse as possible. In this respect Richardson and Andersen (1995) have employed the term 'chunks' which can be easily remembered by the participants. People will not be able to remember the complete structure of the model. What they should be left with is the insights which were gained through the model-building process. These insights will have to guide their future actions and are thus crucial.

Work in Between Sessions and Concluding the Project

Always be prepared that the first session is the most difficult. People have to get used to you and the other way around. In addition, time might be lost by introductions and examples to introduce people to the topic of model-building. So don't be disappointed if the first session does not produce a neat model. It is more important that people have the feeling that the session was worthwhile, because they all got a chance to voice their ideas.

After the session it is important to restructure the model that was built during the session, because this model will generally not be very organized. Redraw the model, but do not change it. Make a list of all discussion topics and questions which were not really answered during the session. Take a critical look at the model from a system dynamics point of view and identify deficiencies (e.g. polarity of causal relationships, formulation of equations). If there will be a second session, summarize the discussion of the first session in the form of a workbook, including the model that was developed and a list of deficiencies in the model. In the workbook, formulate questions for the participants which have to be answered in the next session. If time permits ask participants to send these workbooks to you before the session. It helps you prepare the session and might speed up the process. The agenda for the next session then largely depends on the results of the previous sessions and the workbooks.

It is wise to conclude the group model-building sessions by a 'research report'. It is important that this report only contains conclusions which were formulated by the group during the sessions. Stated differently, the report should be the reflection of the group opinion by the end of the group model-building sessions. The shorter and the more terse these conclusions are, the better it is.

SUMMARY

This chapter has discussed a number of important issues when conducting group model-building projects. The first issue concerns the appropriateness of system dynamics for a specific problem in a particular organization. As stated system dynamics is appropriate when problems with dynamic complexity are involved. I have provided a couple of guidelines with which to decide whether a particular problem lends itself to be analysed with system dynamics. Next, I have shifted attention to the choice between qualitative and quantitative model-building. Qualitative model-building can be extremely useful to help a client organization, but it may be misleading when the robustness of policies have to be judged.

Another important question is who to involve in the group model-building sessions. In general include those who have the power to implement change and from the point of view of platform for change better have one person too many than one too few.

The main part of this chapter has concentrated on the question of whether to use a preliminary model and how to assemble it. Several techniques have been discussed to gather information to construct a preliminary model: interviews, content analysis, questionnaires and workbooks.

Employing written documents entails content analysis as an obvious technique to extract information. In the context of group model-building analysis of written documents frequently involves the production of a cause map or a causal loop diagram. Interviewing basically is an interaction situation in which the interviewer has to foster high quality communication in order to elicit information from the interviewee. Apart from clearly defining the goals of the interview and the type of questions to be asked, the attitude and skills of the interviewer are of primary importance. Both from the point of view of obtaining information and in order to build rapport with the interviewee. Questionnaires are another way of eliciting information. These are less common than interviews, but they are particularly useful when the group of participants becomes larger and group members are geographically dispersed. Most of what was said for interviews also holds for questionnaire design. More than in interviewing attention has to be given to the actual wording of the questions. Pretesting of the questionnaire with a group of persons similar to the target group is essential. Finally, the most dangerous pitfall in mailed questionnaires is the low response rate.

With regard to workbooks I have pointed out that these can best be conceived of as a system dynamics report on a model interspersed with questions and tasks for the participants. They prove extremely useful in between sessions to keep model-building efforts focused.

All these techniques can be seen as a means of preparation for one or more group model-building sessions. I have also briefly discussed the group sessions themselves and work in between sessions. An important ingredient with regard to the success of the group sessions is the role of the facilitator. What a facilitator is and how one can effectively facilitate group model-building sessions is the topic of the next chapter.

Chapter 5

Facilitating Group Model-building Sessions

INTRODUCTION

In the previous chapter I have been talking about the various roles involved in group model-building. Following Richardson and Andersen (1995) I have discussed five different roles: the facilitator, the content coach, the process coach, the recorder, and the gatekeeper. I have pointed out that the most conspicuous and frequently most important role is the facilitator role. Much of the literature on group model-building tacitly assumes that good model-builders will also be effective group facilitators. But constructing system dynamics models is quite different from group facilitation in a number of respects. Characteristics which are essential for model-building are sometimes at right angles to those necessary for effective group facilitation. This chapter will discuss the primary characteristics which are needed for group facilitation. These are based on both empirical research results in the area of small-group decision making, guidelines from literature on group facilitation, and my personal experiences and preferences. (Among the books on small groups which were consulted for this chapter are: Hare (1962); Collins and Guetzkow (1964); Hare, Borgatta and Bales (1965); Steiner (1972); Fisher (1974); McGrath (1984); Hirokawa and Scott Poole (1986); Hackman (1990); Jensen and Chilberg (1991); Worchel, Wood and Simpson (1992). In addition a literature search was conducted on several topics (e.g. group size, power, voting). Note that one has to be careful in using the results of the empirical studies, because several use concocted groups with zero history and results were obtained in the laboratory.)

A number of guidelines for model-builders who want to facilitate a group model-building process will be provided. I will start by explaining what group facilitation is and why it is both useful and necessary. Next, I will address the question of how to be a good facilitator. Any model-builder who wishes to work more closely with groups to make model-building a more effective enterprise will have to make himself acquainted with the contents of this chapter or with the literature mentioned in it.

WHAT IS GROUP FACILITATION?

In order to highlight the specific role of a facilitator let us first make a distinction between content (the subject matter under discussion), procedure or method (the way a problem is tackled), and process (i.e. the way group members interact with each other) in a meeting. Group facilitation concentrates primarily on procedure and process, not on content. In other words, a group facilitator is concerned with how things are done in a meeting. This also implies that the facilitator does not need to be particularly knowledgeable about the subject matter being discussed. Too much knowledge on the subject matter might actually impede the process as we will see in the section on neutrality. On the other hand too little knowledge may also hinder the process. As a facilitator, it is always a good idea to read about the problem or have a couple of interviews in order to be in a position to keep track of the flow of the discussion. However, what is really required in the context of group model-building is a thorough knowledge of system dynamics and extensive model-building skills in order to be able to ask the right questions during meetings.

According to Webster's dictionary to facilitate means: to promote, to aid, to make easy, to simplify. In other words a group facilitator is a person who aids the group in building a model of their problem. Some authors use the term group facilitation as a synonym for training people in group processes (Keltner, 1989), while others use group facilitation to denote group process techniques such as Nominal Group Technique or Synectics (Chilberg, 1989). Group facilitation is also not to be confused with 'social facilitation'. Social facilitation refers to the phenomenon that individuals perform particular tasks better when others are present than when carrying out these tasks in isolation. The reader interested in this phenomenon is referred to McGrath (1984).

Keltner (1989) points out that facilitator styles range from therapeutic to strictly procedural. This is partly related to the type of group. In this book we are primarily concerned with task groups or problem solving groups. The group facilitator is not a trainer but a person who helps the group to build a system dynamics model in order to increase insight into a problem and potential courses of action. The facilitator's role will primarily be procedural and only sometimes lead to interventions in which the group process itself is discussed explicitly. More than being a trainer, a group facilitator in my view functions as a *role model* for a group. The concept of 'moderator' as it is used for instance by Krueger (1988) in his *Focus Groups* is quite similar to the role of facilitator in model-building groups, albeit those focus groups have an information gathering purpose, rather than problem solving or decision making. In short, a facilitator is a person who assists a group in the process of solving a problem or making a decision (Hart, 1992).

The role of group facilitator is often compared to that of a baseball coach or the conductor of a symphony orchestra. As is usual with comparisons, these will not hold water. Both a coach and a conductor 'know' their team and train it in order to increase the team's performance. A group facilitator, on the other hand, does not train a group in decision making skills, but is confronted with a group that he hardly knows and which he has to moderate. A more accurate comparison would be with a conductor who has to conduct an orchestra, that he had not worked with previously and which will be improvising rather than performing a standard piece of music. As Doyle and Straus point out:

> Since the role of facilitator is based on flexibility and accommodation to the needs of the group members, it would be hypocritical and impossible to lay out a step-by-step procedure comparable to 'Robert's Rules of Order'. Unlike the chairperson who can waltz to the regulated music of 'Robert's Rules of Order', the facilitator has to do a combination of tap dance, shuffle, and tango to a syncopated rhythm produced by unpredictable humans. (Doyle and Straus, 1976, 89.)

It is precisely the need for flexibility and the unpredictability of the group process which make the facilitation task so difficult.

WHY GROUP FACILITATION IS IMPORTANT

Empirical research suggests that group facilitation is one of the most crucial elements in effective group model-building (Vennix et al., 1993). Group facilitation is important because meetings are complex phenomena. Apart from the fact that the subject matter (the content) is particularly complex, in the case of messy problems there is also the group interaction process which unfolds simultaneously. Trying to cover both content and process, as is often done by chairmen, is extremely difficult and will frequently decrease a group's potential performance. As Jensen and Chilberg point out:

> Groups are notorious for digressing into irrelevant discussion, pushing through an agenda without finishing important issues, and failing to apply criteria in evaluating alternatives. The person who helps the group manage these procedural difficulties is called the facilitator. In a sense the facilitator has to understand the group process better than he or she understands the group's task. (Jensen and Chilberg, 1991, 94–96.)

It seems useful to have special people attend to the process, so that others can concentrate more fully on the content. This separation of roles will contribute to the success of the group. Some authors have argued that providing groups with discussion guidelines would be equally helpful as introducing a group facilitator. However, Maier and Thurber (1969) found that most groups simply did not employ the guidelines provided to them. Others have suggested that self-directed groups might be as effective as facilitator directed groups. Again empirical research suggests that this is not the case (Conyne and Rapin, 1977). We may assume that a skilled facilitator will thus add to the effectiveness of the group process.

Group facilitation is important because, as is frequently overlooked, the interaction process affects the quality of the outcome and thus process may be considered equally critical as the content or method (Block, 1981). Most of us have been in situations where we have observed this. The way in which you say or do things is often more critical than what it is you say or do (Hackman, 1990). Let me give you an example from my own experience.

George, a colleague of mine in the department where I was working a couple of years ago was responsible for coordination of departmental teaching activities. As part of his task he had calculated everybody's teaching load and concluded that one of my other colleagues (David) was below the norm and I was well above it. So, George decided to transfer one of my courses to David, who did however not agree with this. In the next meeting of our department (in which we had to decide on the plan) David started a discussion in which he fiercely attacked the way the teaching load was calculated (a pretty complicated subject by the way). After this discussion had been going on for about half an hour, I was getting quite tired of it. I suggested to David to let me teach the course, provided that we stop the discussion about it and carry on with the meeting. As soon as I suggested this to the chairman, David turned to me saying: 'but I would like to teach this course to the students'. As you will understand, I was flabbergasted. Later I understood that David in fact very much liked to do the course but that he was rather upset about the fact that he had not been consulted about the decision to assign an extra course to him.

I suppose many readers will be able to provide examples similar to this one albeit maybe not that extreme. Schein provides a case in point:

> If there were too many errors, cost overruns, or other indicators that the program was off target, Ralston immediately and decisively reprimanded the responsible manager under him. I learned later from conversation with others in the division that his immediate subordinates resented the *tone* of these reprimands more than the fact of having the data brought to their attention. (Schein, 1987, 12; emphasis added.)

From the point of view of commitment and getting things done, these examples show that it is not only important to pay attention to what you say or do, but particularly to the *way* you say or do it. (The distinction between what one says and how it is said is purely analytical. In fact, one might argue that how something is expressed actually determines the message. Hence, saying things in a different way means saying something different.) Group facilitation focuses on the way things are said and done in groups in order to decrease the negative effects of inhibiting process characteristics.

The group facilitator, as any interventionist, influences the group process in an important way and sets the stage for group interaction (Mangham, 1978). A facilitator brings more to the group process than just methods and techniques (Block, 1981). Stated differently, the way the facilitator behaves will to a large extent determine the unfolding reality of the group interaction process. In this respect it is interesting to quote a well-known scholar in the field of small group research describing his experiences in editing a book on the effectiveness of groups with the aid of a number of his students. The whole project met with many problems, which were (frankly and admirably admitted by the author) caused by himself as a leader of the group. His conclusion: 'By finally modeling in his own behavior what he expected from others, the leader was able to rescue what many members were beginning to feel was a doomed project.' (Hackman, 1990, xvii.)

In the first chapter I have discussed the nature of reality. I have indicated that from the wealth of information people actively select and interpret information and thus build their mental model of the situation. In turn this mental model determines the way people will behave. Reality as perceived by us is thus largely created by our own actions. Frequently we do not seem to be aware of this or we are resigned to the fact that reality cannot be altered. This is demonstrated by such sayings as: 'that's the way things go around here' or 'that's the reality of organizations'. As a facilitator one has to be aware that the (social) reality in a group, for instance the way group members communicate or interact, will to a certain extent be determined by the way the facilitator behaves. And in turn the way a facilitator behaves will be determined by his or her mental model of the situation. This assumption has profound consequences for the role of the facilitator. It must be assumed that my 'Weltanschauung' (or worldview) as a facilitator determines the way I (inter)act, frequently in subtle and unconscious ways, and in turn helps to create a (social) reality in the group. This point of view has considerable consequences for group facilitation. Let me explain this by means of a couple of examples.

Much research has revealed that power games are a pervasive characteristic of organizational life (Crozier and Friedberg, 1982; Sims, Fineman and Gabriel, 1993; Janis, 1989). Some facilitators argue that one has to take these power games into account. What they mean is that one has to be aware who is the most powerful person in the room and one has to gear one's behaviour to this. As these facilitators say: there are power games, you cannot just ignore them, that is naïve. In my view this type of argument contains two types of mistakes. The first is that it is a descriptive statement. So descriptive theories might point out that power games are a ubiquitous phenomenon. This does not imply however that I have to participate in them. In this chapter on group facilitation we deal with prescriptive statements. The central question is: how best to facilitate a group in such a way that an optimal solution to a problem is developed? A solution with high quality and acceptance among those involved. Power games are generally not very helpful to design this type of optimal solution. The second point is that, from the theory of creation of reality, the idea of power games has to be considered with caution. Because of the mechnism of the self-fulfilling prophecy, the fact that a facilitator *expects* power games in a group may well result in actual power games or an increase in them which did not really exist. Hence my conclusion: the best way to deal with power games is to ignore them altogether. If I am convinced that power games normally produce undesirable outcomes it is best not to pay attention to them. The mechanism works the same way if I want to suppress a thought. The harder I consciously try to repress a thought the more I might end up concentrating on it. The best way to ignore it is to actually concentrate on something else. This suggests that if I want to ignore power games, the best thing to do is to concentrate more on the group task or problem. By doing this the facilitator helps the group to surpass politicking behaviour in the group.

Another example with regard to the construction of the (social) reality in a group relates to processes of face saving. Face saving constitutes an important element in any group interaction process. We rather deny disconfirming information than losing face or self-esteem (Schein, 1987). In that respect Eden (1992a) makes a distinction between negotiated social order and socially negotiated order. Negotiated social order refers to the established social order in an organization, while socially negotiated order refers to the different perceptions of organization members and the way shared meaning is developed. He points out that:

> Because of the power of negotiated social order, negotiation depends on participants devising ways of 'saving face' as they change their mind and attitude about possible outcomes. Face saving reflects a person's need to reconcile the stand he/she takes with principles and with past words and deeds. For the effective balance between socially negotiated order and negotiated social order to be attained, effective negotiators make their contributions with a degree of equivocality so that social order is not destroyed but substantive information is proffered nevertheless. *Equivocality* serves to maintain the balance of order but also provides the fuzziness within which face saving can occur, thus encouraging both a new social order and a new negotiated order. (Eden, 1992a, 209.)

Face saving may sometimes be quite time consuming and frustrating in a meeting. An effective facilitator can break this group interaction pattern by showing no face saving behaviour himself but by frankly admitting a change of stand or a mistake. To a facilitator, maintaining face should be less important than analysing and tackling the problem. As a consequence, other group members start to show similar behaviour and time in a meeting will be used more effectively. In short, the facilitator's behaviour fosters a different social reality in the group. In this respect, it is important to realize that the facilitator's task is primarily to create favourable conditions which will positively affect the process and hence the outcome (see also Hackman, 1990).

Having said this, let us next take a look at what constitutes good facilitation behaviour.

HOW TO BE A GOOD FACILITATOR

What distinguishes a good from a bad facilitator? What are the do's and don'ts of group facilitation? Most of the literature simply states what a good facilitator is supposed to do. (See for instance: Doyle and Straus (1976), Krueger (1988), Jensen and Chilberg (1991), Hart (1992), Heron (1993), Phillips and Phillips (1993), Rees (1991), Westley and Waters (1988).) But the description of these skills might prove to be deceptively simple. For example, one of the skills in group facilitation is to ask questions rather than to present (your own) opinions. As for instance Gibb points out: 'Even the simplest question usually conveys the answer that the sender wishes or implies the response that would fit into his value system.' (Gibb, 1960, 143.) This way of asking questions, or even worse asking questions to put others 'one down', is not very productive. Hence, the simple rule of thumb: 'ask questions rather than give opinions' is much too simple, unless the facilitator understands the rationale behind such a rule. Ideally, such rationales ought to be derived from a scientific theory revealing the determinants of the performance of decision making groups. Unfortunately, such an empirically tested theory is still lacking. In addition, little research has been conducted into the specific phenomenon of group facilitation and how it can be employed to improve group communication and performance (Friedman, 1989; Hirokawa and Gouran, 1989). This implies that we will have to rely on partial theories and available empirical research in this domain.

It seems that for effective group facilitation three elements are of importance, i.e. attitudes, skills, and a number of tangible tasks (which have to be performed before, during and after a group model-building session). These three are not of equal importance and neither are they unrelated. In my view the attitudes are most important, since the right skills will almost automatically follow from the right attitudes, and skills which are not embedded in the right attitude and accompanied by a corresponding behaviour will generate averse effects. As Rees points out: 'In fact some leaders ask for participation and then knowingly or unknowingly discourage it by their actions.' (Rees, 1991, 10.) And as we know: actions generally speak louder than words. Stated differently, if one's actions are not embedded in the right attitudes and both one's actions and non verbal behaviour do not support one's words then one will be pretty ineffective as a group facilitator. Research by Argyris and his colleagues (see for instance Argyris, 1992) has revealed that for most people there is a large discrepancy between what people say they do (espoused theory) and their actual behaviour. His research has also revealed that most people are very much aware of this discrepancy in others, but in general fail to recognize this discrepancy with regard to themselves. This implies the importance of being self reflective. As a facilitator one needs to be aware of one's attitudes and behaviour and how a certain behaviour is likely to affect other people. For instance, we do have to be aware of the fact that what has been said about the limitations of human information processing and the nature of human reality also holds for a facilitator. Research in the tradition of behavioural decision making has demonstrated that the biases and heuristics which play a role in judgement and choice do equally apply to laymen and scientists. Stated differently, when confronted with a decision making task experienced scientists display the same biases and employ the same heuristics as lay persons. I think the lesson we have to draw from this is that even as intervenors we have to be modest when it comes to helping other people. However, this attitude might prove difficult since empirical research has demonstrated time and again that people are generally overconfident with regard to their own judgement (Einhorn and Hogarth, 1978; Lichtenstein, Fischhoff and Phillips, 1982). I am not aware of any empirical evidence which demonstrates that these processes differ significantly between scientists and non scientific persons.

In the final sections of the previous chapter a number of concrete tasks have been described. In the remainder of this chapter we will take a look at appropriate facilitator attitudes and skills.

Facilitation Attitudes

Secord and Backman define an attitude as: '. . . certain regularities of an individual's feelings, thoughts and predispositions to act toward some aspect of his environment.' (Secord and Backman, 1974, 97.) In other words, an attitude is a predisposition to behave in a certain way (Ajzen, 1988; 1991). Thus attitudes affect the way people will respond to certain situations. And in turn, the way a facilitator responds to a situation will (in part) determine the group process and its effectiveness. Certain attitudes will contribute more to the effectiveness of the group process than others. The question then becomes: what constitutes the right set of attitudes for a group facilitator? I think there are several important basic attitudes: a helping attitude, authenticity and integrity, an inquiry attitude, and neutrality. The next sections will discuss these attitudes and the reasons why they are important in more detail.

Helping Attitude

Recently we conducted a project in which we developed an executive information system for John, a marketing manager and vice president of a large Dutch company. At some time during this project someone proposed to do the same kind of project for a group of account managers within this firm. A couple of people asked John to convince the group of account managers of the strategic usefulness and to possibly help them with the development of such an executive information system. However John was a bit reluctant, stating that 'if I have to take everybody in this company by the hand I prefer to quit'. I think that in part this is exactly one of the type of attitudes which promotes organizational inefficiency. I agree with Schein that:

> Effective managers, on the other hand, seem to conceptualize their role and structure their relationships with others very differently. They behave in such a way that subordinates, peers and supervisors get the help they need in order to get things done, to succeed, to achieve the goals that have been set. (Schein, 1987, 6–7.)

In other words, effective managers have a helping attitude, supporting others to get the job done. And this is also one of the basic attitudes for a successful facilitator, since to facilitate implies to help or to make things easier, to help others to structure and solve their messy problems. If one does not have this helping attitude or, even worse, if you display an attitude of knowing things better than your client group you will be useless as a facilitator. Once you start airing your (in your own opinion 'superior') views and criticizing others' views you will generate a lot of resistance within the group (Jensen and Chilberg, 1991).

Pointing out that a helping attitude is required is again a deceptively simple statement. I have met many people who seem to have a helping attitude, or at least think they have. They 'help' others by showing that the problem is in fact very simple and telling them what the 'correct' solution is. Apart from the fact that in the long run this does not really help a person or a group (because one doesn't learn how to solve one's own problems in the future) it is generally counterproductive. Schein (1987) points out that one has to be extremely careful in any helping relationship. Since in most western countries self-reliance is important a client puts himself 'one down' and the helper has to make sure that this situation of non-equilibrium will be restored otherwise the client will do so himself by rejecting the advice. The best way to circumvent this problem is by taking the client and his problem seriously. As experienced psychotherapists say: the best way to help patients is by making them help you.

I have met few instances in which people talked to me about their problems and I knew an immediate answer. As Eden succinctly puts it:

> Most significantly, if problems belong to people and they are thus subjective entities, then it becomes crucial that the consultant understands how the client sees the problem. It is nonsense to suppose that any 'mess' about which a client needs help can be quickly and easily understood by the consultant—if it *were* possible, then we might reasonably wonder why it is that the client needs our help. Similarly, it is an imposition of simplicity to suppose that agreement to the label of the mess is to agree to the nature of the problem. (Eden, 1982, 54.)

In other words, it takes considerable time for a facilitator to fully understand a client's problem, if this is at all possible. In the long run, it proves more effective to try first to understand what a person is really saying to you by asking questions than by providing quick solutions. In other words, the questions and suggestions you make are meant to start a joint thinking process with your client.

Authenticity and Integrity

I know consultants who use 'tricks' to guide the group process. You had better not rely on tricks, since people will see through them, maybe not the first time, but certainly after several times. Tricks will be counterproductive since people will either anticipate them or be irritated by them (Gibb, 1960). Showing integrity and being authentic will prove to be more effective in the long run. Authenticity implies being yourself and displaying genuineness in interaction with other people. Unfortunately, much of what is going on in organizations is not authentic. Much is related to impression management, power games and ways to manipulate people. This leads to lack of confidence and trust between people. Many people acquiesce in this state of affairs. As said before, this is best demonstrated by such typical expressions as: that's the way it goes; such is organizational life. However, as I have indicated before, social reality (or for that matter 'the way it goes') is the result of our own actions. Believing that 'that is the way it goes', implies that we will comply in our behaviour and as a result reinforce 'the way it goes'. By doing this we actually help to sustain a reality which many of us despise and which frequently leads to undesirable outcomes. Changing this state of affairs can only be accomplished by changing our own minds and actions, although this will take time, since people will have to get used to it and respond positively in turn. As Mintzberg states when discussing how to build a better culture in organizations:

These are built slowly and patiently by committed leaders who have found interesting missions for their organizations and care deeply about the people who perform them. To my mind, the critical ingredient is *authenticity*. In fact I believe in a kind of psychic law of management here: that workers, customers, every one involved with a management, no matter how physically distant, can tell when it is *genuine* in its beliefs and when it is just mouthing the right words. (Mintzberg, 1989, 275, emphasis added.)

In other words authenticity and integrity are important factors in creating a favourable climate in organizations, which in turn will augment performance. They are also important in facilitating groups. In my view authenticity and integrity are important factors in building confidence and in creating commitment in the group.

Attitude of Inquiry

One of the most powerful interventions for any facilitator which, if conducted properly, is not threatening to other people, is to ask questions. Part of the reason for this is that people tend not to ask questions in groups. In the 1940s and 1950s Bales and others conducted much research into the behaviour of small problem solving groups. The behaviour of individuals in small groups was observed and coded by means of his Interaction Process Analysis. Bales used 12 different categories in four problem areas: positive reactions, attempted answers, questions, and negative reactions. The interesting thing is that from the total number of scores over a large number of different groups only about 7% fall in the category of asking questions, while more than half (56%) falls in the category of attempted answers (Hare, 1962). Although these studies were done in the laboratory and conducted in the late 1940s and early 1950s, in my opinion this is still a fair representation of how most meetings progress nowadays. People tend to give answers and air opinions rather than ask questions. Now, one could argue whether this is right or wrong. From my experience with meetings I have the impression that participants often talk past each other without being aware of it. Frequently, I tell people that I don't understand what they mean or why they hold a particular opinion and I observe that others in the group are glad that someone asks. The cultural dynamics around face saving, however, prevents these people from asking the question themselves. These type of questions, posed by the facilitator, are thus useful to prevent misunderstandings and to avoid a false feeling of agreement and clarity. As one manager once said to me: 'At the end of a meeting we often feel that we agree, but then the next meeting when we talk it over again it looks as if we are back at the start and did not reach a consensus in the previous meeting' (see also Hackman, 1990, 21). Asking questions to clarify a matter could help to prevent these misunderstandings. On the one hand this creates a possibility for people to explain their thoughts, while on the other it is an effective way to scrutinize these thoughts. To make sure that you understand what someone means, it is best to apply reflective listening skills, a skill which will be discussed in one of the next sections.

Asking questions is meant to foster a problem orientation and an attitude of inquiry within the group. As stated before, however, asking questions has to be embedded in the right attitude. As a facilitator you will have to display an attitude of inquiry. This can best be accomplished if you convince yourself of the fact that what you now consider to be true and thus real, could turn out not to be true or real tomorrow. In other words, the more you are convinced that you are right, the more difficult it will be to ask really neutral questions, i.e. questions without an implied answer. But the more you consider what you know to be preliminary and subject of scrutiny and discussion, i.e. the more you display a learning attitude as opposed to a teaching attitude, the more genuine your questions will be and the more they will foster an inquiry attitude in the group. Focusing on the problem and posing questions is also helpful to avoid politicking and win-lose fights. In that respect a sense of humour will also be very helpful to break the tension when debates might become hostile (see also Krueger, 1988).

Neutrality: Refraining From Voicing Your Opinion

As stated before, content, method (or procedure) and process, although intertwined, have to be considered separately. The facilitator's role is to focus on the procedures and the process. The facilitator must be neutral with respect to the *content* of the discussion (Broome and Keever, 1989; Doyle and Strauss, 1976; Keltner, 1989). The facilitator should refrain from airing his or her personal opinions, nor should the facilitator place evaluations on what is said both verbally and non verbally. An important issue related to the foregoing is to be neutral with regard to group members. Don't show the preferences you might have for some people or ideas. Always take all participants seriously. Avoid getting involved in politicking, and be the first to admit your mistakes. This type of attitude will help you build trust and commitment within the group. As Hackman (1990, 84) reports, the higher the amount of trust between team members, the higher the capacity for learning in the team.

Trying to be neutral is easily said but not very easily done, particularly if you happen to have a strong opinion about the subject matter under discussion. There are a couple of ways to ensure that you as a facilitator do not interfere with the content of the discussion. The first, which we have already mentioned, is an inquiry attitude. Try to have an open mind. The second, which will sound counterintuitive to most consultants, is not to be too knowledgeable about the subject matter of the discussion. The less you know about it the smaller the chances that you as a facilitator will influence the content of the discussion. Of course you can't be totally ignorant about the subject matter, since then you would unnecessarily slow down the process.

Every now and then, however, there will also be situations in which you would like to contribute to the discussion's content. As Doyle and Strauss (1976) point out, be sure that you make it clear to the group that you abandon your facilitator role for the moment and would like to make a comment or present an idea. The best way to do this would be to present your idea to the group and let them decide whether to discuss or ignore it. Another possibility is to invite an outside expert to participate in the group discussions, in order to prevent the group from premature closure.

Facilitation Skills

Thus far we have been concerned with the necessary attitudes for effective group facilitation. I have pointed out that without the right attitudes, skills will be virtually useless, or at least they will be considerably less powerful than when they are embedded in these attitudes. On the other hand, we also have to be aware of the fact that particular skills are needed in order to effectively facilitate (model-building) groups. Possessing the right attitudes without a minimum of the required skills will not be effective. This section discusses a number of basic facilitation skills. Needless to say, system dynamics model-building ability is a necessary prerequisite. The more one is experienced in building system dynamics models the more effective one will be as a group model-building facilitator. There are, however, other skills which are of importance for group facilitation.

Group Process Structuring Skills

Freely interacting groups often perform below their potential (Delbecq, Ven and Gustafson, 1975; Steiner, 1972). The primary reasons are (a) inequal participation, (b) the generation of alternatives is mixed up with their evaluation, and (c) discussions tend to degenerate into battles in which winning the discussion is more important than finding the best solution. In general, these deficiencies tend to get worse when the group becomes larger, as we have seen in the previous chapter. The larger a group, the more difficult it is to keep on track, and maintain high quality communication and a high degree of participation in the discussion.

If size is not under the control of the group model-builder, the problem then becomes how to handle the situation of a larger group. Research indicates that, when dealing with larger groups, introducing structured procedures into the communication process is beneficial (Boje and Murnighan, 1982; Bouchard, 1969, 1972a; Hart et al., 1985).

The facilitator can introduce structure in the group task as well as the communication process. As regards the group task, structure can be obtained by breaking down the decision making task into a number of smaller sequential steps: identifying the problem, generating alternatives and making a choice. Of course each of these steps can in turn be subdivided into smaller substeps if required.

With regard to the communication process, more structure can be accomplished by breaking up a large group into smaller groups, or by working alternately in a nominal (i.e. non-interacting) mode and an interactive mode (as is for instance done in Nominal Group Technique). Further, by employing restricted communication channels (as for instance in Delphi).

Empirical research has demonstrated that introducing structure in the process increases group performance as well as commitment with the decision (White, Dittrich and Lang, 1980). However, research has also indicated that the *type* of structure (or decision making sequence) is of limited importance. (See for instance: Brilhart and Jochem (1964), and Hirokawa (1985).) Simply going through a set of steps will not automatically produce a good decision (Gouran, 1982; Hirokawa,

1985). This observation is clearly corroborated by empirical research results. Hirokawa and Pace (1983), for instance, compared effective and ineffective decision making groups on a number of decision making characteristics. They found that effective groups tended to examine and evaluate the validity of opinions and assumptions introduced into the discussion more carefully. Secondly, effective groups evaluated alternative choices more thoroughly and rigorously. Thirdly, effective groups employed more accurate premises on which to base the decision. Finally, these groups seemed to have influential people who facilitated the group discussion by '. . . asking appropriate questions, introducing or pointing out important information and insights, challenging and persuading the group to reject unwarranted or fallacious assumptions and arguments, clarifying information . . ., and/or keeping the group from digressing into irrelevant discussion tangents.' (Hirokawa and Pace, 1983, 373.)

In other words, empirical research indicates that it is not so much the decision procedure as the degree of vigilance in a group which determines performance (Hirokawa, 1985; 1988; Hirokawa and Rost, 1992). As we will see in the next section one way to increase a group's vigilance is by introducing cognitive conflict.

Conflict Handling Skills

Management teams frequently consist of various and opposing personalities. This can even be augmented when the model-builder strives for diversity in group composition in order to enhance model quality by including a variety of viewpoints. In those cases the group interaction process can be permeated with conflict.

In the literature on small group conflict and conflict management two types of conflict are generally distinguished. One type is affective conflict, also denoted as socio-emotional or personal conflict. Affective conflict is rooted in the interpersonal relations within the group. They concern controversies which relate to the emotional aspects of interpersonal relations as is for instance the case in personal clashes as a result of 'incompatibilité d'humeurs'. In other words, certain personalities do not match and cannot seem to get along easily. One specific personality characteristic which may easily give rise to interpersonal conflict in a group process is self-orientated, individualistic behaviour. Self-orientated need behaviour is mainly focused on the satisfaction of the need itself, regardless of the fact whether it helps the attainment of the group goal (Fouriezos, Hutt and Guetzkow, 1950). Examples of self-orientated behaviour include the need for dependence on authority, intellectual dominance, dominance in social situations and aggression against authority. Studies have revealed that the higher the number of self-orientated statements in a meeting the fewer items are completed in a meeting, while meetings typically take longer. In addition, group members are less satisfied with the group process as well as the way in which the decision was reached. Finally, the more self-orientated behaviour in the group the more difficult it is to reach consensus and the more a group will rely on techniques like voting as a way to resolve conflict (Fouriezos, Hutt and Guetzkow, 1950; Guetzkow and Gyr, 1954; Nemiroff and King, 1975). Elsewhere in this chapter I will discuss the role of voting in group decision making and show the dangers involved in terms of resulting commitment with the decision. It seems safe to conclude that in general affective conflict hinders effective group decision making. Under conditions of affective conflict, groups seem to postpone the consideration of conflict-producing items on the agenda and to withdraw from the discussion.

A second type of conflict is substantive or cognitive conflict. Substantive conflict is related to the group task and generally involves differences of opinion or viewpoint. As I have indicated in the first chapter, differences of opinion are a basic aspect of messy problems.

Research over the last decades has convincingly demonstrated that avoiding substantive conflict by suppressing disagreement negatively affects the quality of a decision. Concurrence seeking groups have repeatedly been shown to arrive at lower quality decisions when compared with groups in which controversy is encouraged. (Results of the effect of suppressing disagreement can be found in Cosier and Rose (1977), Hall and Watson (1971), Nemiroff and King (1975), Harper and Askling (1980), Smith, Johnson and Johnson (1981), and Smith et al. (1986). The effects of concurrence seeking are reported in Tjosvold (1982), Tjosvold and Field (1985), and Smith et al. (1986).) The simple conclusion is to avoid concurrence seeking and to encourage disagreement. In real world decision making there can, however, be powerful forces which act to suppress disagreement and to promote concurrence. For instance, people are in general careful in disagreeing with superiors. Communication from low to high status persons is generally deferential and non-critical (Kelley, 1951; Cohen, 1958; Janis, 1989). Difference in hierarchical positions is not the only force to suppress deviant opinions. The group itself can be another force to discourage disagreement. Substantive conflict in a group is generally introduced by opinion deviates (Pendell, 1990). Laboratory studies have revealed that in cases where an accepted group member expresses a deviant opinion the number of communications directed towards the opinion deviant increase sharply. Evidently, the increased communication towards the deviant is aimed at changing his or her opinion towards the group opinion. This tendency becomes stronger when the pressure towards group uniformity and group cohesiveness is higher. For evidence on this see for instance: Festinger and Thibaut (1951), Schachter (1951), Berkowitz and Howard (1959), and Emerson (1954).

In an extreme form, group cohesiveness may create a pathological phenomenon for which Janis has coined the term 'groupthink'. Groupthink refers to:

> . . . a mode of thinking that people engage in when they are deeply involved in a cohesive in-group, when the members' strivings for unanimity override their motivation to realistically appraise alternative courses of action. . . . Groupthink refers to a deterioration of mental efficiency, reality testing, and moral judgment that results from in-group pressures. (Janis, 1972, 9.)

Groupthink is most likely to occur under conditions of stress when group cohesion is high. The group is primarily occupied with seeking concurrence, maintaining unanimity and suppressing disagreement. The process creates a sense of invulnerability in the group, which in turn reinforces the suppression of disagreement.

Group members are inclined to minimize the importance of their doubts and to suppress counterarguments to decisions made by the group. Many studies have revealed the potential detrimental effects of groupthink. (For examples of studies on the phenomenon and effects of groupthink see for instance Janis (1972), Janis and Mann (1977), Hensley and Griffin (1986), and Herek, Janis and Huth (1987), Hart (1990).)

In short, avoiding conflict and seeking premature consensus negatively affects the quality of the decision regardless of the type of decision making task. But does this also imply that promoting conflict in a group will increase the quality of decision making? The answer is both yes and no. Promoting conflict and controversy is only helpful under certain conditions. Above we discussed situations in which the number of conflicts was low or conflict was totally absent. Promoting controversy in these situations leads to higher quality decisions, because disagreement causes a more thorough investigation of the problem, more information processing and a consideration of more alternatives. As might be expected, however, the relationship between the number of conflicts and quality of decision is curvilinear in shape. More conflict induces higher quality decisions. Beyond a certain point however, decision quality will deteriorate with a further increase in the number of conflicts (Wall, Galanes and Love, 1987). This is illustrated in Figure 5.1.

Typically groupthink situations are located in the lower left hand corner of the figure. Situations of continuous disagreement are in the lower right hand side. Both types of situations are suboptimal. When decision quality is involved the optimal situation is an intermediate level of cognitive conflict in a group. Both too little and too much conflict induces low quality decisions.

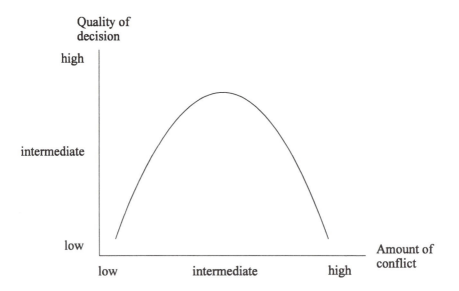

Figure 5.1 Relationship Between Amount of Cognitive Conflict and Quality of Decisions in Small Groups

Not only the amount of conflict is of importance. Another important factor which intervenes between cognitive conflict and decision quality is the way people respond to conflicts. Thomas (1976) developed a two-dimensional model of conflict behaviour. The two dimensions are: cooperativeness and assertiveness. Cooperativeness is related to attempts to satisfy the other party's concerns, while assertiveness involves attempts to satisfy one's own concerns. Based on these two dimensions the author distinguishes five types of conflict behaviour. Unassertive behaviour leads to conflict avoidance when a person is uncooperative and to accommodation if the person is cooperative. Highly assertive behaviour on the other hand, gives rise to competition (uncooperative mode) or to collaboration (cooperative mode). In the middle between all these forms is compromising behaviour, which scores intermediate on both dimensions. As the author points out, each of these types of conflict behaviours is adequate in different circumstances. Avoidance, for instance, can be very useful if one considers an issue trivial. Accommodation can be appropriate when issues are more important to the other party than to oneself. Compromise can be useful to accomplish (temporary) settlements to complex issues. Competitive behaviour seems suitable when others take advantage of noncompetitive behaviour, or when a quick decision is called for. Finally, collaboration is for instance adequate when one wants to merge insights from people with different perspectives.

Since we formulated collaboration as a requirement in dealing with messy problems this seems the way to go in group model-building. The problem is that people do not only respond differently to conflict situations, they also misperceive their own behaviour. Typically, when people have to judge their own behaviour in retrospect of a conflict they tend to view themselves as relatively cooperative while the other party is generally seen as competitive. Under these circumstances most conflicts will tend to drift towards competition rather than collaboration since competitive behaviour breeds competition (Jones, 1977; Kelley and Stahelski, 1970).

In a competitive, conflict situation participants strive to surpass one another. People perceive themselves as having antagonistic interests, and as a result they emphasize the differences. There is a sphere of suspicion, and communication can be hostile and misleading. In those situations people's response to the conflict situation can easily become unregulated (Pood, 1980), i.e. responses are aimed at injuring or eliminating another party. These unregulated responses generally result in a overt power struggle. In a cooperative environment on the other hand, members give priority to the group's goals rather than their personal objectives. Conflict is seen as positive and beneficial, there is mutual trust and open communication. Here responses to the situation are more regulated. Regulated responses aim at information sharing and clarifying the nature of the conflict.

Interestingly, Deutsch (1973) claimed that conflict is more productive in a cooperative than in a competitive environment. Considerable research seems to support Deutsch's assertion. See for instance Pace (1990), Pood (1980), Tjosvold (1982), Tjosvold and Johnson (1977; 1978), and Wall, Galanes and Love (1987). In situations of substantive conflict, cooperative environments produce better decisions than competitive environments. In other words it is not cognitive conflict which is the obstacle, but rather the competitiveness of the situation (Tjosvold, 1982).

But what about the merits of competition? Have we not all been taught about the beneficial effects of genuine competition? Does it not bring out the best in people? And why is competition in cognitive conflict situations disruptive? The answer to these questions might be found in the complexity of the situation. Competition works well in routine, but less well in non-routine situations. As Thibaut and Kelley point out: 'Stated somewhat more generally, any increase in drive will improve the performance of activities that are simple, easy, or well integrated (overlearned) but will lead to deteriorated performance of activities that are complex, difficult, or in general not well learned.' (Thibaut and Kelley, 1959, 58.) In other words, messy problems, which entail non-routine decision making situations, may require non-competitive situations in order not to raise emotions to the level where people will underperform because they are trying too hard (Cosier and Rose, 1977).

From the above we can draw the following tentative conclusions. First, cognitive or substantive conflict in group decision making is beneficial to promote vigilance and to increase the quality of the decision. However, if the group falls prey to personalized conflicts this will deteriorate rather than enhance decision quality. The group facilitator might find it easier to keep discussions focused on the group task, unless he is willing to discuss the group process with the group. But nonetheless the facilitator's task will be more difficult in a heterogeneous group. One guideline which might be helpful in this respect shows that emphasizing this diversity will make matters worse rather than better. Exline (1957) for instance, found that irrespective of actual group composition emphasizing congeniality in groups, led to higher willingness to work with others in the group and greater satisfaction with the progress of the group. Groups in which congeniality was emphasized achieved more adequate task communication as opposed to groups in which no emphasis on congeniality was provided.

Second, promoting cognitive conflict is only useful up to a certain point. If confronted with a concurrence seeking group which looks for premature consensus, the facilitator might promote disagreement by asking critical questions. In order to increase cognitive conflict in a group, the facilitator might even use special conflict promoting techniques. Two well-known techniques are dialectical inquiry (DI) and devil's advocate (DA). The interested reader is referred to Appendix 3 for the specific guidelines for both techniques.

The major difference between DA and DI is that DI leads to a counterplan while DA does not. According to Mason (1969), this is one of the major flaws of DA, since if the plan is rejected there is no alternative available. The debate between proponents and opponents of the superiority of DI over DA has spawned a host of laboratory experiments. Basically, the outcomes of these experiments have revealed that DI and DA are equally effective and both are superior to consensus decision making with regard to decision quality. These experiments have also revealed that groups will only accept a decision which result from the application of these techniques if they have repeated experience with DI and DA. First time use generally leads to lower levels of acceptance. This also holds with regard to the satisfaction within the group, the willingness of team members to work with each other in the future. Unexperienced DA and DI groups also seem to need more time for decision making. For experiments in field settings to establish the usefulness of DI see Mason (1969), and Mitroff, Barabba and Kilmann (1977). Early experiments comparing DA and DI are described in Cosier (1978), Cosier, Ruble and Aplin (1978), Cosier and Aplin (1980), and Cosier and Rechner (1985). Some of these experiments showed a superiority of DA over DI. Cosier's experiments have been criticized by Mitroff and Mason (1981) because of the fact that the these experiments did not employ a true DI approach and some experiments did not really contain an ill-structured decision situation.

Later experiments, taking these criticisms into account, however, also failed to demonstrate the superiority of DI over DA. The conclusion is that both DI and DA are equally effective and both are superior to consensus decision making with regard to decision quality. For details see Schweiger, Sandberg and Ragan (1986), Schweiger, Sandberg and Rechner (1989), and Schweiger and Sandberg (1989). With regard to acceptance of the recommendations and satisfaction with the group one can conclude that when conflict promoting techniques are employed with an unexperienced group, the facilitator will have to employ an adequate conflict resolution style in order to promote acceptance of the recommendations and satisfaction with the group.

In short, if the group is seeking concurrence then conflict should be fostered. On the other hand if group members themselves are already conflict prone, the group facilitator might actually have to try to foster concurrence, in order to arrive at the optimal point of curve in Figure 5.1. Finally, the facilitator will have to take care that a sphere of cooperation rather than competition is created, because in a cooperative climate cognitive conflict will be most beneficial.

Communication Skills

Communication is at the heart of decision making groups. It is the means whereby groups arrive at a decision. In dealing with messy problems, communication is the means through which group members exchange their views about the problem and might come to a shared understanding of the problem and uniformity of opinion (Collins and Guetzkow, 1964). As might be expected communication becomes more important when the problem becomes more complex (Hirokawa, 1990), because viewpoints will be more divergent and more effort is necessary to integrate these perspectives to counteract the divergence (Maznevski, 1994). In other words, the more complex the problem the higher the amount of information which will have to be exchanged between group members. Since, as we have seen in the first chapter, a person's information processing capacity is limited, the group will have to employ means to support and enhance this capacity, for instance by employing visual diagrams or computer simulations.

Not only the amount of information which is exchanged between team members is of relevance. Probably even more important is the *way* in which group members exchange information. Various scholars have emphasized the importance of open or supportive communication and have identified barriers to open and free communication (Gibb, 1960, 1961; Rogers and Roethlisberger, 1988). Rogers for instance, points out that the greatest enemy of open communication is our tendency to evaluate, to approve or disapprove of what is said by someone else. The higher our tendency to judge, the lower our potential to listen carefully to what is being said. And in turn, our tendency to judge depends on the degree to which emotions or feelings are involved as well as the degree to which we are convinced that we are right and the other person must be wrong (Rogers and Roethlisberger, 1988). In his book on *Overcoming Organizational Defenses*, Argyris (1990) presents examples of people communicating with each other about an organizational problem where each person blames the other for the difficulties. One of the things that both sides often think (but not really say in public) about the other side is: 'you do not really understand the issues'. This leads to what might be called communication by convincing, a one-way type of communication, in which there is no real listening to the other. Open communication on the other hand is supposed to be two-way. This type of communication presupposes that one is able to postpone one's judgement.

Closely related to our tendency to evaluate is most people's inability to listen. As Roethlisberger states: 'The biggest block to personal communication is man's inability to listen intelligently, understandingly, and skilfully to another person. This deficiency in the modern world is widespread and appalling. In our universities as well as elsewhere, too little is being done about it.' (Rogers and Roethlisberger, 1988, 25.) Listening intelligently implies that one really tries to understand what is said, not just that one is silent for reasons of politeness. It also presupposes that one attempts to understand the other's thinking, the other person's way of looking at the world.

With regard to understanding, Campbell identified a number of systematic errors in human communication. One is that if the understanding of a message by the recipient is imperfect, the understanding of the message will generally be shorter and less detailed (Campbell, 1958). A recipient has the tendency to reduce gradations in the message, for instance, by losing differentiations. In addition, errors will in general mould messages in such a way that they become similar to the meaning expected by the receiver. Furthermore, according to Collins and Guetzkow, people tend to reduce the content of messages to the dimension 'good versus bad'. 'This principle is represented in the decision making group by the quick evaluation of ideas as either completely good or completely bad.' (Collins and Guetzkow, 1964, 185.) This tendency can be so strong that we even prevent ourselves from finding out what the other person means by a specific concept. A very illuminating example of how easily misunderstanding can occur is presented by Maznevski (1994). The very simple word 'yes' can have strikingly different meaning to different people. Maznevski presents a discussion between two town councillors: Steve and Shawna. Steve presents proposals to which Shawna every now and then answers with a yes. Steve understands this as signalling agreement, while for Shawna it signals comprehension: 'yes, I understand what you mean'. This simple example serves to illustrate the difficulties involved in communicating effectively and preventing misunderstandings.

Apart from our inclination to evaluate and many people's inability to listen, a third inhibiting factor to effective communication is defensiveness. Defensive

routines are habits which we employ to protect ourselves from potential embarrass-
ment when exposing our ideas to others (Schein, 1987; Argyris, 1990; 1994). Their
function is to prevent losing one's face. If for instance we seem to 'lose' the argument in a discussion we have the tendency to start a face saving operation, for
instance by explaining to the other that he did not understand us correctly. A
problem in unmasking defensive routines is that they generally go unnoticed and
they can hardly be discussed openly. 'Accusing' someone of being defensive will
automatically backfire. ('Me? I am not being defensive!'). The way to tackle defensive routines lies in considering them from the perspective of reality creation as
discussed in the first chapter. In other words, the way to break defensive routines is
not to create them, not to be defensive yourself. Just admit your mistakes.

To illustrate characteristics of non-defensive communication let us follow Gibb
(1960) who makes a distinction between defensive and supportive communication.
Supportive communication is characterized by description, i.e. genuine requests for
information as opposed to evaluative statements. It is problem oriented rather than
looking for control in discussions, since control produces defensiveness. Supportive
communication is further characterized by spontaneity rather than strategy. The
latter involves strategies and tricks to fool people. In general people are quick to
perceive this type of strategy which leads to irritation and even violent reactions
according to Gibb. Furthermore supportive communication is also characterized by
empathy and equality.

Gibb not only describes two types of communication, but is also quick to point
out that defensive communication patterns in groups are associated with loss of
communication efficiency. Loss of communication efficiency is in turn associated
with low quality of the resulting decision. Empirical studies have revealed that low
quality communication:

1. increases the time to reach a decision (Fouriezos, Hutt and Guetzkow, 1950);
2. decreases the quality of a group's decision (Leathers, 1972); and
3. may lead to lack of confidence which in turn inhibits creative thinking (Klimoski
   and Karol, 1976).

The conclusion must be that open, supportive communication is a necessary requirement of arriving at high quality decisions. Creating a sphere of open communication is one of the primary tasks of the group facilitator. What skills are required?

First, as a facilitator, do not underestimate miscommunication in groups. By
asking that questions are clarified and checking whether everybody is still in on the
discussion is of the utmost importance. As a facilitator you have to avoid any jargon
or fuzzy, ambiguous language, since this inhibits the communication process
(Leathers, 1972). Be as clear as possible in what you say. For instance, in the
example of the regional management team of the Ministry of Transport that I
presented in Chapter 1, I asked for indicators for 'added value' (of a regional
department of DGPW). But I always pose the question in different ways trying to
explain carefully what I mean, what I expect the group to do. So in the above case I
do not only ask the group to come up with indicators, but I add to this something

like: 'how do you 'see' out there that you produce added value' or 'what is it that you would look at out there in order to determine whether you as a team have added value or not'. Generally, it is also useful to provide an example of what it is that you want team members to do.

Second, an important required skill is active (or reflective) listening: listening and trying to understand what someone means by what he or she says. This implies being able to ask clarifying questions in order to make sure that you understand what is said. The reason for this is not only that you as a facilitator have to understand what is said. More important is that the other team members understand what is meant by someone. Jensen and Chilberg (1991) and Rees (1991) suggest some guidelines which will help in active listening. Some of those are: avoid distractions; use eye contact, head nodding and attentive posture to show that you are listening; do not interrupt and avoid thinking ahead to what you are going to say. Particularly the latter is rather difficult for many people. Listening means that you do not talk (some people tend to forget this obvious logic) and do not think of what you are going to say as soon as you might get a chance, because the other person has to take a breath. An effective way to accomplish reflective listening is to ask questions and reflecting back what you (think you) have heard by sentences such as: 'so, what you are saying is . . .' or 'you mean that . . .'. These sentences have to be stated in a neutral way. They have the sole purpose to check whether you understood what was said. They are not meant to place any values on what was said by someone. As stated previously this skill is not to be used as a trick. On the contrary, it has to be supported by the right attitude: empathy and a real interest in the ideas and opinions of others. If you develop an inquiry attitude you will almost certainly and automatically be an active listener, because you will really become curious about another person's views and opinions.

Active listening and asking questions are also important from the point of view of getting the group into a reflective thinking mode. Be sure that you as a facilitator do not provide answers to your own questions, nor ask questions with an implied answer. Active listening is also critical from the point of view of building commitment. People in groups very rarely listen carefully to someone else, while at the same time each of us likes to be listened to very much. If you are a good listener you will find that you almost automatically build some kind of rapport during discussion.

The Role of Voting in Decision Making Groups: An Aside

Some people argue that open communication and promoting conflict is too time consuming and, if there are differences of opinion which cannot be resolved quickly, it is best to resort to voting as a means of arriving at a decision. Although this might seem right at first sight, the results of empirical research allow a more balanced appraisal.

Laboratory studies have indicated that majority vote does not necessarily lead to faster decision making (Hall and Watson, 1971; Tjosvold and Field, 1983). Tjosvold and Field (1983) showed that voting only leads to faster decisions under a competitive social context, while under cooperative conditions a consensus approach produced the fastest decisions. In the cooperative social context, subjects were instructed to work for mutual benefit and a solution which was best for all. In the competitive condition subjects were instructed to try to win and to demonstrate the superiority of their solutions to others. Within these two conditions some groups were instructed to apply a consensus decision making approach while other groups had to employ a voting procedure. The authors concluded: 'Taken together, these results suggest that the complaint that consensus decision making is time consuming and frustrating holds more when persons try to compete and outdo each other than when they work for mutual benefits.' (Tjosvold and Field, 1983, 505). These latter results, by the way, are remarkably similar to the ones that were found under cognitive conflict in groups. Substantive conflict also proved to be most beneficial under cooperative conditions.

Not only is it questionable whether majority vote leads to faster decision making, frequently decisions under majority vote prove inferior to decisions made under consensus conditions. (See for instance, Barnlund (1959), Burleson, Levine and Samter (1984), Hall and Watson (1971), Holloman and Hendrick (1972), and Nemiroff and King (1975)). Holloman and Hendrick for instance systematically compared five decision making processes. Among these were consensus decision, majority vote and consensus decision after majority vote. (In the latter case the group first takes a vote on an issue and subsequently tries to arrive at a consensual decision). The results of the study clearly revealed that majority vote was inferior to both consensus and consensus after majority vote. Consensus after majority vote proved most superior.

The question might be raised why decisions made under majority vote are inferior and frequently not faster than consensus decisions. In one of the previous sections we have already indicated that voting is frequently used in situations in which the effectiveness of the group process is below its potential. Thus ineffective group process produces win-lose stalemates leading to loss of time which is compensated by voting to reach a timely decision (Hall and Watson, 1971; Nemiroff and King, 1975). In other words it might not be voting which produces lower quality decisions, but rather we might be confronted with a spurious correlation. It might be the ineffective group process which produces both low quality decisions and frustration (and loss of time) which is compensated for by taking a vote on the issue.

There is one other aspect which is important when discussing voting in small groups. Although one might be inclined to believe that voting may sometimes lead to faster decisions this speed may be bought at the cost of commitment with the decision. If majority vote actually means that 51% is in favour and 49% is against the basis for the decision is indeed very small. Whether commitment is built seems to depend primarily on the decision making process and whether group members have the feeling they have had a chance to express their opinion and whether this opinion is taken seriously. The experiment by Tjosvold and Field (1983) discussed above, also revealed that commitment with the decision was highest in the groups which employed a consensus approach (as opposed to a voting procedure), regardless of whether the social context was cooperative or competitive.

In short, empirical research strongly suggests that voting is not always the fastest and most effective way to make a decision. It seems that voting is best used if a group is really unable to reach a consensual decision. This will prove necessary every now and then in almost all groups. However, if a group frequently resorts to majority vote, the question might be whether this is not the result of an ineffective group process. From the point of view of group model-building this also means that the facilitator best attempts to avoid taking votes on an issue or a decision. It is far more effective to try to improve the group's process effectiveness by increasing the quality of communication.

Concentration Skills

As a facilitator, you must be able to fully concentrate on the discussion in the group. In general, discussions have the tendency to go off in all kind of directions (Jensen and Chilberg, 1991). Not only do you have to ask questions, you also have to keep track of the flow of the discussion in relation to the original problem as well as the model which is built. This is done by continuously relating the ongoing discussion to the model under construction. It is not a problem if the discussion gets off target every once in a while. But it is your task as a facilitator to get the discussion back on track by relating it to the model. In order to accomplish this, you can interrupt the discussion, have people take a look at the model, ask them how to proceed with the model or how this discussion relates to what has already been modelled.

Not only do you have to keep the group on track by returning to the model continuously, you will also have to keep in mind the original problem for which the model is built. In other words, every now and then you will have to direct the group's attention to the original problem formulation in order to check whether the model is heading in the right direction. As every experienced modeller knows, model-building is not a linear but rather a cyclical process (Randers, 1980). The discussion in the group should reflect this cyclical process. The discussion may proceed through the same point several times provided that this leads to a more profound understanding of the issues being discussed. As Morris (1966) found, the more difficult the task the more repetitions in the group discussion. Questioning what has been said before is never wrong, because first thoughts on tough issues are not by definition the best thoughts. Questioning also reinforces the reflective mode in the group.

In summary, one might say that in the group process there are two important cycles which have to be covered by the facilitator. The micro cycle goes from discussion to model to discussion to model etc. The macro cycle goes from model to problem to model to problem (see also Morecroft, 1988; 1992). Going through these cycles is also important from the point of view of ownership of the model. You as a facilitator have to make sure that the group owns the model. This can only be established by including ideas of the group members (not your own ideas) and continually checking whether the model helps to solve the problem.

In order to help the group keep track of the discussion and thinking process it is important to summarize parts of the discussion in relation to the model. In addition, it is important that every once in a while you summarize what has been done by the group, contrast this with the original plan, and prepare the next steps in the discussion. As stated, this is necessary to keep the group on target. By the way, if you as a facilitator seem to lose track of the direction of the discussion, remember not to try to cover up and to be defensive. It might be more productive to have the group try to answer the question! Sometimes, it is also useful to take a little break so that you can consult your colleague or the recorder to make a summary and plan the subsequent steps for the discussion.

Team Building Skills

There is a difference between a group and a team. Teams are in general more cohesive. In teams there is an open, informal atmosphere, and mutual acceptance and understanding between team members. Although disagreement frequently occurs, the group is not uncomfortable with this (Dyer, 1977). As opposed to groups, teams have a common goal or mission which they want to accomplish. When it comes to team building, the first step for a group facilitator is to encourage all members to participate, i.e. to state their ideas, to ask questions, etc. Many meetings are characterized by the fact that the 'real' discussions take place outside the actual meeting. One reason for this is that in the meeting participants do not get a chance to voice their ideas, either because they do not feel safe enough to do so or simply because the group is large. In normal group discussions, the larger the group the more skewed the distribution of speaking time among participants. This is not necessarily wrong, but as a facilitator you have the task to continually invite people to participate in the discussion. This is important from the point of view of ownership of the model and commitment with the solutions for the problem. Sometime during a discussion you may see from the face of certain persons that they do not agree with parts of the model, but they do not get a real chance to air their opinion. If you think you notice this, it is important to ask this person what he or she thinks of the model, because if you don't, you will run the risk of 'losing' this individual or worse, if the person does not get a chance to show his or her disagreement, he or she might not support the plan later on. In other words, keep the group together and take people's objections serious and have them discussed by the group. Your task as a facilitator is to create a safe environment in which people have the feeling that they can air their opinions and that these will be given serious consideration. This will in turn encourage people to participate.

In addition, you will have to keep the group focused on the model and the problem which it tackles. This will create a common purpose, i.e. constructing the model and thereby improve understanding of the problem and potential courses of action. In that sense you will also have to take care that you create a 'we' feeling. Be involved in the group process. Employ 'we' sentences which foster team building: do *we* (rather than you) really understand how this works; did *we* model this aspect sufficiently; do *we* agree on this, etc. Also, in the case of personalized conflicts, try to depersonalize these by focusing on the problem and using yourself as a 'lightning-conductor'. For instance, if someone is attacked by the group for uttering a 'bad' idea you might say: I don't understand, why is this such a bad idea? In this case you will help the person who is attacked by giving him or her support and lift this person from his or her solitary position. This will help people to state deviant opinions more easily, which will in turn create cognitive conflict and enhance the quality of the analysis. Remember the experiments performed by Asch (1963), which were discussed in Chapter 1. Subjects in these experiments were placed in small groups, of which all members but one were confederates. They had to indicate which of three lines on a card matched a standard line on another card. The results of these experiments showed that a large proportion of people tended to concur with the opinion of the majority. However, when for instance in a group of four there were not three confederates, but only two who gave the wrong answer while one provided the correct answer, the percentage of people who provided the correct answer increased drastically. In other words, having one partisan in the group as opposed to none seems to make a large difference.

Skills to Build Consensus and Commitment

Frequently, the primary objective of group model-building is not to provide *the* correct analysis and *the* optimal solution. Sometimes consensus and commitment are more important as we have seen in the first chapter. An important factor to create consensus is to give each individual a chance to participate in the discussion. Korsgaard, Schweiger and Sapienza (1995) have demonstrated that in management teams where the leader solicits opinions of group members and takes the team members' inputs seriously, commitment with the decision will be created even when a person does not agree with the final decision. In general, the more people in the group have the feeling that their opinion is heard and considered seriously in the final decision making process, the easier consensus and commitment is created. If the facilitator succeeds in creating a situation in which everyone has the feeling that they had a fair chance to voice their opinion, consensus almost automatically materializes during the process (see also Senge, 1990). And as Schein (1969) has pointed out, consensus might be the best way to reach a decision, because it will also foster commitment with the decision. Vennix, Akkermans and Rouwette (1996) have pointed out that this might be the result of a similarity between the subjective norms of group members. In Ajzen's well-known theory of planned behaviour (Ajzen, 1991) a distinction is made between three factors which affect the intention to perform a specific behaviour: a person's attitude towards the behaviour in question, the subjective norm and the perceived behavioural control. The attitude towards the behaviour is the degree to which a person has a favourable or unfavourable appraisal of the behaviour in question. Perceived behavioural control refers to a person's perception of his ability to perform a particular behaviour. The subjective norm consists of the likelihood that important referents approve or disapprove of performing a behaviour (strength of the normative belief) combined with the person's motivation to comply with these referents (evaluation of the belief). Stated differently, the more the important referents approve of a specific behaviour and the more a person is inclined to succumb to these referents' opinions, then the more likely it is that a person will demonstrate the behaviour in question. If we assume that the group in question contains many important referents for each group member, then the higher the level of consensus on what behaviour is desired, the higher the similarity between each group member's subjective norms and the higher the intention to show a specific behaviour, i.e. commitment with the behaviour. In other words, consensus breeds commitment. Hence, an important task for a facilitator is to test consensus in the group at regular intervals during the group deliberations.

Apart from consensus (which fosters commitment) it is also important to conduct the model-building sessions in such a way that the model is being owned by the group. If this is the case then this will reinforce commitment to the course of action. From the point of view of ownership, it is important to involve the group as much as possible in the model-building process. On various occasions I have experienced that during a model-building session managers step forward in order to start restructuring the model and (partially) take over my role. These are the moments that I step back and let things run their own way, because during these moments the client is really owning the model. I know this might prove difficult for many consultants, because this is as Keltner (1989) points out one of the paradoxes of facilitation: by teaching the group how to help itself, the facilitator essentially eliminates his own role and some people do not like this idea. (If you have difficulties when people take over your role, then it might be good to ask yourself the question why you like to facilitate groups anyway.)

As a facilitator you should not take the fact that people take over as an offense. On the contrary, you are accomplishing what a good facilitator should accomplish: the group starts helping itself! In other words the more the group gets involved in the model-building process and the better the model represents the problem, the higher the resulting commitment will be.

Intervention Skills

Intervention skills in the context of group model-building generally relate to participation in the discussion by various team members. When discussing team-building skills, I have pointed out that the facilitator has to invite all group members to participate in the group's deliberations. A facilitator's efforts to equal participation among group members can be seriously thwarted by so-called problem people in the group. Both Doyle and Straus, and Krueger discuss the issue of problem people. The most difficult persons are the dominant talker, the shy participant and the rambler (Krueger, 1988).

Particularly for the inexperienced facilitator, these type of people can be difficult to handle without appropriate intervention plans. According to Schein (1987) there are four types of intervention tactics, i.e. exploratory, diagnostic, action alternative and confrontive interventions (Schein, 1987). Exploratory interventions encourage a person to go on talking, to tell more. Diagnostic interventions aim at getting the client to think about something (e.g. questions like: what goes on in this meeting? how do you think I could be helpful?). Action alternative interventions focus on questions related to what can be done about something. Finally, confrontive interventions directly focus on a person's own behaviour (for instance: 'John, why don't you shut up and give other people a chance to talk?'). Of the four intervention tactics mentioned by Schein, the confrontive intervention is the most difficult and dangerous, because its results can hardly be predicted. If the person in question loses face he might try to make up for this later in the discussion. Schein suggests that this type of confrontive intervention should only be used when the other three do not produce the desired effects. There are several other ways to deal with dominant talkers or ramblers. One is the use of techniques such as NGT. Another way is to ask clarifying questions. This is particularly useful in case of the rambler who does a lot of irrelevant talking. A very powerful way of stopping a rambler or dominant talker in a group model-building process is to ask this person how his remarks fit into the model. This will help to put this person to silence, while such a question is not really experienced as being confrontive.

Frequently, the shy person or the avoider is much more difficult to handle. In this case too, the use of techniques like NGT will give these people opportunities to state their ideas and opinions. But often the facilitator will have to create an atmosphere in which these people are invited to participate more fully, because they have the feeling that ideas are not evaluated prematurely and are taken seriously. On the other hand, one has to be careful not to force people to air their views. Some people just talk less than others. What is important is that when you as a facilitator notice that these people want to contribute to the discussion you will provide them immediately with a chance to do so.

Handling Types of Cognitive Tasks

A very robust outcome of much small group research is that the characteristics of the task which a group faces is an important determinant of both group interaction patterns and performance (Deutsch, 1951; Morris, 1966; Hackman and Vidmar, 1970). In addition, it seems that determinants of group performance vary over different group tasks (Milliken and Vollrath, 1991). Psychologists specializing in cognitive processes have commonly distinguished between a limited number of general types of tasks. Hackman distinguished between three different types of intellectual tasks: production, problem solving and discussion. Production is a task in which images or ideas have to be generated. Problem solving is concerned with implementation of ideas and involves the development of action plans. Discussion tasks relate to dealing with issues (Hackman, 1968; Hackman and Morris, 1975; Morris 1966). Laughlin (1980) separated intellective tasks from decision tasks. Intellective tasks have a demonstrable correct answer. Examples include mathematical problems, 'Eureka' type of problems, and estimating tasks (e.g. estimating the length of the river Nile). In contrast, decision making tasks do not have a demonstrably correct answer but rather these have a preferred or an agreed upon answer. Most decisions that are made in organizations are of this type. There is no way to determine the absolute correctness of the decision. Rather, 'correctness' of the decisions is determined by the group (Hart, 1985).

The process of constructing a system dynamics model involves a wide variety of activities and cognitive tasks. These range from generating variables to be included in the model, to identifying feedback structure, to establishing system boundary, to evaluating model output, to name only a few. In terms of the tasks distinguished above two types of tasks stand out in the context of group model-building, i.e. generating information (e.g. producing variables to be included in the model) and evaluating information in order to make a choice (e.g. deciding which variables to include in the model, or evaluating the output of the model). Below I will present some results of empirical research with regard to these two task types, which may be helpful to the group model-building facilitator.

Generating Information. Most research in the area of creativity has been conducted with regard to brainstorming. Brainstorming is a technique in which the production of ideas (i.e. ideation) is sharply separated from their evaluation. Osborn (1957) claimed that separating ideation from evaluation would increase both the number of ideas and their quality. Since its inception in 1957, brainstorming has been the subject of a large number of laboratory experiments to examine these claims. Two types of research questions have dominated the scene. The first question focuses directly on Osborn's claim: do brainstorming groups produce more and better ideas than non-brainstorming groups? With regard to this question research indicates that groups working under conditions in which ideation is separated from evaluation indeed produce more and better ideas than groups in which these two processes are combined. In other words, separating the production of ideas from their evaluation, as is the rule in brainstorming, produces more and higher quality ideas. For evidence of the positive effects of postponing evaluation see: Brilhart and Jochem (1964), Maier and Thurber (1969), Parnes and Meadow (1959), Collins and Guetzkow (1964).

It is also claimed that brainstorming in a group will produce more ideas than individual brainstorming because through interaction in the group people will build on each other's ideas. This claim has also spawned a host of laboratory experiments. In these experiments interacting brainstorming groups are compared with nominal (i.e. non-interacting) brainstorming groups. In the latter case the results of the individual brainstorming are pooled by the investigator to create the group result. Contrary to what one would expect, these experiments have revealed that nominal groups tend to produce more ideas (and frequently better quality ideas) than interacting groups. (For evidence on the superiority of nominal groups in brainstorming see: Dunnette, Campbell and Jaasted (1963), Vroom, Grant and Cotton (1969), Bouchard (1972a, 1972b), Lamm and Trommsdorf (1973), Graham (1977), Jablin (1981), Diehl and Stroebe (1987, 1991)). As was pointed out in the section on group size, larger groups yield diminishing returns (Gibb, 1951) and large nominal groups tend to produce more ideas than large interacting groups (Bouchard and Hare, 1970).

Three main causes of this productivity loss have been identified, i.e. social inhibition, social loafing and production blocking. The first factor refers to a person's apprehensiveness to express his or her ideas in a group. It is supposed that in groups people are hesitant to air their ideas, because others might disapprove of them (Jablin, Seibold and Sorenson, 1977). Social loafing refers to free-riding: once working in groups some people tend to become inactive and leave the work to be done by others. This phenomenon tends to increase in significance in larger groups. Finally, production blocking means that it is the brainstorming process itself which blocks persons to express their ideas, since only one person can talk at a time and people obviously do not use waiting time effectively (Stroebe and Diehl, 1994). Again, contrary to what one would expect, experiments have revealed that production blocking is primarily responsible for the production loss in brainstorming groups (Diehl and Stroebe, 1987, 1991). The latter conclusion seems to be corroborated by experiments with electronic brainstorming devices. In computer supported brainstorming participants are in a position to continuously type in ideas and are not blocked by the fact that only one at a time can talk. Cooper, Gallupe and Bastianutti (1990) have shown that electronically supported brainstorming groups perform equally well, or even better than nominal groups without computer support.

In the light of this overwhelming evidence of the relative ineffectiveness of the brainstorming technique in interacting groups, it is strange that the technique is still being employed frequently in today's organizations. This becomes even more strange since research has also indicated that ideas developed in interacting brainstorming groups are not accepted more readily than those developed in nominal groups (Graham, 1977).

One explanation for the lingering popularity of brainstorming might be the illusion of group effectivity. In retrospect, participants of nominal and interacting brainstorming groups were asked to indicate which of the list of ideas were (a) suggested by themselves (b) suggested by someone else but had also occurred to them, and (c) suggested by other group members and had not occurred to them. The largest discrepancy between nominal and interacting groups was found in the second category, i.e. participants in interacting brainstorming groups typically claim that a large proportion of the ideas suggested by others had also occurred to them during the session. In addition, it seems that people in interacting groups seem more satisfied than individuals in nominal groups (Stroebe and Diehl, 1994).

In the context of facilitating group model-building one may conclude that, if productivity is important, the cognitive task of generating information can best be done by individuals in isolation (e.g. at their office) or in nominal groups. If interacting groups are employed it seems wise to keep these as small as possible.

Evaluative Tasks. While interaction during the idea generation phase is dysfunctional it seems to promote a group's performance when evaluating complex situations (Hall, Mouton and Blake, 1963; Vroom, Grant and Cotton, 1969; Hart et al., 1985).

In this category of evaluative tasks, psychologists have made a distinction between judgement and choice. Quantitative judgement involves estimating the value of a parameter (e.g. the height of a person, or the value of a parameter in model-building). Choice on the other hand involves the selection from a set (e.g. which variables to include in the model, or which sensitivity or policy runs to conduct).

When it comes to judgement one might be inclined to think that two heads are better than one. Indeed, early research confirmed this notion (Gordon, 1924). Stroop (1932) however, demonstrated that this is a statistical rather than a social phenomenon. Pooling the estimates of group members to form the group's judgement increases group performance when individual estimates are unbiased and as a result individual estimates involve random error (Farnsworth and Williams, 1936; Einhorn, Hogarth and Klempner, 1977). In addition, the larger the group the better the accuracy of the judgement. But, although pooling individual estimates into a group average might improve group performance, research has also revealed that groups have been found to perform under the level of their best member, i.e. the member with the most accurate judgement (Miner, 1984). This is particularly true when there is systematic bias in the individual estimates (Einhorn, Hogarth and Klempner, 1977). In order to increase the accuracy of group judgement the problem is then to identify the best member in the group. Research results on this issue are mixed. Miner (1984) demonstrated that four person groups were unable to correctly identify their best member, while Henry (1993) found that in three person groups selection of the best member by group members by far exceeded chance expectation.

When in group model-building the group might for instance have to estimate a model's parameter and the group is capable of identifying the expert in the group it seems wise to take this person's estimation as the group's quantitative judgement. When the group is unsure about who their 'best member' is, research seems to indicate that judgement is best done in interacting groups provided that individuals first make their own individual estimates before a discussion and subsequent group decision (Miner, 1984; Sniezek and Henry, 1990). Sniezek and Henry also show that in this case commitment with the group decision is higher than if a group decision process is started without prior individual estimation. In addition, carefullly facilitating the group will assist in improving the accuracy of the estimate (Reagan-Cirincione, 1994).

I do have to point out however that the task of finding an accurate value of a model parameter is less critical than a number of other estimation tasks. Once a group establishes a parameter value this group's estimate will have to be implemented in the model and evaluated on its accuracy based on the subsequent model's output. In other words, the group will receive some kind of feedback on the acceptability of their estimate and can subsequently adjust the value of the parameter if deemed necessary.

Next to estimation, the other task in evaluation involves choice, i.e. the selection from a set of alternatives. If the choice has to be made on the basis of one criterion only, matters are uncomplicated. If price is the criterion, then, unless one wants to spend a great deal of money, one just selects the cheapest alternative. Most choice situations, however, involve multiple criteria on which to evaluate a choice. For instance in the context of group model-building a policy may have to satisfy several criteria simultaneously. The policy has to: decrease unemployment, not increase the budget deficit, not increase wage costs etc. Generally, the evaluation of policies with the simulation model is conducted in an intuitive way. Several policies are simulated and compared with regard to their efficacy on these multiple criteria. No official and explicit weights are given to the criteria to calculate the scores for each of the policies. A more formal evaluation of policy alternatives would involve the application of Multi Attribute Utility Decision making (von Winterfeldt and Edwards, 1986). Special software is available with which the evaluation and choice of policies can be conducted in a flexible manner. A full discussion of the use of this technique in the context of group model-building is beyond the scope of this book. For examples of the application of multi criteria decision analysis to the selection of the best policy the reader is referred to Gardiner and Ford (1980) and Reagan-Cirincione et al. (1991).

SUMMARY

This chapter has discussed the role of the group facilitator in the context of group model-building. I have started by indicating what facilitation is and why it is important. The facilitator focuses on method, procedure and process in order to increase the quality of the group's deliberations. An important insight is that the facilitator does not just bring techniques to the process, but also him- or herself. The group interaction process is to a large extent determined by the facilitator's behaviour, which is in turn a function of his or her attitudes. I have discussed a number of important attitudes: a helping attitude, authenticity and integrity, an enquiry attitude, and neutrality. Apart from the right attitudes, specific skills are required: process structuring, conflict handling, communication, concentration, team-building, interventions skills, and skills to handle types of cognitive tasks and to build consensus and commitment. Each of these have been discussed in detail, together with important insights from the small group process literature. With regard to group size for instance, we can conclude that larger groups will decrease member satisfaction. Although there is no clear evidence that smaller groups produce higher quality decisions than larger groups, when groups become larger it is wise to introduce more structure in the group communication process. However, solely relying on methods and procedures to enhance group performance can be misleading. Communication and decision making procedures must be employed in order to increase a group's vigilance, which in turn will affect the quality of the decision. Defensive communication will lower group performance and the quality of the discussions. Open, supportive communication needs to be fostered. This is an important task for the facilitator.

One way to increase vigilance in the group is to introduce cognitive conflict. Suppressing differences of opinion and concurrence seeking may lead to groupthink-like phenomena and deteriorate decision quality. On the other hand, if differences of opinion arise continuously and no common ground can be established then there might be no decision at all. In this case too the group facilitator will have to try to find an optimal level of group conflict. Not only the amount of conflict but also the way a conflict is handled will affect the group process and decision quality. An integrative conflict resolution style will enhance decision quality, while a distributive style will decrease it.

As pointed out, the facilitator's skills need to be embedded in the right attitudes in order to be effective. In that sense, the facilitator frequently determines, to a large extent, the success of the project. The messier the problem, and the higher the level of conflict in the group, the more critical the role of the facilitator. This will be demonstrated in the examples discussed in the next chapters. These chapters will integrate a number of the insights discussed in the previous chapters. They will demonstrate the process of group model-building in action. In addition they will also demonstrate the suitability of a couple of special group process techniques (i.e. NGT and delphi) in the context of group model-building.

Chapter 6

Group Model-building in Action: Qualitative System Dynamics

INTRODUCTION

The previous chapters have focused on a number of ingredients which are required for group model-building. In this and the following chapters we will shift our attention to actual examples of group model-building projects. Selection of cases is restricted by the fact that some projects are confidential. From non proprietary projects I have selected three group model-building projects for description. They have deliberately been chosen in such a way that a variety of approaches is demonstrated, in order to give the reader an idea of the range of possibilities with group model-building approaches and to stimulate creativity. (For more examples on group model-building the reader is referred to: Morecroft and Sterman (1994), Andersen and Richardson (1994), Lane (1993), Akkermans (1995) and the special issue of *System Dynamics Review* (Vennix, Richardson and Andersen, forthcoming).)

As I have pointed out in Chapter 4, no two group model-building projects are the same. Each project will have to be tailor-made to the specific client needs and adapted to the constraints of the particular case. In addition, the discussion of the three cases and the learning that took place in the teams show the unpredictability of (a) the actual outcomes of a group model-building process, and (b) the moment when these outcomes will occur during the process. As an introduction to the chapters I will give a short description of each of the cases below.

In the first case the primary purpose proved to be consensus building with regard to a course of action on a support programme for the Dutch commercial fleet. This case was introduced in the opening of the first chapter of the book. In this project there was a clear conflict of opinions and interests. A qualitative system dynamics model was developed with a group of nine people, which led to a consensual decision where previously the group had grappled uselessly with this issue for over a year. As I have pointed out in Chapter 1, in this project there was no time for preparatory interviews. The whole project consisted of three sessions of three hours each and took about six weeks to complete. The model-building process was started from scratch with the group. To structure the sessions use was made of a modified version of the Nominal Group Technique.

The focus in the second case was on providing more insight concerning the health care cost problem from a system dynamics point of view. The reader may recall from the first chapter that the health care insurance organization had originally embarked on a policy to try to reduce referral rates in order to cut health care costs. However, potential side-effects of this policy were largely ignored. A qualitative system dynamics model was built in order to increase systemic understanding in the organization. Because of the complexity of the health care system and in order to build a basis for decision making a large group of participants was invited to participate in the process. Due to this large group the group model-building process had to be highly structured. Use was made of a Delphi approach because of the geographical dispersity of group members and the limited time that participants had available. This project will demonstrate in detail the development of a preliminary model from document analysis and the use of questionnaires and workbooks in group model-building.

In the third case, which will be discussed in the next two chapters, we will turn our attention to the problem of housing associations in the Netherlands. In the past housing associations used to be subsidized by the Dutch government. For some time however, these associations have had to operate independently from the Dutch government in a free market. One of the umbrella organizations of these housing associations felt the need to design a quantitative system dynamics model in order to explore the chances of survival of Dutch housing associations under the new situation. In this case the initial number of people who helped to design the system dynamics model was quite small varying from three to five over the sessions. There was a moderate level of conflict about the goals to be studied with the model, some wanting to concentrate on the problems of financial continuity, and others on the problem whether associations would be able to maintain their social objectives.

The three projects differ on a number of important characteristics. These have been summarized in Table 6.1.

The first two projects primarily employ qualitative system dynamics, while the housing association project employs a quantitative model. In addition, there is a difference in the number of participants and, as a consequence, in the structure of the project. The health care project needed to be highly structured because of the large number of participants, the Dutch fleet project because of the high level of conflict, while the housing project was conducted with a relatively small group and a moderate level of cognitive conflict. Because of the large number of participants and the limited time available for participants, the health care project also employed a preliminary model.

Project time also differs considerably between projects, the Dutch fleet project requiring only six weeks and three sessions, while the health care project took over a year to complete. The latter was partially due to the delphi rounds which take time to finish. Questionnaires and/or workbooks were employed in all three projects, albeit in different ways and forms. Finally, in all projects the project team consisted of one or more model-builders and one or two persons from the client organization acting as the gatekeeper.

Table 6.1 Primary Differences Between the Group Model-building Projects

Characteristics	Project		
	Dutch fleet	Health care	Housing association
Number of participants	Middle (10)	High (20–60)	Low (3–6)
Level of cognitive conflict	High	Low	Moderate
Quantification and simulation	No	No	Yes
Total project time	Six weeks	One year	Six months
Preliminary model	No	Yes	No
Questionnaires/workbooks	Yes	Yes	Yes
Group process technique	NGT based	Delphi based	Facilitated freely interacting group
Project group: modellers + gatekeeper	2 + 1	2 + 2	2 + 1

This chapter will focus on the first two projects in which qualitative system dynamics was applied. I will start the discussion with the case of the Dutch Shipping and Maritime Affairs with which the book opened in the first chapter.

MODELLING THE DUTCH FLEET: THE NOMINAL GROUP TECHNIQUE

From the first chapter the reader may recall that, during a demonstration session at the Department of Transportation and Public Works I was approached by two members of the strategic staff of the Directorate General for Shipping and Maritime Affairs (DGSM) with the request if I was interested in conducting a couple of model-building sessions for the Long Term Strategy Group of DGSM. According to these two people, the issue to be modelled was related to the Dutch-registered merchant fleet. For economic reasons many shipowners had decided to resort to so-called 'flags of convenience'. In the past the Dutch government had financially supported the commercial fleet, but because of its relative ineffectiveness the secretary of Transportation, Public Works and Water management (DTPW) was contemplating ceasing this financial support. Since this decision was fast approaching there was no time to conduct any preparatory interviews and hence it was decided to plan three sessions with a group of about nine people. As pointed out in Chapter 1, it was agreed that after three sessions the situation would be evaluated and a decision would be made whether to continue model-building or not. To further speed up the model-building process the three sessions would be interspersed with workbooks. Normally these workbooks are designed by the project group (as will be seen in the next case), but in this case one of my two spokespersons, who acted as the Long Term Strategy Group's secretary, took care of this. This person also acted as a gatekeeper during the project (Richardson and Andersen, 1995; Eden and Simpson, 1989).

The reader will also remember that during the first session it became clear that there were sharp differences of opinion within the organization on the question of whether to support the commercial fleet. However, I was largely unaware of this before the first session and I thus planned this first session to include a short introduction on system dynamics and to start with a modified version of the Nominal Group Technique.

The Nominal Group Technique for Group Model-building

The Nominal Group Technique (NGT) is a procedure to generate and evaluate a number of ideas on an issue with a group of persons joining together in a session. As we have seen in the previous chapter, idea generation can best be done in a nominal group mode. Hence, in NGT the stage of idea generation is strictly separated from the evaluation of ideas. The process consists of the following steps (Delbecq, Van de Ven and Gustafson, 1975):

1. individuals silently write down ideas;
2. ideas are listed in a round-robin fashion on a flip chart;
3. each idea on the list is discussed for clarification and evaluation;
4. individual rank-ordering or rating of ideas and voting.

The group decision is mathematically derived from the voting procedure in the final step. Empirical studies have shown that NGT groups outperform interacting and delphi groups and would thus be useful in group model-building to improve group performance. (For evidence on the superiority of NGT see Gustafson et al. (1973), Van de Ven and Delbecq (1974), Rohrbaugh (1981), and Reagan-Cirincione (1991).) As I have discussed in the previous chapter, voting might leave certain people unsatisfied because they disagree with the decision and cognitive conflict might remain unresolved. In the example presented below, the reader will note that no use is made of voting, primarily because it can be skipped without harming the group model-building process.

Apart from the fact that the voting procedure seems unsatisfactory, NGT primarily focuses on the listing and evaluation of ideas rather than on structuring ideas (Hart et al., 1985). Hence, application of NGT to group model-building is only useful in the first session at the start of the model-building process. As pointed out in the previous chapter, NGT is particularly helpful to get the process started quickly.

The First Session

I started the first session with a brief one hour introduction to system dynamics and group model-building. The presentation was illustrated by an example of a previous project in order to demonstrate to group members what was expected from them and what they in turn could expect from the sessions.

After this short introduction, I initiated the group model-building process by introducing the problem of the declining size of the Dutch-registered merchant fleet. As mentioned in Chapter 1, this produced a heated debate between advocates and opponents. Opponents argued that the focus of DGSM should be shifted towards the other two strategic areas: the Dutch ports and sea traffic at the North Sea. Gradually it became clear to me that there were truly divergent perspectives within the division about its preferred strategy. I have also described in the first chapter that the deadlock was overcome by suggesting to the group that system dynamics model-building would most probably reveal that the three strategic areas were strongly interrelated. This at least temporarily convinced the sceptics and the process was started by modelling the Dutch fleet problem. The decline in the number of ships flying the Dutch flag served as the reference mode of behaviour.

During the discussion I had noted that group members held ideas and opinions which were rather rigid, something which frequently happens when a group is not able to reach a consensual decision. In such cases people generally increase their efforts to convince others of the correctness of their viewpoint (which generally produces the opposite effect). As a result the group had a communication problem: people hardly listened to each other's arguments and made frequent interruptions. The Nominal Group Technique is particularly suited to break through such an ineffective communication pattern. Below I will describe how it can be used in the context of group model-building to start the process. The approach is similar to the one explained in Chapter 4 (Figure 4.2).

After defining the initial problem, participants are invited to generate relevant variables in silence and write these down. After the group has finished this step, the facilitator invites group members in a round-robin fashion to name one variable from their list. Each variable is written on a magnetic hexagon (Hodgson, 1992) and put on a white board (see left hand part of Figure 6.1). (Magnetic hexagons were developed by Hodgson (see Hodgson, 1992) and are distributed by Idon Ltd, Edradour house, Pitlochry, Pertshire, Scotland PH16 5JW.) When no more variables are generated, the facilitator starts building the causal diagram by selecting the problem variable (in this case the 'number of ships flying the Dutch flag') and putting it on a separate white board. Next, he asks participants to identify the causes for increases or decreases in the number of ships by looking at the list of generated variables. These are then transferred to the other white board and built into the diagram as can be seen in the right hand part of Figure 6.1. They show up as incoming arrows for the problem variable. As the reader may understand, not all of the variables are included directly in the model and sometimes new variables can come up during the modelling process which were not mentioned in the 'brainstorming' phase.

Having completed this step, the facilitator then asks the group to consider the consequences of changes in the problem variable, again by looking at the list of variables. These will show in the diagram as arrows 'leaving' the problem variable.

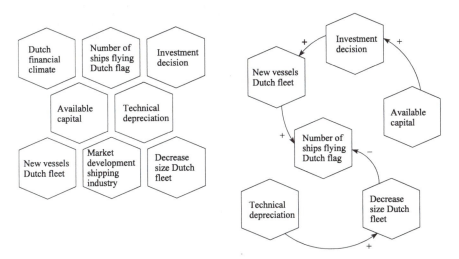

Figure 6.1 Use of Hexagons in NGT Approach to Group Model-building. (Reprinted by permission of Kluwer Academic Publishers)

(Incoming arrows denote causes, while arrows 'leaving' a variable show the consequences of a change in this variable for other variables. See also the explanations in Chapter 4.) Simultaneously, the facilitator invites the group to look for connections between consequences and causes, i.e. consequences which in turn can be considered as causes of the 'original' causes. This will lead to the identification of potential feedback loops. The latter two steps will be illustrated in the next sections, where I will describe the second and third session.

As a consequence of the introduction and the discussion on which problem to model, the actual model-building time in the first session was limited. The session ended with a causal diagram (Figure 6.2) which only identified a number of causes of the decreasing number of ships flying the Dutch flag.

This diagram was sent to the group members with a couple of accompanying tasks in the form of a small workbook. Three tasks had to be performed. First, the participant was asked to further complete the diagram. Second, to indicate which variables represented the most urgent problems for DGSM, and finally to identify potential consequences of a decrease of the Dutch fleet size.

In previous projects I had always had good experiences with workbooks as a means to speed up the model-building process and to prepare participants for the next session (Vennix et al., 1990; Vennix, Akkermans and Rouwette, 1996). Unfortunately, in this case only two out of nine participants reacted to the questions. One of the potential reasons for this lack of cooperation was that people tried to protect their positions by an attempt to postpone or prevent a strategic decision to be taken by the organization. Although the number of reactions was disappointing, I proceeded as normal and added the changes made in the diagrams of the two workbooks to the causal diagram that resulted from the first session. This adapted diagram was taken as a starting point for the second session.

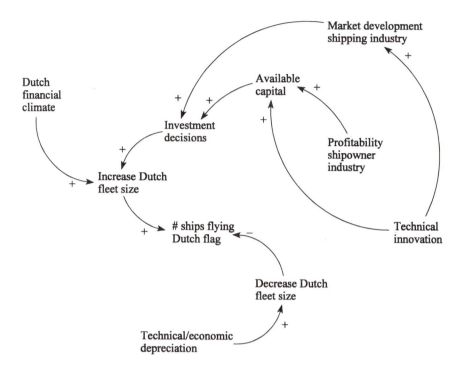

Figure 6.2 Causal Diagram after First Session: Causes of Problem. (Reprinted by permission of Kluwer Academic Publishers)

The Second Session

Another problem was that some people were a little reluctant to participate in the sessions. They did not attend the second session but (at our specific request) sent substitutes. Although this disturbed the process, it also proved beneficial in the longer run because more persons from DGSM got involved in the strategic discussion, often leading to new and fresh perspectives on the matter.

The second session was started with the adapted diagram from the first session. The basic idea was to improve the diagram and in particular to focus on the consequences of the decreasing fleet size. However, one of the substitutes, who was very knowledgeable about the process of investment by shipowners, came up with a more detailed diagram of the investment decision process of shipowners. I invited him to present it to the group. After having discussed his diagram the discussion shifted to the question of the consequences of the decreasing size of the Dutch fleet for the DGSM organization. At this point the discussion waned. Obviously thinking of likely future consequences is more difficult than generating causes of a problem (Russo and Schoemaker, 1989). In order to stimulate thinking about this issue I made the group conduct a 'mental simulation' by asking the following question: 'Suppose that the number of vessels flying the Dutch flag would gradually but

Table 6.2 Potential Effects of a Decrease in the Size of (1) a Dutch Managed Fleet, and (2) Merchant Fleet Flying the Dutch Flag for (a) DGSM and (b) the Maritime Policy Area in General

Decrease in size of	Effects for	
	DGSM organization	Maritime policy area
Dutch managed fleet	• Weaker position within DTPW • Loss of technical/nautical know-how • Smaller organization	• Weaker international influence • Decrease contribution to GNP
Fleet flying the Dutch flag	• Smaller organization • Loss of technical/nautical know-how • Weaker position of DGSM within DTPW • Less 'qualitative' departments • Increase in attention to Dutch ports and Dutch coast	• Decrease contribution to GNP • Weaker position in international maritime organizations • Increase in attention to Dutch ports and Dutch coast • Loss of sailors (with consequences for maritime education) • Loss of technical/nautical know-how

within a few years decrease to zero. What do you think would happen?' (For the concept of 'mental simulation' see Kahneman and Tversky (1982) and Sims (1986).)

This question helped to produce some interesting reactions. It was felt by the group that a distinction had to be made between the effects of no vessels flying the Dutch flag versus no vessels being managed in the Netherlands. In addition, potential effects for DGSM were separated from those for the maritime policy area. A four cell matrix was applied in order to arrange potential consequences as can be seen in Table 6.2.

With regard to the causal diagram only the lower half of the matrix is important, since it shows the potential effects of a sharp decline in the size of the fleet flying the Dutch flag. We started including these potential effects (of the lower half of the matrix) into the diagram. Some of these were rather straightforward and easy to include. Some were more difficult because there was no consensus on them and a couple led to the identification of (what would later prove to be crucial) feedback loops. Rather straightforward were the effects on the number of sailors, the Dutch economy (balance of payments), and the loss of technical know-how. Most of the discussion focused on the effects on the position of DGSM within the Department of Transportation and Public Works (DTPW). Of course this position is determined by all three strategic areas: the size of the ports, maritime traffic at the North Sea and the size of the Dutch fleet. With regard to this latter variable the group was convinced that a sharp decrease in the size of the Dutch-registered merchant fleet would undermine the strength of the position of the division within the department

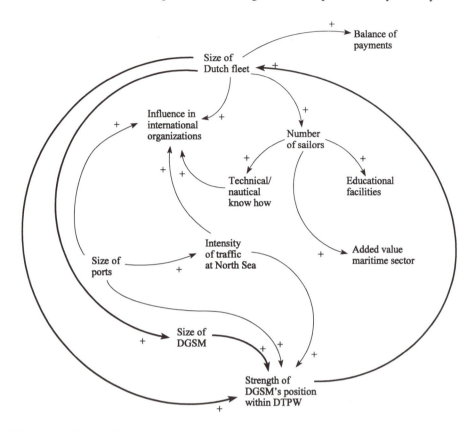

Figure 6.3 Causal Diagram after Second Session: Consequences of Problem. (Reprinted by permission of Kluwer Academic Publishers)

of DTPW. In addition it would decrease the size of DGSM itself which would further reinforce the latter process. The weakened position of DGSM would in turn lead to a further decline of the Dutch fleet, because it was felt that no other agency had the appropriate network nor experience to develop effective policies for it. As a result of these discussions, two positive feedback loops emerged in the diagram as can be seen in Figure 6.3. The loops are indicated by the bold arrows.

This figure is the result of the discussions on the potential *consequences* of a decreasing Dutch fleet size (as opposed to causes in the previous diagram). The two positive feedback loops indicate a self reinforcing process, i.e. a process of a declining fleet will reinforce itself and hence lead to a further reduction in the fleet size. Due to the emergence of these feedback loops the first real doubts arose within the group about abandoning support for the Dutch fleet, since in the long run this might undermine the strength of DGSM within DTPW as well as the influence in international organizations, which in turn might affect the potential to carry out the other two strategic tasks effectively. Although these latter thoughts did not yet neatly materialize in the above diagram it started to dawn in people's minds that the three strategic areas were more closely interrelated than they were previously inclined to believe. For those who were still in doubt this notion would be strongly reinforced in the third session by another feedback loop which was to emerge in the diagram.

The Third Session

One of the effects in the matrix, which had not been discussed in the second session, was the tacitly assumed increase in DGSM's attention to the other two strategic tasks (i.e. ports and coast), once no more attention would have to be given to the Dutch fleet. However, no consensus could be reached on plausible causal links to be put in the causal diagram to support this notion. Quite the contrary. The discussions and the emerging feedback loops were suggesting that the smaller the Dutch fleet the *more difficult* it would be to carry out the other strategic tasks. This conjecture which had already surfaced by the end of the second session was now strongly reinforced by a new feedback loop which emerged in the diagram as a result of the discussions in this third session.

Until 1992, support of the Dutch fleet had primarily been defended because of its direct contribution to the Dutch economy through ship building and repair yards, employment in the ports, training of crews, etc. In the third session, a new notion was added to this argument while discussing the role of the Netherlands in the whole logistical chain of storage, trans-shipment and distribution in Europe. Some people argued that a strong reduction of the number of vessels flying the Dutch flag would in the long run lead to an outflow of a number of shipowners. Without Dutch shipowners the amount of maritime traffic through the Netherlands, and the size of the Dutch transportation sector, would also decline. As a consequence, this would reduce the distribution function of the Netherlands in Europe. This in turn would impede the growth of the Dutch ports, which would then further weaken DGSM's position within DTPW and thus lead to a further decrease in the number of ships flying the Dutch flag and a declining contribution to the Dutch GNP, as can be seen in Figure 6.4. Again the important feedback loops are indicated by bold arrows.

Figure 6.4 contains the final diagram of the potential consequences of a decreasing fleet size as it existed at the end of the third session. From a system dynamics perspective the causal diagram is not really finished. There are for instance several 'open loops'. In addition, no efforts were made to quantify the conceptual model. However, as stated earlier, we had previously agreed that at the end of the third session a decision would be made whether to continue the model-building process. Although some persons agreed with me that the model was not finished, the majority of the group felt that no further sessions were required, a situation which is not uncommon in group model-building, probably because the client group feels that their problem is solved (Lane, 1992; Wolstenholme, 1992).

By the end of the third session three important conclusions stood out. The first was that abandoning support for the Dutch fleet would most probably jeopardize DGSM's position within DTPW. Second, the indirect contribution of the Dutch fleet to the economy by enhancing the Dutch position as a distributor of goods to Europe proved to be far more important (particularly in the future) than its direct

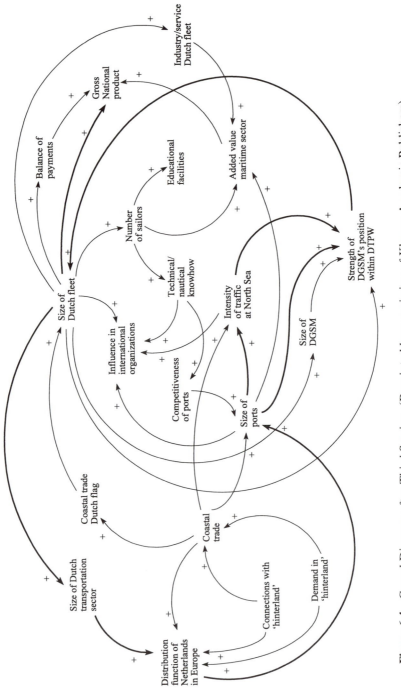

Figure 6.4 Causal Diagram after Third Session. (Reprinted by permission of Kluwer Academic Publishers)

contribution to the economy. Third, without a Dutch commercial fleet it would be hard for the Netherlands to maintain its role in international trade as a distributor of goods for Europe.

These three insights changed several people's minds and helped to create consensus within the Long Term Strategic Group about the appropriateness to try to find ways to continue governmental support for the Dutch fleet. In a sense the whole group was now ready to back up the policy document from the Sea Fleet Policy Unit, which this Unit had initiated at the beginning of 1991.

Results: The Policy Document

What happened to the causal diagrams and how was the strategic decision making process affected? As stated, the diagrams were never revised or neatly redrawn, nor has there ever been an attempt to formalize and quantify the causal model into a full-blown system dynamics simulation model. In parallel with the system dynamics sessions the Long Term Strategic Group was still discussing the structure and contents of the final version of the policy document, which was to be presented to the Secretary to get support for the Dutch fleet. This policy document was published in September 1992, about four months after the last session (DGSM, 1992). Interestingly enough there is also a draft version of this policy document dating back to January 1991, more than one and a half years before. This document was produced by the Sea Fleet Policy Unit but was not supported by the whole DGSM organization as we have seen in the first chapter. It was exactly about this document that no consensus within the Long Term Strategy Group could be reached.

Comparing both policy documents leads to a couple of interesting findings and demonstrates the way the model-building sessions affected the strategic decision making process. As might be expected, the contents of both policy documents largely overlap. However, there are also a couple of significant arguments in the final version which are missing in the draft version. These arguments can, at least in part, be traced back to the discussions in the group model-building sessions and the causal diagrams.

The first is related to the influence of the Netherlands in international maritime organizations. In discussing safety and environmental matters and the role of various international organizations the policy document emphasizes that:

> The strong international character of the maritime sector constrains the possibilities of self regulation by the industry. International organizations, like the International Maritime Organization (IMO) of the United Nations, are required to arrive at international agreements.

> The size of a national fleet determines to a large degree the influence a country can exert on decision making within these organizations. (DGSM, 1992, 7, translation J.V.)

The second is that the final version contains at least six references to the importance of the role of the Netherlands as a distribution country and its importance for the

Dutch economy. It is also clearly argued that this function can only be maintained by means of a Dutch fleet.

> And in particular a modern, high quality Dutch fleet with the shipowner as logistic service agent is of great importance for the further reinforcement of the Dutch distribution function for Europe. (DGSM, 1992, 9.) And:

> For a number of flows of goods the shipowner is the director of the logistical chain. . . . From their role as worldwide carriers they attempt to direct as many flows through the Netherlands as possible, because they also have financial interests in Dutch transshipment and distribution companies. This will strengthen the position of 'Netherlands distribution country' as gateway to Europe. (DGSM, 1992, 10.)

The importance of the latter arguments is reinforced by the fact that these are specifically mentioned by the Secretary in her accompanying letter of the policy document to the Lower Chamber:

> The Netherlands have always been an important maritime trading nation. Shipping is an essential link in 'Holland distribution country'. Strengthening this distribution function can best be accomplished if shipping activities are tied with the Netherlands. In order to accomplish this it is necessary to maintain ships flying the Dutch flag.

In other words, the Secretary, first unwilling to continue support to the Dutch fleet was now arguing that financial support was necessary in order for the Netherlands to be able to fulfil a significant distribution function for Europe. Obviously the arguments produced in the policy document (combined with a lobby of a number of shipowners) had aided in convincing both the Secretary of Finance and DTPW to reconsider their original position to abandon the financial aid programme. This is not to say that they had uncritically changed their mind and were now all of a sudden inclined to provide unlimited support to the Dutch fleet. The Secretary of DTPW also pointed out that in the long run the Dutch fleet ought to be fully competitive and this type of financial support programme had to be made redundant. In order to accomplish this it was also proposed that international agreements had to be negotiated to abolish financial aid programmes in maritime countries in the future. As a result, the policy document suggested to provide financial support for a limited time period of five years.

The policy document was used as a basis for the decision in the Lower and Upper Chambers. Obviously the arguments in the document were also convincing to the members of these two Chambers, because it was decided to agree with a financial support to the Dutch-registered merchant fleet amounting to about dfl. 150 million per year for a limited period of five years.

Project Results

At the end of the process there were at least two tangible results. First, as participants indicated on a questionnaire, there was a high level of consensus and commitment with regard to the strategic choice. Something which was clearly lacking at the beginning of the process. Second, as a result of this, DGSM accomplished to obtain a financial support of dfl. 150 million per year to protect the Dutch fleet.

The interesting question is to what degree and how system dynamics group model-building contributed to this success. (Note: thus far, little empirical research has been conducted to support the claims made by model-builders about the useful functions of models, i.e. learning, communication, building shared vision etc. In the past, I have initiated and supervised a number of PhD studies to study this topic. One related to theoretical and philosophical foundations of GDSS (Scheper, 1991). This study focused among others on the question of shared meaning and the problems associated with its measurement in empirical research. Another study (Verburgh, 1994) replicated my own study on mental models (Vennix, 1990). The major differences between Verburgh's and my own study is that in the latter (a) a system dynamics model was used (as opposed to an econometric model in my study), and (b) real policy makers in health care were involved (as opposed to students). A third study, which I supervised, had a more exploratory character (Akkermans, 1995). A number of participative model-building projects in real world settings were evaluated by means of questionnaires (Vennix, Scheper and Willems, 1993) and interviews with participants in the process. The interested reader is referred to the above literature.) Insight into the above question can be gained because participants who attended at least two sessions were requested to fill out a questionnaire at the end of the project. Participants were asked to indicate their opinion on a number of (five-point) Likert items ranging from strongly agree to strongly disagree. From their answers we may conclude that three factors are responsible for the success of this project.

These three factors partially relate to the most important problems this particular group was facing at the start of the project. The first is that the model-building process produced new and fresh insights in the strategic issues. A sceptic might, for instance, argue that it is hard to imagine that people would not have been aware of the importance of the Netherlands as a distribution country and the fact that shipowners play a role in this process. It would be difficult to deny this. One of the beneficial effects of the group model-building process, however, was that it restructured existing, but scattered, knowledge by putting it in a systemic perspective. It thus revealed relationships between various elements and in that way created new knowledge for the group. Lack of systemic perspective was for instance demonstrated in the discussion in the first session on which problem to select for the model-building sessions. An indication of this can also be found in an answer from one participant to a question in one of the workbooks: 'No, we know almost everything there is to know about this subject, but I have the feeling that we do not interrelate all that we know in an appropriate way'.

Second, the process aided in improving the quality of communication within the group. As stated in the previous chapter low quality communication negatively affects group performance. This is corroberated by this case. The Long Term Strategy Group had discussed their strategic plans for more than a year without making any real progress. Hence, one of the first prerequisites to improve performance within this group was to enhance the quality of group communication. This was accomplished in several ways. First, by the use of structured group process techniques (e.g. NGT). In addition, employing causal diagrams in front of the group creates a visual group memory retaining the flow of the group discussion. The facilitator then fostered an open communication atmosphere by reinforcing supportive and by avoiding defensive communication.

Finally, the group model-building process was successful in fostering consensus and commitment with the final decision. When it comes to commitment three persons agree and two strongly agree that they *fully* stick to the conclusions which were formulated. Two persons agree nor disagree and one person disagrees. In part consensus and commitment were created through the systemic insights gained during the model-building process. The notion that abandoning the Dutch fleet might in the long run have serious repercussions for the whole DGSM organization must have helped to create this consensus.

Commitment is also affected by appropriate facilitation behaviour. Vennix, Scheper and Willems, (1993) evaluated four different group model-building projects, which included this case. Their data suggest that the facilitator is probably the most important factor in creating commitment with the decision. Moreover in all four projects participants indicated that in their opinion, it was the facilitator who contributed most to the overall success of the project. These results are in agreement with other research in the field of Group Decision Support Systems (Bostrom, Anson and Clawson, 1993; Clawson, Bostrom and Anson, 1993). In short, the role of the facilitator can hardly be overestimated, particularly in situations where there is conflict of interest and viewpoint.

Conflict of interest is not a pervasive characteristic of the next project to be described. In the second case the primary problem was the large number of participants to be handled. As I have pointed out in one of the foregoing chapters, the larger the group the more structure needs to be introduced in the process. The next case provides a detailed example of how structure can be provided in a group model-building process.

MODELLING THE HEALTH CARE SYSTEM: A DELPHI BASED APPROACH

In this case the client was a regional Dutch Health Care Insurance Organization (HCIO). As I have described in Chapter 1, the organization had embarked on a policy to reduce referral rates of family doctors in their region. In particular doctors with high referral rates had been approached. As the reader may recall, these doctors had, however, indicated that their high referral rates were caused by a particular composition of their practice population. At that point the organization had approached me and one of my colleagues in order to statistically correct these referral rates. During the first discussion we had with one of the persons of this organization, we could convince him of the fact that their intervention in the health care system might well produce unanticipated side-effects of which they were largely unaware. This discussion alerted the organization of the need to take a system dynamics view to the problem of health care cost reduction. After one more meeting with a group of persons from the organization it was decided to start a model-building project in order to increase insight in the systemic relationships between processes in the health care system.

As mentioned above, the organization was eager to involve a large number of doctors and other people in the process of model-building, partly because their knowledge would be needed, partly because through the process one hoped to build a basis for decision making with regard to the control of health care costs. Because of the large group size a special process was designed to structure the group model-building project. Delphi seemed a promising alternative, because of its iterative nature and design for dispersed groups.

Delphi in the Process of Group Model-building

Delphi was originally designed to reduce the inhibiting effects of interacting groups while at the same time preserving the power of combined knowledge from a group of experts (Dalkey, 1969; Linstone and Turoff, 1975). This is accomplished by an anonymous procedure employing a series of mailed questionnaires. Results of one iteration are fed back to the panel in the next iteration. The number of cycles is limited by a predetermined criterion, e.g. the level of consensus in the panel or stability in the response patterns. Delphi has particularly been employed in technological forecasting. Since the 1970s a number of alternatives emerged. The most well-known of these is the policy delphi, which focuses on structuring policy issues rather than on forecasting (Linstone and Turoff, 1975). An advantage related to delphi is that time investment for participants is about one half to one third when compared to an interacting group or the Nominal Group technique (NGT). This is accomplished at the cost of a doubling in time investment for the delphi administrator (Delbecq, Van de Ven and Gustafson, 1975). This can be prevented by applying a modern version of delphi, embedded in a Group Decision Support System, as was for instance developed by Kenis (1995).

Another advantage of delphi is its iterative character, which matches with the cyclical nature of model-building. However, one has to keep in mind that the conventional forecasting delphi has been harshly criticized by Sackman (1975), among other things, because of methodological deficiencies in questionnaire design, the disproportionate emphasis on consensus and the sloppy execution of most delphi studies. Moreover, when estimation or prediction tasks are involved, most empirical studies have revealed that delphi processes do not outperform interacting groups, although there are counterexamples. (See for instance Gustafson et al. (1973), Fischer (1981), Stewart (1987), Rohrbaugh (1979) and Sniezek (1990). An exception is Sniezek (1989), who found that delphi outperformed a freely interacting group.)

When it comes to idea generation Van de Ven and Delbecq (1974) found that delphi significantly outperformed interacting groups and performed almost as well as the Nominal Group Technique. On the other hand, with regard to satisfaction of participants with the procedure, NGT clearly scored better than both delphi and the interacting group. One reason the authors suggest for the lower level of participant satisfaction is the lack of opportunity for interaction and clarification of ideas in a delphi (see also Nelms and Porter, 1985; Van Dijk, 1990).

In summary, one may conclude that delphi is potentially useful in cases where there is a large number of participants who are geographically dispersed. Its iterative character makes it appropriate for group model-building as well as the fact that it cuts down considerably on the participant's time investment. However, delphi in its original form is not suited because of its completely anonymous character. In order to make group model-building effective in terms of learning it will always need group discussions, in which people can exchange viewpoints. It seems that the best way to apply delphi is as a focusing device in the first stages of group model-building and to conclude with one or more cycles in which participants gather to discuss the model. This approach is also in line with the conclusion that brainstorming tasks can best be done by individuals working at home, since these tasks generally happen in the first stages of model-building.

The Case of the Health Care System

The approach employed in this case was based on the above ideas and consisted of several stages. After a preliminary definition of the policy problem, in the first stage a small project group constructed a preliminary conceptual model based on a review of the relevant literature and insights within the project group (see also Hart et al., 1985). This preliminary model was used as a basis for the second stage in which the actual participation took place. In the first cycle of this second stage a questionnaire is employed. The questionnaire aims at eliciting comments from the participants with regard to the significance of concepts and relationships between concepts employed in the preliminary model. The questionnaire is followed by a so-called workbook in the second cycle. This workbook provides feedback about the results of the questionnaire. In addition, it invites participants to comment on more complex submodels constructed by the project group on the basis of the information generated in the questionnaires. Both the questionnaire and the workbook are filled out by participants working individually at home. In the third cycle a structured workshop concludes the group model-building process. In this workshop participants discuss their comments on the workbook's submodels in more detail. In this sense the first two cycles serve as a focusing function: they identify those elements in the preliminary model on which participants do not agree. In sum, the three cycles lead to considerable adaptation of the preliminary model, which results in a final conceptual model. The above mentioned stages are exhibited in Figure 6.5.

The Policy Problem

The project group consisted of two planners from the Health Care Insurance Organization (HCIO) and two experienced system dynamics modellers. In addition, some five HCIO staff members assisted in assessing the preliminary model, the

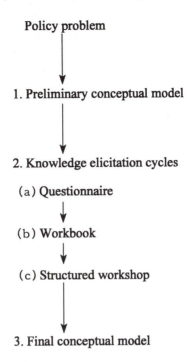

Policy problem

1. Preliminary conceptual model

2. Knowledge elicitation cycles

(a) Questionnaire

(b) Workbook

(c) Structured workshop

3. Final conceptual model

Figure 6.5   Stages in Group Model-building of the Dutch Health Care Project

questionnaire, the workbook and the workshops. The policy problem is related to the gradual but persistent rise in health care costs. From 1968 to 1985 total health care costs in the Netherlands increased from about 6% of the net National Product to about 10% (Grünwald, 1987). The reader will recognize that this rise in health care costs over time served as our reference mode of behaviour (see Chapter 2). The problem definition for the model-building project consisted of three specific questions:

1. What factors have been responsible for the increase in health care costs in the past?
2. How will health care costs develop in the future?
3. What are the potential effects of policy options aimed at reducing these costs?

The above three questions guided the design of the preliminary model by the project group.

The Construction of the Preliminary Conceptual Model

The process of designing the preliminary model was started by a two hour session within the project group in which a flow diagram of the system was constructed. The diagram is shown in Figure 6.6.

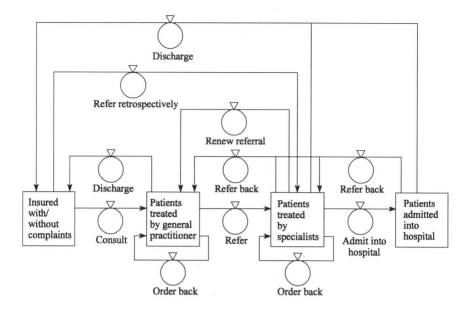

Figure 6.6 Patient's Flow in the Health Care System

Persons with health complaints initially consult their general practitioner (GP), who decides whether a patient:

- has to return (order a patient back); or
- will be referred to a medical specialist; or
- will be discharged.

The medical specialist, in turn, decides whether his patients

- have to return (order back); or
- will be discharged; or
- will get a renewed referral from the general practitioner (which is necessary after one year of treatment by a medical specialist); or
- will be admitted into hospital, and
- when they will be discharged from hospital.

Health care costs for the general practitioner are generated by his decision to perform certain required medical treatments or to prescribe one or more drugs. With regard to medical specialists health care costs are generated by a decision to (re)examine a patient, to apply medical surgery (medical transactions) and/or to prescribe a drug. Most of these decisions have a quantity and a cost component. For instance: the number of prescriptions by a general practitioner or a specialist (quantity) and the price of the drug prescribed (cost).

Table 6.3   Potential Factors Affecting Decisions in Patients' Flow Model

Consultation	Order back GP	Refer to specialist	Order back specialist
• Patient's age • % of women (perceived) • Severity of complaint • Duration of complaint • GP's view of job • GP's view of patients • Urbanization	• Patient's age • Check patients • Chron. disease • GP's workload to be referred	• Patient's age • % women • Chron. disease • Patient's pressure	• Specialist's workload
Admit into hospital	# Prescriptions by GP/specialist	# Medical transactions by specialist	Cost of medical transactions
• Patient's age • Specialist's view of job	• Patient's age • Workload	• Specialist's view of job • Patient's age	• Patient's age • # beds

(Source: adapted from Poppen, 1987)

The next step in the model-building process is to identify a number of factors which affect the decisions discussed above and to include these in the flow model of Figure 6.6. A literature search was carried out and content analysis was employed to find relevant factors and relationships which could be used in developing the preliminary model. Table 6.3 summarizes the results of this literature search.

Interestingly enough as can be seen from the table most studies concentrate on the 'forward' flow process, i.e. consultations, referrals and admissions into hospital. Almost no research was found on factors affecting flow processes in the opposite direction, i.e. discharges from the general practitioner, the medical specialist and from hospital. Hence, we decided to first concentrate on this 'forward' flow process in the construction of the preliminary model. Most of the variables in the table were used in this construction process. Variables which could not be causally related to the decisions of the actors in the system were left out (e.g. urbanization), which is not to say that these could never be incorporated in the model. As we will see in the next section participants are invited to add factors to the preliminary model which they consider important. In this respect it is important to point out that no effort was made by the project group to make this preliminary model perfect, since it primarily served a 'trigger' function to start the group model-building process. It was argued that a 'perfect' preliminary model would hardly be motivating for participants and would most probably not give them a feeling of 'ownership' over the conceptual model. The preliminary model is shown in Figure 6.7. The model shown in this figure served as a basis for the first step in the knowledge elicitation process: the questionnaire.

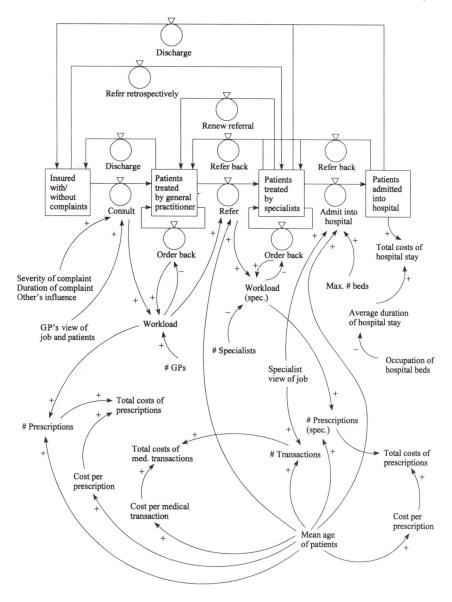

Figure 6.7 Preliminary Conceptual Model

The Questionnaire

To avoid receiving one-sided, biased information we incorporated a variety of persons with different backgrounds. The participants belong to various organizations in three fields, i.e. the health care system (e.g. general practitioners, medical specialists), the policy making system (e.g. planning institutions) and research institutions (e.g. university health care research units). Participants were selected in a two-step procedure. First, relevant organizations were listed. Next within these organizations we identified some 60 potential participants, fairly well spread over the three fields. As stated in Chapter 4, the greatest danger in using a mailed questionnaire is the low response rate. Several precautions were taken to avoid low response. For example, we enclosed with the questionnaire an abstract of an article written on the construction of the preliminary model. In addition, we pointed out to the participants that we needed their expert opinion in order to be able to improve the preliminary model. These precautions paid off. The response rate exceeded 95%, which is very high for a mailed questionnaire. Chapter 4 discussed the use of questionnaires to elicit viewpoints in the context of group model-building and the issue of employing open and closed questions. I stated there that one should first establish the objectives of the questionnaire before designing questions. Let us now take a closer look at the way the questionnaire was designed.

The purpose of the questionnaire was to find out (a) if participants agreed with relationships in the model, (b) if they would like to add other factors not identified by the project group, and (c) what factors were deemed most important in describing the health care system. The questionnaire was divided in a number of sections which carefully match with the decisions as represented in the model, e.g. consultations by patients, prescriptions by family doctors, etc.

The actual wording of questions was derived by translating causal relationships of the conceptual model into verbal statements. For instance, in Figure 6.7 the accompanying verbal statement for the arrow running from 'mean age of patients' to 'refer' is: 'older patients are referred more often to a medical specialist than younger patients'. As shown in Chapter 4, we first asked participants whether they agreed, partially agreed or disagreed with the statement and second we invited them to indicate *why* they agreed or disagreed. From the point of view of group model-building this second part of the question is particularly interesting, since it provokes causal arguments from the participant's mental model. For example, most participants agree with the above statement presenting explanations such as the following:

- older patients have more and more serious complaints;
- they have more pathology;
- the chances of serious pathology are much greater;
- more polypathology;
- polypathology, more complex diagnosis, more complex therapy, etc.

The task of the project group is twofold. First, if possible, to combine concepts employed in these arguments into a smaller number of categories. Second, to apply qualitative content analysis in order to derive a causal structure from these argumentations. In the latter case a couple of people from the project group made initial suggestions from the written material which were in turn checked by the other two persons from the project group. Discussions in the project group then led to a final decision for each of the statements. For instance, from the arguments presented on the above statement, the project group derived the following causal argument: 'older patients frequently have more polypathology. This impedes a correct diagnosis, hence a specialist's opinion is needed, which causes older patients to be referred more often'. Rather than the two original variables (average age and number of referrals) one now has four variables related into a causal chain: (a higher) average age, (gives rise to more) polypathology, (which leads to a higher number of) complex diagnoses and (to a higher) number of referrals.

In the second cycle (workbook) this elaborated argument is reported back to the participants and they are invited to indicate whether they agree with this formulation or not. The example presented above is clear and one of the most straightforward examples of eliciting causal arguments from the participants' mental models. This does of course not happen in all cases. Sometimes no arguments are presented or it is pointed out that the statement itself is obvious.

However, causal arguments are not the only type of interesting information which can be derived from the questionnaire. Interesting information was also derived from the 'why' part of the questions, which related to the concepts themselves. In Chapter 4 it was shown that people who agreed with the statement 'the higher a general practitioner's workload the higher the number of prescriptions' in general employed a different definition for workload than those persons who disagreed with this statement. A similar example on the concept of the 'general practitioner's view of his job' will be discussed in the next section when we will show a sample of part of the workbook. Interpretations like these (made by the project group) were reported back in the workbook and participants were asked to comment on it.

As stated, the questionnaire was divided into a number of sections each dealing with one decision (or dependent) variable, e.g. number of referrals or number of prescriptions by general practitioners. This can be seen in Figure 6.8, in which a sample of the questionnaire is reproduced. Each of these sections in turn contained a number of statements together with 'why' questions. In the figure a couple of questions are shown (under a. Statements) for the section on ordering patients back.

At the end of each section (after: a. Statements) we asked participants to add variables (affecting the dependent variable) which were not included in the preliminary model (see under b.). As will be clear, this resulted in a large number of factors, which cannot all be included in the model. Hence, the last question in each of the sections to indicate the three most important factors (see under c.). From the last question in each section, we calculated frequency distributions and the three factors mentioned most frequently as important were used to develop submodels around a dependent variable in order to carry the conceptual model-building process one step forward.

The Workbook

In order to be able to develop more complex submodels and have these criticized by the participants we employed a so-called workbook in the second cycle. In

Introduction and explanation

...

...

Section 1: Consulting the general practitioner

a.

b.

c.

Section 2: Ordering patients back by general practitioners

a. *Statements*

1. The higher a general practitioner's workload the more patients he will refer to a specialist.
   - agree
   - partially agree
   - disagree

   because: ————————————————————————————————————

   ——

2. The broader a general practioner's view of his job, the more patients he will order back.
   - agree
   - partially agree
   - disagree

   because: ————————————————————————————————————

   ——

3. etc.

b. *Considering the number of referrals by general practitioners, do you think there are any other factors, apart from the ones mentioned above, which affect the number of referrals?*

   ——

   ——

c. *Which three of the above mentioned factors (including the ones you added in the previous question) do you consider most important in explaining the number of referrals? Please indicate the most important first, etc.*

   1. ——

   2. ——

   3. ——

Section 3: Referrals by general practitioners

a.

b.

c.

Section 4: Prescriptions by general practitioners

a.

b.

c.

Figure 6.8 Sample of the Questionnaire Used in the Health Care Project

Chapter 4 it was pointed out that a workbook is best conceived of as a research report on the model, interspersed with a number of questions for the participant. The workbook in this case consisted of about 30 pages (including diagrams and space for comments). In the workbooks we explained in more detail the process of model-building and the diagramming tools, we fed back the results of the questionnaire and again we invited participants to comment on the submodels developed in the workbook. The workbook was also meant to prepare the participants for the third stage in the process: the structured workshop. Two subsets of nine respondents (from the original 60) were selected to fill out the workbooks and to participate in one of two workshops. We selected 18 participants spread over the three fields mentioned above (i.e. health care system, policy making organizations, research institutions) who presented us with the most detailed comments and arguments in the questionnaires. All 18 filled out the same workbook. The workbooks and the two workshops both covered that part of the model which is related to the first echelon (general practitioners), since a number of medical specialists (the second echelon) refused to cooperate because of a conflict between their interest group and the central government.

As in the questionnaire, the workbook contained four submodels, centred around four decision (or dependent) variables in the preliminary model, i.e. consultation by patients on the one hand and prescriptions of drugs, referrals and 'back orders' by general practitioners on the other. These four submodels were developed by the project group using the preliminary model and the results of the questionnaires. Although the questionnaires provided us with the three most important variables affecting each of the above 'dependent' variables and with intermediary links between two variables this information was not always sufficient to produce a submodel. Hence, the project group frequently had to fill in 'causal gaps' between these dependent and independent variables where the questionnaires did not provide that information. Again research literature was consulted and discussed within the project group to generate the necessary information.

In order to simplify matters for the participants the submodels were built up gradually in the course of the workbook. This was accomplished by first linking the most important independent variable (mentioned in the questionnaire) to the dependent variable. Next, variables were identified which could explain this independent variable and so on until a network of causal relationships was constructed. The verbal explanations were summarized by means of a causal diagram, in which the participant could indicate comments and suggestions for adaptations. The same procedure was followed with regard to the second and third most important variable. In order to illustrate the procedure used in the workbooks, we have reproduced part of the workbook (on the phenomenon of ordering patients back) in Figure 6.9.

Once a submodel was complete, the participant was invited to summarize his comments by indicating disagreements with the submodel as shown in Figure 6.10. The participant was next requested to continue with the next submodel.

The completed workbooks were sent to the project group one week before the workshop. They were used to determine the topics for discussion and to organize the subgroups.

The Workshop

Since two workshops were held, it was important that they matched as closely as possible. For the actual design of the workshop we relied on our experience with previous workshops and guidelines found in the literature. (See for instance Duke (1981), Hart et al. (1985), Mason and Mitroff (1981), Vennix and Geurts (1987).) In addition we employed a few conclusions from the research literature on small groups which was discussed in detail in the previous chapter. One is that introduction of structure in group activities drastically improves group performance (Bouchard, 1969). Another is that participation can be improved by using small subgroups (Eden, 1985; Hart et al., 1985) and a group facilitator to structure plenary discussions. There were also some impediments that we had to take into account. For example, since general practitioners participated in the workshops these could not be held during daytime. Hence we started at 4 p.m. and had to be finished by 9 p.m. In order to use the available time as efficiently as possible and to improve participation in the discussions we formed three subgroups of three persons to allow in depth discussions of different submodels during the workshop. Subgroups were composed of persons with similar comments on the submodels. Each of the three subgroups discussed one of the submodels. From the four submodels in the workbook we selected the three that received most criticism in the workbooks. The programme for the workshop was as follows:

4.00–4.15 p.m.	welcome to participants
4.15–5.00	introduction and explanation
5.00–6.00	subgroup discussions
6.00–7.30	plenary session
7.30–8.15	dinner
8.15–9.00	discussion on feedback loops
9.00–9.15	evaluation and conclusion

In order to facilitate work in the subgroups each was assisted by one member of the project team. To structure subgroup activities we used a few aids. First, each group member was assigned a role with accompanying responsibilities. For instance, one person was responsible for time management, another for presentation of the results of the subgroup discussions in the plenary session. Second, to feed back the results from the workbook and as a potential starting point for discussion we provided each group with a copy of the submodel diagram. On these diagrams we indicated by means of different colours which person had criticized what part of the submodel (see also Figure 6.10). The diagrams provided to the participants were used as a kind of scribbling-paper during discussion about the submodels. The diagrams could be modified by participants as they saw fit. In addition, we returned the workbooks to participants as an aid in the discussion. At the end of the subgroup session one person recorded the final changes in a large format diagram, which was put on the wall in the plenary session room. The spokesperson of the first subgroup was then given ten minutes to explain the changes in the submodel. After answering any clarifying questions, there was a 20 minute plenary discussion about

1. Consultation by patients
...
...

2. Back orders by the general practitioner

In the previous section we focused on the decisions of patients to consult their general practitioner. In this and the next two sections we discuss three decisions of general practitioners: ordering patients back, prescribe drugs, refer to a medical specialist or combinations of these. In this section we focus on factors affecting the process or ordering patients back.

2.1 Results of the questionnaire

From the questionnaire we conclude that with regard to the number of patients ordered back by a general practitioner the uncertainty of the general practitioner is considered the most important factor. About 90% of the respondents agrees with the statement that more uncertainty leads to more patients being ordered back. From the argumentations presented with the statements, however, it turns out that the statement cannot be maintained in its current form. We will refer back to this in section 2.2 of this workbook. The second most important factor is the general practitioner's view of his job (about 75% agrees with this statement). This statement too will have to be elaborated as we will see in section 2.3 of this workbook. The third most important factor is the general practitioner's workload. We will discuss this in section 2.4.

2.2 A general practitioner's uncertainty

Most respondents indicate that uncertainty leads to more control behaviour, which in turn increases the number of patients ordered back. There is a problem however. A number of respondents states that more uncertainty can also lead to more *referrals* to medical specialists. In our opinion this depends on the aspect about which a general practitioner is uncertain. We distinguish three kinds of uncertainty, i.e. uncertainty with regard to:
- the diagnosis,
- the expected progress of the disease,
- the potential effect of the therapy.

In our opinion the first kind of uncertainty will lead to either more referrals or more prescriptions or both. We will return to that in Chapters 3 and 4 of this workbook. The second and the third kind of uncertainty of a general practitioner will lead to more patients being ordered back. We formulate the following statements:

1. The more often a general practitioner is uncertain about the expected progress of the disease, the more often he will order patients back.
2. The more often a general practitioner is uncertain about the effects of the therapy, the more often he will order patients back.

A number of respondents point out that the uncertainty of the general practitioner will decrease with his number of years of experience. Some assume that this is amongst others related to the fact that he will know more about his patients. Hence:

3. The more experienced a general practitioner is in his profession, the better he is informed about the history/background of his patients and the less uncertain he will be.

Using a causal diagram the above statements can be visualized as below.

Task 1:
Please indicate in this diagram with which parts you do not agree by crossing these out. Please write down any comments in the space below.

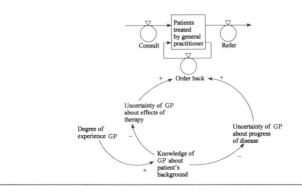

Figure 6.9 Sample of the Workbook in the Health Care Project

2.3 The general practitioner's view of his job

The general practitioner's view of his job also leads to some differences of opinion between respondents. Most probably this is due to a difference in the interpretation of the concept of 'view of his job' (as was the case above with uncertainty). Those respondents agreeing with the statement that a broad view will lead to more patients being ordered back argue that a general practitioner with a broad view will carry out more therapeutic and diagnostic transactions and will check more patients himself (rather than refer to a specialist) and hence will order back more patients. These general practitioners will also refer less in those respondent's opinion. Those respondents who do not agree with the statement, point out that a general practitioner with a broad view will provide better and more specific aid to his patients, which will lead to less patients being ordered back. This contradiction between the two groups can in our opinion be explained form the fact that different persons interpret the concept 'view of job' in different ways. One group considers 'view of job' as the number of tasks the general practitioner considers to be part of his job. The other group seems to interpret the concept as the way the general practitioner handles his patients. From here on we will define 'view of job' as the number of tasks the general practitioner considers to be part of his job. The way a general practitioner handles his patients will be denoted by the concept 'GP-patient relationship'. Below we will first focus on the GP-patient relationship:

4. The more susceptible the general practitioner is to the patient's complaint, the higher the quality of the discussion during consultation.
5. If the quality of the discussion during consultation increases, the patient will get more confidence in his general practitioner.
6. The more confidence a patient has in his general practitioner, the more information (quantitatively and qualitatively) he will provide about his complaint to the general practitioner.
7. The more information a patient provides, the higher the quality of the discussion during consultation.
8. The higher the quality of the consultation discussion, the less a general practitioner will order patients back.

Adding these three factors to the previous figure results in the figure below.

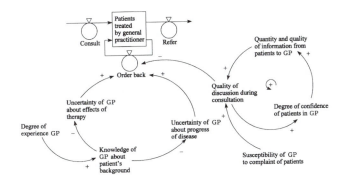

Task 2:
Please indicate in this diagram with which parts you do not agree by crossing these out. Please write down any comments in the space below.

2.4 A general practitioner's workload
...
...

3. **Prescriptions by general practitioners**
...
...

4. **Referrals by general practitioners**
...
...

Figure 6.9 Sample of the Workbook in the Health Care Project (continued)

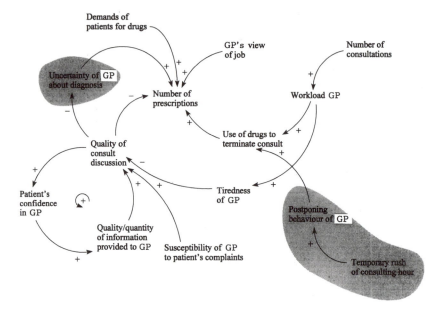

Figure 6.10   Conceptual Submodel on 'Number of Prescriptions' from Workbook

the submodel. This procedure was repeated for the other two submodels. After the break for dinner there was a discussion on the notion of feedback loops that could be identified within the model.

Participants were quite involved in the discussions and were very satisfied that there was a clear timetable, which was followed quite strictly. Although there was consensus on many issues, it also became clear that several processes in health care are poorly understood. Here the group model-building process was arrested at the point where there were only vague conjectures. This was, for instance, true with regard to the number of 'back orders' by a general practitioner. As I have indicated in the first chapter lack of knowledge on general practitioners' back orders is largely due to disinterest of the insurance companies. The reader will recall that as far as mandatory insurance is concerned, a change in the number of back orders does not affect the number of payments to general practitioners. Hence, the disinterest in this phenomenon.

Project Results

In this case several tangible results materialized from this conceptual model-building stage. These are related to the quality of the conceptual model, the definition of the policy problem and the structuring of future research efforts in health care processes. In our view, the quality of the conceptual model was increased drastically on a number of aspects. First, with regard to the number of variables included in the model. This number increased considerably during the process. Our preliminary model contained about 40 variables and the final model contains more than 80. Although a larger conceptual model is not necessarily better, the increase was primarily caused by refinement of the concepts and relationships in the preliminary model. The project group considered that as an important improvement of the quality of the model. I have presented several examples indicating that concepts used in the research literature and in discussions about health care are frequently too ambiguous. Concepts like workload, general practitioner's view of his job and uncertainty of a general practitioner were refined considerably. I have also presented examples of refinement of relationships, sometimes identifying new feedback loops, during the process of model-building (see also Vennix et al., 1990).

The model-building process also had an impact on the definition of the policy problem of cost reduction. Before starting the model-building process various people were quite convinced that the best way to cut health care costs would be by reducing the number of referrals by general practitioners. This seems obvious, since transactions by medical specialists are much more expensive than those by general practitioners, particularly if patients are admitted into hospital. As indicated in the first chapter, during the model-building process it became clear that there are feedback processes which might counteract the cost reduction effect from the reduction of the number of referrals. For instance, through an increase in the number of transactions by medical specialists to compensate for the loss of new patients.

A third result which materialized relates to further empirical research into health care processes. As I have stated, the discussions in the workshop showed that various parts of the system are ill-understood. This was for instance true with regard to ordering patients back by family doctors. I have explained above that lack of interest in this phenomenon was because it was considered not to have any financial consequences. The model however, revealed that indirectly (through workload) ordering back policies might prove more influential on health care costs than initially thought. As a result a research project has been started aimed at filling in the gaps in knowledge on the factors determining back orders by general practitioners.

As this project demonstrates (particularly when compared with the previous one) the results of group model-building projects can hardly be predicted and can take on a variety of forms, including redefinition of the policy problem, a focused research project (on ordering patients back) and abandoning an intended policy. One of the results of the project has also been that the organization has intensified its contacts with medical specialists to find ways to control health care costs. In addition, parts of the model have been formalized and quantified and have been used as a computer based learning environment in the organization. The interested reader is referred to Verburgh (1994) for a more detailed description.

SUMMARY

This chapter has discussed examples of group model-building with qualitative system dynamics. Both cases differed significantly on a number of aspects. In the first case time pressure was high and there was a large conflict of interest. In the second, both these characteristics were absent, but the group of participants was quite large. The case descriptions show how under different circumstances different methods were applied to fit in carefully with the needs of the projects. The next chapter will provide a detailed description of group model-building with a quantified system dynamics model.

Chapter 7

Group Model-building in Action: Quantitative System Dynamics

INTRODUCTION

This and the next chapter discuss an example of quantitative system dynamics in the context of group model-building. The example explores some of the dynamics of the housing market from the perspective of housing associations. I have selected this case for two reasons. The first is related to the difficulty of understanding the rich background of an issue that is the subject of modelling. Describing a complex model to an outsider in an understandable way is not an easy matter. Understanding can further be complicated by the fact that the subject matter is largely unfamiliar territory to the reader. The first reason why this case was selected is therefore that readers will have at least a basic understanding of the processes which are involved in renting or buying a house. This will help to understand the model, particularly for those who are unexperienced with system dynamics. The second reason is because the material used in this case is not subject to proprietary rights. Many model-building projects conducted for business corporations contain confidential material which impedes publication. Although this also holds with regard to individual housing associations, in this chapter I will describe the process of construction of a prototype model which can be considered as a model of an 'average' medium sized housing association.

In the opening sections I will provide a brief description of the background of the project and the problem to be tackled. Subsequent sections will describe the way the model was constructed with the group of the client organization. While this chapter discusses the process, the next chapter will present a couple of analyses and policy experiments with the model. Since the construction of workbooks (and their analysis) and the role of the facilitator have been discussed extensively in the previous chapter, this chapter will place more emphasis on the process of model construction and analysis.

THE CLIENT AND THE PROBLEM

The case under discussion has as its subject the problem of building and financing (low cost) housing. In contrast with the two previous projects in this case, a full-blown simulation model was constructed. The process was started by identifying the relevant flows and by building a small prototype model. This was accomplished with the cooperation of people from Marco Polis Advice (MPA), the consultancy department of the Dutch Christian Institute for Housing (DCIH). The DCIH constitutes an umbrella organization for a number of Dutch housing associations. Housing associations administer a number of houses and apartments. One of their goals is to rent these houses to low income families who cannot (or do not want to) buy a house of their own. Typically, a small association would own about 1000 housing units while the large ones would possess over 30 000 units.

The primary client in this project was Marco Polis Advice (MPA), who wanted to use a simulation model in their strategic consultancy projects with allied associations. The idea was to build a canonical situation model which could be adapted to the specific circumstances of MPA's clients and could then be used in strategic workshops for these clients. Remember the discussion in Chapter 3 on generic structures (Lane and Smart, 1996). There a distinction was made between (a) canonical situation models, (b) abstracted micro-structures, and (c) archetypes. Canonical situation models are case specific, which are reduced to their essentials and are thus applicable to more than one case. The goal of these workshops is to provide management teams of individual housing associations with the opportunity to discuss and test future strategies with regard to the new situation which had originated in the early 1990s.

Until the end of the 1980s, housing associations were largely subsidized by the Dutch government. As a result, associations did not really have to worry about their continuity, since this was in fact guaranteed by the Dutch government through subsidies. However, starting in 1988 the Dutch government initiated a programme to make associations independent from the central government. In other words, in the future, associations are supposed to operate on a free market and to generate their own sources of revenues with which they can finance their housing policies. This government programme presents housing associations with new strategic questions and challenges which they have never faced before. Some of these relate of course to the new financial situation. Others to the future mission and strategic goals of associations.

Our client, MPA, had in the past already been involved in the construction of a simulation game of the new situation. This board game was used as an experiential learning device for associations. It was supposed to put them in a position to experiment with a number of aspects of the new situation in a safe environment. The construction of the game had been conducted by one of my colleagues and its use proved to be very successful. However, it was felt that the game lacked a thorough quantitative basis with which to assess the effects of various strategies. My colleague then advised members of MPA to consider system dynamics as a means of building a computer-based learning environment in which people could actually test the robustness of strategies to deal with the new situation. This idea was discussed in a meeting in which a number of representatives of MPA were present. In this meeting I gave a short description of system dynamics and its use in strategic decision making. After some deliberation it was decided that my colleague and I would build a small model in order to explore the possibilities of system dynamics to support the strategic learning process of individual housing associations. The first step in this process involved the construction of a prototype system dynamics simulation model, with the aid of a couple of people from the MPA. Since the group of participants was relatively small (between three to six people), no restrictions were placed on the communication process as was the case in the previous projects. A number of separate sessions were conducted in which participants provided the necessary information to construct the model. The two model-builders used the time in between sessions to actually construct parts of the model. Each time these were fed back to the MPA representatives in the subsequent session. Four sessions were held in which a model was constructed. Then the process was interrupted, because the client wanted to check whether managers of allied housing associations were interested in using this model to support their strategic decision making processes. In order to test the water, two (identical) conferences were conducted, for which managers of these housing associations were invited. The conferences consisted of a couple of lectures on the new situation for housing associations in the future, followed by a demonstration of the system dynamics model. Since the reactions to the model were quite positive, it was decided to continue the group model-building process, and three additional sessions were organized.

Although total project time took about one year, the work was abandoned for about six months in order to prepare and conduct the conferences. Actual project time was thus about six months, and in these six months a total of seven, three hour, sessions was conducted. In the next sections I will first describe the model and the way it was developed in the four sessions preceding the conferences.

The First Session: Problem Identification

In this session four representatives of MPA were present. We will call this group the core group. One member of this group acted as the gatekeeper. The session was further guided by two system dynamicists, one serving as a facilitator and the other as a recorder. After a brief introduction to the topic of system dynamics (explaining the concepts of stocks and flows, feedback and the model construction process) the discussion was started with the identification of the problem to be modelled.

Participants initially disagreed about the problem to be addressed with the model. One group member emphasized the new financial situation for housing associations. His concern was for a sound financial basis for the associations in the future, given the fact that they would be made independent from the central government. While it used to be the central government who largely financed the social housing market, in the new situation housing associations would have to become self supporting. Revenues would have to be generated with which housing associations could accomplish their objectives on the housing market. According to this person, the primary question in the future would be how associations could secure their financial continuity.

Another member of the group disagreed and explained the dangers in focusing on financial issues. She stated that housing associations had originally been called into being in order to serve a social goal, i.e. to supply sufficient housing for low income groups. This had been the result of the Dutch government's policy to guarantee housing for all Dutch citizens regardless of their income level. As she pointed out, housing associations had been founded exactly to help accomplish this objective. In her opinion one might expect that, although associations will be completely independent in the future, the central government will still evaluate whether housing associations accomplish their social goals. She argued that focusing on financial issues in the model construction process might lead to neglecting the primary tasks of housing associations and thus to the construction of a model which would prove relatively useless.

A third view on the matter was that in the future housing associations would have to operate independently on the housing market and in competition with other associations in the same region. This issue concerned the continuity of the associations in terms of product market combinations and their position on the housing market relative to competing associations in the region. It may be assumed that over a longer time frame shifts may occur in the demand for houses, for instance due to changes in the composition of the population and changes in the housing demands from new people entering the housing market. The question for an association would then be how to anticipate these changes and how to decide what type of houses to build given the long life time of houses.

These three different purposes were discussed at length and it was difficult to arrive at an immediate choice for one of these three issues. Each group member argued from its own position and wanted to use the model for his or her own area of expertise when advising associations. Each was probably afraid that if the model was developed with one of the three purposes in mind it could not be used for the other two. The facilitator argued that this need not necessarily be the case. Focusing on the financial goals would not necessarily mean an exclusion of the social goals. On the other hand, as was also argued by one of the group members, focusing solely on the social goals would exclude an important limiting condition, i.e. the money to accomplish these goals. In other words, it is not just a matter of accomplishing one goal, rather the question is how to accomplish a viable balance between multiple competing objectives. In this respect even the third goal might be incorporated. When discussing this issue further it turned out that the third issue (i.e. product market combinations) would most probably lead to a very complex model. Most associations distinguish between no less than 15 types of houses, a number which might even grow in the future. As a result, it was felt by the group that it would be better to first focus on the other two goals. And rather than selecting one of these two, it was agreed that it might be interesting to use the model to try to find out how competitive these two objectives are by incorporating both into one single model. As a result of the discussion the preliminary problem was formulated as: how can a housing association maintain low cost housing (social goal) and at the same time guarantee its (financial) continuity?

It is important to point out that in this case no historic reference mode of behaviour was available to guide the model construction process, since the future situation would be radically different from the past. We could not rely on data from the past decades since these figures were contaminated with the subsidies provided by the government. This would have required the building of quite a different model, because of the complex nature of subsidy regulations. Since these regulations would be abolished in the future it was felt by the group that it would be more useful to attempt to model the new situation rather than the old or the transition period. As stated in the third chapter, although a reference mode of behaviour is missing, it is still perfectly possible to construct a model of an association which includes a number of financial variables (e.g. level of current account, solvency, and profitability) which can be simulated over time. Problems occur when one attempts to check the model's validity by applying a replication of the reference mode of behaviour. This proves unfeasible. In that respect we had to rely primarily on face validation of the model's structure and its dynamics by experts in the field. The validation issue will be taken up in more detail in the next chapter.

Based on the preliminary problem definition a first rough flow model was built during this first session. The model primarily focused on one type of housing units, i.e. single-family houses. Five flows were discussed in this first session: demand for houses, supply of houses, cash flow, land, and of course loans. The rough sketch of the model was taken home by the model-builders and used as a basis to construct a first version of the model. This model will be discussed in more detail below. I will start the discussion with the demand for houses and their supply.

In Figure 7.1 two flows are portrayed. The above flow represents the demand for family houses, while the flow below pictures the production and supply of this type of house. Let us take a closer look at the demand flow first.

The first stock in this flow depicts the number of families on the waiting list (wait–list). It is assumed that every month a number of families will register for houses (inflow–wait–list) and will be put on the waiting list. The second stock (fam–in–

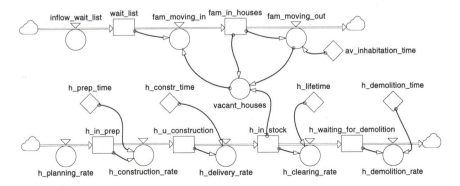

Figure 7.1 Flow Demand and Supply Houses

houses) represents the number of families actually inhabiting a house of the association. The number of families in houses will increase as a result of people coming from the waiting list and moving into houses (fam–moving–in). The number of families in houses will decline as people move out of their houses (fam–moving–out). The number of families moving out every month is calculated by dividing the number of families inhabiting houses by the average time a family inhabits the house (av–inhabitation–time). In the model it is assumed that on average families will stay in a house for about 10 years (120 months). For the moment it is assumed that the average inhabitation time is constant over the run of the simulation. (In Powersim constants are depicted by a rhombus.)

As soon as families move out of their houses (fam–moving–out) this will generate vacant houses which will create the possibility to move families from the waiting list into the houses of the association (fam–moving–in). In other words, if we assume for the moment that the stock of houses is constant, the number of families moving in each month, equals the number of families moving out. In general houses are always occupied. Even if people decide not to move in immediately, the fact remains that a family will have to pay the rent starting from the first day after another family has moved out. Hence, we assume no really uninhabited houses as a result of families moving in and out of houses.

Naturally, the total number of houses will not be constant since houses will be demolished and new houses will be constructed. The number of vacant houses is thus not only determined by the number of families who move out, but also by the difference between the number of houses in stock (h–in–stock) and the number of houses occupied by families. If for instance houses under construction are finished and are delivered (h–delivery–rate) this will increase the number of houses in stock and will create extra vacant houses and additional families (above those moving in, because others moved out) will be able to move into these new houses. As might be anticipated, the number of families moving in, can never exceed the number of families on the waiting list. As a result, the number of families moving in will be equal to either the number of people on the waiting list or the number of vacant houses, whichever of the two is smallest. In other words, the mathematical equation for families moving in becomes: families moving in = MIN (wait list, vacant houses). As we will see later on in this chapter this conceptualization of the process proved to be wrong when the consistency of dimensions were checked in a later stage.

The lower flow in Figure 7.1 represents the flow of houses. In this flow four states are identified, i.e. the number of houses in preparation (h–in–prep), houses under construction (h–u–construction), houses in stock (h–in–stock), and houses waiting to be demolished (h–waiting–for–demolition).

The number of houses in preparation represents the number of houses taken into planning for which the required permits are being obtained. On average, the whole preparation process takes about six months in the Netherlands. As a result, the outflow of this stock, i.e. houses which are going from planning to construction (h–construction–rate), is equal to the number of houses planned divided by the average preparation time (h–prep–time). The inflow for houses in preparation (h–planning–rate) depends among other things on available land to build houses. This will be discussed in more detail below when we address the issue of available land.

The outflow of houses in preparation (h–construction–rate) constitutes the inflow for houses under construction. On average construction time takes about nine months and as a result each month ⅑th of the number of houses under construction will be finished (h–delivery–rate) and will flow into the stock of houses of the association (h–in–stock). This is the actual stock of houses which can be rented. After a number of years houses will have to be pulled down. In general, the normal house life time is assumed to be about 50 years. In other words each month the stock of houses will be depleted with the number of houses in stock divided by 600 (i.e. 50 years × 12 months). These houses will be cleared and wait for demolition (h–waiting–for–demolition). On average it takes about six months (h–demolition–time) before these houses are actually pulled down.

Thus far, I have discussed two important flows for a housing association: demand and supply. At least three important additional flows for a housing association can be identified: available land, loans, and the current account. These flows have been incorporated in the previous model and are depicted in Figure 7.2.

The upper part of the diagram is similar to Figure 7.1, i.e. the demand for houses and its supply. The flow representing the availability of land is depicted in the lower left hand corner. Two states for available land are identified: unprepared and prepared land. Both states represent land which is unoccupied by houses. Only prepared land can be used to build houses, hence the arrow from prepared land to potential number of houses (pot–number–of–h). The amount of square metres of prepared land divided by the average amount of land needed for a house (land–per–house) will produce the potential number of houses which can be built by the association. If for instance the amount of available prepared land equals 10 000 square metres and the amount of land per house equals about 200 square metres (which is not uncommon for inexpensive houses in the Netherlands), the potential number of houses which can be taken into planning will amount to 50. The potential number of houses thus represents the upper limit for the number of houses which can be taken into planning. Simultaneously, once a number of houses are taken into planning the available prepared land is reduced by the number of houses taken into planning multiplied by the average amount of land required per house. Hence, the arrows running from land per house and houses planning rate to land used for houses (l–using–rate). So if in the previous example 10 houses are taken into planning then the amount of prepared land is reduced by 10 × 200 = 2000 square metres (l–using–rate) and from the original 10 000 square metres of prepared land 8000 will be left.

In turn the amount of prepared land can be increased by either preparing available land (l–preparation–rate) or by demolishing houses. Preparing land (including permits and the like) will take on average about six months (land–prep–time). Demolishing houses will provide new prepared land (land–from–demolished–h), because it is assumed that during the demolition process the land will simultaneously be prepared. Hence, the arrow running from h–demolition–rate to land from demolished houses. For the reader who is not familiar with Powersim I

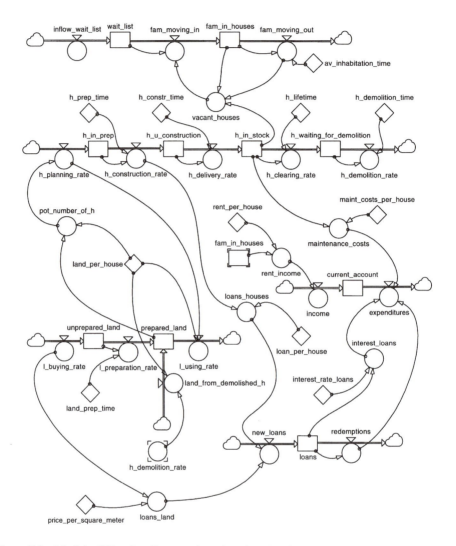

Figure 7.2   Model of Housing Corporation after One Session

have to point out that normally this arrow would run from demolition to land from demolished houses. However, in order to keep the diagram orderly I have employed a copy of the original h-demolished variable and placed this near the variable land-from-demolished-houses. Copies of variables are represented by a circle with four corners surrounding it.

Finally, the amount of available unprepared land can be increased by buying land (l–buying–rate). Buying land will generally increase the amount of loans, a flow which is depicted in the lower right hand part of the diagram and to which we will turn our attention now.

The total amount of loans is increased by new loans which consists of loans for land (loans–land) and loans for houses (loans–houses). The amount of land bought multiplied by the price per square metre (dfl. 25.00) produces the loans for land, assuming that the association is financing through outside capital, which is normally the case. A similar argument can be made for the loans for houses. The number of houses taken under construction in one month (h–construction–rate) multiplied by the average mortgage per house (loan–per–house) produces the total loans for houses (loans–houses). As stated, both types of loans (for land and houses), which are negotiated in a particular month produce new loans, which increase the total amount of loans. On the other hand the total amount of loans is decreased by redemptions made by the association. In this version of the model it is assumed that loans will be amortized in 30 years.

Redemptions constitute expenditures for the association, which will decrease its current account, hence the arrow from redemptions to expenditures. Other expenditures are the interest paid on loans and the maintenance expenditures (maintenance–costs). The interest paid on loans is set equal to the amount of loans multiplied by the interest rate on loans. The maintenance costs are derived by multiplying the number of houses in stock with the average maintenance expenses per house per month (maint–costs–per–house).

While the three expenditures discussed previously (redemptions, interest and maintenance costs) decrease the current account, income increases it. An important income source for a housing association is the total amount of rent received each month (rent–income). This amount is equal to the average rent per house per month (rent–per–house) multiplied by the number of families inhabiting houses of the association (fam–in–houses).

The Second Session

As pointed out before, the model discussed in the previous section was constructed by the model-builders based on the information provided by the participants in the first session. The second session thus started with a brief explanation of the model to the core group, who were then given the opportunity to indicate where they agreed and disagreed. No simulation run with the model was shown because of the very preliminary character of the model.

The primary problem felt was that the model only contained one type of family house. This seemed in conflict with the purpose of the model to show under what circumstances an association would be able to maintain low cost housing for its primary client group. It was decided that a distinction had to be made between at least three types of family houses, i.e. low, middle and high class houses.

A second omission, which was discussed by the group, related to houses under renovation. After about 50 years, most houses are renovated, which increases their average life time to another 30 years, bringing the total life time of houses to 80 years, on average. Simultaneously, these houses are temporarily (6 months) withdrawn from the stock of houses and cannot be rented during that time. It was felt that this process needed to be incorporated in the model.

A third issue concerns the inclusion of revenues, losses and financial reserves of the association. As stated before, the primary source of income for the association are the rents received. Another important source (particularly in the future) will be the interest received on investments. More and more associations will either invest in funds in order to earn additional income or use surpluses to increase the internal rate of financing for instance by paying additional redemptions.

Finally, two other points were mentioned. The first relates to the inclusion of an increase in the rent over time. In this version of the model rents are constant, while in reality rents are increased with a particular percentage each year thus creating a positive feedback loop. The second point relates to a topic which will become increasingly interesting for housing associations, i.e. the possibility of selling houses in order to generate income.

The alterations which were discussed in this session were again implemented by the modellers at their office and the resulting model is depicted in Figure 7.3.

In comparison with the first model this model includes: (a) a flow of houses under renovation, (b) a flow of financial reserves with accompanying profits and losses (bottom of diagram), (c) a variable indicating the rate with which rents are increased each year (see centre of diagram: rent–increase–rate), and (d) a subdivision of the flow of houses and the demand in three categories. The latter can be seen in Powersim by the double lines in the symbols for levels, rates and auxiliaries, indicating that there are several parallel flows. These parallel flows relate primarily to the demand and supply of houses. It is assumed that for an average housing association a reasonable distribution of houses over the three classes is 60%, 25%, and 15% for the low, middle and high class respectively (NCIV, 1994). The initial number of houses for the three classes are thus: 1800, 750 and 450 houses, totalling 3000 houses at the start of the simulation, which makes this a prototype of a (lower range) middle large association. The same figures apply to the number of families in houses, implying no unoccupied houses at the start of the simulation.

In the next session the model was presented, together with a couple of simulation runs. Figure 7.4 shows an example of three runs in which the rent increase rate was fixed at 0.00%, 0.25%, and 0.50% respectively. Since the model in its current form does not include inflation, a 0.00% rent increase rate implies an increase in rent which is equal to the inflation rate.

The curve labelled -1- represents the situation of no increase in the rent, i.e. during the whole of the simulation the rent equals dfl. 600 for the low category (and dfl. 800 and dfl. 1200 for the other two classes (NCIV, 1994)). The curve labelled -2- represents the situation of an increase of 0.25% in rent per year, while the curve labelled -3- shows the behaviour of the model when the rents are raised by 0.5% (above inflation) annually. As can be seen from this figure, in all three runs, the financial reserves show the tendency to rise at an exponential rate. This is not surprising for the simulations in which the rent is increased, because this is a self-reinforcing loop. (In this model the rent increase is calculated as: initial rent × rent increase rate$_{time}$.) However, it might be surprising for the situation in which the rent is kept constant. The explanation for this phenomenon is that over the whole simulation period income exceeds expenditures and revenues exceed costs. When

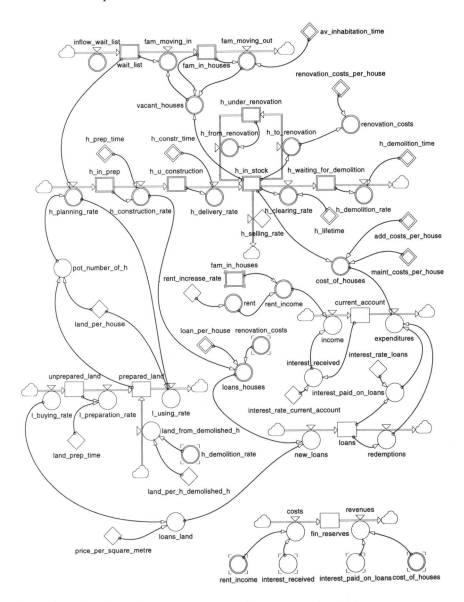

Figure 7.3   Model of the Housing Association after Two Sessions

the current account rises this will in turn increase the interest received and thus boost the current account. Once rents are collected these are put into funds which will generate interest, which in turn augments the amount of the current account, etc. This also creates a reinforcing feedback loop.

As a result of this output, a lively discussion originated. The unlimited exponential growth in financial reserves and current account was recognized from other

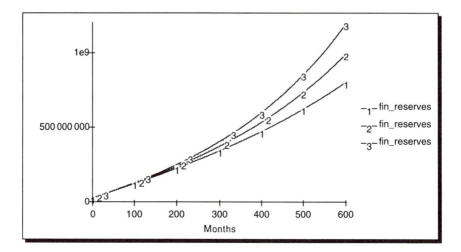

Figure 7.4 Three Runs with Rate of Rent Increase at 0% (-1-), 0.25% (-2-) and 0.5% (-3-)

financial models which were employed by MPA. It was also in line with what was expected by a number of people in the housing domain. However, group members were a bit surprised by the fact that the curves exhibited exponential growth, without first showing a dip. Group members explained that initially (roughly over the first 10 years) new houses have higher costs than revenues. However, since rents increase more rapidly than costs, after the tenth year the balance is switched and revenues start to exceed costs. In other words, losses in the first years are re-earned in later years. Hence, group members expected the curves for financial reserves and current account to fall first and then rise.

Although this argument seems valid at first sight, the facilitator pointed out that their argument might be correct for one house, but it would fail if considered at an aggregate level when the stock of houses would consist of both new and old houses. Losses suffered on new houses would on an aggregate level be compensated by revenues earned on old houses. The discussion was arrested at this point, because no agreement could be reached on which argument was correct. In fact this version of the model could not be used to clarify the debate, because no distinction could be made between different age classes of houses in stock. In addition, the runs with the model might be misleading since it contained no depreciation of houses. As will be seen, the issue of exponential growth re-emerged and was rediscussed several times during subsequent sessions, until it was finally resolved.

Subsequent Meetings

As was seen, the second version of the model was the subject of further discussions. Because of the fact that financial continuity was one of the primary problems to be addressed by the model, it was felt that additional financial expertise would be required to develop the model further. Two sessions were conducted, one with two financial specialists from MPA and one with an external financial specialist who had participated in the construction of an econometric model of housing associations (cf. Berkhout, Hopstaken and Vegt, 1993). As might be expected, discussions with these financial specialists led to considerable adaptations of the model, although the basic structure was preserved. The most important changes involved adding variables related to inflation, the association's solvability and its profitability. These with a couple of other alterations, produced the prototype model of the housing associations which was used as a basis for the demonstration at the conferences. This model is shown in Figure 7.5.

Although this model looks more complicated than the previous ones, the basic structure has remained unaltered. When compared with the previous versions, this model contains a number of minor and major modifications. A minor modification concerns the inclusion of one more stock for land: land in use. The model thus now includes the total amount of land owned by the association. This is more correct since if, for instance, houses are sold, land will in general be sold with it, which reduces the amount of land owned by the association. This is an example of a minor change which does not really affect the dynamics of the model (except for the case mentioned before). Major additions and changes in the model are discussed in the sections below.

Inflation Rate, Inflation Effect and Rent Increase

As stated above, an important variable which was added to the model was the rate of inflation. The inflation rate can be seen in the upper right hand part of the figure and is a constant in the current version of the model: the inflation rate equals 3% per year. The inflation rate affects three other variables in the model: (a) the interest rate on loans, (b) the rent increase rate, and (c) the increase in inflation effect. Let me explain each of these effects in more detail.

With regard to the interest rate on loans (right hand part of diagram), it is assumed that this rate will equal the sum of the inflation rate (3%) and the real interest rate (4%). As a result, the interest rate on loans equals 7%.

The rent increase (centre of the diagram) is modelled with the aid of a stock called rent (indicating the actual amount of rent) and a flow, called rent increase (indicating the increase in rent). The level of the rent is used as a basis to calculate the increase of it, thus forming a reinforcing loop: the higher the rent the higher the rent increase and the higher the rent increase the higher the rent. The initial value of the rent per house equals dfl. 600, dfl. 800 and dfl. 1200 per month for the three classes (NCIV, 1994). The rent increase is equal to the level of the rent multiplied by the rent–increase–rate. The rent increase rate is determined by two factors: (a) the inflation rate, and (b) the effect of the market (eff–of–market–on–rent). This is depicted in the formula below:

rent–increase–rate = inflation–rate + eff–of–market–on–rent

In a sense, the inflation rate constitutes the base rate for the increase in the rents. The inflation rate (3%) is taken as a starting point to calculate the rent increase

Figure 7.5 System Dynamics Model Used at the Conferences

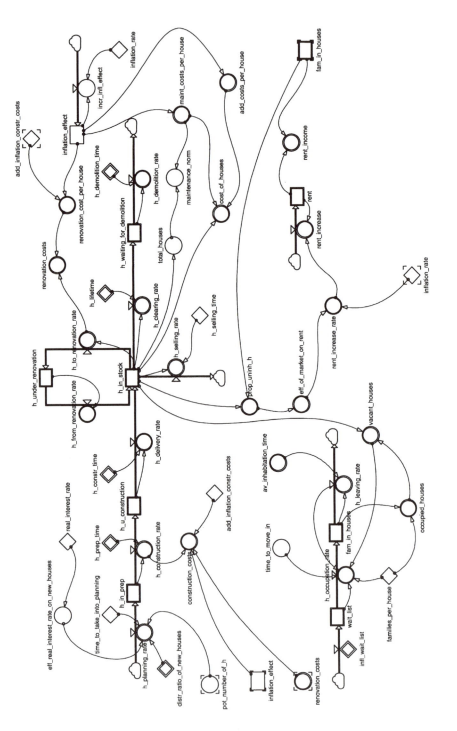

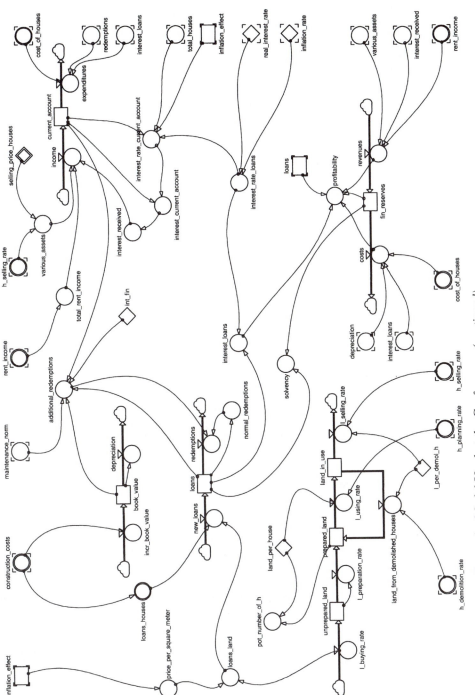

Figure 7.5 System Dynamics Model Used at the Conferences (*continued*)

rate. This base rate can be altered by the effect of the market situation on the rent, more specifically the proportion of uninhabited houses (prop–uninh–h). If demand falls short of supply in a structural manner this will produce a number of uninhabited houses, which will augment the proportion of uninhabited houses. As a result, one may expect rents to start falling. In the model it is assumed that when the proportion of empty houses equals zero there will be no effect on the rent increase rate. If the proportion of empty houses increases, however, the effect of the market upon the rent increase rate will gradually move toward –1.0%. In other words, if the proportion of uninhabited houses increases the rent increase rate will be lowered with a maximum of 1.0%. So, if the inflation rate equals 3% and there is a large proportion of uninhabited houses the maximum rent increase rate will equal: 3.0% – 1.0% = 2.0%.

Thus far, I have discussed the effect of the inflation rate on the interest rate and the rent increase. Let us now turn our attention to the third effect of the inflation rate: its impact on the inflation effect. This effect might be more difficult to understand. As is the case with compounded interest, price increases affect themselves forming a positive feedback loop. So, if prices increase by 3% annually, then the price increase over a number of years will show exponential growth, because previous price increases form the basis for current price increases. There are several ways to model this. In this model we chose to employ a stock variable (inflation–effect) with an initial value of 1.0. Each year this stock variable is increased with an increase in inflation (incr–infl–effect), which itself depends on the level of the stock, and will thus produce exponential increase.

The inflation effect is thus determined by the inflation rate and in turn influences a number of other variables in the model. These include: (a) the price per square metre of land (left hand lower corner of diagram), (b) the maintenance costs and other costs of houses (close to the inflation effect in the diagram), (c) the renovation costs per house (upper right hand part), and last but not least (d), the construction costs of houses. The latter costs are also affected by so-called additional inflation costs (0.5%), because prices of building materials are assumed to rise somewhat faster than other prices.

To provide the reader with an idea of the actual amounts involved: the price for land is set at dfl. 25 per square metre. The maintenance costs amount on average to dfl. 166 per month and the additional costs per house are dfl. 75 (NCIV, 1994). These additional costs reflect such costs as salaries and office costs of the association. Renovation costs are set at dfl. 40 000, 60 000, and 80 000 for the three classes, while the construction costs amount to: dfl. 140 000, dfl. 170 000, and dfl. 250 000 respectively. Each of the above costs are affected by the inflation effect. For instance the initial maintenance cost per house (next to the inflation effect in the diagram) in the lower category of houses amounts to dfl. 1992 per year (12 × dfl. 166.00) at the start of the simulation. This price is multiplied by the inflation effect bringing the maintenance costs after 80 years at about dfl. 8486.00. A similar argument holds for the other costs.

As stated before, rents provide the primary source of income for a housing association. Because of the large amounts of money involved a secondary source of revenues is formed by the interest on investments. Let us now turn our attention to the current account and the interest on current account.

Current Account and Interest on Current Account

In the previous version of the model it was simply assumed that money on the current account would generate interest, which was added to the level of the current account through the revenues. In that model the interest rate was independent of the level of the current account. This is of course unrealistic. When income exceeds expenditures the additional money will be invested in funds in order to create additional income. In other words, the higher the current account the more money will be transferred to accounts with a higher interest rate, which creates additional interest at the current account and thus interest income. In order not to make matters too complicated, we have assumed in the model that the higher the level of the current account the higher the interest rate will be, because money will be invested in more profitable funds.

Financial Reserves, Solvency and Profitability

The previous version of the model already included financial reserves as a separate flow. Financial reserves (lower right hand part of the diagram) are increased through profits (rents, interest received, and various assets) and decreased through losses (cost of houses, interest paid on loans and depreciation of houses). Important financial indicators are an association's solvency and profitability. Profitability of the association is calculated as the sum of revenues and interest on loans decreased by costs, the result of which is divided by the sum of financial reserves and loans.

The solvency of the housing association (lower middle part of the diagram) is defined as the amount of financial reserves divided by the total of assets and liabilities. The higher the financial reserves in relation to the loans, the higher the association's solvency: revenues will increase the solvency, while costs (which decrease financial reserves) and increased loans will decrease it.

The loans have also been discussed in the previous version of the model. It was demonstrated that loans increase through new loans for houses and land and decrease through redemptions. The only difference with the previous version of the model is that in this model, next to normal redemptions, there are so-called additional redemptions. These depend on the redemption policy of the association. It is assumed that if the association owns enough money it will pay additional redemptions to a level called the desired proportion of internal financing (int–fin). In the model this desired level of internal financing is arbitrarily set at 10% of the book value of the houses in stock. This implies that if the total amount of loans surpasses the value of 90% of the book value, the association will pay additional redemptions in order to have the loans at the desired value of 90% of the book value. Whether additional redemptions will be paid, will of course also depend on the level of the current account. The minimum level for the current account is assumed to be the desired current account. For most associations this desired level is roughly equal to twice the value of the so-called maintenance norm. The maintenance norm is the amount of money needed for maintenance costs per year. This amount equals the number of houses in stock (in our case about 3000 houses) multiplied by the maintenance costs per house per year (dfl. 1992, per year). The desired level of the current account at the start of the simulation thus equals almost dfl. 12 million. If the actual current account is below the desired level no additional redemptions will be paid. Only if the current account exceeds this minimum level will the association pay additional redemptions. If the latter is the case this will naturally positively affect the solvability of the housing association.

Demand for Houses: Changing Model Structure as a Consequence of Dimension Inconsistency

The attentive reader may have noticed that in the upper part of the diagram the flow for the demand for houses has changed slightly in comparison with the previous models. These alterations became necessary, because it proved when the dimensions were checked by the modellers, that the original conceptualization was wrong. (Actually, this inconsistency (and a couple of others) was revealed by David Lane, when he was invited to check the model.) Let me explain this in more detail, because it demonstrates the value of checking dimensions. In the original model (see Figure 7.3) we had assumed two stocks in the demand flow: a waiting list and a stock of families in houses. Problems arise in the flow from the waiting list to families in houses: families moving in. The equations for families moving in and for vacant houses were formulated as:

$$\text{fam--moving--in} = \text{MIN (wait--list, vacant houses)}$$
$$[F \div M] = \text{MIN} ([F], [H])$$

$$\text{vacant houses} = \text{fam--moving--out} + (\text{h--in--stock} - \text{fam--in--houses})$$
$$[H] = [F \div M] + ([H] - [F])$$

Now, 'families moving in' needs a timescale, because it represents a flow. The dimension of this variable is families per month: $[F \div M]$. But the waiting list is defined as families $[F]$, and vacant houses as houses $[H]$. Hence, a dimensional error occurs in the first equation above: families per month is neither equal to families nor to houses. A similar argument can be provided with regard to the formula for vacant houses. Hence, we had to adapt the model slightly. Obviously we had ignored the timescale 'time to move in', when it came to vacant houses in the formula for families moving in. On the other hand, when it came to the waiting list in the same formula we obviously needed a 'translator' from families to houses occupation rate (as the variable 'families moving in' is now called). This translator is the number of houses per family. As a result the house occupation rate is now defined as:

$$\text{h--occupation--rate} = \text{MIN } \{(\text{wait--list} \div \text{families--per--house}) \div \text{time--to--move--in}, (\text{vacant--houses} \div \text{time--to--move--in}) + \text{h--leaving--rate}\}$$

In other words, the house occupation rate is equal to either the wait list divided by the number of families per house and the time to move in, or the number of vacant houses divided by the time to move in plus the houses leaving rate, whichever of the two is smaller. The corresponding dimensions for the variables in the equation are: wait list [F], families–per–house [F÷H], time–to–move–in [M], vacant–houses [H], and h–leaving–rate [H÷M]. The check below demonstrates the correctness of the dimensions.

$$[H \div M] = MIN \{([F] \div [F \div H]) \div [M]), ([H \div M\} + [H \div M]\}$$

To make the translation from families into houses we introduced the variable occupied houses. The number of vacant houses is now defined as the difference between the number of houses in stock and the number of occupied houses. The latter in turn is equal to the number of families in houses divided by the number of families per house.

vacant–houses = h–in–stock – occupied–houses
[H] = [H] – [H]

occupied–houses = fam–in–houses ÷ families–per–house
[H] = [F] ÷ [F÷H]

The example, demonstrates the usefulness of the check on dimension consistency when conceptualizing a model. Let us turn back to the process of model construction with the group.

THE CONFERENCES

As I have pointed out in the beginning of this chapter, the model was constructed by MPA to be used as a tool to support strategic decision making of their clients. As a result, members of MPA were curious whether managers of housing associations would be interested in actually using this new tool. In order to test the water, it was decided to plan a conference in the beginning of 1995. (Since the interest was overwhelming we actually had to organize two conferences.) Each of the two conferences was attended by some 40 managers of housing associations. The conference consisted of three presentations on issues concerning the newly emerging situation for the housing associations in the future. One presentation focused on demographic trends and scenarios. The second on the new financial situation which would emerge in the future. As might be expected, most associations underwent a profound change. In the past it would have been hard for an association to go bankrupt, while this became a real possibility under the new situation, without government support. Managers were looking for means to help them decide how to run their associations and how to develop robust policies to accomplish their goals. In that sense, the third presentation and demonstration of the system dynamics model was offered as one possibility to explore the potential long term effects of intended policies. Reactions to the demonstration were quite favourable, because many participants realized the potential of such a tool. As a result of these conferences the group model-building process was taken up again after having been interrupted for almost six months. In the meantime, one model-builder was added to the team.

SESSIONS AFTER THE CONFERENCES

The first meeting with the group after the conferences started with a short explanation of the version of the model which was used for demonstration at the conferences. The explanations proved necessary to refresh memories, since almost six months had passed since the last meeting of the group.

The First Session After the Conferences

As might be expected, the explanation by the facilitator gave rise to new discussions on the model's structure. One involved the notion of the availability of land. Thus far we had assumed that land could be bought from an infinite source and that the price per square metre was only affected by the inflation rate. In the Netherlands scarcity of land is an important issue, which is becoming more and more urgent. The more scarce available land becomes, the higher the price per square metre. The discussion indicated that an additional stock (available land) had to be built into the model indicating a finite stock. The smaller the stock the higher the price per square metre. The phenomenon is interesting, since by buying land from a finite stock an association would thus be a reinforcing factor in driving up the prices for land by diminishing the stock of available land. The more land is bought by an association, the more expensive land becomes. As we will see, this issue was taken up in the workbook which was prepared for the second session.

After these explanations and some discussion, the modellers showed the base run of the model which was used at the conferences. As was the case with the previous model, this model also showed an exponential growth in financial reserves and current account. The model was simulated with a rent increase rate which was equal to the inflation rate +0.5%. This rate was assumed by most associations to hold for a number of years. Figure 7.6 shows the results of a simulation run with the model when the rent increase rate is fixed at inflation rate +0.5%.

It is clear that financial reserves rise exponentially to the level of over dfl. 3 billion. Even when corrected for the inflation rate over the 50 years of the simulation, the end result is a financial reserve of over dfl. 700 million (initial value: dfl. 28 million). Consequently, solvency rises to almost 80%.

As a result of this run, three issues were discussed in the session. The first involved identifying the *causes* for the exponential growth, while the second focused again on the question why there was no initial dip in the curve for financial reserves. The third issue focused on the question of how realistic would be such an exponential increase and extreme level of financial reserves.

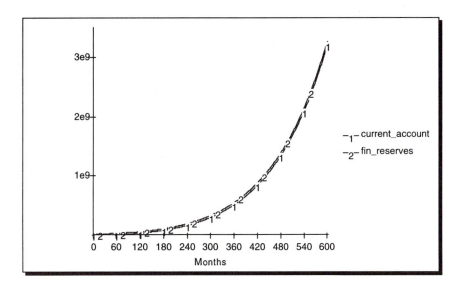

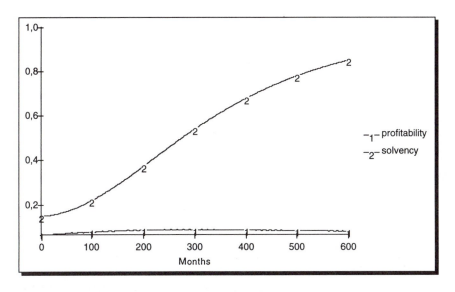

Figure 7.6 Graphs of Financial Indicators with Rent Increase at Inflation Rate +0.5%

With regard to the first issue, a number of runs with the model were performed in which a number of factors were deactivated gradually. Remember that the most important sources of income for a housing association are rents and interest received. Hence, the first experiment was to assume a rent increase rate which would equal the inflation rate (rather than inflation + 0.5%). Although in this case the end result is somewhat lower (dfl. 1.7 billion for financial reserves and solvency over 75%), the exponential increase in financial reserves remained. Even when we set the inflation rate and additional inflation on construction costs at 0%, the exponential curve remained intact. Financial reserves still grew to dfl. 500 million and solvency to over 70%. Only when, in addition to the above changes, the rents received on the current account were set at 0% did the exponential curve change and growth levels off. In this case the curve of financial reserves showed the tendency to grow towards an equilibrium value of dfl. 130 million, while solvency reaches a value of 35%.

The group was a little puzzled about the results. Since in our model, rents and interests were the only income sources, we had to come to the conclusion that even when these income sources were fixed at zero the association did not go bankrupt, something which should have been expected to happen, particularly when new houses were built which would increase costs over revenues. In other words, since under all of the above conditions the financial reserves were continually increasing, the conclusion had to be that revenues exceeded costs over the whole 600 months of the simulation run. And this was in sharp contrast with what was known by financial experts. As I have stated in one of the previous sections, it was expected that particularly when new houses were built, financial reserves and solvency would first drop and then start to rise.

During the session, several explanations were offered why this dip in the beginning of the simulation did not occur. The first focused on the way redemptions to loans as well as the depreciations were determined. Both were calculated based on the 'rest value', while in fact loans are redeemed by means of an annuity system. The effect was, for instance, that the interests paid on loans would be lower than would be under an annuity regime. Although this is correct for one house, the facilitator pointed out that if an association would own new as well as old houses the system of redemptions and interest might better be modelled as a linear system. High amounts of interest would be paid on new houses, but relatively low amounts of interest on old houses.

Another potential explanation for the lack of the initial dip in the financial reserves which was offered by one of the group members, was that the initial book value and loans would be too low. The initial values for book value was dfl. 180 million and for loans 0.9 × 180 million = 162 million. (The figure of 0.9 is derived from the fact that in the model the amount of external financing was set at 90%, as was explained in one of the previous sections.) In order to check this explanation we increased the book value to dfl. 240 million and the loans to dfl. 216 million. This indeed produced an initial dip in the financial reserves. At that point it was however not quite clear what we were doing in the model. Were we artificially creating a model outcome, just by arbitrarily changing parameters in the model? The answer to this question remained a bit obscure and would not be solved before the next session.

In the final part of the session the facilitator confronted the group with the question of whether it would be realistic to assume the exponential growth in financial reserves and current account to go on indefinitely. The group agreed that when associations would become that profitable, it could be expected that the Secretary of Housing matters would intervene in the rent increase rate. In system dynamics terms, this implies a feedback link from the financial situation of the association to the rent increase rate. As the reader may have noticed, rather than discussing feedback loops directly, the behaviour of the model is taken as a starting point to ask questions about pressures building up in the system, which may lead to counter pressures. This way of identifying feedback loops is suggested by Richardson and Andersen (1995) as a natural way of bringing the feedback issue up in a group model-building session.

In the discussion, two financial indicators were selected which would most probably be used to assess an association's prosperity: the average ratio of revenues versus costs and the solvency position. The reader may wonder why two indicators were selected, particularly because the revenues and costs affect solvency. At first sight it seems that this is superfluous. However, two indicators were deemed necessary, in order to be able to identify associations which might have a relatively 'normal' cost benefit ratio, but might have built up large reserves in the past. It was assumed that associations with a normal cost benefit ratio but a high solvency, due to high financial reserves, might also come under pressure when it came to an increase in rents.

Building a link from these two indicators to rent increase rate would automatically create two balancing loops: the better the financial situation of an association, the more downward pressure on the rent increase rate. This would in turn lower the revenues, and thus the solvency and the revenue to cost ratio. However, when over time the financial position deteriorates, this will in turn produce an upward pressure on the rent increase rate, etc. The actual link between the variables was not explicitly discussed in the group. Since time ran out, it was decided that the modellers would adapt the model and would put the results into a workbook, which could be used as a preparation for the next session.

The Workbook After the First Session

The workbook contained a summary of the discussions which were held in the foregoing session. It also summarized a number of questions which had not been answered satisfactorily thus far. One of these included the identification of the indicators for the social goals of the association, another was the lack of the initial dip in the financial reserves.

The workbook then introduced the balancing loops from financial situation through rent increase to financial situation. As stated, two indicators were identified: the revenue to cost ratio and the solvency. According to the financial experts, a housing association, on average, wants revenues to exceed costs by at least 5% under normal circumstances. This implies that when, on average, profits do not exceed losses by a minimum of 5%, the rents will be increased above the inflation rate. If, on average, profits do exceed losses by about 5% or more the rent increase rate will be below the inflation rate. A secondary factor in the financial situation is the association's solvency position. Here it is assumed that if the solvency rises above 15% this will have a decreasing effect on the rent increase rate. If the solvency drops below 15% this will produce an upward effect on rents. Figure 7.7 shows how these two effects were built into the model.

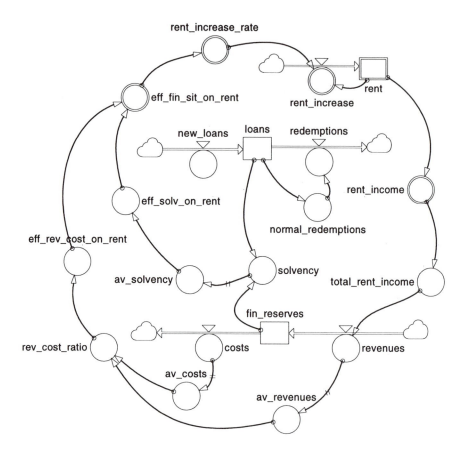

Figure 7.7 Effect of Financial Situation on Rent Increase Rate

The figure clearly shows the feedback processes involved. When rents are increased (upper right hand corner), this will boost total rent income, which raises (a) revenues, and (b) the financial reserves. The increase in (average) revenues will push up the revenue cost ratio, and thus produce a downward effect on the rent increase rate, which will lower rent income. A rise in financial reserves will raise solvency and will thus also produce a downward effect on the rent increase rate through the effect of the solvency on the rent (eff–solv–on–rent).

Let me explain in more detail how the actual effects of revenue cost ratio and solvency upon rent increase rate were built into the model and presented in the workbook. Let us first turn our attention to the effect of the profits and losses on the rate with which rents are increased. To build this effect into the model we employed the concept of revenue–cost ratio. This ratio is calculated by dividing the average profits in a particular period (i.e. the past year) by the average costs in the same period. The point at which the effect of this amount changes from upward into a downward effect on the rent increase is at 1.05. At that point revenues exceed

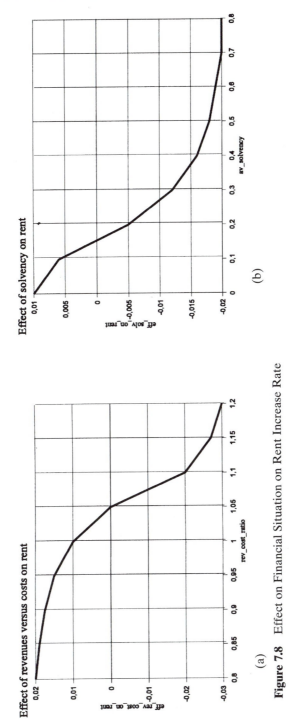

Figure 7.8 Effect on Financial Situation on Rent Increase Rate

costs by 5%. If the amount rises above 1.05, the effect on the rent increase rate becomes more and more negative, with a minimum value of 2%. On the other hand, if the amount drops below 1.05, there is an upward effect on the rent increase with a maximum of 2%. This is shown in Figure 7.8 (a).

Let us now turn to the second factor: the solvency effect. In the model it is assumed that the higher the solvency the more rent increase will come under pressure and vice versa. The effect of the solvency on the rent increase rate can be seen in the right hand part of Figure 7.8 (b). The turning point is at a solvency of 15%. Above 15% solvency there is a downward effect on rent increase rate of maximally 1%. The maximum upward effects was set at 1%.

Both these graphs were presented in the workbook and accompanied by three questions, asking whether:

1. the turning point was determined correctly,
2. the upper limit was correct, and
3. the lower limit was correct.

In addition, the results of a simulation run with the model were presented, which included both these feedback effects. As could be expected, the model now revealed no exponential growth, because of the balancing loops, as can be seen in Figure 7.9.

Because of the feedback loops controlling the rent increase rate, the current account and financial reserves grow in a linear fashion. The growth is primarily determined by inflation. In other words, the final value of financial reserves, if corrected for inflation, is about dfl. 20 million, which is close to the initial value. The current account shows a little erratic behaviour, which is primarily due to the additional redemptions. Each time the amount of loans rises above 90% of the book value, additional redemptions take place, which lower the current account. Solvency initially tends to grow and then gradually declines. This is caused by the fact that loans increase somewhat faster than financial reserves. Profitability is quite constant and this is what would be expected. Even in cases when high profits are made, profitability will level off, because profits (which appear in the numerator of the profitability fraction) are added to the financial reserves (which appear in the numerator). As stated, these graphs with accompanying explanations were presented in the workbook, in order to show the effects of the feedback loops on the behaviour of the model.

Next, the workbook presented a submodel which represented the limited amount of land available and the effects of a decrease in available land on the price per square metre. Rather than thinking of land as coming from an infinite source, the stock of available land is now limited to the amount of potential land (pot–land) in a region. The submodel is shown in Figure 7.10.

The stock of potential land can be depleted when land is purchased by the association (l-buying–rate) or by other parties operating in the region (comp–l–buying-rate). As can be seen the price per square metre is determined by the normal price (which is in turn affected by the inflation effect) and the effect of the

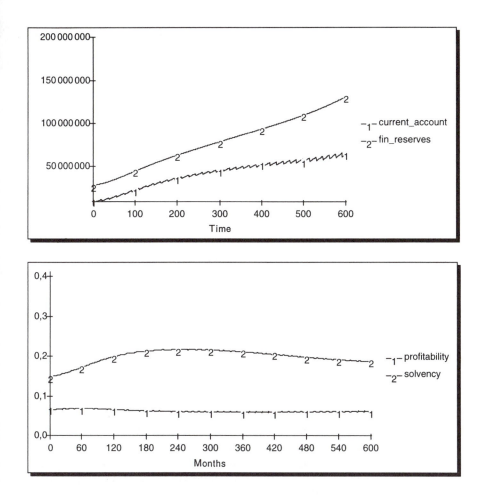

Figure 7.9 Model Behaviour after Including Feedback Loops Controlling Rent Increase

available land (eff–land–on–price–land). The smaller the amount of potential land available in a region, the higher the price will be. The submodel also reveals that by buying land a housing association will thus help to increase prices. Again use was made of a graph function to model the effect of available land on the price per square metre. The minimum effect, when land abounds, was assumed to be 1.0, while the maximum effect, when scarcity approaches zero, was set at 10.0. In the workbook, a question similiar to the ones for the previous graphs was added, i.e. whether the upper and lower limits were correctly identified. As a discussion in one of the next sessions revealed, this upper limit seems on the safe side. There are parts in the Netherlands where the price per square metre exceeds 20 times the normal price.

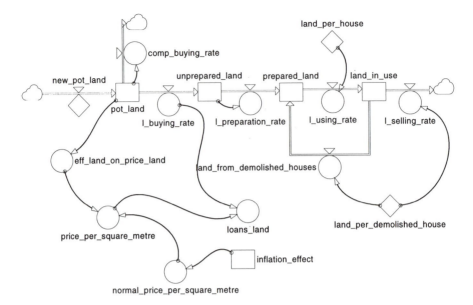

Figure 7.10 Partial Model of Land and Effect on Price Per Square Metre

The Second Session After the Conferences

Unfortunately, the workbook was not ready in time for the participants to study extensively at their office. Hence, we decided to work through the workbook during the session. With regard to the first question on the social and financial indicators, it was decided that people of MPA would discuss this issue over the next couple of weeks, and would come up with these indicators in the next session. The discussion then focused on the summary of the previous session and returned to the point of the exponential growth and the absence of the initial dip. This discussion was partly induced by our questions in the workbook whether an increase in the initial values of book value and loans was not an arbitrary choice in order to create the initial dip. Our argument, as modellers, was that if an association would have a number of houses which would be distributed equally over age categories, this dip should not occur, because losses on 'young' houses would be cancelled out by profits on 'older' houses. (The reader may recall that for newly built houses costs exceed revenues, a situation which is reversed after 10 years.) In order to test this hypothesis, one would have to decompose the level of houses in stock into a number of age categories. One would then be in a position to simulate situations of associations with (a) an equal distribution of houses over various categories, (b) a high number of old houses, and (c) a high number of new houses. Discussing these matters in more detail, however gradually clarified the issue, which had persisted thus far. After all, changing the initial values of the book value and the loans, in fact represented these different situations. The more old houses an association owns, the lower the initial book value and the level of the loans. On the other hand, the more the distribution of houses would be skewed towards the 'young' end, the higher the initial value of book value and loans. And as we have seen, the higher the initial values of these two variables (indicating many 'young' houses), the larger the initial dip in the financial reserves and solvency. In that sense the model thus behaved as expected. In addition, although somewhat roughly, we would be able to simulate associations with different distributions of houses, without further decomposing the level of houses in stock for the time being.

The discussion then shifted to the balancing loops controlling the rent increase rate. The group agreed with the graphs, but disagreed with the lower limits. The lower limits we selected, in combination with the additional character of the way the rent increase was calculated could result in an actual *decrease* of the rent below zero. In the most extreme situation the rent increase rate could turn out to be: 3% (inflation rate) minus 3% (i.e. the revenue cost effect) minus 2% (solvency effect), which would result in a rent decrease rate of 2% below zero. It was felt by the group that in general rent increases would not drop below zero percent. As a result, the lower limit for the revenue cost effect was set at 2% and for the solvency effect at 1% in order to meet this criterion.

After this, the facilitator introduced the results of a run with the model in which a large piece of land was bought. The run revealed that under these circumstances, the association started to build extra houses, because the potential number of houses was increased due to the growth in available land. Because of these extra houses, the waiting lists were emptied which resulted in the construction of houses while there were uninhabited houses. The model run thus showed that the decision to construct houses was not modelled correctly and that some feedback loop was missing. Thus far the only factor determining the construction of houses was available land. This is of course quite correct: if no land is available, no houses can be constructed. On the other hand, if land is available houses will only be constructed under certain conditions. The group identified two factors which enter the decision to construct or not. The first is whether houses, once constructed, will be occupied. The primary determinant is the so-called 'demand pressure'. This indicator is calculated by dividing the waiting list by the total stock of houses. After some deliberation the group agreed that if this indicator rises above 10% no restrictions will in general be placed on the construction of houses by an association. On the other hand if this indicator drops below 5% (low demand) housing construction will be arrested, in order to prevent future losses due to uninhabited houses.

A further result of this discussion was that one person indicated that available land and demand are not the only factors affecting the decision to construct houses. One additional determinant is the possibility of negotiating loans. This is to a large degree determined by the financial position of the association. Most financiers are quite silent about the exact criteria they employ (Berkhout, Hopstaken and Vegt, 1993). In the current situation the so-called 'Waarborgfonds Sociale Woningbouw' (Guarantee Fund Social Housing) provides a guarantee which, if obtained, is a sufficient condition for a financier to issue a loan to a housing association. In general, if the solvency is negative and it cannot be assumed that within the next five years the solvency will be restored to a positive value, a guarantee is not provided and it will almost be impossible for an association to negotiate a loan. Below this level, if no loans can be negotiated by an association it has to turn to the Central Fund, which may assist associations when they are financially in trouble. To the reader it may seem strange that associations can negotiate loans at such a low (or even negative) level of solvency. One has to keep in mind however, that changes in demand and supply are quite slow on the housing market, particularly in the Netherlands, where houses are scarce. Although in this model we have assumed that below this level of the test no loans can be negotiated, in practice sometimes loans are provided but under more stringent conditions.

Back Office Modelling and Second Workbook

The modellers added the ideas discussed in the second session to the model and put the results in a workbook. The first item, which had been contained in the previous workbook, but which was not discussed satisfactorily in the session, was the availability of land. Hence, we decided to bring up this issue in the second workbook. In addition, we presented the way in which we had incorporated the effect of 'demand pressure' and the solvency on the decision to build houses. The effect of the solvency was quite straightforward. If solvency drops below zero and it may be expected to stay below zero for the next five years no loans can be negotiated. Technically, this was modelled by taking a projection of the solvency (solv–projection) for the next five years. If solvency drops below zero and the projection of solvency over the next five years also predicts no positive value for solvency, no loans can be negotiated and the number of potential houses which can be constructed drops to zero.

The effect of demand pressure proved more cumbersome. We decided to employ a graph function, which would produce an effect on the decision to take new houses into planning (h–planning–rate). As indicated by the group in the previous meeting, if demand pressure in some categories drops below 5%, the effect of demand pressure on new houses becomes zero, thus arresting the process of house construction. If demand pressure rises to 10% the effect gradually rises to 1.0, which results in the construction of all potential houses. However, when we tested the model it turned out that it did not behave the way we expected it to behave. In particular, when we decreased the inflow on the waiting list for one category (and thus decreased demand pressure), it turned out that indeed the number of houses constructed in this category dropped, but, contrary to what we expected, this did not imply that more houses were built in the other two categories to decrease demand pressure there. This was caused by the fact that the model still contained a constant distribution ratio. In other words the potential number of houses which could be built were distributed over the three categories according to initial conditions: 60%, 25%, and 15% for the low, middle and high class. And if demand drops in one category, then, although potentially houses can be constructed, this process is arrested by the lack of demand pressure. But there is no mechanism which ensures that those houses will be built in other categories where they might be needed. In order to solve this apparent inconsistency, we decided to make the distribution ratio variable. We took the demand in each category and divided this by total demand and thus created a variable distribution ratio which always totalled to 1.0. The idea was presented in the workbook and participants were asked whether they agreed or disagreed with this solution.

The Third Session After the Conferences

In this session four issues were discussed. The first related to the availability of land and its effect on price. It proved that not enough expertise was available in the group to estimate the actual parameters involved. It was decided that this part of the model would have to be discussed in more detail with a specialist.

The second issue related to the social indicators. From a list which had been collected from the literature and discussions with specialists in this domain, three indicators were selected. The first indicator, which proves crucial, is the demand pressure, in particular in the low and the middle class. The lower the demand pressure in these classes, the better the social goals are accomplished. The second indicator is the average increase in rent over the years. This indicator can be calculated as the increase in rent over the simulation (actual rent minus initial rent at some point in time) divided by the initial rent, the result of which is in turn divided by the time elapsed.

The third social indicator, which is closely related to the previous one, is the actual rent increase rate per year. Not only the average increase over a number of years, but also the scale of the actual rent increase rate each year is of importance, since this is what people actually pay attention to. People do not normally calculate the average rent increase over the last 20 years.

Having discussed the selection of the social indicators, the next issue to be discussed was the effect of the demand pressure on the decision to build houses. As explained, we introduced a variable distribution ratio in the workbook by dividing demand in each class by the total demand in the three classes. Although participants agreed with this idea, it was felt that the distribution ratio should depend on the demand pressure rather than the demand versus total demand, as we had assumed. In other words, the distribution ratio should depend on the relative demand pressure in each of the classes.

The relative demand pressure in a particular category is calculated as the demand pressure in that category, divided by the sum of the demand pressures in the three categories. This is similar to what we had proposed, albeit with a different indicator. The submodel in Figure 7.11 shows the effect of demand pressure on the inflow on the waiting list. Demand pressure in each of the classes is determined by dividing the waiting list by the number of houses in stock. On the one hand demand pressure affects the planning rate of new houses. If demand pressure rises above 10% then all potential houses are taken into planning. Below 5% no new houses are taken into planning. On the other hand demand pressure affects the distribution ratio of new houses. The lower the demand pressure in a category, the lower the percentage of houses built in that particular category. The introduction of demand pressure thus creates a balancing loop. The higher the demand, the more houses will be constructed, the higher the number of houses in stock will be and the lower the demand pressure. The reader may wonder why two separate effects of demand pressure on the decision to construct new houses are needed, in particular because both are related. If demand pressure drops in a particular category, this will lower the distribution ratio for this category and thus automatically lower the number of houses built for this class. However, if this would be the only balancing loop, then if demand pressure drops below 10%, new houses will still be constructed in this category, although at a low rate. Since houses do have a long life time, this may then lead to a situation of uninhabited houses when demand continues to drop. By introducing the second effect this danger is diminished.

Discussing these matters focused attention on demand and on the fact that demand was an exogenous factor. But under the new circumstances it might be expected that associations would operate on a competitive market. Hence, it was felt by one group member that we would need to include a variable called 'competitive power'. This variable would indicate the relative attractiveness of the association for tenants who would normally hesitate between renting or buying a house. In order not to complicate matters, it was assumed that the price to be paid for buying a house would follow the inflation rate. If an association increases rent above the inflation rate, it would thus lose potential tenants who would then decide to buy rather than to rent a house. On the other hand staying below the inflation rate would attract demand. This is depicted in Figure 7.11.

The figure portrays the effect of competitive power. If competitive power increases (rent increases are lower than inflation), this will be perceived by renters (perc–comp–power), which will increase the inflow on the waiting list. This will in turn increase the pressure to construct houses. On the other hand, if competitive power drops, this will decrease the inflow. Although the direction of the effect of competitive power on the inflow is clear, the group had a difficult time in actually determining its magnitude. It was felt that the magnitude of the effect would be different for the three categories. The effect was considered to be most pronounced in the high class and less so in the lower ones. It was assumed that the maximum effect, when competitive power would be highest, would be 1.25 for the high, 1.15 for the middle and 1.1 for the lowest class. This situation is reached when the association has a zero rent increase rate as compared to the inflation rate. The normal inflow will thus be increased by multiplying it with the above effect in each of the categories. When the association follows the inflation rate in its rent increase policy the effect for each of the classes is 1.0, which will make the actual inflow on the waiting list equal to the normal inflow. Finally, in extreme cases, when rent increases are five times as high as inflation the demand inflow in the highest category will drop to zero. In the lowest category this effect is less pronounced, demand inflow will drop to 50%, while in the middle category it will drop to 75% of the normal inflow. Although this issue was discussed during the meeting, there was no time to actually build this into the model during the session and no runs could be made to check the validity of these assumptions.

The modellers added the results from the third meeting into the model and the result can be seen in Figure 7.12.

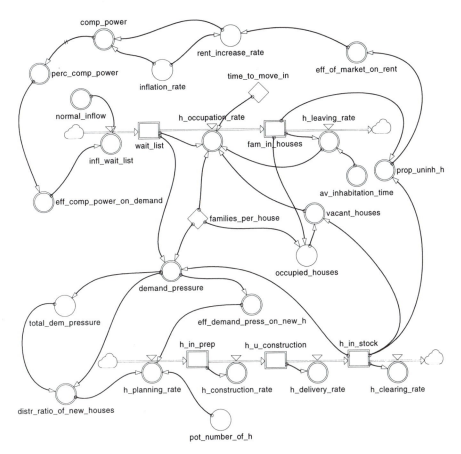

Figure 7.11 Effect of Demand Pressure on House Construction and Competitive Power on Demand

As can be seen this model is already quite complex. Throughout this chapter it was explained how it was constructed. I will not summarize the model here. In the next chapter I will discuss a number of analyses of the model in order to reveal its behavioural characteristics. There I will present a causal loop diagram which may assist the reader in better understanding the structure of the model.

INSIGHTS GAINED

This third session was the last one planned with the group and it was decided to temporarily stop the model construction process in order to test its applicability in a strategic workshop with a 'friendly' allied association. As pointed out in the beginning of this chapter, the model will be used as a means to support strategic workshops with management teams of allied housing associations of MPA. Since

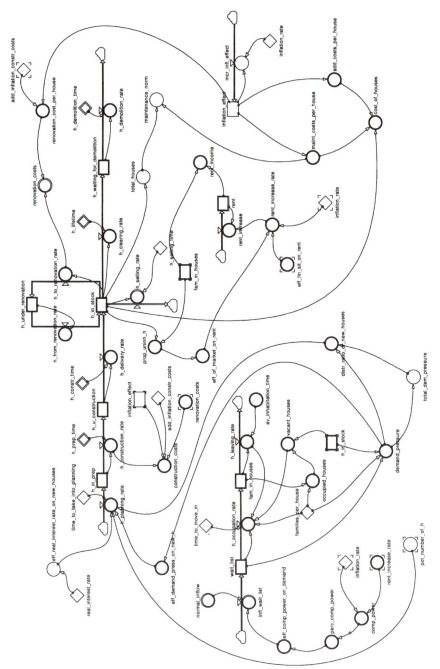

Figure 7.12 System Dynamics Model of Housing Association

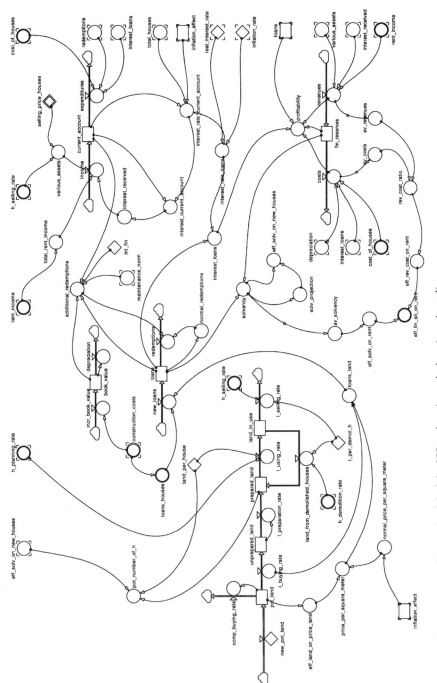

Figure 7.12 System Dynamics Model of Housing Association (*continued*)

strategic problems can vary widely between associations, each time the model is used, it will have to be adapted to the specific situation of a particular association. As such, it was felt by the group that rather than developing this model further, it might be wise to conduct a couple of test workshops with a couple of 'friendly' management teams, in order to find out if the model was actually well-suited.

A number of important insights were gained by the client during the model construction process. The first and foremost was the feedback perspective. Although at first our client was a bit reluctant to introduce feedback loops, simulation runs with the model revealed that exponential behaviour produced unrealistic results. Part of their reluctance derived from the fact that participants were afraid that the model would behave like an 'automatic pilot', which would be useless in strategic workshops. They wanted their clients to be able to set all kinds of parameter values (e.g. rent increase rate, inflow on the waiting list), rather than having these controlled by feedback loops. We explained that there were at least two reasons to introduce the feedback processes: first, to be able to explore the dynamics of the model in depth. Second, even if one would like the client to 'play' with the model parameters, this could be accomplished under various scenarios. For instance, the participant may control the rate of rent increase, but the effects may be studied under varying conditions. For example, under different assumed effects of rent increase on demand inflow. Alternatively, the participant may want to control the process of negotiating loans and the proportion of internal financing, while the effects can be studied under various conditions of government control over rent increase rates. In other words, we explained to the group that the best strategy was to start by identifying the full set of relationships and feedback loops and in the second step decide, with their client, which parameters and/or feedback loops would be put under control of the participants in the strategic workshops. This argument helped to lower the client's resistance towards feedback loops.

A second insight related to the character of the exponential development. The model clearly showed that exponential growth could be expected and this was in line with what the client knew from other financial models. What was less known, was that the exponential increase showed a tendency to continue into the far future, even when rent increase rates tended to follow the inflation rate. The model, by the way, also clearly revealed that this situation could differ drastically for various associations depending on the 'age distribution' of their houses. In this respect the answer to the question of whether the social and financial goals could be accomplished simultaneously depended, among other things, on the age distribution of the houses in stock of a particular association. The more skewed the distribution is towards the young end the more difficult it may be to accomplish both goals simultaneously. In that case an association may find it difficult to guarantee its financial continuity, particularly when many houses have to be constructed in the low category.

The model-building process also helped to lift our client from the 'complex' perspective to a more abstract level of dynamic processes in the housing domain. Rather than focusing on one complex of houses as is usually done, the emphasis was now on the whole set of interrelated processes within a housing association. This holistic view also affected the way consultancy projects with clients were handled.

The model-building process also had an effect on the organization itself and the way consultants handled their clients. In the organization, the model-building process induced a communication between various specialists and the model revealed the interrelatedness of the various areas. This also percolated through to the consultancy processes with clients. In the past different specialists tended to advise their clients in a piecemeal fashion. Each specialist tended to provide advice on one aspect of a housing association: demand, supply, finances etc. Currently, advice processes tend to take a more holistic view towards the client's problem, which in turn produces more consistent advice for the client.

SUMMARY

This chapter has described the process of building a system dynamics model with a client group of MPA. I have attempted to show how the client group participated in the model construction process and how runs with the model lead to adaptations of the model and in particular to the identification of a number of feedback loops in the model.

As the reader may gather, the model, as I have discussed it so far, is not finished in the sense that it has been tested thoroughly. In this chapter I have only shown a couple of runs with the model. In order to assess the model and to demonstrate some analyses of the current model for the novice reader, the next chapter will focus on sensitivity analyses and policy experiments. I will start with the presentation of the whole model and next introduce causal loop diagrams to highlight the structure of the model.

Chapter 8

Analysis of the Housing Association Model

INTRODUCTION

In the foregoing chapter I have described the process by which the housing association model was constructed. In this chapter I will present a number of analyses to assess the current version of the model and to illustrate the process of model analysis for the reader who is not familiar with system dynamics model-building. The primary purpose is to illustrate the process of model analysis. Assessment is the secondary purpose. I will start with a summary of the model in the form of a causal loop diagram. Next the base run will be presented. The remainder of the chapter will discuss a number of sensitivity analyses and policy experiments.

A CAUSAL LOOP DIAGRAM OF THE MODEL

As we have seen at the end of the previous chapter the housing model is already quite complex. In order to keep the diagram orderly I used a number of 'ghost' variables. These have the advantage that one does not need to draw arrows over long distances in the model, which quickly creates the idea of disorderliness. However, there is also a disadvantage to it, because one easily loses track of the feedback structure of the model. In order to assist the reader in grasping the feedback structure of the model, I will discuss this with the aid of a causal loop diagram as shown in Figure 8.1.

In order not to replicate the flow diagram and in an attempt to clarify the structure I have left out (a) variables which are not embedded in any feedback loop, and (b) intermediating variables within feedback loops, which do not add to our understanding of the structure. As can be seen from the causal loop diagram the model contains several reinforcing as well as balancing loops. Let us first take a look at the reinforcing loops.

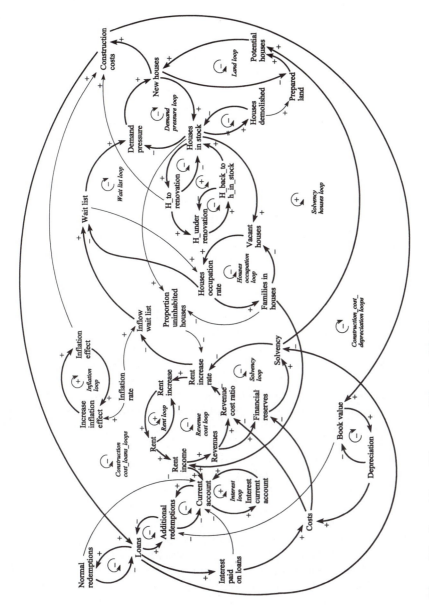

Figure 8.1 Causal Loop Diagram of Housing Model

Reinforcing Loops

The model contains three important reinforcing loops: (a) the rent loop, (b) the inflation loop, and (c) the interest loop. The rent loop indicates a positive feedback process between rent increase and rent, even when the rent increase rate is constant. In the previous chapter we have seen that this positive loop is quite strong in affecting the model's behaviour. The inflation loop is similar to the rent loop. Finally, the interest loop refers to the phenomenon of interest upon interest with regard to the current account.

The reader may have noticed, that a positive feedback loop can also be identified from solvency back to solvency through the potential number of houses, new houses, houses in stock, vacant houses, families in houses, rent income and thus back to solvency via revenues and financial reserves (the 'solvency houses loop'). If solvency drops below zero, no new houses can be constructed which leads to less families in houses and less rent income which will negatively affect the solvency. The solvency houses loop is thus a reinforcing loop. As will be clear this loop only operates under the extreme condition that solvency drops below zero. If this is not the case the loop is not active.

Balancing Loops

The model also contains a number of balancing loops. First, there are a number of direct balancing loops, including only two variables. For instance, the loop between houses in stock and houses demolished. The more houses in stock, the higher the demolition rate and thus the lower the number of houses in stock. This negative loop contains a larger delay, because of the long life time of houses. Comparable balancing loops can be found between (a) houses in stock and houses to renovation, (b) houses under renovation and houses back to stock, (c) book value and depreciation, and (d) loans and (additional) redemptions. The higher the loans in comparison with the book value the higher the additional redemptions. On the other hand, the higher the additional redemptions, the lower the current account, which will in turn decrease the amount of additional redemptions.

In the upper right hand part of the diagram, there are four mutually linked balancing loops. One of these is the 'demand pressure loop'. This loop runs from demand pressure through new houses and houses in stock, back to demand pressure. The higher the demand pressure the more new houses will be constructed, which will increase the number of houses in stock, which will in turn decrease demand pressure. The second is the 'wait list loop'. This one also runs from demand pressure, which, if increased, boosts the number of new houses and houses in stock, creating vacant houses, a higher houses occupation rate, which empties the waiting list and thus reduces demand pressure. The third loop, the 'houses occupation loop', runs from houses occupation rate through families in houses and vacant houses back to the occupation rate. The higher the occupation rate, the higher the number of families in houses (if the waiting list exceeds the number of vacant houses), which decreases the number of vacant houses and thus the occupation rate.

Another balancing loop, which is connected to the previous ones, is the 'land loop'. The more prepared land is available the higher the number of potential houses, which augments the number of new houses constructed, which reduces the amount of available land.

Two important balancing loops which have been discussed in the previous chapter are: the 'revenue cost loop' and the 'solvency loop'. The 'revenue cost loop' can be described as follows: if rents increase, this will augment rent income (for each of the three different classes of houses) and thus the total rent income for the housing association. The increase in rent income will boost revenues and thus the revenue cost ratio. This will in turn produce a downward effect on the rent increase rate, which reverses the process. Simultaneously, increased revenues will raise financial reserves, which makes solvency go up. And in turn the higher the solvency the more the downward pressure on the rent increase rate. As we have seen in the previous chapter, these loops control model behaviour to a large degree, they changed a situation of exponential growth into one of linear growth. In one of the experiments in this chapter, I will investigate which of these two loops is most important in producing this effect in the model.

Five additional balancing loops are the three 'construction costs – loans' loops, and the two 'construction costs – depreciation' loops. The first two loops can be described as follows. The higher the number of new houses, the higher the construction costs, which increases the loans. This produces two effects, the first of which has two branches, hence three loops: (a) higher interests to be paid on loans, which produces costs and decreases the revenue cost ratio as well as the financial reserves and the solvency (two branches), and (b) a lower solvency. All three produce an upward pressure on the rent increase rate, which decreases the inflow on the waiting list, which decreases demand pressure and thus the number of new houses and construction costs. A similar process can be described for the construction costs–depreciation–rent increase loops. Increasing construction costs produce a higher book value, more depreciation, more costs, and thus (via the two known routes) an upward pressure on the rents, which decreases the inflow on the waiting list and the number of new houses and construction costs.

An additional balancing loop (actually three loops as before) can be found from rent income through current account, additional redemptions, loans, interest paid on loans, cost and via revenue cost ratio (and solvency) back to rent income. The effect of this loop is, however, clearly subordinate to the revenue cost loop. In other words, if the revenue cost ratio changes this will almost immediately affect the rent increase rate, an effect which is more direct and stronger than the loop(s) discussed above.

THE BASE RUN OF THE MODEL

Before discussing the base run I have to remind the reader that the model was built with this question in mind: can sufficient low cost housing be built while simultaneously insuring the financial continuity of the association? The primary indicators for the financial situation of the association are its profitability and its solvency. The primary indicators for the social goal are: the demand pressure in the lower categories and the rent (average) increase rates. In presenting simulation runs with the model these variables will thus be presented (see Figure 8.2).

As can be seen from this run, the model now behaves in a more stable fashion than the run shown in the previous chapter. This is primarily caused by two balancing feedback loops: the revenue cost loop and the solvency loop.

As a result of increasing rents in the beginning of the simulation run and interest received, revenues exceed the costs. This boosts the financial reserves which improves the solvency of the association, from 14 to over 20%. The revenues which surpass the costs by about 8%, in combination with the rising solvency start a downward effect on the rent increase rate. Due to the decrease in the rent increase rate after the first couple of years, the financial reserves start to show declining growth and the solvency slightly drops until it reaches a value of 18.5% at the end of the 50th year. The profitability of the association follows a comparable pattern. It starts off at 6.6% and climbs to about 7% in the first 10 years. After that there is a slow decline towards a value of 6% by the end of the simulation.

Since solvency (and the revenue cost ratio) both increase in the beginning of the simulation the rents are slightly decreased (0.7%) below the inflation, which results in a decrease of the average real rent increase rate. When this decrease produces lower margins and lower solvency, rents tend to go up again. Since the developments in rent is the same for all three classes I have only reproduced the rent increase for the lowest class 1. The initial erratic behaviour of the averages is partly caused by initial changes in the rent increase rate and partly by the fact that the elapsed time period is relatively short, which ensures that changes have a relatively large effect. In addition, rents are adapted once every twelve months which also produces an erratic pattern.

Although the association performs well financially, the social goals are not entirely met. The rent increase is mild and stays on average below inflation. However, the demand pressure in the lowest category is high and it grows from 60 to 72.2%. For the middle category the pressure rises slightly from 25 to 29%, while in the highest category it ends at 15%, which is equal to the value in the beginning of the simulation. In one of the policy experiments we will explore how this situation might be changed. In the next sections I will discuss a couple of tests with the simulation model.

DEACTIVATING FEEDBACK LOOPS: THE EFFECT OF THE FINANCIAL SITUATION ON THE RENT INCREASE

An important way to gain understanding of the model is to conduct a number of controlled experiments or tests with the model. One important test of system dynamics models is to deactivate one or more feedback loops to study their effects. In one of the previous sections I have discussed two important balancing feedback loops controlling the model's behaviour. These loops control the rate with which the rent is increased as a result of the financial situation of the association. Two effects of the financial situation were employed: the ratio of average revenues

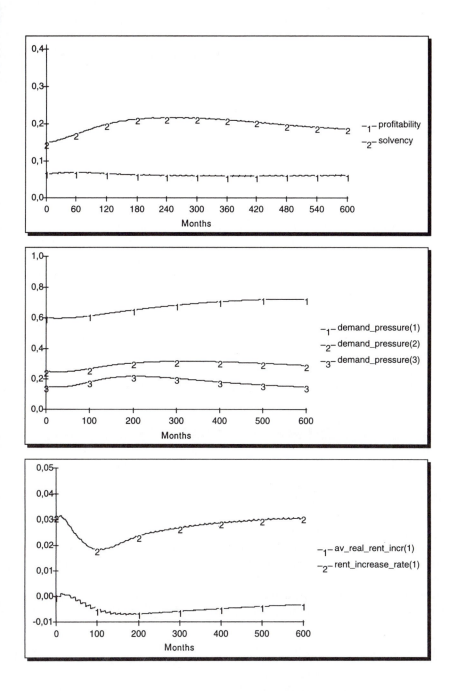

Figure 8.2 Base Run of the Housing Model

versus costs and the association's solvency. The two balancing loops ensure that the financial situation of the association remains within specified limits. In the previous chapter we have seen that without these loops the financial reserves rise to over dfl. 3 billion and the solvency rises to 75%. This exponential increase was the primary reason to build these feedback loops into the model. In the base run, when these two loops are added to the model, the financial reserves rise to about 125 million (in a linear fashion) and the solvency reaches a value of 18.5% after 50 years. Since there are two loops controlling this process, the question may be raised which of the two is stronger. This can be studied by deactivating one loop at a time. The results are shown in Figure 8.3.

The runs with an odd number represent runs in which the revenue cost loop is 'switched off'. The rent increase is solely controlled by the solvency loop. The runs with an even number show the results when the rent increase is controlled by the revenue cost ratio loop only. The differences between both runs are substantial and reveal that the revenue cost ratio loop is the strongest of both loops. When the rent increase is controlled by the solvency loop, solvency grows to almost 40%, while the revenue cost loop ensures that solvency never exceeds 25%. This also holds for the average rent increase. Curves labelled -2- and -4- show that when the rent increase is controlled by the revenue cost ratio it drops faster than when the solvency loop is active. Finally, differences between demand pressure are found. These are largely due to the fact that in the case of the solvency loop, rents stay at a higher level, which produces a downward effect on the inflow of the waiting list, while in the case of the revenue cost loop rents decrease rapidly, which then attracts additional tenants on the waiting list, through the increase in competitive power.

SENSITIVITY ANALYSES

One important stage is conducting sensitivity analyses with the model. One reason for conducting sensitivity analyses is to increase confidence in the model. The question is whether, if parameters in the model are changed within plausible limits, the model reveals reasonable behaviour. As stated, sensitivity analyses are primarily meant to establish sensitive parameters in the model. Generally sensitivity analyses also result in learning about the model's structure and dynamics. As an example, I will present a couple of sensitivity analyses below. I do have to point out that because of the prototype character of the model and the fact that numerous analyses can be performed, these just serve as examples as is the case for the policy experiments which will be discussed in the subsequent section.

The Inflation Rate

A very straightforward example of a sensitivity analysis would be to vary the value of the inflation rate to see how the model would react to such a change. I have made three runs with the model where the rate of inflation is 1%, 3% and 5%. Figure 8.4 shows the results on a number of variables.

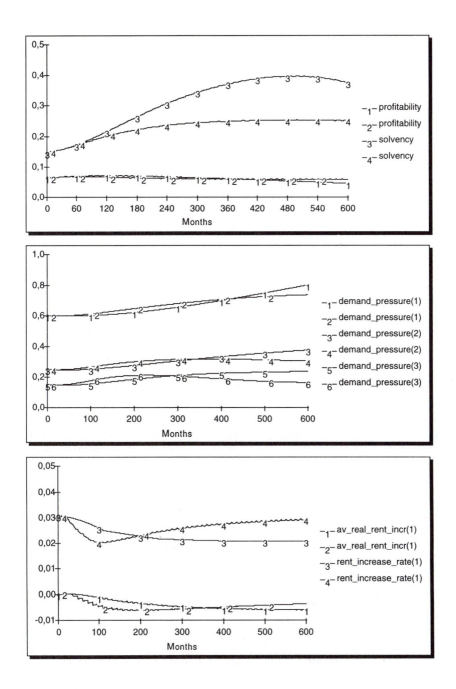

Figure 8.3 The Effect of Deactivating the Revenue Cost Ratio Loop and the Solvency Loop

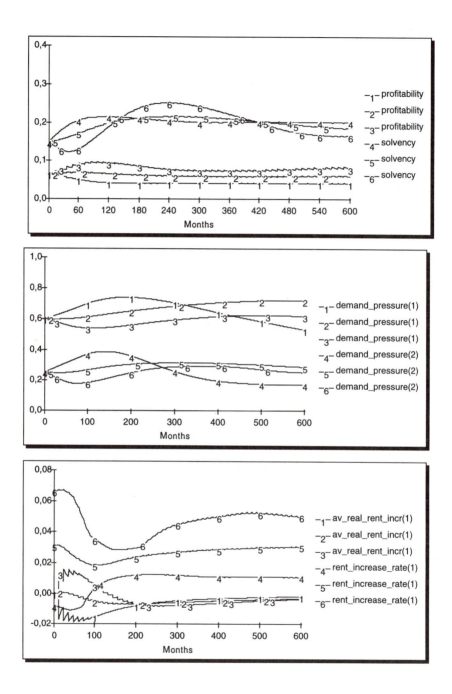

Figure 8.4 Sensitivity Analysis with Inflation Rate at 1%, 3% and 5%

In the diagrams the curves labelled -1- (and -4-) represent the situation of 1% inflation rate. Curves labelled -2- (and -5-) represent 3% inflation rate and curves -3- (and -6-) illustrate the situation of 5% inflation rate annually. Note that the curves labelled -2- and -5- (with a 3% inflation rate) will be identical to the base run, which provides a basis for comparison. The most conspicuous result is that most variables show much larger swings when the inflation rate increases. This is understandable because prices will increase faster, which makes rents go up quicker and boosts the current account and the profits. When we observe the rent increase rate, one may expect that the nominal increase will be largest in the run with 5% annual inflation (curve -6-). But when we look at the real annual increase (corrected for inflation) there is slight decrease similar to the base run, as can be seen in the figure.

A couple of things deviate from the base run. For instance in the situation of a 1% inflation rate, the solvency starts to rise immediately (curve -4-), while in the case of a 5% inflation rate solvency first drops considerably (curve -6-). This is due to the fact that when the inflation rate is 5%, the interest rate paid on loans rises to 9% rather than 7% as is the case in the base run. As a result, costs increase rapidly, which reduces the financial reserves and hence the solvency. In the longer run solvency recovers, because, as can be seen in the figure, rents are rapidly raised (curve -6- in lower graph), which in turn increases revenues and restores the financial reserves and the solvency. Profitability on the other hand, shows quite a different picture. In this case the sharpest rise happens initially in the run when the inflation rate is set at 5%. Because of this inflation rate, the interest on loans is high, which increases the profitability. (Remember that the numerator of the profitability fraction contains the rents paid on loans. I have to point out that in this model the interest rate follows the inflation rate. In reality the percentages of interest are converted once in a number of years which make the adaptation of interest levels to the inflation much more erratic.)

Interestingly, the differences in the inflation rate also affect the demand pressure. In order to keep the figure legible, I have only selected to print the demand pressure for the two lower classes. When the inflation rate is 1%, the lower graph shows that rents are lowered considerably below the inflation level (curve -4-). This in turn attracts extra tenants to the waiting list, which increases the demand pressure. When demand pressure in the lower category rises, this in turn affects the distribution ratio of houses. More houses are built in the lower category and, as a result, demand pressure starts to fall off, due to the 'demand pressure loop'. This effect is reinforced by the fact that when real rents start to increase, demand pressure starts to drop, because inflow on the waiting list will decrease.

Initial Values for Book Value and Loans

In the session with the client group, the discussion has focused several times on the exact value for the initial book value and the loans. Below is the result of three experiments with initial values of dfl. 180, 200 and 220 billion for book value and the corresponding initial values at 90% of the book value for loans: dfl. 162, 180 and 198 billion. The results of these three experiments are shown in Figure 8.5.

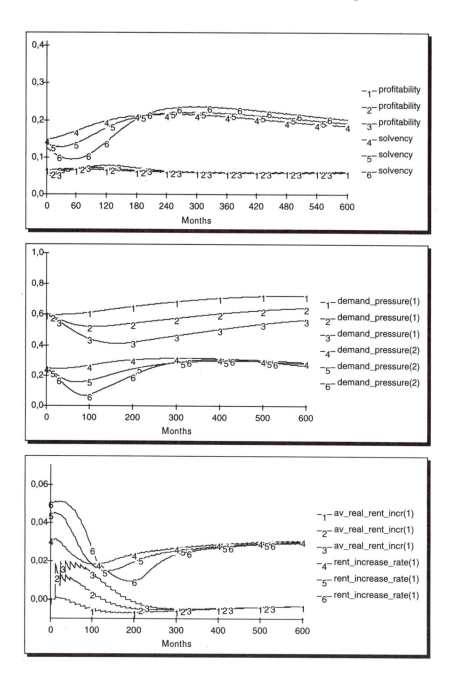

Figure 8.5 Effect of Different Initial Values for Book Value and Loans

The runs show that changing the initial values of the loans and the book value has a marked effect on the model's output. The solvency shows the tendency to drop initially (curve -6-), the higher the initial values are. This is understandable, since the higher the book value, the higher the depreciations, and the higher the initial value of the loans, the higher the interest to be paid on loans. As we have seen in the previous chapter, the situation with high initial values represent associations with a high proportion of 'young' houses. On the other hand, associations with a high proportion of old houses have a low book value and level of loans. The reader may recall that I have indicated in the previous chapter that initially houses have higher costs than revenues. This is compensated when in later years revenues start to exceed costs (because in general, rents increase faster than costs, as I have explained previously). In this sense the model shows behaviour which would be expected. The higher the proportion of 'young' houses for an association (and thus a high book value and level of loans) the higher the costs in comparison with the revenues, which explains the initial drop in solvency. As houses mature, revenues start to exceed costs and solvency quickly starts to rise. In this model this is partly caused by the feedback loops controlling the rent increase rate. In the case of high initial costs, the revenue cost ratio and the solvency will be low, which will produce an upward effect on the rents, hence the rise in solvency after the first five years. As can be seen in the high book value/loans situation (curve -6-), solvency even overtakes the low book value/loans situation (curve -4-) after about 200 months. As stated, this is largely due to the two feedback loops. When these are deactivated, financial reserves rise exponentially and solvency increases towards a value of 75%, as we have seen in the previous chapter. If we increase the initial values for book value and loans (and deactivate both loops), we see the same initial dip in solvency, but, contrary to when the loops are activated, solvency does *not* overtake, because the rent increase has become constant. In other words, the fact that solvency overtakes is caused by the corrective actions of the feedback loops. Similar arguments can be made with regard to profitability.

The graphs also show that the rent increase rate behaves markedly different in the three situations. When the initial values of loans and book value are increased, rents are raised quickly because of the low revenue cost ratio and solvency. In the highest initial values for loans and book value the average real rents increase with more than 2% (curve -3-), which implies a nominal rent increase rates of 5% (curve -6-). Again, the reader is reminded that the erratic behaviour is partly caused by an annual (rather than monthly) rent increase and the fact that in the beginning, changes in rents play a larger role in the average rent increase than in later years.

Finally, the simulation run shows that demand pressure falls when initial values for loans and book value are increased. This is caused by the fact that rents are increased, which reduces the inflow on the waiting list. The effects are more pronounced for category two than one, because changes in rents are supposed to affect the second category to a larger degree: if rents rise people in this category will more quickly respond by buying houses rather than renting them. In turn when demand pressure falls the construction cost loans loops become active and less new houses are constructed, which slightly reduces the amount of loans and thus lowers the rent increase.

Simulating an Event: Pulling Down Houses

In the next experiment, let us suppose that all of a sudden 10% of the houses in the lower category have to been emptied and pulled down, because the quality of the concrete has deteriorated rapidly. This can be simulated by increasing the clearing rate for houses with a pulse of 10% of the houses in stock in category one. The pulse is set at the 60th month, i.e. after five years from the start of the simulation. One would expect that in this case the demand pressure in the lowest class would increase. As a result the distribution ratio of new houses would be skewed towards the lowest class and this would lead to an increase in the demand pressures in the other two classes too. The results of this simulation run are shown in Figure 8.6.

As was expected, demand pressure in the low category rises sharply, due to the houses which have been pulled down. The rise in demand pressure is higher than would be expected. If 10% of the houses in the low category are demolished (i.e. 180 houses) one would expect demand pressure to increase by 10%. Initially, demand pressure is $1080 \div 1800 = 0.60$. Now demand pressure becomes: $1080 \div 1620 = 0.67$. The extra increase to almost 80% in the graph of Figure 8.6 is caused by the waiting list loop. Extra houses demolished means less houses in stock, which creates less vacant houses and a lower houses occupation rate, which further increases the waiting list and the demand pressure. This is what happens initially. From the demand pressure loop and the waiting list loop, however, one would expect that increasing demand pressure would lead to the construction of more new houses and over time demand pressure would then fall again. This is indeed the case, because the number of houses pulled down increases the amount of prepared land, which temporarily increases the potential number of houses to be constructed, which if constructed, take up the land and the houses planning rate decreases, a process caused by the 'land loop'.

As stated, one would expect demand pressure to rise in the other categories too, because of a change in the distribution ratio towards the low category. Strangely, this proves not to be the case. Contrary to what one might expect, the demand pressure in the other two categories drops when demand pressure in the lowest category increases. How can this counterintuitive behaviour be explained? In order to find an answer to this question, we will have to look for changes in other variables in the model. Since demand pressure is defined as demand divided by houses in stock, when demand pressure in the other two categories drops, this can only be the result of the fact that: (a) the demand in these classes drops, or (b) the number of houses in stock increases (or both). Studying the figures in the model reveals that the latter is not the case. On the contrary the distribution ratio for these two classes of houses decreases and so does the stock of houses. Then demand must have dropped, which is indeed the case. The waiting list decreases because the inflow falls. And the latter is caused by a sudden increase in the rents after the 60th month, which causes the competitive power of the association to deteriorate rapidly. But why would rents increase suddenly? This is caused by the fact that a number of houses had to be emptied and pulled down. This results in a loss of rent income and hence the revenue cost ratio drops sharply. This in turn

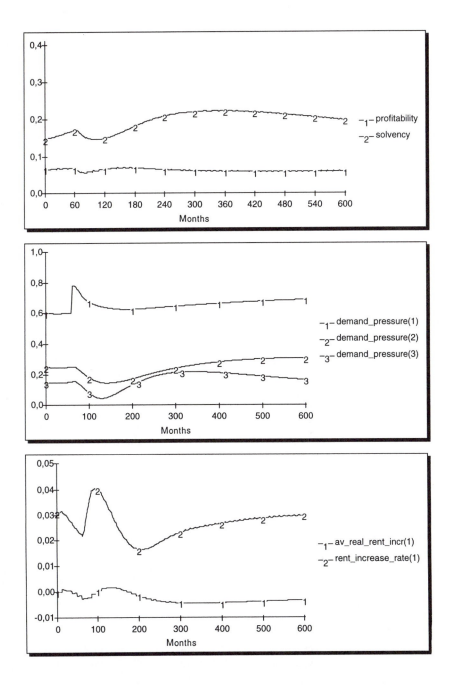

Figure 8.6 Exogenous Scenario: 10% of Houses in Category 1 have to be Pulled Down

augments the rents. In addition, there is an effect from the construction cost loans loops and the construction cost depreciation loops. New houses are constructed at the spot where others have been pulled down. This creates extra construction costs, which in turn increases the rents. The rent increase rate rises to 4% and remains above 3% (the inflation level) from about the 80th to the 130th month, i.e. for more than four years. This can be seen in curve -2- of the lower graph. And particularly in the highest income category such an increase in rents produces a large effect on the inflow, as we have seen at the end of the previous chapter. In this category, the inflow drops most sharply and so does demand pressure.

As a result of the increase in rents, however, revenues start to rise again which results in a stabilization of the rents. Additionally, construction costs will fall again when demand pressure has been decreased due to an increase in rents, which decreases the inflow on the waiting list and thus demand pressure and construction cost, which in turn lowers the rate of rent increase.

Interestingly, this experiment also revealed a flaw in the model. What normally happens is that people whose houses have to be pulled down are rehoused into vacant houses. This implies that the inflow into houses (h–occupation–rate) is temporarily stopped until all relevant families have been rehoused. What happens in the model, however, is that people who are inhabiting houses, which have to be pulled down, are sent back to the waiting list, because of the equation for vacant houses. Vacant houses are calculated as the difference between occupied houses and houses in stock. Since the number of houses in stock is suddenly decreased (through the PULSE on the houses clearing rate), the number of vacant houses becomes negative, which produces a negative houses occupation rate and in turn a negative outflow of the waiting list, which actually implies an inflow on this list.

This experiment was discussed with the client, but although there clearly was a conceptual gap in the formulation of the model, the client was not too worried, because the reassuring thing was that in terms of figures the effects remain the same. Whether the model sends people back to the waiting list or whether the outflow of the waiting list is temporarily arrested in order to have people rehoused into other houses. Although this argument may be correct, the conceptual structure of the model will have to be corrected to match the actual process as it is supposed to operate in reality.

I have shown this example, because it neatly demonstrates that this simulation run with the model reveals a defect which gives rise to a change of the model's structure. This is what modellers mean when they say that model-building is an iterative process. From a particular stage in the process (model analysis) the modeller will have to go back to a previous stage (conceptualization). I do have to remind the reader that this can happen with every new simulation run which is made. That is one of the reasons why testing the model, although time consuming, is an absolute requirement, before 'real' policy conclusions can be drawn. Although our model does not prove to be complete, I will conduct a policy experiment for illustrative purposes.

POLICY EXPERIMENTS

As discussed in the chapters on system dynamics, the ultimate goal of a quantitative system dynamics model is to perform a number of policy experiments to find robust policies. Although in this case we only have a prototype model, which is not geared towards one particular housing association, I will use the model to demonstrate the way policy experiments are conducted with system dynamics models.

The analyses thus far have revealed that the housing association will perform well on the financial indicators if the inflation rate is taken as the basis for the rent increase rate. One important indicator on the social goals on which performance leaves to be desired is the demand pressure, particularly for the low income category. As we have seen in the base run, demand pressure for the low income category rises from 60 to 72% at the end of the simulation. One way to solve this problem would be to initiate a policy in which priority is given to the construction of houses in the low category. However, initiating such a policy would automatically be at the expense of the other two waiting lists. The reason for this is that we have assumed that our association follows a conservative housing construction policy. The association just replaces demolished houses, but does not actively look for ways to expand the stock of houses. As a consequence, if the association starts to change the distribution ratio in favour of the low income category, this will automatically raise the demand pressure in the other categories. One way to solve this problem would be to buy additional land on which extra houses could be built. The question might be how much extra land would be needed if demand pressure in all three categories should have to drop. In order to investigate this issue I have performed three runs with the model. In all three situations I have assumed that the distribution ratio for the three categories will be fixed at 70% (low), 20% (middle) and 10% (high). The reader may recall that the normal ratios were 60, 25, and 15% respectively. The new situation thus favours the low and middle income categories at the expense of the high income class. In the first run, no extra land is bought, in the second it is assumed that the association will buy 5000 square metres every five years, starting after five years. In the third situation the amount of land bought is increased to 10 000 square metres every five years. The results are depicted in Figure 8.7.

In order to keep the graphs legible, I have depicted the demand pressure for the low and high class. The middle class is in between these two. In the graph the curves -1- to -3- represent the three situations described above for the low income class: (1) 70% distribution ratio and no extra land, (2) 70% distribution ratio and 5000 square metres every five years, and (3) 70% distribution ratio and 10 000 square metres every five years. The curves -4- to -6- represent the situation for the high category under the same conditions with a 10% distribution ratio.

As the graphs reveal, when no land is bought the change in distribution ratio (from 60 to 70%) produces a decline in demand pressure in the low class to under 40% (curve -1-), but a high increase in the high class (curve -4-). As was predicted, changing the distribution ratio will favour the low class at the expense of the high class: the demand pressure rises to almost 100% in the high class. When 5000 square

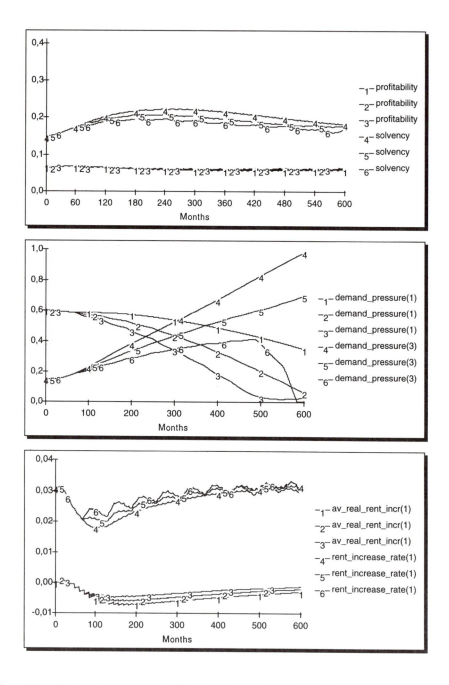

Figure 8.7 Experiments to Reduce Demand Pressure in Lowest Category

metres is bought every five years (which implies an extra 25 houses are constructed), the demand pressure in the low category drops to about 10% (curve -2-), while the increase in category three is to over 60% (curve 5). Finally, when 10 000 square metres are bought, demand pressure in the low class tends to approach zero. In that situation the effect of demand pressure on the construction of new houses becomes active and it reduces the number of houses constructed in the low class to zero. What is strange, however, is that when demand pressure in category one drops to zero, demand pressure also starts to drop in category three. The reader might be inclined to think this is natural since more houses can be built in the second and third category, if no houses have to be built in the first. Remember, however, that we have fixed the distribution ratio: it is constant rather than variable. Even when no houses are built in the first category, this does not mean that more houses will be built in the other two. The reader may recall from the previous chapter that this was exactly the reason why a variable distribution ratio was built into the model.

Since, in the case of a fixed distribution ratio the explanation cannot be a shift in the construction of houses between classes, then what is the explanation? The first thought which comes to mind is a potential decrease in the inflow of the waiting list, because rents are increasing. This would produce a fall in demand pressure, which was the case in a couple of the previous runs. In the current situation, however, this does not seem to be the case. Graphs (not shown here) reveal no particular drop in the inflow in the waiting list for the third category. If demand does not reveal a dramatic change, then the explanation has to be found on the supply side of the demand pressure. The only explanation left, is that more houses are built in category three. Indeed, the graphs show that when the house planning rate for the first category drops to zero more new houses are planned in the other two categories. This happens after about the 480th month, as can be seen in curves -2- and -3- in Figure 8.8.

The figure also reveals why more houses are planned in these two categories. The explanation for this is not the distribution ratio (which is fixed), but has to be found in the land loop. The amount of prepared land increases as a result of the fact that no houses are constructed in the first category. This leaves prepared land unoccupied in month t, which increases the number of potential houses in month $t+1$, and this increases the number of houses which can be built in the second and third category, even when the distribution ratio is constant. This in turn decreases the amount of prepared land. By the end of the simulation there is enough land so that supply starts to exceed demand and the demand pressure in the other two categories also starts to drop to zero.

If we maintain the idea that land will be bought every five years, the experiment reveals that in order to lower the demand pressure in all three categories, the association would have to buy an amount of land between 5000 and 10 000 square metres every five years. More simulation runs could narrow this range down more carefully. Alternatively, as was discussed in Chapter 3, optimization procedures could be used to find the optimal policy. This, however, requires a thoroughly tested and validated model.

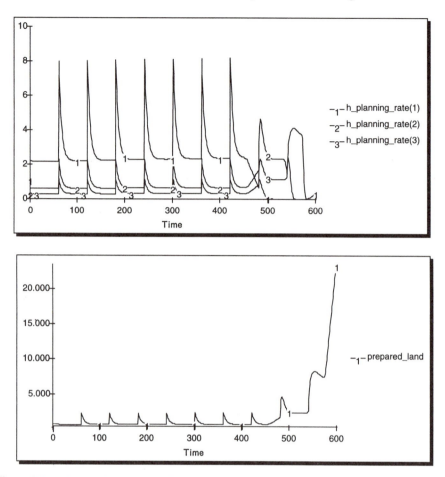

Figure 8.8 Effect of Diminishing Pressure on Land and New Houses

MODEL VALIDITY AND USEFULNESS

In the previous sections I have discussed a couple of simulation runs with the model
of an average housing association. One element which has not yet been discussed is
the validity of the model. Two things have to be kept in mind when discussing the
model's validity. First, this is not a model of a specific association and hence no test
on the reproduction of the reference mode of behaviour can be performed. This is
also complicated by the fact that this model simulates a completely new situation
without government support for housing associations, a situation which contains
many uncertainties and about which no historical data are available. Second, the
model is still under construction, it is not finished and has to be subjected to more
tests. Both previous remarks need not be a problem. As I have pointed out in
Chapter 3, Forrester and Senge (1980) see validation as a process of building

confidence in the model, a point of view with which I agree. The authors present a variety of tests, and the rule is that the more tests are passed the higher the confidence will be in the model. So, the replication of the reference mode of behaviour is not the only test to be relied upon and validity is not established once the model is finished but rather it has to permeate the whole model-building process.

Several tests on the validity of the model have been performed thus far. The first is the dimensional consistency check. All equations of the model have been checked for dimensional consistency, a procedure which was discussed in Chapter 3. In the previous chapter I have shown that this consistency test revealed a flaw in the model's conceptual structure with regard to the waiting list and houses occupation rate. This led to an adaptation of the model in order to have dimensional consistency and a more realistic conceptual structure. In addition, the structure of the model has been identified in close cooperation with experts within Marco Polis Advice. A couple of things will have to be altered to better match the model and what is known about housing associations. One such change involves the way depreciation and redemptions are calculated. I have discussed this issue in the previous chapter. Most of the structure of the model, however, does not seem to contradict expert knowledge on the system. On the contrary, MPA representatives seem to feel confident enough to organize a couple of try outs with the model in strategic workshops. In addition, the parameters of the model have been established based on research reports from DCIH (1994), in which a number of typical figures for allied housing associations are presented.

As stated before, one test which cannot be performed is the replication of the reference mode of behaviour, simply because the model was built for the new situation after 1995 for which no data are available yet. However, with regard to the behaviour of the model, and particularly the financial indicators, it seems that the model behaves in accordance with what is known from other financial models as employed by MPA and other housing institutions. I have discussed the issue of exponential growth and an initial dip in financial indicators, which is related to the distribution of houses over age categories. In addition, the model has been tested, amongst others, by conducting thought experiments and by checking these with the aid of the model. As described in the previous chapter, during one of the sessions the inflation rate, the rent increase rate, and the interest rate on the current account were fixed at 0%. Under such a scenario one would expect the financial situation of the association over time to be relatively stable, if the distribution of age categories of houses is relatively normal. The run with the model under such conditions revealed that the model indeed showed the tendency to grow to an equilibrium value. Another thought experiment would be to stop constructing new houses. This experiment was also discussed in the previous chapter, in combination with the experiment above. In this case one would expect financial reserves and solvency to grow again (rather than remain stable), because no new construction costs and loans would emerge. A run with the model confirmed this.

Although a number of tests have been carried out, and have sometimes led to considerable model improvements, there are still a number of tests which will have to be conducted, before the model can be used reliably in the strategic workshops. In particular, a whole range of systematic sensitivity analyses will have to be performed, the results of which will be discussed with the client group. In addition, structure will have to be added in order to reveal so-called substitution effects, i.e. people moving from apartments to houses and to senior homes when of that age.

The previous paragraphs all talk about *model* validity. As Lane (1995) points out, different model uses and processes of constructing a model can be identified. A modeller can, for instance, decide to build a model himself. This is a situation which is quite different from group model-building. As a result different types of validity tests may be applied. With regard to group model-building the effectiveness of the intervention is not only determined by model validity, but also by the process effectiveness of the intervention. This process effectiveness test checks how participants respond to the process of model construction rather than just the model. Elements include the time and cost of the intervention, the trustworthiness of the system dynamicists, the meaningfulness and communicability of the policy insights and recommendations and the congruence of these with the organization's culture. It seems that in our case participants have responded well to the model construction process. Although meetings have been distributed over a whole year (due to the interruption of the conferences), interest has not waned. Given the model as it stands now, time and costs have been relatively low, at least for the participants. In addition, it seems that the meaningfulness and the communicability of the model results have been quite good. On the one hand the model produces results which have been recognized, on the other the model has revealed insights which were new to participants. I do have to point out however, that our situation is a little different in the sense that the model is constructed to be used in strategic workshops with allied housing associations. In this sense the model still has to stand the test of use with these groups regarding the increase of the information processing capabilities of a management team and exploring the robustness of potential strategies.

SUMMARY

This chapter has discussed a number of simulation runs with the housing model. As stated, the primary purpose of this chapter has been to illustrate the model analysis process for the non-system dynamicist. The simulation runs which were shown have on the one hand revealed that the model behaves as expected, on the other hand they have shown that there is room for further improvement. Currently the model is subject to a number of tests and adapted to the specific circumstances of the strategic workshops.

Chapter 9

Summary and Reflections

This book has discussed the role of system dynamics in tackling complex, messy problems. I set out in the first chapter to identify a number of recurrent flaws that arise when teams have to deal with complex, messy problems. A central characteristic of this process is the difference of viewpoints within a team. People are bound by their limited information processing capacity and by selective perception. The nature of the selectivity in perception is induced by such factors as personality, training and education as well as one's position in an organization. Processes like selective perception and selective memory lead to the construction of a mental model, which in turn forms the basis for our behaviour. Through this behaviour we help to construct a reality, which in turn is perceived by us with the aid of the mental model. Several psychological processes, e.g. selective perception and looking for confirmatory evidence, ensure that we are capable of maintaining our interpretation of reality even when conflicting evidence is clearly available. Expectations largely guide our perceptions and help to create a reality that we assumed to be there in the first place, a phenomenon known as self-fulfilling prophecy. We frequently demonstrate that we are not aware of these subtle processes by such expressions as: 'that's the way it works in organizations' or 'that's the way life is'. Obviously, we do not see that in an important way we are actually creating the reality that we assume to exist independent of our own actions. Understanding these processes may be helpful to acknowledge the fact that others might have different viewpoints which might be equally valid as our own.

A second important issue with regard to tackling messy problems refers to the limited information processing capabilities of humans and teams. People have difficulty viewing 'the whole'. Rather, they tend to focus on parts and to design piecemeal solutions to complex problems. I have presented a couple of examples from my own projects to illustrate this phenomenon. A system's point of view is helpful to 'lift' team members to the system's level and to create a holistic view in a team, by merging various piecemeal viewpoints. However, without any formal aids to store information and to visualize people's points of view it is almost impossible to keep track of the vast amount of ideas, knowledge and opinions addressed in a meeting. I have demonstrated that employing diagramming techniques to visualize a messy problem can be extremely helpful to clarify the strategic debate and to arrive at consensus. Moreover, visualization and diagramming tools are helpful to force team members to accurately articulate their opinions. They help to surface tacit (causal) assumptions which will prevent miscommunication.

Many of the above flaws could be prevented by almost any system's methodology. However, I have also indicated that managers largely ignore feedback processes and thus might get haunted by their own policies. Just creating awareness of feedback processes, although useful, does not necessarily prevent this, because the human mind is ill-suited in anticipating the dynamic consequences of a complex feedback structure. Computer models are helpful in this respect by simulating the behaviour of these systems so that our understanding of a problem is enhanced. One of the most important functions of system dynamics and group model-building is to learn about the system that we have selected to investigate. This way policies can be tested before they are actually implemented. Many of the unanticipated side-effects of proposed policies can thus be prevented and robust policies can be designed.

In Chapter 2, I introduced qualitative system dynamics. I pointed out that it is important to start the process of model-building with a clear problem identification. The subsequent step entails the construction of a conceptual model either in the form of a causal loop diagram or as a flow diagram. For the non-experienced modeller I have included a number of exercises with the construction of causal loop diagrams. I have indicated that qualitative system dynamics can be a very useful approach to deal with messy problems. In particular, because it integrates various viewpoints of team members into one overall problem description. Examples of the usefulness of qualitative system dynamics have been discussed in Chapter 6. In the chapter on how to design group model-building projects I have also discussed the dangers in trying to derive dynamic conclusions from either of these two types of diagrams. In particular causal loop diagrams have to be approached with care. But even for a simple flow diagram it may be too difficult for the human mind to derive its dynamic implications. Hence, the need for quantification and simulation.

Quantitative system dynamics and simulation were introduced in Chapter 3. As stated, if one is serious about establishing the dynamics of a system then quantification and simulation are prerequisites. As the reader may have gathered, quantification is considerably more difficult than qualitative model-building. This can also be seen from the example of the housing association in the previous chapters. However, this example also shows that once a model is constructed it allows for a variety of experiments in order to increase our understanding of it and to develop robust strategies. As is the case with qualitative modelling, experience comes with practice. Although I have included a couple of exercises in Chapter 3 I do realize that these only constitute a beginning. Later on in this chapter I will discuss the question of what the novice could undertake in order to improve one's model-building capacities.

The first three chapters produced the necessary ingredients to make the step to group model-building. In Chapter 4 I have discussed a number of issues which relate to the design of group model-building projects. Of course the most important issue is to decide whether system dynamics is an appropriate method to tackle a problem. Unfortunately, this is also the most difficult question. I have attempted to provide some guidelines which may be helpful. The most important is dynamic complexity and the differences between short and long term developments. On the more pragmatic side it is helpful to think in terms of a reference mode of behaviour and in terms of flow processes within a system. Chapter 4 has also discussed the question of the applicability of qualitative and quantitative system dynamics.

Another important issue in group model-building is whether to apply a standard methodology or not. Many scientists and practitioners prefer a standard methodology. This might also apply to group model-building. A sceptic might argue that obviously the method is still in an infant stage because there is no clear method and steps to guide the process and the practitioner. As I have pointed out throughout the book, the particular way of handling group model-building projects largely depends on a number of contingencies like, for instance, the size of the group, the geographical dispersion of group members, and the degree to which there is disagreement about the topic to be modelled.

Let me remind the reader that the construction of a system dynamics model can be (and is) standardized to a large extent. This does not mean however, that by following the required steps in model-building an adequate model will automatically be the result. Hence, the stages and steps in system dynamics model-building just serve as helping guidelines. They should never be applied without careful reflection. This also applies to the group model-building process. There are a number of approaches and helpful techniques some of which have been demonstrated in this book. The central issue however remains the need to continue being responsive to the group's needs. Stated more vehemently, the primary purpose is to solve the group's problem. Group model-building is an aid in that process and not a goal in itself.

My opinion is that there is *not* one best method to conduct group model-building. Although employing standard procedures might look attractive at first sight, there is a danger that these are applied in an unreflective manner and the method will prevail over the problem. This is probably one of the best guarantees that the client's problem will *not* really be addressed. A method prevailing over a problem is likely to occur at two levels: at the project level and at the model level. At the project level a problem is frequently suited to the method rather than the other way around. At the micro level there is the danger that a standard procedure for group model-building is conducted without asking oneself the question whether this approach is the best in the given circumstances. Building the model then becomes more important than solving the problem. This is also recognized by system dynamicists working with standard approaches. Richmond, one of the developers of Ithink and the Strategic Forum, states: 'With all of these advantages the "sequence of exercises" approach is still not always the best way to go. Some groups clearly prefer to grope in an unstructured manner toward an enhanced, shared understanding. The structure imposed by a preconceived set of exercises is antithetical to their accustomed way of doing business. When the unstructured process works, it can be extraordinarily effective!' (Richmond, 1987, 8.)

As a general rule, it is the quality of the thinking process which determines the value of a project and not the specific technique used. As Steven Schnaars puts it when it comes to the construction of scenarios: 'Herman Kahn was probably not far off the mark when he noted that the most important part of scenario analysis is simply to think about the problem.' (Schnaars, 1987, 128.)

I prefer to think of group model-building as a flexible method where a facilitator can make a selection from a toolbox which contains several techniques to guide the process (see also Lane, 1992, 1993). Applying a standard methodology in all cases and for all problems is similar to always taking your car no matter what your destination is. In general we select our way of travelling to match the distance and a number of other constraints. So why not apply this way of reasoning to group model-building projects? I prefer an open approach where system dynamics is taken as the methodology and the group model-building project is designed to best meet the needs of the client organization and to take the specific circumstances into account. As stated, important factors which have to be considered in the design of a specific group model-building project are amongst others: divergence of opinions and/or interests, number of participants, time and money constraints. In that re-spect I have presented a couple of approaches and methods to elicit people's viewpoints. One important choice is whether to start from scratch or to employ a preliminary model. A preliminary model may be useful when a group is large or when time is limited. However, there is a clear trade-off between saving on the participant's time investment and the ownership felt over the model by the group.

A preliminary model can be developed from discussions with individual group members or from documents. The first case leads to the use of interviews while the second calls for techniques in the realm of content analysis. In addition, I have discussed the use of questionnaires and workbooks. In the examples of group model-building projects discussed in the previous chapters I have illustrated the use of a number of these techniques in the context of group model-building.

When it comes to dealing effectively with messy problems and differences of viewpoints the facilitator is frequently more important than the specific methodol-ogy which is applied. Freely interacting groups have been shown to lead to process losses. Effective facilitation behaviour can enhance group performance consider-ably. In Chapter 5 I have discussed small group interaction processes and group facilitation behaviour. I have made a distinction between attitudes and skills. In my opinion the right attitudes are more important to be effective than the right skills for two reasons. First, because the right attitude frequently leads automatically to the required skills and second, because the skills will then not be used as a trick but rather will be embedded in the right attitude which will make them so much more effective. Of course, total lack of skills will render it difficult to be effective as a facilitator.

Among the most important attitudes are: a helping attitude, authenticity and integrity, an enquiry mode, and neutrality. The first skill which is of importance is system dynamics model-building skills. Other skills include: group process structur-ing, conflict handling, communication, concentration, team-building, appropriate intervention skills and skills to foster consensus and to create commitment. Each of the attitudes and skills was discussed extensively in Chapter 5 along with typical characteristics of group interaction processes.

With regard to the group process I have discussed a number of factors which are known to affect group performance. These can be summarized as follows. When it comes to group size, the larger the group the harder it is to keep it focused. Introducing structure in the communication and problem solving process will be necessary to overcome the dangers of digressing into irrelevant issues and lack of focus in the discussions. When it comes to group size, a trade-off will often have to be made between size, which one might want to keep as small as possible, and involvement of a large number of people in the organization, to create commitment and a platform for change. Group composition is also a factor to be taken into account. The more heterogeneous a group the more diverse the points of view, which is positive in itself, but on the other hand the more difficult the process. In heterogeneous groups the likelihood of conflict of viewpoints will naturally be higher. As I have indicated this need not be a problem, provided that conflicts are handled in an integrative way. This can be achieved when (a) these conflicts are discussed in an open atmosphere, (b) there is clear communication, and (c) cognitive conflict is not dominating discussions all the time. Remember that cognitive conflict will enhance a group's vigilance and that complete lack of differences of viewpoints might lead to such undesirable phenomena as premature consensus and even groupthink. When there are large differences of opinion, restriction of communication can be helpful to make the group process successful. Have people talk one at a time (for instance by means of NGT) and create an open communication climate. The latter is best induced by not evaluating opinions of group members and by not being defensive about one's opinion. The facilitator should always try to have team members postpone their evaluations in order to keep the communication unambiguous. However, be aware of the limited use of structured procedures. More important than methods and techniques is increasing a group's reflective qualities and vigilance. In addition, quality of communication seems of vital importance. In particular supportive, as opposed to defensive communication, is helpful to increase the quality of group discussions and decisions. High quality communication can also prevent a quick decision on issues through voting. Remember that voting will generally only be helpful if discussions do not lead to a form of consensus. There is always the chance that some team participants will still disagree. Only if there is consensus in the team that they should take a vote, will participants be willing to accept the majority vote. Finally, I have also emphasized that a group model-builder needs to be aware of the various types of cognitive tasks which have to be performed by a team. In particular brainstorming tasks have been found to be performed best by individuals (or nominal groups for that matter).

In Chapters 6 and 7 I have discussed a number of projects in order to illustrate the process of group model-building in more detail. These projects varied considerably in the way the group model-building process was handled. This was largely due to the differences in the type of problems and the circumstances under which the projects had to be carried out. The case descriptions also revealed the unpredictability of the outcomes of a group model-building project as well as when these outcomes may occur.

HOW TO PUT IT INTO PRACTICE

The use of group model-building to help client organizations is escalating rapidly. When it comes to messy problems, organizations will increasingly rely on consultants who work from a process point of view rather than in an expert mode. Less and less will organizations need people who tell them what to do and more and more, people in organizations will rely on their own thinking process to figure out what to do. As the examples in this book demonstrate, group model-building constitutes a powerful method to deal effectively with messy problems. If experienced in the methodology, the practitioner has an extremely powerful tool to help organizations to function more effectively. The reader may be left with the question how to make sure to be effective?

The answer to this question may differ for different readers. For those who are not experienced in system dynamics, the first and foremost skill which needs to be developed is the skill of building system dynamics models. Without this skill one will be a poor help to a management team. Model-building skills can only be improved by much training and practice. This book has presented a number of basic exercises to start building these skills but they may not be considered sufficient. For the interested person there are several ways to proceed. The first is to consult other textbooks which contain more exercises in system dynamics model-building. A number of these are listed in Appendix 1. A second way is to start to build models from problems that you encounter for instance in newspapers, or to start modelling problems in your own organization. The third way would be to start practising with one of the software packages which were mentioned in the Introduction. Most of these contain exercises which will further introduce you to system dynamics model-building. The fourth way is to follow one of the courses in system dynamics which are offered in many different countries. As a general rule model-building skills only come with practice. Once this practice builds up one can start to think of facilitating group model-building sessions. A good way to start would be with a non-controversial topic, which is well-suited for system dynamics, in a safe environment. For instance, with a student group or with a couple of colleagues in your organization whom you may consider to be a friendly audience. At first it may seem wise to limit oneself to qualitative model-building, because, all else being equal, this is less complicated than constructing quantitative models. Particularly in the case of building quantified models with groups, unless one has extensive experience in constructing system dynamics models, it seems wise to extend the model-building process over several sessions. This will give you and the project group an opportunity to do some backroom work. Only when a large amount of experience has been built could one try to build quantified models at the spot with a group. In this latter case the group meets off-site in a special environment and is guided through the model-building process in a two-day workshop. Conducting group model-building projects this way demands a high level of expertise in system dynamics model-building as well as group facilitation. In particular when the goal is to build a quantified model the model-builder needs to be a person who has had a thorough training in and extensive experience with building system dynamics models and, even then, at least two or three people will be required to guide the process (Richardson and Andersen, 1995).

When it comes to developing group facilitation skills things may be more complicated because this is not just a cognitive skill, but, as I have indicated, it is largely a matter of the right attitude and personality. It is a misunderstanding to think that group facilitation skills can only be developed by working with groups. A lot can be done before actually working with groups. Take one or more regular meetings and start to implement one of the skills mentioned in this book. Watch for instance how things will start changing in group interaction if you start asking questions rather than providing answers. Many of the attitudes and skills can be developed in your daily work by careful self reflection. It is a serious misconception to think that these attitudes and skills can only be displayed when in the role of group facilitator. This would imply that you behave differently as a facilitator than you would in daily life. But as stated, to be effective as a facilitator, your attitudes are most important and these cannot just be switched on and off. Developing the right attitudes is a gradual learning process, which may involve many mistakes. But you should be aware that displaying these attitudes and skills, particularly in daily life in your own organization, is extremely effective in creating a different social reality. You have the opportunity to change the teams in which you are working into more effective teams, creating more statisfied people and thus improving team and organizational performance. It is up to you whether you take the opportunity to accomplish this.

Appendix 1

SUGGESTED FURTHER READING

There is a host of literature on system dynamics and topics closely related to it. Sastry and Sterman (1993) composed an annotated bibliography containing numerous books and articles in the field. Cooper and Steinhurst (1992) have composed a complete list of over 3000 system dynamics articles, papers, books and the like. These are available in computer readable format and can be obtained from Mrs. Julie S. Pugh, 49 Bedford Road, Lincoln, MA 01773, USA.

When compared to the two previous sources, this appendix contains a limited list of books suggested for further reading for the reader who has become interested in the topic of system dynamics and group model-building. I have grouped the titles under a couple of headings. It may be helpful to know that many of the books which were originally published by MIT Press are now issued by Productivity Press.

HANDBOOKS ON SYSTEM DYNAMICS

There are several high quality handbooks, which discuss the stages in the construction of a system dynamics model. A pedagogical approach is provided in Roberts et al. (1983). This book is very easy to understand and is used to teach system dynamics to high school students.

A comprehensive overview is Richardson and Pugh's *Introduction to System Dynamics Modeling with DYNAMO* (1981). This is one of the classic handbooks in system dynamics. It treats all topics in the construction of system dynamics models in much more detail than was done in this book. Although the book uses the computer language DYNAMO (which sometimes differs slightly from other software packages) to explain system dynamics, it is an invaluable reference book.

There are also a couple of books which primarily focus on the relationship between structure and dynamics in the form of exercises for the reader. One of the classics in this field, and still worth reading, is Forrester's *Principles of Systems* (1968). This book explains the basics of feedback systems and the relationships between structure and dynamics in a quite understandable manner. Only a basic knowledge of algebra is required to understand and complete the exercises in this book. Another book worth pursuing is Michael Goodman's *Study Notes in System Dynamics*. It provides numerous exercises of conceptualization and understanding the relationship between structure and behaviour.

EXAMPLES OF MODEL-BUILDING TO SOLVE PROBLEMS

Books in this category discuss examples of system dynamics models to analyse and solve real world managerial problems. They do not focus particularly on group model-building, but provide examples of how system dynamics is applied to help solve managerial problems. One book which focuses primarily on a manufacturing firm is Lyneis' *Corporate Planning and Policy Design* (1980). This starts with a simple model and gradually extends it through the book. Edward Robert's book *Managerial Applications of System Dynamics* provides examples in a variety of fields including: manufacturing, marketing and distribution, research and development, financial applications and societal problems. Other examples can be found in Wolstenholme's *System Enquiry* (1990).

EXAMPLES OF GROUP MODEL-BUILDING PROJECTS AND ORGANIZATIONAL LEARNING

The best known book on the relationship between systems thinking and organizational learning is Peter Senge's *The Fifth Discipline* (1990) (and the accompanying Fieldbook). It deals with the five so-called disciplines for effective learning organizations: mental models, team learning, personal mastery, systems thinking and shared vision. It does not explicitly deal with the topic of group model-building.

One interesting source on group model-building and modelling for learning is *Modelling for Learning Organizations* (1994) (edited by Morecroft and Sterman). It was originally published as a special issue of the *European Journal of Operational Research* (Morecroft and Sterman, 1992) and later reissued by Productivity Press. These contain case descriptions of group model-building. Other examples can be found throughout editions of the *System Dynamics Review* and its special issue on group model-building (Vennix, Richardson and Andersen, forthcoming).

GROUP FACILITATION

Although there are a number of books and articles on the topic of group facilitation, one of the books I have found most useful in understanding the nature and role of facilitation is Edgar Schein's *Process Consultation* (1969). His book explains much about processes involved in helping other people. On the lighter side the reader might consult a couple of the books mentioned in the chapter on group facilitation.

HISTORICAL BOOKS AND THE IMPACT OF MODELS ON POLICY MAKING

Although there are no books on the history of system dynamics proper, a collection of seminal papers by the founder of system dynamics can be found in *Collected Papers of Jay W. Forrester*, Cambridge, Wright-Allen Press, 1975. From a historical point of view an important source on the history of feedback thought is George Richardson's *Feedback Thought in Social Science and Systems Theory* (1991). A more critical look on the history and impact of system dynamics is provided in Bloomfield's *Modelling The World* (1986). Other sources dealing particularly with the impact of models on policy making processes are *Groping in the Dark* (Meadows, Richardson and Bruckmann, 1982), which describes the first decade of global modelling, and *The Electronic Oracle* (Meadows and Robinson, 1985).

SYSTEM DYNAMICS IN THE CONTEXT OF SYSTEMS THINKING AND SYSTEMS THEORY

For those interested in the relationship between system dynamics and other systems approaches a good place to start would be the special issue of the *System Dynamics Review* edited by Richardson, Wolstenholme and Morecroft: 'Systems thinkers, systems thinking' (1994). The relationship between system dynamics and soft OR is discussed in Lane (1994a).

Appendix 2

SUGGESTED SOLUTIONS TO EXERCISES

This appendix contains suggested solutions to the exercises provided in Chapter 2

1. Investments $\xrightarrow{+}$ Employment

2. Employment $\xrightarrow{-}$ Unemployment

3. Motivation of workforce $\xrightarrow{+}$ Productivity per person

4. Social security outlays $\xrightarrow{+}$ Government budget deficit

5. Hours worked $\xrightarrow{+}$ Grades

6. Number of people participating in politics $\xrightarrow{-}$ Disinterest

7. Quality of product $\xrightarrow{+}$ Sales of product

8. Height of taxes $\xrightarrow{+}$ Size of black circuit

9. ??? $\xrightarrow{?}$ Unemployment rate

10. Quality of arguments $\xrightarrow{+}$ Chances of winning the discussion

Suggested Solutions for Exercise 2.1

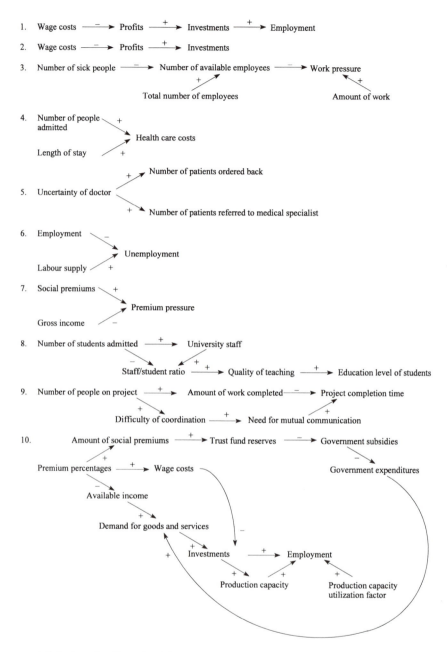

Suggested Solutions for Exercise 2.2

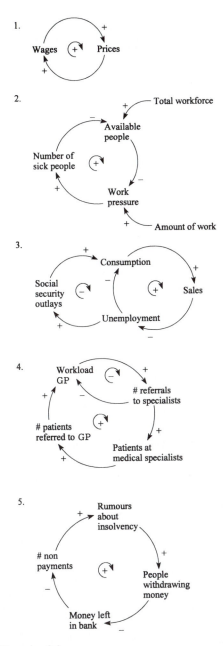

Suggested Solutions for Exercise 2.3

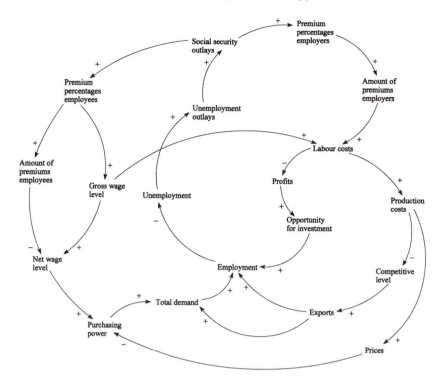

Suggested Solutions for Exercise 2.4

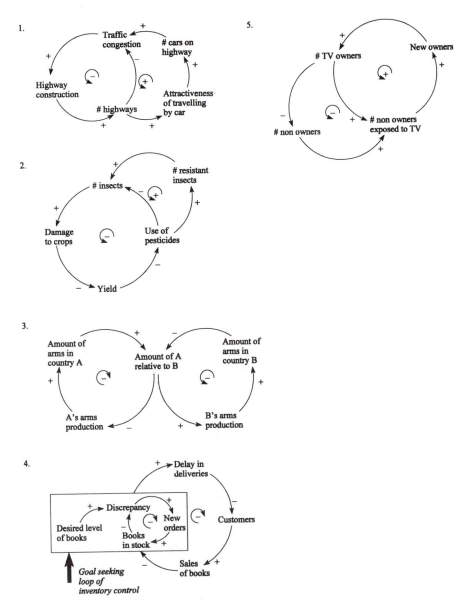

Suggested Solutions for Exercise 2.5

Appendix 3

GUIDELINES FOR DEVIL'S ADVOCATE AND DIALECTICAL INQUIRY

Since substantive conflict seems to enhance decision quality several researchers have advocated conflict promoting techniques in order to increase the quality of decision making. Two of these techniques are: Dialectical Inquiry and Devil's Advocate. Mason (1969) has proposed that Dialectical Inquiry (DI) could be propitious for strategic planning. DI is a procedure which involves the presentation of a strategic plan with supporting assumptions and a counterplan based on entirely different assumptions than the original plan. It is presumed that the decision maker, faced with two opposing plans, will be forced to think through his decision thoroughly and to come up with a synthesis of both plans which will be more objective than both the original and the counterplan. More specifically the guidelines for Dialectical Inquiry include:

1. Divide the group in two subgroups.
2. One subgroup develops written recommendations accompanied by arguments which are supported by all key assumptions, facts and relevant data.
3. The other subgroup awaits the list of all key assumptions produced by the first group. Then it generates plausible assumptions which negate the assumptions produced by the first group. Based on these 'counter' assumptions the group produces an alternative plan.
4. Both groups then present to the other group their recommendations and the assumptions, facts and data underlying these.
5. After this debate is completed the whole group decides which assumptions have survived the debate.
6. Using the surviving assumptions the group then develops final recommendations.

Janis has suggested an alternative conflict promoting technique: Devil's Advocate. He recommends that at every meeting involving decisions, one or more members should be assigned the role of devil's advocate (Janis and Mann, 1977). In the DA a strategic plan is attacked by one or more persons playing the devil's advocate who try to demonstrate all that is wrong with the plan. More specifically the steps involved in DA are:

1. Divide the group into two subgroups; one subgroup is assigned the role of devil's advocate.
2. One subgroup (not the devil's advocate) develops written recommendations accompanied by arguments which are supported by all key assumptions, facts and relevant data.
3. The first subgroup presents its written recommendations to the devil's advocate group.
4. The devil's advocate group develops a formal written critique in which they attempt to uncover all that is wrong with the recommendations, assumptions etc.
5. The critique is presented to the first group, which next revises its original recommendations based on the other's group critique.
6. These steps are repeated until both subgroups can accept the recommendations.
7. The final recommendations are written down.

Empirical research has demonstrated the effectiveness of DA in individual decision making. Schwenk (1988) for example demonstrated that the use of a devil's advocate procedure considerably reduced the effect of escalating commitment with a prior failing decision, i.e. reducing the tendency to throw good money after bad. In other words, when DA was used people were more willing to abandon a failing decision (e.g. an unremunerative investment) than in situations when DA was not used.

Most empirical research however has concentrated on the question of which of the above two approaches is more effective (see Chapter 5).

References

Ackoff, R.L. (1979) *The Art of Problem Solving*. New York, Wiley and Sons.

Ackoff, R.L. (1981) *Creating the Corporate Future*. Chichester, Wiley and Sons.

Ajzen, I. (1988) *Attitudes, Personality and Behavior*. Chicago, Dorsey Press.

Ajzen, I. (1991) The theory of planned behavior. *Organizational Behavior and Human Decision Processes* **50**, 179–211.

Akkermans, H.A. (1995) *Modelling with managers: participative business modelling for effective strategic decision-making*. Ph.D. dissertation, Eindhoven Technical University, the Netherlands.

Andersen, D.F. and Richardson, G.P. (1994) Scripts for group model-building. In: *Proceedings of the 1994 International System Dynamics Conference: Problem-solving Methodologies*, 25–34.

Anderson, J.R. (1980) (3rd ed.) *Cognitive Psychology and its Implications*. New York, W.H. Freeman and Co.

Argyris, C. (1970) *Intervention Theory and Method*, Reading (MA), Addison-Wesley.

Argyris, C. (1990) *Overcoming Organizational Defenses, Facilitating Organizational Learning*. Boston, Allyn and Bacon.

Argyris, C. (1992) *On Organizational Learning*. Cambridge, Blackwell.

Argyris, C. (1994) Good communication that blocks learning. *Harvard Business Review* July–August, 77–85.

Argyris, C. and Schön, D.A. (1978) *Organizational Learning: a Theory of Action Perspective*. Reading (MA), Addison-Wesley.

Asch, S.E. (1963) Effects of group pressure upon the modification and distortion of judgments. In: H. Guetzkow (ed.), *Groups, Leadership and Men: Research in Human Relations*. New York, Russel & Russel.

Axelrod, R. (1976) *Structure of Decision: the Cognitive Maps of Political Elites*, Princeton (NJ) Princeton University Press.

Baker, J.P. and Crist, J.L. (1971) Teacher expectancies: A review of the literature. In: J.D. Elashoff and R.E. Snow (eds.), *Pygmalion Reconsidered*. Worthington (OH), Charles A. Jones.

Bales, R., Strodtbeck, F.L., Mills, T.M., Rosebourgh, T.M. and Mary, E. (1951) Channels of communication in small groups. *American Sociological Review* **16**, 461–468.

Barnard, C. (1938) *The Functions of the Executive*. Cambridge (MA), Harvard University Press.

Barnlund, D.C. (1959) A comparative study of individual, majority, and group judgment. *Journal of Abnormal Social Psychology* **58**, 55–60.

Bell, J.A. and Senge, P.M. (1980) Methods for enhancing refutability in system dynamics modelling. In: Legasto A.A., J.W. Forrester, and J.M. Lyneis (eds.), *TIMS Studies in Management Science* **14**. Amsterdam, North-Holland.

Berger, P. and Luckmann, T. (1966) *The Social Construction of Reality*, New York, Penguin Books.

Berkhout, P., Hopstaken, P. and Vegt, C. v.d. (1993) *Het noodzakelijke weerstandsvermogen van woningcorporaties* (The required potential for financial endurance for housing associations), Stichting voor Economisch Onderzoek der Universiteit van Amsterdam (Foundation for Economic Research of the University of Amsterdam).

Berkowitz, L. and Howard, R.C. (1959) Reactions to opinion deviates as affected by affiliation need and group member interdependence. *Sociometry* **22**, 81–91.

Block, P. (1981) *Flawless Consulting: a Guide to Getting Your Expertise Used.* University Associates, 8517 Production Avenue, San Diego, CA 92121, USA.

Bloomfield, B.P. (1986) *Modelling the World, the Social Constructions of Systems Analysts.* Oxford, Basil Blackwell.

Boje, D.M. and Murnighan, J.K. (1982) Group confidence pressures in decisions. *Management Science* **28**(10), 1187–1196.

Bostrom, R.P., Anson, R., Clawson, V.K. (1993) Group facilitation and group support systems. In: L. Jessup, J. Valacich (eds.), *Group Support Systems: New perspectives.* New York, Macmillan, 146–168.

Bouchard, T.J. (1969) Personality, problem solving procedure and performance in small groups. *Journal of Applied Psychology* **53**, 1–29.

Bouchard, T.J. (1972a) A comparison of two group brainstorming procedures. *Journal of Applied Psychology* **56**(5), 418–421.

Bouchard, T.J. (1972b) Training, motivation and personality as determinants of the effectiveness of brainstorming groups and individuals. *Journal of Applied Psychology* **56**(4), 324–331.

Bouchard, T.J. and Hare, M. (1970) Size, performance and potential in brainstorming groups. *Journal of Applied Psychology* **54**(1), 51–55.

Bray, R.M., Kerr, N.L. and Atkin, R.S. (1978) Effects of group size, problem difficulty, and sex on group performance and member reactions. *Journal of Personality and Social Psychology* **36**, 1224–1240.

Brehmer, B. (1980) In one word: not from experience. *Acta Psychologica* **45**, 223–241.

Brehmer, B. (1987) Systems design and the psychology of complex systems. In: J. Rasmussen and P. Zunde (eds.), *Empirical Foundations of Information and Software Science III.* New York, Plenum.

Brehmer, B. (1989) Feedback delays and control in complex dynamic systems. In: P.M. Milling and E.O.K. Zahn (eds.), *Computer-based Management of Complex Systems.* Proceedings of the 1989 International Conference of the System Dynamics Society, Berlin, Springer Verlag, 189–196.

Brilhart, J.K. and Jochem, L.M. (1964) Effects of different patterns on outcomes of problem-solving discussions. *Journal of Applied Psychology* **48**(3), 175–179.

Broome, B.J. and Keever, D.B. (1989) Next generation group facilitation: proposed principles. *Management Communication Quarterly* **3**(1), 107–127.

Bryant, J. (1989) *Problem Management, a Guide for Producers and Players.* Chichester, Wiley and Sons.

Burleson, B.R., Levine, B.J. and Samter, W. (1984) Decision-making procedure and decision quality. *Human Communication Research* **10**(4), 557–574.

Campbell, D.T. (1958) Systematic error on the part of human links in communication systems. *Information and Control* **1**, 334–369.

Castaneda, C. (1968) *The Teachings of Don Juan.* Berkeley (CA) University of California Press.

Checkland, P. (1981) *Systems Thinking, Systems Practice.* Chichester, Wiley and Sons.

Checkland, P. (1985) From optimizing to learning: a development of systems thinking for the 1990s. *Journal of the Operational Research Society* **36**(9), 757–767.

Checkland, P. and Scholes, J. (1990) *Soft Systems Methodology in Action.* Chichester, Wiley and Sons.

Chilberg, J.C. (1989) A review of group process designs for facilitating communication in problem solving groups. *Management Communication Quarterly* **3**(1), 51–70.

Clawson, V.K., Bostrom, R.P. and Anson, R. (1993) The role of the facilitator in computer-supported meetings. *Small Group Research* **24**(4), 547–565.

Cohen, A.R. (1958) Upward communication in experimentally created hierarchies. *Human Relations* **11**, 41–53.

Cohen, M.D., March, J.G. and Olsen, J.P. (1972) A garbage can model of organizational choice. *Administrative Science Quarterly*, 1–25.

Collins, B.E. and Guetzkow, H. (1964) *A social psychology of group processes for decision-making*. New York, Wiley and Sons.

Conyne, R.K. and Rapin, L.S. (1977) Facilitator- and self-directed groups: A statement-by-statement interaction study. *Small Group Behavior* **8**, 341–350.

Cooper, K. and Steinhurst, W. (1992) *The system dynamics society bibliography*. System Dynamics Society, 49 Bedford Road, Lincoln MA 01773, USA.

Cooper, W.H., Gallupe, R.B. and Bastianutti, L.M. (1990) Electronic versus non-electronic brainstorming. *Proceedings of the 50th Annual Meeting of the Academy of Management*, 237–241.

Cordaro, L. and Ison, J.R. (1963) Observer bias in classical conditioning of the planaria. *Psychological Reports* **13**, 787–789.

Cosier, R.A. (1978) The effects of three potential aids for making strategic decisions on prediction accuracy. *Organizational Behavior and Human Performance* **22**, 295–306.

Cosier, R.A. and Aplin, J.C. (1980) A critical view of dialectical inquiry as a tool in strategic planning. *Strategic Management Journal* **1**, 343–356.

Cosier, R.A. and Rechner, P.L. (1985) Inquiry effects on performance in a simulated business environment. *Organizational Behavior and Human Decision Processes* **36**, 79–95.

Cosier, R.A. and Rose, G.L. (1977) Cognitive conflict and goal conflict effects on task performance. *Organizational Behavior and Human Performance* **19**, 378–391.

Cosier, R.A., Ruble. T.L. and Aplin, J.C. (1978) An evaluation of the effectiveness of dialectical inquiry systems. *Management Science* **24**, 1483–1490.

Coyle, G. (1977) *Management System Dynamics*. Chichester. Wiley and Sons.

Crozier, M. and Friedberg, E. (1982) *Actors and Systems*. Chicago. The University of Chicago Press.

Dalkey, N. (1969) An experimental study of group opinion: the Delphi method. *Futures* **1**, 408–426.

Davis, D.R., and Sinha, D. (1950) The influence of an interpolated experience upon recognition. *Quarterly Journal of Experimental Psychology* **2**, 43.

Dearborn, DeWitt, C. and Simon, H.A. (1958) Selective perception: a note on the departmental identifications of executives. *Sociometry* **21**, 140–144.

Dess, G.G. (1987) Consensus on strategy formulation and organizational performance: competitors in a fragmented industry. *Strategic Management Journal* **8**, 259–277.

Delbecq, A.L., Ven, A.H., v.d. and Gustafson, D.H. (1975) *Group Techniques for Program Planning: a Guide to Nominal Group and Delphi Processes*, Glenview (Ill.), Scott, Foresman and Co.

DeStephen, R.S. (1983) High and low consensus groups: a content and relational interaction analysis. *Small Group Behavior* **14**(2), 143–162.

Deutsch, M. (1951) Task structure and group process. *The American Psychologist,* 324.

Deutsch, M. (1973) *The Resolution of Conflict: Constructive and Destructive Processes*. New Haven and London, Yale University Press.

DGSM (1992) *Voortvarend naar de volgende eeuw*. (Energetically towards the next century) Den Haag, Directoraat Generaal Scheepvaart en Maritieme zaken, Ministerie van Verkeer en Waterstaat.

Diehl, E. and Sterman, J. (1995) Effects of feedback complexity on dynamic decision making. *Organizational Behavior and Human Decision Processes* **62**(2), 198–215.

Diehl, M. and Stroebe, W. (1987) Productivity loss in brainstorming groups: toward the solution of a riddle. *Journal of Personality and Social Psychology* **53**(3), 497–509.

Diehl, M. and Stroebe, W. (1991) Productivity loss in idea-generating groups: tracking down the blocking effect. *Journal of Personality and Social Psychology* **61**(3), 392–403.

Dijk, J.A.G.M. van (1990) Delphi questionnaires versus individual and group interviews: a comparison case. *Technological Forecasting and Social Change* **37**, 293–304.

Dipboye, R.L. (1982) Self-fulfilling prophecies in the selection-recruitment interview, *Academy of Management Review* **7**, 579–586.

Dörner, D. (1980) On the difficulties people have in dealing with complexity. *Simulation and Games* **11**(1), 87–106.

Doyle, M. and Straus, D. (1976) *How to Make Meetings Work*. New York, Jove Books.

Drucker, P. (1988) The coming of the new organization. *Harvard Business Review* **66**(1), 45–53.

Duke, R.D. (1981) A paradigm for game design. In: C.S. Greenblat and R.D. Duke (eds), *Principles and Practices of Gaming-simulation*, Beverly Hills/London, Sage, 63–72.

Dunnette, M.D., Campbell, J. and Jaastad, K. (1963) The effect of group participation on brainstorming effectiveness for two industrial samples. *Journal of Applied Psychology* **47**(1), 30–37.

Dyer, W.G. (1977) *Team-building: Issues and Alternatives*. Reading (MA), Addison-Wesley.

Eden, C. (1982) Problem construction and the influence of O.R. *Interfaces*, 50–60.

Eden, C. (1985) Perish the thought. *Journal of the Operational Research Society* **36**(9), 809–819.

Eden, C. (1987) Problem solving or problem finishing. In: M.C. Jackson and P. Keys (eds.), *New Directions in Management Science*. Aldershot, Gower.

Eden, C. (1992a) A framework for thinking about Group Decision Support Systems (GDSS). *Group Decision and Negotiation* **1**(3), 199–218.

Eden, C. (1992b) Strategy development as a social process. *Journal of Management Studies* **29**(6), 799–811.

Eden, C. (1994) Cognitive mapping and problem structuring for system dynamics model-building. *System Dynamics Review* **10**(2/3) 257–276.

Eden, C. and Radford, J. (1990) *Tackling Strategic Problems: the Role of Group Decision Support*, London, Sage.

Eden, C. and Simpson, P. (1989) SODA and cognitive mapping in practice, In: J. Rosenhead (ed.), *Rational Analysis For a Problematic World*. Chichester, Wiley and Sons, 43–70.

Eden, C., Jones, S. and Sims, D. (1983) *Messing About in Problems: an Informal Structured Approach to Their Identification and Management*, Oxford/New York, Pergamon Press.

Einhorn, H.J. (1980) Learning from experience and suboptimal rules in decision-making. In: Thomas S. Wallsten (eds.) *Cognitive Processes in Choice and Decision Behavior*. Hillsdale, N.J., Erlbaum.

Einhorn, H.J. and Hogarth, R.M. (1978) Confidence in judgment: persistence of the illusion of validity. *Psychological Review* **85**, 395–416.

Einhorn, H.J. and Hogarth, R.M. (1986) Judging probable cause. *Psychological Bulletin* **99**, 3–19.

Einhorn, H.J., Hogarth, R.M. and Klempner, E. (1977) Quality of group judgment. *Psychological Bulletin* **84**(1), 158–172.

Emerson, R.M. (1954) Deviation and rejection: An experimental replication. *American Sociological Review* **19**, 688–693.

Espejo, R. (1994) What is systemic thinking? *System Dynamics Review* **10**(2/3), 199–212.

Exline, R.V. (1957) Group climate as a factor in the relevance and accuracy of social perception. *Journal of Abnormal Social Psychology* **55**, 382–388.

Exline, R.V. and Ziller, R.C. (1959) Status congruency and interpersonal conflict in decision-making groups. *Human Relations* **12**, 147–162.

Farina, A, Allen, J.G. and Sal, B.B. (1968) The role of the stigmatized person in affecting social relationships. *Journal of Personality* **36**, 169–182.

Farnsworth, P.R. and Williams, M.F. (1936) The accuracy of the median and mean of a group of judgments. *Journal of Social Psychology* **7**, 237–239.

Festinger, L. and Thibaut, J. (1951) Interpersonal Communication in small groups. *Journal of Abnormal Social Psychology* **46**, 92–99.

Fischer, G.W. (1981) When oracles fail: a comparison of four procedures for aggregating subjective probability forecasts. *Organizational Behavior and Human Performance* **28**, 96–110.

Fisher, B.A. (1974) *Small Group Decision-making*. New York, McGraw-Hill.

Fischhoff, B. (1975) Hindsight does not equal foresight: the effect of outcome knowledge on judgement under uncertainty. *Journal of Experimental Psychology: Human Perception and Performance* **1**, 288–299.

Fischhoff, B. and Beyth, R. (1975) I knew it would happen. *Organizational Behavior and Human Performance* **13**, 1–16.

Flood, R.L. and Jackson, M.L. (1991) *Creative Problem Solving: Total Systems Intervention*. Chichester, Wiley and Sons.

Forrester, J.W. (1958) Industrial dynamics: a major breakthrough for decision makers. *Harvard Business Review* July–August, 37–66.

Forrester, J.W. (1961) *Industrial Dynamics*. Cambridge (MA), MIT Press.

Forrester, J.W. (1968) *Principles of systems*. Cambridge (MA), MIT Press.

Forrester, J.W. (1969) *Urban Dynamics*. Cambridge (MA), MIT Press.

Forrester, J.W. (1973) *World Dynamics*. Cambridge (MA), MIT Press.

Forrester, J.W. (1975) Industrial dynamics—after the first decade. In: *Collected Papers of J.W. Forrester*, Cambridge, Wright-Allen Press. (Original paper in *Management Science* **14**(7), 398–415, 1968.)

Forrester, J.W. (1980) Information sources for modelling the national economy. *Journal of the American Statistical Association* **75**, 555–574.

Forrester, J.W. (1987) Lessons from system dynamics modelling. *System Dynamics Review* **3**(2), 136–149.

Forrester, J.W. (1992) Policies, decisions and information sources for modelling. *European Journal of Operational Research* **59**(1), 42–63.

Forrester, J.W. and Senge, P.M. (1980) Tests for building confidence in system dynamics models. In: A.A. Legasto, J.W. Forrester and J.M. Lyneis (eds.), *TIMS Studies in the Management Sciences* **14**, 209–228.

Fouriezos, N.T., Hutt, M.L. and Guetzkow, H. (1950) Measurement of self-oriented needs in discussion groups. *The Journal of Abnormal and Social Psychology* **45**, 682–690.

Fox, W.M. (1987) *Effective Group Problem Solving*. San Francisco, Jossey-Bass.

Friedman, P.G. (1989) Upstream facilitation: a proactive approach to managing problem solving groups. *Management Communication Quarterly* **3**(1), 33–50.

Gardiner, P.C. and Ford, A. (1980) Which policy run is rest, and who says so? In: A.A. Legasto, J.W. Forrester and J.M. Lyneis (eds.) *TIMS Studies in the Management Sciences* **14**, 241–257.

Gardner, H. (1987) *The Mind's New Science, a History of the Cognitive Revolution*. New York, Basic Books.

Gehani, R.R. (1993) Fighting fires: pressed for time, today's manager needs imperfect answers to messy problems. *OR/MS Today* June, 8–9.

Geus, A.P., de (1988) Planning as learning. *Harvard Business Review* March–April, 70–74.

Gibb, J.R. (1951) The effects of group size and of threat reduction upon creativity in a problem-solving situation. *The American Psychologist*, 324.

Gibb, J.R. (1960) Defensive communication. *The Journal of Communication* **10**, 141–148.

Gibb, J.R. (1961) Defence level and influence potential in small groups. In: L. Petrullo and B.M. Bass (eds.) *Leadership and Interpersonal Behavior*. New York, Holt, Rinehart and Winston, 66–81.

Goodman, M.R. (1974) *Study Notes in System Dynamics*. Cambridge (MA), MIT Press.

Gordon, K. (1924) Group judgements in the field of lifted weights. *Journal of Experimental Psychology* **7**, 398–400.

Gouran, D.S. (1982) Making decisions. *Choices and Concepts*. Glenview, (IL), Scott Foresman.

Gouran, D.S., Brown, C. and Henry, D. (1978) Behavioral correlates of perceptions of quality in decision-making discussions. *Communication Monographs* **45**, 51–63.

Graham, A.K. (1980) Parameter Estimation in System Dynamics Modelling. In: J. Randers (ed.), *Elements of the System Dynamics Method*. Cambridge (MA), MIT Press, 143–161.

Graham, W.K. (1977) Acceptance of ideas generated through individual and group brainstorming. *The Journal of Social Psychology* **101**, 231–234.

Greenberger, M., Crenson, M.A. and Crissey, B.L. (1976) *Models in the Policy Process: Public Decision Making in the Computer Era*, New York, Russell Sage Foundation.

Grünwald, C.A. (1987) *Beheersing van de gezondheidszorg* (Control of health care), VUGA, Den Haag.

Guetzkow, H. and Gyr, J. (1954) An analysis of conflict in decision-making groups. *Human Relations* **7**, 367–382.

Gustafson, D.H., Shukla, R.K., Delbecq, A. and Walster, G.W. (1973) A comparative study of differences in subjective likelihood estimates made by individuals, interacting groups, delphi groups and nominal groups. *Organizational Behavior and Human Performance* **9**, 280–291.

Hackman, J.R. (1968) Effects of task characteristics on group products. *Journal of Experimental Social Psychology* **4**, 162–187.

Hackman, J.R. (1990) *Groups That Work (and Those That Don't)*. San Francisco, Jossey-Bass.

Hackman, J.R. and Vidmar, N. (1970) Effects of size and task type on group performance and member reactions. *Sociometry* **33**, 37–54.

Hackman, J.R. and Morris, C.G. (1975) Group tasks, group interaction process, and group performance effectiveness: A review and proposed integration. In: L. Berkowitz, (ed.). *Advances in Experimental Social Psychology* **8**, New York, Academic Press.

Hall, R.I. (1984) The natural logic of management policy making: its implications for the survival of an organization. *Management Science* **30**(8), 905–927.

Hall, E.J. and Watson, W.H. (1971) The effects of a normative intervention on group decision-making performance. *Human relations* **23**(4), 299–317.

Hall, E.J., Mouton, J.S. and Blake, R.R. (1963) Group problem solving effectiveness under conditions of pooling vs. interaction. *The Journal of Social Psychology* **56**, 147–157.

Hampden-Turner, C. (1990) *Charting the Corporate Mind: From Dilemma to Strategy*. Oxford, Basil Blackwell.

Hanneman, R.A. (1988) *Computer-assisted Theory Building: Modelling Dynamic Social Systems*. Beverly Hills/London, Sage.

Hare, A.P. (1962) *Handbook of Small Group Research*. New York, The Free Press of Glencoe.

Hare, A.P., Borgatta, E.F. and Bales, R.F. (1965) *Small Groups: Studies in Social Interaction*. New York, Alfred A. Knopf.

Harper, N.L. and Askling, L.R. (1980) Group communication and quality of task solution in a media production organization. *Communication Monographs* **47**, 77–100.

Hart, L.B. (1992) *Faultless Facilitation*, London, Kogan Page.

Hart, S.L. (1985) Toward quality criteria for collective judgments. *Organizational Behavior and Human Decision Processes* **36**, 209–228.

Hart, S.L., Boroush, M., Enk, G. and Hornick, G. (1985) Managing complexity through consensus mapping: Technology for the structuring of group decisions. *Academy of Management Review* **10**, 587–600.

Hart, P.'t (1990) *Groupthink in Government, a Study of Small Groups and Policy Failure*. Ph.D. dissertation, University of Leiden, Netherlands.

Henry, R.A. (1993) Group judgment accuracy: Reliability and validity of post discussion confidence judgments. *Organizational Behavior and Human Decision Processes* **56**(1), 11–27.

Hensley, T.R. and Griffin, G.W. (1986) Victims of groupthink: The Kent State University Board of trustees and the 1977 gymnasium controversy. *Journal of Conflict Resolution* **30**(3), 497–531.

Herek, G.M., Janis, I.L. and Huth, P. (1987) Decision making during international crises: is quality of process related to outcome? *Journal of Conflict Resolution* **31**(2), 203–226.

Heron, J. (1993) *Group Facilitation: Theories and Models for Practice.* London, Kogan Page.

Hickling, A. (1990) 'Decision spaces': A scenario about designing appropriate rooms for group decision management. In: C. Eden and J. Radford (eds.), *Tackling Strategic Problems: the Role of Group Decision Support*, 169–177.

Hirokawa, R.Y. (1980) A comparative analysis of communication patterns within effective and ineffective decision-making groups. *Communication Monographs* **47**, 312–321.

Hirokawa, R.Y. (1985) Discussion procedures and decision-making performance, a test of a functional perspective. *Human Communication Research* **12**(2), 203–224.

Hirokawa, R.Y. (1988) Group communication and decision-making performance: A continued test of the functional perspective. *Human Communication Research* **14**, 487–515.

Hirokawa, R.Y. (1990) The role of communication in group decision-making efficacy: a task-contingency perspective. *Small Group Research* **21**(2), 190–204.

Hirokawa, R.Y. and Gouran, D.S. (1989) Facilitation of group communication, a critique of prior research and an agenda for future research. *Management Communication Quarterly* **3**(1), 71–92.

Hirokawa, R.Y. and Pace, R. (1983) A descriptive investigation of the possible communication-based reasons for effective and ineffective group decision making. *Communication Monographs* **50**, 363–379.

Hirokawa, R.Y. and Poole, M.S. (1986) *Communication and Group Decision Making.* Beverly Hills, CA, Sage.

Hirokawa, R.Y. and Rost, K.M. (1992) Effective group decision making in organizations: field test of the Vigilant Interaction Theory. *Management Communication Quarterly* **5**(3), 267–288.

Hodgson, A.M. (1992) Hexagons for systems thinking. In: J.D.W. Morecroft, and J.D. Sterman (eds.), *Modelling for Learning, Special Issue of the European Journal of Operational Research* **59**(1), 220–230.

Hoffman, L.R. (1959) Homogeneity of member personality and its effect on group problem-solving. *Journal of Abnormal Social Psychology* **58**, 27–32.

Hogarth, R. (1987) (2nd ed.) *Judgement and Choice*, Chichester, Wiley and Sons.

Holloman, C.R. and Hendrick, H.W. (1972) Adequacy of group decisions as a function of the decision-making process. *Academy of Management Journal* **15**, 175–184.

Holsti, O.R. (1969) *Content Analysis for the Social Sciences and Humanities.* Reading (MA), Addison Wesley.

Huff, A.S. (1990) *Mapping Strategic Thought.* Chichester, Wiley and Sons.

Jablin, F.M. (1981) Cultivating imagination: factors that enhance and inhibit creativity in brainstorming groups. *Human Communication Research* **7**(3), 245–258.

Jablin, F.M., Seibold, D.R. and Sorenson, R.L. (1977) Potential inhibitory effects of group participation on brainstorming performance. *Central States Speech Journal* **28**, 113–121.

Janis, I.L. (1972) *Victims of Groupthink, a Psychological Study of Foreign-policy Decisions and Fiascoes.* Boston, Houghton Mifflin Company.

Janis, I.L. (1989) *Crucial Decisions: Leadership in Policy Making and Crisis Management.* New York, The Free Press.

Janis, I.L., and Mann, L. (1977) *Decision Making: a Psychological Analysis of Conflict, Choice and Commitment.* New York, The Free Press.

Jensen, A.D. and Chilberg, J.C. (1991) *Small Group Communication. Theory and Application.* Belmont (CA), Wadsworth Publishing Company.

Jones, R.A. (1977) *Self-fulfilling Prophecies: Social, Psychological and Physiological Effects of Expectancies.* New York, Wiley and Sons.

Johnson Abercrombie, M.L. (1960) *The Anatomy of Judgement.* Harmondsworth, Penguin Books.

Jussim, L. (1986) Self-fulfilling prophecies: A theoretical and integrative review. *Psychological Review* **93**(4), 429–445.

Kahn, R.L. and Cannell, C.F. (1957) *The Dynamics of Interviewing, Theory, Technique, and Cases.* London/Sydney, Wiley and Sons.

Kahneman, D. and Tversky, A. (1982) The simulation heuristic. In: D. Kahneman, P. Slovic and A. Tversky (eds.), *Judgment Under Uncertainty: Heuristics and Biases*. Cambridge, Cambridge University Press, 201–208.

Kahneman, D., Slovic, P. and Tversky, A. (1982) *Judgment Under Uncertainty: Heuristics and Biases*. Cambridge, Cambridge University Press.

Kelley, H.H. (1951) Communication in experimentally created hierarchies. *Human Relations* **4**,39–56.

Kelley, H.H. and Stahelski, A.J. (1970) Social interaction basis of cooperators' and competitors' beliefs about others. *Journal of Personality and Social Psychology* **16**, 66–91.

Keltner, J.S. (1989) Facilitation, catalyst for group problem solving. *Management Communication Quarterly* **3**(1), 8–32.

Kenis, D. (1995) *Improving Group Decisions: Designing and Testing Techniques for Group Decision Support Systems Applying Delphi Principles*. PhD dissertation, Utrecht University.

Kleijnen, J.P.C. (1995) Sensitivity analysis and optimization of system dynamic models: regression analysis and statistical design of experiments. *System Dynamics Review* **11**(4), 275–288.

Kleinmuntz, D.N. (1993) Information processing and misperceptions of the implications of feedback in dynamic decision making. *System Dynamics Review* **9**(3), 223–237.

Klimoski, R.J. and Karol, B.L. (1976) The impact of trust on creative problem solving groups. *Journal of Applied Psychology* **61**(5), 72–74.

Korsgaard, M.A., Schweiger, D.M. and Sapienza, H.J. (1995) Building commitment, attachment, and trust in strategic decision-making teams: the role of procedural justice. *Academy of Management Journal* **38**(1), 60–84.

Krippendorff, K. (1981)(2nd printing) *Content Analysis, an Introduction to its Methodology*. Beverly Hills/London, Sage Publications.

Krueger, R.A. (1988) *Focus Groups: a Practical Guide for Applied Research*. Newbury Park, Sage.

Lamm, H. and Trommsdorf, G. (1973) Group versus individual performance on tasks requiring ideational proficiency (brainstorming): a review. *European Journal of Social Psychology* **3**(4), 361–388.

Lane, D.C. (1989) *Modelling as Learning: Creating Models to Enhance Learning Amongst Management Decision Makers*. Paper presented at the European Simulation Conference, Edinburgh.

Lane, D.C. (1992) Modelling as learning: A consultancy methodology for enhancing learning in management teams. In: J.D.W. Morecroft and J.D. Sterman, *Modelling for Learning, Special Issue of European Journal of Operational Research* **59**(1), 64–84.

Lane D.C. (1993) The road not taken: observing a process of issue selection and model conceptualization. *System Dynamics Review* **9**(3), 239–264.

Lane, D.C. (1994a) With a little help from our friends: how system dynamics and soft OR can learn from each other. *System Dynamics Review* **10**(2/3), 101–134.

Lane, D.C. (1994b) Social theory and system dynamics practice. *Proceedings of the 1994 International System Dynamics Conference: Methodological and Technical Issues*, 53–66.

Lane, D.C. (1995) The folding star: a comparative reframing and extension of validity concepts in system dynamics. *Proceedings of the 1995 International System Dynamics Conference*, 111–130.

Lane, D.C. and Oliva, R. (1994) The greater whole: towards a synthesis of SD and SSM. *Proceedings of the 1994 International Systems Dynamics Conference: Problem Solving Methodologies*, 134–146.

Lane, D.C. and Smart, C. (1996) Reinterpreting 'generic structure', evolution, application and limitations of a concept. *Systems Dynamics Review*, **12**(2).

Larkin, J.H. and Simon, H.A. (1987) Why a diagram is (sometimes) worth ten thousand words. *Cognitive Science* **11**, 65–99.

Laughlin, P.R. (1980) Social combination processes of cooperative, problem-solving groups as verbal intellective tasks. In: M. Fishbein (ed.), *Progress in Social Psychology* **1**, Hillsdale (NJ), Erlbaum.

Lazarsfeld, P.F. (1944) The controversy over detailed interviews, an offer for negotiation. *Public Opinion Quarterly* **8**, 38–60.

Leathers, D.G. (1972) Quality of group communication as a determinant of group product *Speech Monographs* **39**(1), 166–173.

Lichtenstein, S., Fischhof, B. and Phillips, L.D. (1982) Calibration of probabilities: the state of the art to 1980. In: D. Kahneman, P. Slovic and A. Tversky: *Judgment Under Uncertainty: Heuristics and Biases*, Cambridge, Cambridge University Press, 306–334.

Lindblom, C.E. (1959) The science of muddling through. *Public Administration Review*, 79–88.

Linstone, H.A. (1978) The delphi technique. In: J. Fowles (ed.) *Handbook of Futures Research*. London, Greenwood Press, 273–300.

Linstone, H.A. and Turoff, M. (1975) *The Delphi Method: Techniques and Applications*. New York, Wiley and Sons.

Lippitt, G.L. (1983) (new edition) *A Handbook for Visual Problem Solving: a Resource Guide for Creating Change Models*. Bethesda (MA) Development Publications.

Littlepage, G.E. and Silbiger, H. (1992) Recognition of expertise in decision-making groups: effects of group size and participation patterns. *Small Group Research* **23**(3), 344–355.

Lorge, I. and Solomon, H. (1959) Individual performance and group performance in problem solving related to group size and previous exposure to the problem. *Journal of Psychology* **48**, 107–114.

Lyneis, J.M. (1980) *Corporate Planning and Policy Design: a System Dynamics Approach*. Cambridge, MIT Press.

Maier, N.R.F. and Thurber, J.A. (1969) Limitations of procedures for improving group problem-solving. *Psychological Reports* **25**, 639–656.

Majone, G. (1984) A good decision is more than a right decision. *Acta Psychologica* **56**, 15–18.

Mangham, I. (1978) *Interactions and Interventions in Organizations*. Chichester, Wiley and Sons.

March, J.G. and Simon, H.A. (1958) *Organizations*. Cambridge, Blackwell.

March, J.G. and Olsen, J.P. (1976) *Ambiguity and Choice in Organizations*. Bergen. Universitetsforlaget.

Mason, R.O. (1969) A dialectical approach to strategic planning. *Management Science* **15**, B403-B414.

Mason, O.M. and Mitroff, I.L. (1981) *Challenging Strategic Planning Assumptions, Theory, Cases and Techniques*. New York, Wiley and Sons.

Maznevski, M.L. (1994) Understanding our differences—performance in decision making groups with diverse members. *Human Relations* **47**(5), 531–552.

McGrath, J.E. (1984) *Groups: Interaction and Performance*. Englewood Cliffs, Prentice-Hall.

McGraw, K.L. and Harbison-Briggs, K. (1989) *Knowledge Acquisition, Principles and Guidelines*. Englewood Cliffs, Prentice-Hall.

Meadows, D.H. and Robinson, J.M. (1985) *The Electronic Oracle: Computer Models and Social Decisions*. Chichester, Wiley and Sons.

Meadows, D.H., Richardson, J. and Bruckmann, G. (1982) *Groping in the Dark: the First Decade of Global Modelling*. Chichester, Wiley and Sons.

Meadows, D.H., Behrens, W.W., Naill, R.F., Randers, J. and Zahn, E.K.O. (1974) *Dynamics of Growth in a Finite World*. Cambridge, Wright-Allen Press.

Merton, R.K. (1957) *Social Theory and Social Structure*, New York, The Free Press.

Miller, G.A. (1956) The magical number seven, plus or minus two: some limits on our capacity for processing information. *The Psychological Review* **63**(2), 81–97.

Milliken, F.J. and Vollrath, D.A. (1991) Strategic decision making tasks and group effectiveness: insights from theory and research on small group performance. *Human Relations* **44**(12), 1229–1253.

Miner, F.C. (1984) Group versus individual decision making: an investigation of performance measures, decision strategies, and process losses/gains. *Organizational Behavior and Human Performance* **33**, 112–124.

Mintzberg, H. (1978) Patterns in Strategy Formation. *Management Science* **24**(9), 934–948.

Mintzberg, H.(1989) *Mintzberg on Management: Inside our Strange World of Organizations.* New York, The Free Press.

Mitroff, I.I. and Mason, R.O. (1981) The metaphysics of policy and planning: a reply to Cosier. *Academy of Management Journal* **6**(4), 649–652.

Mitroff, I.I., Barabba, V.P. and Kilmann, R.H. (1977) The application of behavioral and philosophical technologies to strategic planning: a case study of a large federal agency. *Management Science* **24**, 44–58.

Morecroft, J.D.W. (1983) System dynamics: portraying bounded rationality. *Omega* **11**, 131–142.

Morecroft, J.D.W. (1988) System dynamics and microworlds for policy makers. *European Journal of Operational Research* **35**, 301–320.

Morecroft, J.D.W. (1992) Executive knowledge, models and learning. In: J.D.W. Morecroft, and J.D. Sterman (eds.), *Modelling for Learning, Special Issue of the European Journal of Operational Research* **59**(1), 9–27.

Morecroft, J.D.W. and Sterman, J.D. (1994) *Modelling for Learning Organizations.* Portland, Productivity Press. Previously published as: *Modelling for Learning, Special Issue of the European Journal of Operational Research* **59**(1), 1992.

Morris, C.G. (1966) Task effects on group interaction. *Journal of Personality and Social Psychology* **4**(5), 545–554.

Naftulin, D.H., Ware, J.E. and Donnely, F.A. (1973) The doctor Fox lecture: a paradigm of educational seduction. *Journal of Medical Education* **48**, 630–635.

N.C.I.V. (1994) Nederlands Christelijk Instituut voor de Volkshuisvesting: *NCIV-Kengetallen 1992*, De Bilt. (Dutch Christian Institute for Housing: DCIH-indicators 1992).

Nelms, K.R. and Porter, A.L. (1985) EFTE: an interactive delphi method. *Technological Forecasting and Social Change* **28**, 43–61.

Nemiroff, P.M. and King, D.C. (1975) Group decision making performance as influenced by consensus and self-orientation. *Human Relations* **28**(1), 1–21.

Osborn, A.F. (1957) (rev. ed.) *Applied Imagination.* New York. Scribner.

Overmier, J.B. and Seligman, M.E.P. (1967) Effects of inescapable shock upon subsequent escape and avoidance responding. *Journal of Comparative and Physiological Psychology* **63**, 28–33.

Pace, R.C. (1990) Personalized and depersonalized conflict in small group discussions: an examination of differentiation. *Small Group Research* **21**(1), 79–96.

Paich, M. (1985) Generic structures. *System Dynamics Review* **1**(1), 126–132.

Paich, M., and Sterman, J.D. (1993) Boom, bust, and failures to learn in experimental markets. *Management Science* **39**(12), 1439–1458.

Parnes, S.J., and Meadow, A. 1959. University of Buffalo research regarding development of creative talent. In: Calvin W. Taylor (ed.), *The Third University of Utah Research Conference on the Identification of Creative Scientific Talent.* University of Utah.

Patton, M.Q. (1980) *Qualitative Evaluation and Research Methods.* Newbury Park/London/ New Delhi, Sage.

Pen, J. and Gemerden, L.J. van (1977) *Macro Economie* (Macro economics). Utrecht, Het Spectrum.

Pendell, S.D. (1990) Deviance and conflict in small group decision making: an exploratory study. *Small Group Research* **21**(3), 393–403.

Peterson, D.W. (1980) Statistical tools for system dynamics. In: J. Randers (ed.). *Elements of the System Dynamics Method.* Cambridge, MIT Press.

Phillips, L.D. (1984) A theory of requisite decision models. *Acta Psychologica* **56**, 29–48.

Phillips, L.D. (1989) Requisite decision modelling for technological projects. In: C. Vlek and G. Cvetkovich (eds.), *Social Decision Methodology for Technological Projects.* Dordrecht, Kluwer, 95–110.

Phillips, L.D. and Phillips, M.C. (1993) Facilitated work groups: theory and practice. *Journal of the Operational Research Society* **44**(6), 533–549.

Pood, E.A. (1980) Functions of communication: An experimental study in group conflict situations. *Small Group Behavior* **11**(1), 76–87.

Poppen, H.J. (1987) *In den eersten lijn gemeeten, een systeemdynamische benadering van de huisartsgeneeskunde* (Measured in the first echelon, a system dynamics approach of general practitioner health care). Master's Thesis, State University of Groningen, Netherlands.

Post, D. and Been, P. (1988) Kostenontwikkeling van prescriptie (Cost development of prescriptions). *Medisch Contact* **43**, 1485.

Powers, W.T. (1973) Feedback: beyond behaviorism. *Science* **179**, 351–356.

Randers, J. (1977) *The Potential in Simulation of Macro-social Processes, or How to be a Useful Builder of Simulation Models.* Gruppen for Ressursstudier, Oslo, Norway.

Randers, J. (1980) *Elements of the System Dynamics Method.* Cambridge, MIT Press.

Reagan-Cirincione, P. (1991) *Improving the Accuracy of Forecasts: A Process Intervention Combining Social Judgment Analysis and Group Facilitation,* PhD dissertation, Rockefeller College of Public Affairs and Policy, State University of New York at Albany.

Reagan-Cirincione, P. (1994) Improving the accuracy of group judgement — A process intervention combining group facilitation, social judgment analysis, and information technology. *Organizational Behavior and Human Decision Processes* **58**(2), 246–270.

Reagan-Cirincione, P., Schuman, S., Richardson, G.P. and Dorf, S.A. (1991) Decision modelling: tools for strategic thinking. *Interfaces* **21**(6), 52–65.

Rees, F. (1991) *How to Lead Work Teams: Facilitation Skills.* San Diego, Pfeiffer & Co.

Richardson, G.P. (1986) Problems with causal-loop diagrams. *System Dynamics Review* **2**, 158–170.

Richardson, G.P. (1991) *Feedback Thought in Social Science and Systems Theory.* Philadelphia, University of Pennsylvania Press.

Richardson, G.P. and Andersen, D.F. (1995) Teamwork in group model-building. *System Dynamics Review* **11**(2), 113–137.

Richardson, G.P. and Pugh, A.L. (1981) *Introduction to system dynamics modeling with DYNAMO.* Cambridge (MA), MIT Press.

Richardson, G.P., Andersen, D.F., Rohrbaugh, J. and Steinhurst, W. (1992) Group model-building. In: J. Vennix, J. Faber, W. Scheper, and C. Takkenberg (eds.), *Proceedings of the 1992 International System Dynamics Conference.* Utrecht, Netherlands, 595–604.

Richardson, G.P., Wolstenholme, E.F. and Morecroft, J.D.W. (1994) 'Systems thinkers, systems thinking'. *System Dynamics Review* **10**(2–3).

Richmond, B. (1987) *The Strategic Forum: From Vision to Strategy to Operating Policies and Back Again,* High Performance Systems, Lyme (NH), Netherlands.

Rittel, H.W.J. and Webber, M.M. (1973) Dilemmas in a general theory of planning. *Policy Sciences* **4**, 155–169.

Roberts, E.B. (1978) Strategies for effective implementation of complex corporate models. In: E.B. Roberts (ed.). *Managerial Applications of System Dynamics.* Cambridge, MIT Press, 77–85.

Roberts, E.B. (1978) *Managerial Applications of System Dynamics.* Portland (OR), Productivity Press.

Roberts, N., Andersen, D.F., Deal, R.M., Grant, M.S. and Schaffer, W.A. (1983) *Introduction to Computer Simulation: a System Dynamics Modelling Approach.* Reading (MA), Addison-Wesley.

Rogers, C.R. and Roethlisberger, F. J. (1988) Barriers and gateways to communication. In: Joh. J. Gabarro (ed.), People: managing your most important asset. Special edition of articles. *Harvard Business Review*, 19–25.

Rohrbaugh, J. (1979) Improving the quality of group judgment: Social Judgment Analysis and the Delphi technique. *Organizational Behavior and Human Performance* **24**, 73–92.

Rohrbaugh, J. (1981) Improving the quality of group judgment: Social Judgment Analysis and the Nominal Group Technique. *Organizational Behavior and Human Performance* **28**, 272–288.

Rosenhead, J. (ed.) (1989) *Rational Analysis for a Problematic World: Problem Structuring Methods for Complexity, Uncertainty and Conflict.* Chichester, Wiley and Sons.

Rosenthal, R. (1966) *Experimenter Effects in Behavioral Research.* New York, Appleton-Century-Crofts.

Rosenthal, R., and Jacobson, L. (1968) *Pygmalion in the Classroom, Teacher Expectations and Pupils' Intellectual Development.* New York, Holt, Rinehart and Winston, Inc.

Russo, J.E. and Schoemaker, P.J.H. (1989) *Decision Traps: Ten Barriers to Brilliant Decision-making and How to Overcome Them.* New York, Doubleday.

Sackman, H. (1975) *Delphi Critique: Expert Opinion, Forecasting and Group Process.* Lexington (MA), D.C. Heath and Co.

Sastry, M.A. and Sterman, J.D. (1993) Desert island dynamics: an annotated survey of the essential system dynamics literature. In: E. Zepeda, J.A.D. Machuca, *Proceedings of the 1993 International System Dynamics Conference.* Cancun, Mexico, 466–475.

Schachter, S. (1951) Deviation, rejection, and communication. *Journal of Abnormal Social Psychology* **46**, 190–207.

Schein, E.H. (1969) *Process Consultation: its Role in Organizational Development.* Reading (MA), Addison-Wesley.

Schein, E.H. (1987), *Process Consultation (vol. II).* Reading (MA), Addison-Wesley.

Schein, E.H. (1988) *Organizational Culture and Leadership.* San Francisco, Jossey-Bass

Scheper, W.J. (1991) *Group Decision Support Systems: an Inquiry into Theoretical and Philosophical Issues.* PhD dissertation, Tilburg University, Netherlands.

Scheper, W.J., and Faber, J. (1994) Do cognitive maps make sense? In: Ch. Stubbart, J.R. Meindl and J.F. Porac (eds.), *Advances in Managerial Cognition and Organizational Information Processing.* Greenwich: JAI Press.

Schnaars, S.P. (1987) How to develop and use scenario's. *Long Range Planning* **20**(1), 105–114.

Schoemaker, P.J.H. (1993) Multiple scenario development: its conceptual and behavioral foundation. *Strategic Management Journal* **14**, 193–213

Schön, D.A. (1987) *Educating the Reflective Practitioner: Towards a New Design for Teaching and Learning in the Professions.* San Francisco, Jossey-Bass.

Schutz, A. (1962) *Collected Papers I: the Problem of Social Reality.* The Hague, Martinus Nijhoff, Netherlands.

Schutz, W.C. (1955) What makes groups productive? *Human Relations* **8**, 429–465.

Schwartz, P. (1991) *The Art of the Long View.* New York, Doubleday.

Schweiger, D.M. and Sandberg, W.R. (1989) The utilization of individual capabilities in group approaches to strategic decision-making. *Strategic Management Journal* **10**, 31–43.

Schweiger, D.M., Sandberg, W.R. and Ragan, J.W (1986) Group approaches for improving strategic decision making: a comparative analysis of dialectical inquiry, devil's advocacy, and consensus. *Academy of Management Journal* **29**(1), 51–71.

Schweiger, D.M., Sandberg, W.R. and Rechner, P.L. (1989) Experiential effects of dialectical inquiry, devil's advocacy, and consensus approaches to strategic decision-making. *Academy of Management Journal* **32**(4), 745–772.

Schwenk, C.R. (1988) Effects of devil's advocacy on escalating commitment. *Human Relations* **41**(10), 769–782.

Secord, P.F. and Backman C.W. (1974) (2nd ed.) *Social Psychology.* London, McGraw-Hill.

Seligman, M.E.P. and Maier, S.F. (1967) Failure to escape traumatic shock. *Journal of Experimental Psychology* **74**, 1–9.

Senge, P. (1990) *The Fifth Discipline: The Art and Practice of the Learning Organization.* New York, Doubleday.

Shannon, R.E. (1975) *Systems Simulation: The Art and Science.* Englewood Cliffs (NJ), Prentice-Hall.

Shoham, Y. (1990) Nonmonotonic reasoning and causation. *Cognitive Science* **14**, 213–252.

Silverman, D. (1975) *Reading Castaneda: A prologue to the Social Sciences.* London, Routledge and Kegan Paul.

Simon, H.A. (1948) *Administrative Behavior: a Study of Decision-making Processes in Administrative Organizations.* New York, Macmillan.

Simon, H.A. (1960) *The New Science of Management Decision.* New York, Harper and Row.

Simon, H.A. (1985) Human nature in politics: The dialogue of psychology with political science. *The American Political Science Review* **79**, 293–304.

Sims, D. (1986) Mental simulation: an effective vehicle for adult learning. *International Journal of Innovation in Higher Education* **3**, 33–35.

Sims, D., Fineman, S. and Gabriel, Y. (1993) *Organizing and Organizations.* London, Sage.

Slater, P.E. (1958) Contrasting correlates of group size. *Sociometry* **21**, 129–139.

Smith, K.A., Johnson, D.W. and Johnson, R.T. (1981) Can conflict be constructive? Controversy versus concurrence seeking in learning groups. *Journal of Educational Psychology* **73**(5), 651–663.

Smith, K.A., Petersen, R.P., Johnson, D.W. and Johnson, R.T. (1986) The effects of controversy and concurrence seeking on effective decision making. *The Journal of Social Psychology* **126**(2), 237–248.

Sniezek, J.A. (1989) An examination of group process in judgmental forecasting. *International Journal of Forecasting* **5**, 171–178.

Sniezek, J.A. (1990) A comparison of techniques for judgmental forecasting by groups with common information. *Group and Organization Studies* **15**, 5–19.

Sniezek, J.A. and Henry, R.A. (1990) Revision, weighting, and commitment in consensus group judgment. *Organizational Behavior and Human Decision Processes* **45**, 66–84.

Stasson, M.F., Kaoru Ono, Zimmerman, S.K. and Davis, J.H. (1988) Group consensus processes on cognitive bias tasks: A social decision scheme approach. *Japanese Psychological Research* **30**(2), 68–77.

Steiner, I.D. (1972) *Group Process and Productivity.* New York, Academic Press.

Stenberg, L. (1980) A modelling procedure for public policy. In: J. Randers (ed.), *Elements of the System Dynamics Method.* Cambridge (MA), 292–312.

Stephan, F.F. (1952) The relative rate of communication between members of small groups. *American Sociological Review* **17**, 482–48

Sterman, J.D. (1985) The growth of knowledge: testing a theory of scientific revolutions with a formal model. *Technological Forecasting and Social Change* **28**(2), 93–122.

Sterman, J.D. (1989a) Misperceptions of feedback in dynamic decision making. *Organizational Behaviour and Human Decision Processes* **43**, 301–335.

Sterman, J.D. (1989b) Modelling managerial behaviour: misperceptions of feedback in a dynamic decision-making experiment. *Management Science* **35** (3), 321–339.

Stewart, T.R. (1987) The delphi technique and judgmental forecasting. *Climatic Change* **11**, 97–113.

Stroebe, W. and Diehl, M. (1994) Why groups are less effective than their members: on productivity losses in idea-generating groups. In: W. Stroebe and M. Hewstone (eds.), *European Review of Social Psychology* **5**, 271-303. Chichester, Wiley and Sons.

Stroop, J.R. (1932) Is the judgement of the group better than that of the average member of the group. *Journal of Experimental Psychology* **15**, 550–560.

Tank-Nielsen, C. (1980) Sensitivity analysis in system dynamics. In: J. Randers (ed.), *Elements of the System Dynamics Method*, 187–204.

Taylor, D.W. and Faust, W.L. (1952) Twenty questions: Efficiency in problem solving as a function of size of group. *Journal of Experimental Psychology* **44**, 360–368.

Thibaut, J.W. and Kelley, H.H. (1959) *The Social Psychology of Groups.* New York, Wiley and Sons.

Thomas, E.J. and Fink, C.F. (1963) Effects of group size. *Psychological Bulletin* **60**, 371–384.

Thomas, K. (1976) Conflict and conflict management. In: M.D. Dunette (ed.), *Handbook of Industrial and Organizational Psychology.* Chicago, Rand-McNally, 889–935.

Thomas, W.I. and Thomas, D.S. (1928) *The Child in America: Behavior Problems and Programs.* New York, Alfred Knopf.

Tjosvold, D. (1982) Effects of approach to controversy on superiors' incorporation of subordinates' information in decision making. *Journal of Applied Psychology* **67**(2), 189–193.

Tjosvold, D., and Field, R.H.G. (1983) Effects of social context on consensus and majority vote decision-making. *Academy of Management Journal* **26**, 500–506.

Tjosvold, D. and Field, R.H.G. (1985) Effect of concurrence, controversy, and consensus on group decision-making. *The Journal of Social Psychology* **125**(3), 355–363.

Tjosvold, D. and Johnson, D.W. (1977) Effects of controversy on cognitive perspective taking. *Journal of Educational Psychology* **69**(6), 679–685.

Tjosvold, D. and Johnson, D.W. (1978) Controversy within a cooperative or competitive context and cognitive perspective-taking. *Contemporary Educational Psychology* **3**, 376–386.

Tucker, D.H. and Rowe, P.M. (1979) Relationship between expectancy, causal attributions, and final hiring decisions in the employment interview. *Journal of Applied Psychology* **64**(1), 27–34.

Tversky, A. and Kahneman, D. (1974) Judgment under uncertainty: heuristics and biases. *Science* **185**, 1124–1131.

Tversky, A. and Kahneman, D. (1981) The framing of decisions and the psychology of choice. *Science* **211**, 453–458.

Underwood, S.E. (1984) *An Evaluation of a Participative Technique for Strategic Planning.* University of Ann Arbor, unpublished paper.

Ven, A.H. van de, and Delbecq, A.L. (1974) The effectiveness of nominal, delphi and interacting group decision making processes. *Academy of Management Journal* **17**, 605–621.

Vennix, J.A.M. (1990) *Mental Models and Computer Models: Design and Evaluation of a Computer-based Learning Environment for Policy Making.* PhD dissertation, University of Nijmegen, Netherlands.

Vennix, J.A.M. (1995) Building consensus in strategic decision making: system dynamics as a group support system. *Group Decision and Negotiation* **4**(4), 335–355.

Vennix, J.A.M. and Geurts, J.L.A. (1987) Communicating insights from complex simulation models: a gaming approach. *Simulation and Games* **18**, 321–343.

Vennix, J.A.M., Scheper, W. and Willems, R. (1993) Group model-building: what does the client think of it? In: E. Zepeda and J. Machuca (eds.), *The Role of Strategic Modelling in International Competitiveness, Proceedings of the 1993 International System Dynamics Conference.* Mexico, Cancun, 534–543.

Vennix, J.A.M., Akkermans, H.A. and Rouwette, E.A.J.A (1996) Group model-building to facilitate organizational change: an exploratory study. *System Dynamics Review*, **12**, 39–58.

Vennix, J.A.M., Richardson, G.P., Andersen, D.F. (forthcoming) Group model-building, *Special Issue of the System Dynamics Review.*

Vennix, J.A.M., Gubbels, J.W., Post, D. and Poppen, H.J. (1990) A structured approach to knowledge elicitation in conceptual model-building. *System Dynamics Review* **6**, 194–208.

Vennix, J.A.M., Andersen, D.F., Richardson, G.P. and Rohrbaugh, J. (1992) Model-building for group decision support: issues and alternatives in knowledge elicitation. In: J.D.W. Morecroft, and J.D. Sterman (eds.), *Modelling for Learning, Special Issue of the European Journal of Operational Research* **59**(1), 28–41.

Vennix, J.A.M., Ikink, T., Scheper, W.J. and Huijgen, F. (1994) *Eindverslag onderzoek lidmaatschap KNMG en beroepsverenigingen* (Final research Report membership Royal Dutch Medical Association and professional associations). Department of methodology, Nijmegen, Netherlands.

Verburgh, L.D. (1994) *Participative Policy Modelling: Applied to the Health Care Insurance Industry.* PhD dissertation, Nijmegen University, Netherlands.

Voorlopige Raad voor Verkeer en Waterstaat. (1992). *Advies over de nota 'Maritiem Nederland in het jaar 2010'* (Advice on the policy note: 'Maritime Holland in the year 2010'). Den Haag, Netherlands.

Vroom, V.H., Grant, L.D. and Cotton, T.S. (1969) The consequences of social interaction in group problem solving. *Organizational Behavior and Human Performance* **4**, 77–95.

Wack, P. (1985a) Scenarios: uncharted waters ahead. *Harvard Business Review* September–October, 73–89.

Wack, P. (1985b) Scenarios: shooting the rapids. *Harvard Business Review* November–December, 139–150.

Wagenaar, W.A. and Sagaria, S.D. (1975) Misperception of exponential growth. *Perception and Psychophysics* **18**(6), 416–422.

Wagenaar, W.A. and Timmers, H. (1978) Extrapolation of exponential time series is not enhanced by having more data points. *Perception and Psychophysics* **24**(2), 182–184.

Wagenaar, W.A., and Timmers, H. (1979) The pond-and-duckweed problem: three experiments on the misperception of exponential growth. *Acta Psychologica* **43**, 239–251.

Wall, V.D. jr., Galanes, G.J. and Love, S.B. (1987) Small, task-oriented groups: conflict, conflict management, satisfaction and decision quality. *Small Group Behaviour* **18**(1), 31–55.

Watt, K.H. (1977) Why won't anyone believe us? *Simulation*, 1–3.

Watzlawick, P. (ed.) (1984) *The Invented Reality, How do we Know What we Believe we Know?* New York/London, W.W. Norton & Company.

Weil, H.B. (1980) The evolution of an approach for achieving implemented results from system dynamic projects. In: J. Randers (ed.), *Elements of the System Dynamics Method.* Cambridge (MA), 271–291.

Weiner, B. (1985) 'Spontaneous' causal thinking. *Psychological Bulletin* **97**(1), 74–84.

Westley, F. and Waters, J.A. (1988) Group facilitation skills for managers. *Management Education and Development* **19**(2), 134–143.

White, S.E., Dittrich, J.E. and Lang, J.R. (1980) The effects of group decision-making process and problem situation complexity on implementation attempts. *Administrative Science Quarterly*, 428–440.

Winterfeldt, D. von and Edwards, W. (1986) *Decision Analysis and Behavioral Research.* Cambridge, Cambridge University Press.

Wittenberg, J. (1992) On the very idea of a system dynamics model of Kuhnian science. *System Dynamics Review* **8**(1), 21–33.

Wolstenholme, E.F. (1982). System dynamics in perspective, *Journal of the Operational Research Society* 33, 547–556.

Wolstenholme, E.F. (1990) *System Enquiry, a System Dynamics Approach*, Chichester, John Wiley and Sons.

Wolstenholme, E.F. (1992). The definition and application of a stepwise approach to model conceptualisation and analysis, *European Journal of Operational Research* **59**, 123–136.

Wolstenholme E.F. and Coyle, R.G. (1983). The development of system dynamics as a methodology for system description and qualitative analysis. *Journal of the Operational Research Society* **34**, 569–581.

Wolstenholme, E.F. and Al-Alusi, A-S. (1987) System dynamics and heuristic optimization in defence analysis. *System Dynamics Review* **3**, 102–116.

Worchel, S., Wood, W. and Simpson, J.A. (1992) *Group Process and Productivity*. Newbury Park, Sage.

Zakay, D. (1984) The evaluation of managerial decisions' quality by managers. *Acta Psychologica* **56**, 49–57.

Index

Organizational Transformation and Learning
A Cybernetic Approach to Management

Raul Espejo, Werner Schuhmann, Markus Schwaninger & Ubaldo Bilello

Today's managers are increasingly busy and less inclined than ever to cope with difficult theoretical propositions. *To this very reason, the managers to whom this book will appear daunting are the ones who have most to gain.* This book aims to make their own jobs, and the organizations they work for, more satisfying and humane.

Organizational Transformation and Learning is more than theory in isolation. The ideas have been worked out in practice to approach five fundamental issues:

- How can organizations cope with increasing environmental complexity?
- How can they maintain viability and develop further at the same time?
- How can organizational action become more effective?
- How can managers cope with increasing organizational complexity?
- How can their action become more effective?

Given that complexity is the core issue for organizations to deal with in the future, **Organizational Transformation and Learning** shows in theory and practice how organizational and managerial cybernetics can contribute to dealing with this core issue. It provides a framework to relate and organize the myriad activities common to contemporary business. The book will change the reader's appreciation of their role in the organization and make each action more effective.

In plain terms, the authors believe that organizational transformation begins with individual transformation, and intend that this book will encourage that individual transformation.

0471 96182 5 £24.95 March 1996 HB